FROM TRANSNATIONAL RELATIONS TO TRANSNATIONAL LAWS

This book approaches law as a process embedded in transnational personal, religious, communicative and economic relationships that mediate between international, national and local practices, norms and values. It uses the concept 'living law' to describe the multiplicity of norms manifest in transnational moral, social or economic practices that transgress the territorial and legal boundaries of the nation-state. Focusing on transnational legal encounters located in family life, diasporic religious institutions and media events in countries such as Norway, Sweden, England and Scotland, it demonstrates the multiple challenges that accelerated mobility and increased cultural and normative diversity is posing for Northern European law. For in this part of the world, as elsewhere, national law is challenged by a mixture of expanding human rights obligations and unprecedented cultural and normative pluralism enhanced by expanding global communication and market relations. As a consequence, transnationalization of law appears to create homogeneity, fragmentation and ambiguity, expanding space for some actors while silencing others. Through the lens of a variety of important contemporary subjects, the authors thus engage with the nature of power and how it is accommodated, ignored or resisted by various actors when transnational practices encounter national and local law.

From Transnational Relations to Transnational Laws

Northern European Laws at the Crossroads

Edited by

ANNE HELLUM
University of Oslo, Norway

SHAHEEN SARDAR ALI
University of Warwick, UK

ANNE GRIFFITHS
Edinburgh University, UK

Routledge
Taylor & Francis Group
LONDON AND NEW YORK

First published 2011 by Ashgate Publishing

2 Park Square, Milton Park, Abingdon, Oxon OX14 4RN
711 Third Avenue, New York, NY 10017, USA

Routledge is an imprint of the Taylor & Francis Group, an informa business

First issued in paperback 2016

British Library Cataloguing in Publication Data
From transnational relations to transnational laws :
Northern European laws at the crossroads. -- (Law, justice
and power series)
1. Legal polycentricity--Europe, Northern. 2. Conflict of
laws--Europe, Northern. 3. Law and globalization.
4. Culture and law.
I. Series II. Hellum, Anne. III. Ali, Shaheen Sardar.
IV. Griffiths, Anne M. O.
340.1'15'094-dc22

Library of Congress Cataloging-in-Publication Data
From transnational relations to transnational laws : northern European laws at the crossroads / by Anne Hellum, Shaheen Sardar Ali, and Anne Griffiths.
p. cm. -- (Law, justice and power)
Includes index.
ISBN 978-1-4094-1896-2 (hardback)
1. Legal polycentricity--Europe, Western. I. Hellum, Anne. II. Ali, Shaheen Sardar. III. Griffiths, Anne.

KJC383.F76 2010
340.9094--dc22

2010029872

ISBN 978-1-4094-1896-2 (hbk)
ISBN 978-1-138-26106-8 (pbk)

Contents

List of Contributors

Anne Hellum is a lawyer and anthropologist holding a Doctor Juris Degree from the University of Oslo. She is professor at the Department of Public and International Law at the University of Oslo and Director of the Rights, Culture and Society Program (RIKS) at the Faculty of Law. She is part of the research group on transnational relations in the interdisciplinary research program Cultural Complexity in the New Norway (CULCOM). Her research has generally focused on the relationship between human rights, gender and legal pluralism in Zimbabwe, South Africa, Pakistan and Norway. Substantive areas of research are discrimination and equality law, social and economic human rights related to reproduction, land and water. Her most recent publications are *Human Rights, Gendered Realities and Plural Legalities* (with Shaheen Sardar Ali *et al.* Weaver Press 2007), *Discrimination and Equality Law* (with Kirsten Ketscher, Norwegian University Press 2008) and *Justice* (with Beatrice Halsaa Norwegian University Press 2010). She is visiting professor at the Southern and Eastern African Centre of Women's Law (SEARCWL) at the University of Zimbabwe and has had visiting appointments at the Human Rights Study Centre at the University of Peshawar and the Department of Anthropology at Michigan State University. She is currently holding a grant at the Centre for Advanced Studies at the Norwegian Academy of Science as part of the International Research Project – *Why States Ratify Human Rights* – where she is directing the CEDAW project.

Anne Griffiths holds a personal chair in the Anthropology of Law at the School of Law at Edinburgh University. Her research focuses on anthropology of law, comparative and family law, African law, gender, culture and rights and juvenile justice. Her most recent publications include *The Power of Law in a Transnational World: Anthropological Enquires* (2009); *Spatializing Law: An Anthropological Geography of Law in Society* (2009) and *Mobile People, Mobile Law: Expanding Legal Relations in a Contracting World* (2005) co-edited with F. and K. von Benda-Beckmann. Over the years she has held visiting appointments at various institutions including Distinguished Visiting Professor, Faculty of Law, University of Toronto, The Max Planck Institute for Social Anthropology, Halle/Saale, Germany, The International Institute for the Sociology of Law Oñati – Gipuzkoa, Spain, The University of Texas at Austin, School of Law and the Southern and Eastern African Regional Centre for Women's Law at the University of Zimbabwe. She is currently a member of the Executive Body of the Commission on Legal Pluralism, a branch of the International Union of Anthropological and Ethnological Sciences, of which she was President from 2003–2009. Her current research, funded by the Leverhulme Trust (2009–2010) is on the *Gendered Dynamics of Land Tenure in Southern Africa.*

Shaheen Sardar Ali Professor of Law, University of Warwick, UK, Professor II, at the Department of Public Law at the University of Oslo, Norway and Vice-Chair, United Nations Working Group on Arbitrary Detention. Her research interests include human rights, women's human rights, children's rights, Islamic law and jurisprudence, gender and the law. She has written more than sixty articles and chapters for books, authored five books and edited two, the most widely read of which is *Gender and Human Rights in Islam and International Law: Equal Before Allah, Unequal Before Man?* She was awarded the British Muslims Annual Honours achievement plaque in the House of Lords in May 2002 and the Asian Woman of Achievement Award in the Public Sector in 2005.

Dr Samia Bano is a lecturer in Family Law at the University of Reading. Her research interests include gender, migration, Islam, Muslim family law, human rights and multiculturalism and the law. She has worked on a number of research and policy initiatives in the area of gender, migration and human rights. Her current work explores the relationship between informal religious legal systems, state law and gender relations within South Asian Muslim communities in the UK and is due to be published as a book in Autumn 2010 (Palgrave Macmillan).

Elisabeth Eide is Associate Professor (PhD) in Journalism studies at Oslo University College, and also holds a position with Infomedia at the University of Bergen. She has published a number of books and articles related to journalism research in a postcolonial perspective. Lately she has co-edited two volumes on the international coverage of the Mohammed Cartoon Crisis (2007, 2008) and co-authored a book on Pakistan (2010) and leads a global researchers' network studying media coverage of climate change. She has spent three years in India and Pakistan and frequently travels to Afghanistan. This experience has inspired the publication of five novels.

Thomas Hylland Eriksen is Professor of Social Anthropology at the University of Oslo and directed the interdisciplinary research programme CULCOM (Cultural complexity in the new Norway) from 2004 to 2010. His research has focused on the politics of identity, cultural dimensions of globalization and forms of cultural mixing, but he has also published books and articles in other fields inside and outside of anthropology, ranging from Darwinism to the quality of life. His most recent books in English are *Engaging Anthropology* (2006), *Globalization: The Key Concepts* (2007), *Small Places, Large Issues*, third edition (2010), *Ethnicity and Nationalism*, third edition (2010) and the co-edited books *Flag, Nation and Symbolism* (2007), *Paradoxes of Cultural Recognition* (2009) and *A World of Insecurity* (2010).

Mohamed Hussein Gaas has received his MSc degree in Development Studies from the Norwegian University of Life Sciences. He has since then researched on the linkage between diasporas' engagement in conflict, peace building and developing their countries of origin, focusing on the Horn of Africa region and its diaspora in Nordic countries. More recently, he conducted research on maritime piracy off the Somali coast and the Gulf of Aden.

Randy Kandel has JD from New York University School of Law and a PhD in anthropology from the City University of New York. She is a part-time associate professor in the Department of Anthropology at John Jay College of Criminal Justice and an Administrative Law Judge for New York City. She has published numerous articles and chapters about the intersection of law, anthropology and children, many with her colleague Anne Griffiths, about the legal process in the UK and Scotland. The latest article is Custody and Coming of Age: Three American Cases in *Parenting after the Century of the Child* (2010).

Lena Larsen is a Research Fellow at the Norwegian Centre for Human Rights, University of Oslo, studying the development of Islamic legal thought in Western Europe. She has a scholarship from the interdisciplinary research project CULCOM (Cultural Complexity in the New Norway). She is coordinator of the Oslo Coalition on Freedom of Religion or Belief, co-editor of *New Directions in Islamic Thought* (2009), associate editor of *Facilitating Freedom of Religion or Belief: A Deskbook* (2004) and a former Chair of the Islamic Council in Norway.

Abdul Paliwala has been Professor of Law and Professorial Consultant at the University of Warwick. He has previously lectured at the Queen's Belfast, Dar es Salaam and Papua New Guinea Universities. He is a member of the International Development Law and Human Rights Research Group and Director of the Electronic Law Journals Project. His recent work includes *A History of Legal Informatics* (2010) and his recent interests include law development and social justice, global digital regulation and e-learning in law.

Annika Rabo is Professor in the Department of Social Anthropology, Stockholm University. She has conducted fieldwork in the Middle East, mainly in Syria, since the late 1970s focusing on a variety of topics related to state-citizens relationships. She is currently involved in projects focusing on transnational connections and has recently finished a project on transnational Syrian families and family law.

Marit Melhuus is Professor of Social Anthropology at the University of Oslo. She has previously worked in Argentina and Mexico publishing on economic anthropology, gender and morality, including *Machos, Mistresses, Madonnas* (Verso 1996). Over the past years she has been researching issues of kinship, biotechnology, and law, and published widely on these interlinked themes. Tangentially she has addressed the theme of transnational flow of concepts and substances, co-editing *Holding Worlds Together: Ethnographies of Knowing and Belonging* (Berghahn 2007).

Farhat Taj is research fellow at the Center of Interdisciplinary Gender studies at the University of Oslo. She is working on a PhD thesis at the Department of Criminology and Sociology of Law, University of Oslo. Her thesis title is: 'Legal Pluralism, Gender and Islam among Norwegian-Pakistanis in Oslo, Norway'. She holds an MPhil degree in Gender and Development from the University of Bergen. Taj is the author of *Women and Women Police Station, Peshawar, NWFP, Pakistan* published by VDM Verlag Dr. Müller.

Sarvendra Tharmalingam is a PhD Research Fellow at University of Oslo's strategic research programme 'Cultural Complexity in the New Norway (CULCOM)' affiliated to the Department of Sociology and Human Geography. He holds a Bachelor Degree in the field of Commerce at the University of Jaffna in Sri Lanka and two master degrees, one in the field of Education in Science, Society and Technology (ESST) at the University of Oslo in Norway and the State University of Limburg (Now Maastricht University) in the Netherlands, and the other in Development Studies at the University of Life Sciences in Norway.

Knut Papendorf is Associate Professor at the Institute for Criminology and Sociology of Law, University of Oslo, Norway. His special research interest is in criminal policy, sociology of law and control politics.

Preface

To come to grips with the complex intersections of transnational social, economic and legal life, the chapters in this book are based on empirical studies that draw on disciplines like law, social anthropology, anthropology of law, sociology of law, media studies, gender studies, religious studies and social geography.

The book is the outcome of the international interdisciplinary research program, *Cultural Complexity* (CULCOM), led by professor Thomas Hylland Eriksen at the University of Oslo. The Transnational Law Project, which was initiated by professor Anne Hellum, formed a part of CULCOM's broader study of the relationship between transnationalism and cultural complexity. It started out with an international conference on Transnational Law arranged by CULCOM in Oslo in 2007. The Conference was followed up with a book seminar hosted by the research group Rights, Individuals, Culture and Society (RIKS) at the Faculty of Law at the University of Oslo in 2009.

We are grateful to Anne Marit Hessevik (CULCOM) for the organization of the CULCOM conference and Elisabeth Wenger Hagene (RIKS) for the organization of the book seminar. Margo Bedingfield edited the chapters. Funding for this book project was provided by CULCOM, the Norwegian Research Council's Immigration Program (IMER) and the research group RIKS at the Faculty of Law.

Anne Hellum
Oslo, October 2010

Introduction

Transnational Law in the Making

Anne Hellum, Shaheen Sardar Ali and Anne Griffiths[1]

Introduction

Transnationalization of personal, economic, communicative and religious relations has profoundly affected the role of state law and international law in all parts of the world. Accelerated mobility of people, norms, capital and technology is reflected in the current state of legal flux where local, national and international regulatory domains are constantly reconfigured (F. and K. von Benda-Beckmann and Griffiths 2005). To describe and understand how the normative plurality and complexity resulting from transnationalization is played out in Northern Europe, particularly in Norway, Sweden, England and Scotland, this book explores encounters between international, national and local norms and practices in four interrelated spheres of life and law: family, religion, media and market. Our aim is to provide an empirical foundation for a critical assessment of the assumptions and presumptions underlying legal discourse in what used to be perceived as culturally homogenous societies bounded by national borders (Twining 2000).

The chapters all provide an actor's perspective from below. They uncover the legal constraints, inconsistencies or conflicts that individuals, groups or enterprises face in their search for secure livelihoods, freedom or economic gain. Focusing on transnational legal encounters embedded in family relationships, diasporic Islamic institutions, transnational media events and global economic transactions, the chapters provide a window into the conflicts and dilemmas that increased mobility poses for Northern European state law as to how to strike a balance between equality and difference. The Norwegian case studies are set in a Northern European protestant culture where difference is seen as a shortcoming of some kind (Gullestad 2001:54). They reveal how narrow nationalist ideas of sameness underlying legal policies that make claim to universality often result in inequalities between the majority and minority population. How laws and policies endorsing multiculturalist claims may reinforce existing inequalities within minority groups is demonstrated by the British experiences. The study of the British *Shari'a* Councils opens up space to see in evidence the multicultural project in its attempt to reconfigure social and legal discourse in matters of family law and the ambiguous experiences of British Pakistani Muslim women using

1 We would like to thank Thomas Hylland Eriksen for insightful comments to this chapter.

such fora. Faced with a situation where rights claims are embedded in overlapping and conflicting identities in terms of religion, ethnicity, gender and social status, Northern European state law, as the chapters show, is indeed at the crossroads.

Embodying both universality and diversity, human rights are often seen as the key to the challenges that increased mobility and cultural diversity and complexity have set off in Northern Europe (Hellum 2006). The increasing body of international and regional human rights instruments and institutions has become the location of claims for welfare, justice, freedom and dignity from women, refugees, migrants and ethnic, religious and sexual minorities who until recently stood excluded from the Western equality project. Norway, Sweden, England and Scotland, the locations of this book, are facing challenges from both above and below. A growing body of international and regional human rights obligations along with an unprecedented cultural and normative diversity is challenging the national legal identity (Gorashi, Eriksen and Algashi 2009).[2] Accelerating international human rights obligations that call the assumed cultural homogeneity underlying national law into question and, as such, challenge privileged positions of status and power, are met with increasing state resistance in both the South and the north. In the Nordic countries there is increasing concern about the dynamic interpretation of regional human rights challenging national laws, policies and practices. In Norway, a recent study on 'Power and Democracy' raised concerns about incorporating international conventions into the law which served to undermine national sovereignty (NOU 2003:19). One hypothesis purporting to explain this growing state resistance to incorporating international human rights in the Nordic countries' legislation is the prevalence of communitarian narratives that depict these countries as ethnically and culturally homogenous and egalitarian nations with a strong emphasis on grassroots movement and participatory local democracy (Føllesdal and Wind 2009:132).

Yet the human rights arena is only one of the multiple avenues that people who fall outside the scope of national law pursue. People's search for security, justice, freedom or economic gain is increasingly reflected in social and economic arrangements drawing upon norms and values that transgress both national and international law. For the actors engaged in these endeavours, neither international nor national laws are the sole mechanisms for regulating their affairs. The concept of legal pluralism draws attention to the coexistence within the same social space of more than one body of law, pertaining to the same set of activities (Griffiths 1986, F. von Benda-Beckmann 2001, Griffiths 2002). The historical and ethnographic record shows considerable variation in the effectiveness of state laws in comparison with coexisting non-state legal orders (F. and K. von Benda-Beckmann 2006). Globalization, in terms of transnational human mobility and flows of capital, technology, ideas and norms, has had the effect of creating transnational social, economic and religious communities that to a large extent

2 This is one of the theoretical propositions of the interdisciplinary and comparative research conducted in the research project, 'Cultural Complexity in the New Norway', of which this book is a part.

regulate their own affairs. To understand the role of both international and national law in this changing sociolegal landscape, this book explores the norm-generating processes embedded in transnational personal, social, religious and economic relations. Thus we investigate the social and legal factors and forces that inform family determinations, religious decrees, media events, inter-governmental regulations or contracts regulating exchange of labour, services and goods, at the various levels at which they occur.

To come to grips with these complex intersections of social, economic and legal life, the chapters are based on empirical studies conducted by researchers who, in their engagement with transnationalism, draw on disciplines like law, social anthropology, anthropology of law, sociology of law, media studies, gender studies, religious studies and social geography:

- In Part I, Marit Melhuus, Annika Rabo, Farhat Taj and Anne Hellum rely on field research and individuals' lived experiences to explore the moral, political and legal contestations that transnational family lives are giving rise to in Norway and, to a certain extent, in Sweden. A common theme is how gay and lesbian Norwegians, Syrian Christians in Sweden and Pakistani Muslim women in Oslo create a way around social, religious and legal stereotypes that disregard their quest for welfare, belonging, equality, dignity and choice.
- In their explorations of 'living Islamic law' in the Northern European diaspora in Part II, Shaheen Sardar Ali, Lena Larsen and Samia Bano draw on a combination of written and oral sources as well as field observations. Analyzing *fatwas* from the Internet, the European Council of *Fatwa*s and Research and the practices in informal *Shari'a* Councils in Britain, they draw a picture of Islam in all its pluralities with focus on the position of women. Viewed from this perspective, what emerges is the homogenizing character of these discourses and the lack of engagement with human rights principles.
- Part III illustrates the multiplicity of laws, norms and other regulatory mechanisms at work in providing governance in its varying forms, whether in relation to family intervention, business lawyers, the Internet or economic transactions. Anne Griffiths and Randy Kandel draw on data from children's panels in Scotland; Knut Papendorf interviews Norwegian and German business lawyers; Sarvendra Tharmalingam, Mohamed Husein Gaas and Thomas Hylland Eriksen examine Somali families remitting money from Norway to Somalia and Abdul Paliwala confronts the challenges of regulating cyberspace. They all describe the multi-directional aspects of regulation deriving from differentially constituted institutions and networks. A plurality of non-state actors, such as companies, non-governmental organizations and intergovernmental networks, are today involved in rule-making which until recently was considered the domain of the nation-state or the United Nations General Assembly.

- In their analyses of transnational public media events, Elisabeth Eide and Thomas Hylland Eriksen in Part IV show the complex effects of the new world order of transnational communication on the construction of identities and rights at multiple levels of law and society. Through a comparative approach they describe how universal human rights, like freedom of speech and gender equality, become transformed into standardized and static notions of cultural difference in the process.

What emerges as a common feature of these diverse and dynamic transnational fields of life and law is the plurality of formal and informal norms invoked by the different actors in their efforts to carve out viable solutions to emerging social, moral and economic challenges. To reappraise the role of the nation-state and its relationship with law, society and culture, the studies in our book locate law as a process embedded in transnational relationships that mediate between international, national and local practices, norms and values. Situating social, economic and legal activities in transnational family life, transnational procreative practices, global media events, global lawyering, Internet communication and religious regulation, this book provides a relational perspective on the making of transnational law. Asking who within a social group or community has the power and authority to define, interpret, implement and enforce law at the multiple levels at which it operates, this work seeks an understanding of how relationships of inequality, domination or control are created, reinforced or unmade in these processes. Exploring how women embedded in transnational relationships negotiate the multiple norms that have a bearing on their lives in different contexts and settings, it follows the line of investigation carved out by sociolegal women's law studies in the post-colonial South (Hellum, Stewart, Ali and Tsanga 2007:xix). Pursuing this line of investigation, the book draws the ambiguous relationship of gender, legal pluralism and power into attention by exploring how transnationalism challenges established perceptions of family, gender and sexuality in a Northern European context.

Living Transnational Law

As actors in transnational social spaces, people are subject to a multitude of restricting, conflicting and incoherent bodies of state laws, religious norms and customary practices that govern their lives. In response to the diverse and often conflicting legal, social and economic circumstances that surround their activities, they are in pursuit of ways and means of reconfiguring law to meet their needs. Describing how these efforts are manifest in practices constituting creative efforts to reconfigure legal relations, this book is about 'living law' in the era of globalization. 'Living law', we suggest, is manifest in transnational moral, social or economic practices, norms and values that transgress the territorial and legal boundaries of the nation-state.

The concept of 'living law' originates from the Austrian legal scientist Eugene Ehrlich (1862–1922). His main work, *Fundamental Principles of the Sociology of Law* (1962), contains a fundamental criticism of the assumption that law only arises from juristic law or state law. To give a realistic picture of law Ehrlich maintained that the main objective of legal science is an investigation of the 'living law'. According to Ehrlich this was 'the law that dominates in life itself, even though it has not been posited in legal propositions' (Ehrlich 1962:493–494). In his view, 'the concrete usages, the relations of domination, the legal relations, the contracts, the articles of association, the disposition of will by testament, yield the rules according to which they regulate their conduct.'

Instead of studying norms and actions as parallel or congruent forms we are attempting to come to grips with the living law, focusing on transnational sociolegal life as process. To understand the complex and multi-sited processes of sociolegal life that transnational relationships give rise to, following the legal anthropologist Sally Falk Moore's concept of 'law as a semi-autonomous social field', we extend the line of investigation to transnational social fields. Law, as Falk Moore suggested in 1978, should be studied as a process observable to the anthropologist in small social fields 'in terms of its semi-autonomy – the fact that it can generate rules and customs and symbols internally, but that it is vulnerable to rules and decisions and other forces emanating from the larger world that it is surrounded by' (Moore 1978:55, 56). Addressing legal pluralism in terms of the existence of several normative orders in a social field, Falk Moore, at that point in time, emphasized that semi-autonomy, in terms of interacting state laws and customary and religious norms, was not a phenomenon exclusively related to tribal communities but a feature of all nation-states in the world. Similarly, John Griffiths (1986), among others, has argued that legal pluralism is not just a product of the colonial counter but is to be found in all states, whether situated in the North or South, in the 'developed' or 'underdeveloped' world. Henrik Zahle and Hanne Petersen use the term 'polycentricity' in an effort to capture the consequences of legal pluralism in Northern European law (Petersen and Zahle 1995). Describing how, in the era of globalization, law is constituted in an intersection of different legal orders, Boaventura de Sousa Santos uses the term 'interlegality' to characterize the mixed and porous character of law (Santos 1987:208). In dealing with the multiple positionalities of people living transnational lives, methodological approaches that analyze the interaction between international, national and local norms in postcolonial Africa and Asia are highly relevant in Northern Europe (Hellum 1999, Ali 2000, Hellum *et al.* 2007:xix).

Pursuing this line of investigation the chapters in this book show how the dynamics of accelerated mobility of people, technologies and laws reinforce the semi-autonomous character of law. In Northern Europe, the geographical location of this book, national law is under pressure from above, below, within and without. Its semi-autonomy and porosity is, as the chapters show, closely linked to expanding human rights obligations and unprecedented cultural and legal pluralism embedded in increasingly transnational families, expanding religious institutions and global market relations. The living law that is emerging in these overlapping and conflicting transnational semi-autonomous social fields is embedded and shaped by networks of power in terms of resources and information. How relationships of inequality, domination or control are created, reinforced or unmade in the course of these processes is the overall focus of this book. Locating the case studies in Northern Europe, the book explores, through a sociolegal lens, the relationship between both national majorities and minorities and between majorities and minorities within the minority groups. The diverse and ambiguous outcomes of these transnational processes in terms of gender, class and status demonstrate the advantages and disadvantages that legal pluralism poses for differentially situated actors in various contexts and settings.

Family Lives and Family Laws: Transnational, National and Local Sites of Contestation

Increased mobility of people, technologies and laws have turned family lives and family laws into a site of moral, political and legal contestation in all parts of the world. In Norway, Sweden and England a plurality of family forms challenges the cultural sameness that was a precondition for national family law (even if it never fully realized its aspirations). A recurrent concern of individuals within minority groups, ranging from gay and lesbian Norwegians to Syrian Christians in Sweden and Pakistani Muslims in Norway and Britain, is to find a way around social, religious and legal stereotypes that disregard their quest for welfare, belonging, equality, dignity and choice. In an attempt to escape undesired control of economic, sexual, procreative and marital relationships embedded in state-law, custom or religion, people manoeuvre within and between different national, social and religious norms. Liberal democracies in Scandinavia and Britain are confronted with a dilemma concerning laws and regulations affecting these increasingly diverse and complex family relations. Women's multiple identities as individual citizens and members of ethnic and religious minorities epitomize the conflicts and dilemmas that arise.

Facilitating new forms of procreation, the global availability of new reproductive technologies opens up family space by including previously excluded and stigmatized categories of people. Marit Melhuus (Chapter 2) addresses the question of childlessness that drives Norwegian women and men to pursue procreation as a form of belonging through the use of new reproductive technologies. She explores encounters between the imageries of belonging that stem from new reproductive technologies on offer in a global market that are at odds with the narrow family norms and values regulated by national laws embedded in Norwegian legislation. In a series of efforts to uphold the ideal of the heterosexual, married couple as the natural unit of family life, Norwegian legislators have curtailed people's access to assisted procreation. Melhuus shows how national legal efforts to circumscribe people's procreative choices fail in a situation where reproductive technologies, such as egg and embryo donation, are available through service providers in countries that have more liberal legislation than Norway.

Annika Rabo (Chapter 1) draws attention to the legal intricacies that Syrian orthodox Christians face in their country of origin and in the West. Many of the early Syrian orthodox migrants who came to Sweden were happy to be resettled in what they believed to be a Christian country. They were happy to escape the minority position of Christians under Syrian law, which constitutes a bifurcated family law system based on religion as opposed to universal citizenship. Yet Christian Syrians living in Sweden and Syria are not, as Annika Rabo demonstrates, a homogenous group. Religious authorities in the Christian Syrian community are critical of Swedish law and decision makers who see it as their duty to help liberate women and children from male control legitimized by Syrian state law. A Syrian orthodox priest interviewed by Rabo in Syria in 2008 underlined the fact that Europe is not good for Syrians from the point of view of family life: 'People divorce over small differences. A sick spouse is cast aside and old parents are not cared for by their children.' Yet many ordinary Christian Syrians do not want Syrian orthodox family law to be applied to their situation in Sweden. They want recognition and respect for their particularity but do not consider Swedish family norms to be completely negative. Many take the view that family relations in Sweden might be 'cold' but they are 'fair', particularly where state intervention is involved. According to Rabo, many Syrians with experience from Scandinavia are impressed by the way the best interest of the child, for example, predominates over parents' interests in cases of divorce.

Set in the context of Norway's uniform legal system that on paper applies equally to all citizens, Anne Hellum and Farhat Taj (Chapter 4) explore tensions between Norwegian family law, Pakistani law, Islam and custom. They explore how the relationship between Norwegian state law and coexisting religious and customary norms are mediated through civil society interventions. Towards this end they describe how a Pakistani women's organization in Oslo (PAKWOM) tries to make Norwegian law available, accessible and acceptable to women embedded in transnational family relationships. They show how the women in the non-governmental organization have created an environment that facilitates choice and empowerment by drawing on multiple sources and networks within both the local Pakistani community and the Norwegian legal community. The outcome of this process is an enabling space where in the spirit of free and informed choice women are defining a place for themselves in the context of conflicting moral, religious and legal expectations and pressures deriving from husbands, in-laws, religious institutions and Norwegian authorities. Facilitated through cooperation between Pakistani and Norwegian women, the process stands in contrast to the confined normative repertoire that guides Internet *fatwas* or the mediation that takes place within religious institutions, as described by Shaheen Sardar Ali and Samio Bano in Part II of this book.

How the rights of sexual, social and ethnic minorities can be safeguarded without perpetuating an unequal distribution of rights, duties and power among group members – particularly between women and men and parents and children – is a highly complex and controversial issue. How should a unified family law system aiming at substantive equality strike a balance between individual women, men and children's rights as individuals while in the same vein recognizing their common cultural identity? Or is a multiculturalist model assigning different family law regimes to different ethnic and religious groups the way forward? Learning from the lifeworlds of individual men and women, it is important to bear in mind the complex and multi-sited situations people embedded in transnational relationships face. Standardized notions of gender, sexuality and family are at work both in unified family law systems in Western welfare states like Norway or segregated multicultural family law systems based on religion, like that of Syria. As the case studies show, family law regimes upholding narrow and static moral categories that exclude and stigmatize single women and sexual or religious minorities, are resisted and circumvented. To accommodate women and children's quest for protection and recognition under state law there is clearly a need to rethink established notions of the relationship between gender, sexuality, marriage and family under Northern European law.

Recognizing that international and national law can never be an abstract neutral position there is need to develop a united set of principles that, without losing focus on difference, can provide a form of equality under the law. Anne Hellum (Chapter 3) suggests we take a closer look at the global equality and non-discrimination standard embedded in the United Nation's Convention on the Elimination of All Forms of Discrimination Against Women (CEDAW). In her view it constitutes an important mechanism for including different categories of women that have been excluded in national and local contexts on the basis of legal, social and religious paradigms that derive from narrow stereotypical perceptions of gender, sexuality or ethnicity. Due to its recognition of cultural differences that fall outside the scope of dominant national family and gender values, the global equality and non-discrimination standard often meets with state resistance. State resistance is not limited to states that make reservations to the Convention with reference to religious and customary family law regimes. The Norwegian state's reluctance to make existing reproductive technologies available on a non-discriminatory basis epitomizes the tension between the notions of equality based on cultural sameness and equality based on cultural difference in the context of a state that has ratified CEDAW without reservations. By limiting access to certain technologies the Norwegian Biotechnology Act reproduces the dominant ideal of cultural sameness whereby those who fall outside the scope of the Act are deemed inferior.

Calling the assumed cultural homogeneity underlying national law into question, in Northern Europe the acceleration of international legal obligations and sociocultural diversity have led to a revitalization of national cultural and legal values (Gorashi, Eriksen and Algashi 2009). This development is reflected in inconsistent and ambiguous legal responses. Ruling that a prohibition against the *hijab* in the workplace constitutes indirect gender discrimination, the Norwegian

Gender Equality Appeals Board, as shown by Hellum, is engaging with difference to achieve equality of result. This speaks to a process whereby the equal status norm is re-embedded in social relationships so as to prevent women from being excluded from the national equality project. On the other hand, inequalities between majority and minority women are often ascribed to cultural differences. Addressing judicial responses to cultural defence in honour killing cases, Hellum also shows how human rights principles ensuring women equal protection under the law is transformed through a nationalist legal discourse that reinforces popular nationalist sentiments assuming cultural sameness. Rendering women equal protection under the law, the Norwegian judiciary, like that of India and Pakistan, uses language that relegates honour crimes to other spaces, less civilized than the law of the nation state. By using a legal discourse clustering around a civilized/uncivilized divide, the national judiciary is upholding a dichotomy between what is embraced as the 'self' and what constitutes the 'other'. In a similar vein, Hellum and Taj point out how national information campaigns directed at migrant women and their families in Norway have almost exclusively focused on female genital mutilation, forced marriages and honour killings. Not a single campaign has been carried out to inform migrant women about the laws that protect them against discrimination on the basis of gender and ethnicity. So the inequalities between majorities and minorities in Norway, in spite of the dominant equality rhetoric, often appear to be ascribed to the migrant's own culture and not to any discrimination related to the majority's stereotypical perception of migrant women. Law and policy makers in this field thus use egalitarian ideas in ways that, in Marianne Gullestad's terms, '... marginalize specific groups by simultaneously creating dichotomies asking for sameness' (Gullestad 2001:54).

Transnational Religious Relations: Muslims in the European Diaspora

The oft-repeated remark that Islam is not simply a religion but a code of life is pertinent to our present discussion as it provides a theoretical framework for understanding why and how the *Shari'a* as the overarching umbrella of principles permeates every sphere of life. Islamic law therefore will always be more than the black letter law; it is the law in its sociological, political, moral and economic context. Islamic law through its secondary sources, including *'urf* (custom, practice of communities), has a robust living law dimension that has played an important role in its transformative processes over the centuries. The contributions in Part II of this book mirror this reality, where the actors seek out and accept certain principles of *Shari'a* and Islamic law while at the same time challenging, resisting and interpreting these in accordance with their individual sociolegal contexts.

The very construction of the European Muslim diaspora with its fluid and transnational nature offers a fascinating canvas where 'classical' notions of Islamic law are reinterpreted against a contemporary backdrop. A departure from historical *Siyar* (Islamic international law) lies in the fact that Muslims have voluntarily and permanently settled in a non-Muslim jurisdiction while maintaining channels of relationship and communication with their countries of origin. Are they now part of an international *ummah* subscribing to a 'pristine' universal *Shari'a* and Islamic law or a transnational community navigating diverse laws and regulatory norms (of Islamic law, the new home country and the country of origin)? These questions are critical as they inform how individuals and communities order their lives and regulate themselves and how they interact with the host country's national laws. What are the mechanisms employed by the European Muslim diaspora to cope with their new identity?

Two opposing trends are visible from the case studies in this book; the first is the diaspora as a site of contestation for the various ethnic, racial and cultural identities of Muslims now living as 'European Muslims'.[3] The desire for an overriding Muslim identity and freedom from a particular ethnicity is visible in all three studies. A number of strategies are employed in this regard. For instance, in Bano's study of *Shari'a* Councils, Muslim communities in Britain assert their 'Muslim-ness' by creating informal dispute resolution institutions. In Ali's study of cyberspace *fatwas*, young women of Pakistani origin are advised to subsume their South Asian culture in a universal *ummah* identity, whereas in Larsen's study of the European Council of *Fatwa* and Research, a minority *fiqh* (*fiqh al-aqalliyat*) is being generated to respond to the diasporic existence of European Muslims. Thus the Islamic juristic techniques of *darura* (necessity/duress) and *maslaha* (public interest/good) are invoked to make permissible what would normally not be accepted in a Muslim country or jurisdiction.

Simultaneously, and in consonance with the pluralist Islamic legal tradition, the second trend is a resistance against this uniformity of norms. The *Shari'a* Councils of Britain do not invoke *fatwas* of the European Councils in their opinions; neither do the Internet *fatwas* cite the opinions of the *Shari'a* Councils (of Britain).

A third element running through the living law of the European Muslim is the use of Islam and Islamic norms as a regulatory mechanism. It is at the level of communities that living Islamic law emerges as both a liberating factor and a controlling device. Thus Muslims of Norway resist the non-South Asian version of the 'triple' divorce despite *fatwas* and other exhortations to the contrary. British Muslim women are forced to approach the *Shari'a* Councils to validate their divorce despite clear injunctions to use the mainstream English legal system as enunciated in minority *fiqh*.

Departing from the traditional doctrinal approach to the study of Islamic law, this book turns attention to the living law of Muslim diasporic communities in Europe. Locating themselves in emerging Muslim institutions, such as the unofficial *Shari'a* Councils in the United Kingdom, the European Council for *Fatwa* and Research

3 These trends are described by An-Na'im's term in his work entitled, 'Global citizenship and human rights: from Muslims in Europe to European Muslims', in *Religious Pluralism and Human Rights in Europe: Where to Draw the Line?*, edited by M.L.P. Leonen and J.E. Goldschmidt. Antwerpen: Intersentia, (2007) 13–55.

(ECFR) and the numerous 'global' *fatwa*-giving websites, Samia Bano, Lena Larsen and Shaheen Sardar Ali offer insights beyond Islamic law as described in the books. Drawing on Islamic doctrine and how it is reconfigured in the diaspora, their studies offer an empirical, contextual and dynamic approach to understanding the tenuous relationship between cultural diversity, religious pluralism and human rights and equality before the law in contemporary Europe and beyond. These chapters demonstrate how diasporic, religio-cultural constituencies are formulated and strategies devised to resist the dominant socio-political order as well as to control communities and appropriate power and authority within them. The focus for all three case studies is women, gender relations and dispute resolution in the sphere of family law, indicating the centrality of these issues within Muslim discourse in general and in the diaspora in particular. The case studies also show the selectivity and limits of transnational flows of normative principles in the field of family law.

Samia Bano's study of unofficial non-statutory *Shari'a* Councils in Britain (Chapter 7) describes how family law matters are resolved according to Muslim family law. Her work opens up space to see in evidence the multicultural project in its attempt to reconfigure social and legal discourse in matters of family law and the ambiguous experiences of British Pakistani Muslim women using such fora. Drawing upon fieldwork data she argues that Muslim women's capacities and potential for autonomy, agency and choice within the formations of social and religious legal pluralism cannot be understood within the dichotomous variables of insider/outsider, Muslim/non-Muslim and state law/religious law. Instead she draws upon the narratives of the women themselves and embraces notions of complexity and ambiguity. Bano's contribution is cast within the framework of 'multicultural legalism'. She highlights the difficulties inherent in the British state's attempts to respond to its obligations to its minority citizens through its legal system. These attempts have inevitably brought Muslim communities (among others) into conflict with the dominant and official legal system in the area of family law, leading to unofficial parallel institutions within these communities, like the *Shari'a* Councils. Bano's work gives an example of members of Muslim communities creating unofficial 'legal' space to resolve family law issues 'Islamically' as a strategy for appropriating authority within their communities and as a controlling mechanism over Muslim women. This is supported by Bano's research findings where the majority, if not all, applicants to the *Shari'a* Councils are women. In an historic context the 'Muslim woman', both within and beyond the European Muslim community, is seen as the repository of Islamic values.

Lena Larsen focuses on questions related to family law and personal status (Chapter 6). Cases dealt with by the European Council for *Fatwa* and Research (ECFR), a *fatwa*-giving body established to serve Muslims in Western Europe, are presented and analyzed with focus on the position of women. Her study highlights the complex interplay between transnational understandings of religion, culture and tradition in emerging diasporic Muslim space. The composition of the European Council for *Fatwa* and Research (in its membership) reflects this transnationality, negotiating between *fiqh* and the imperatives of social reality within a fast globalizing diaspora. Larsen's analysis depicts the Council as a project to define Western Europe as a 'local' jurisdiction using minority jurisprudence as a strategy for acquiring authority over Europe. Larsen's study of the Council also highlights the fact that Muslim women are seen as markers of community identities, especially within a diasporic context, and thus an important constituency not to be neglected. This is borne out by the *fatwas* that invariably address Muslim women in response to questions addressed to the Council.

Shaheen Sardar Ali (Chapter 5) takes this discussion of *fatwas* forward, broadening it out to explore the discourse of Internet *fatwas* relating to women and gender relations and its potential implications for transnational and international family law norms within a plural Islamic legal tradition. Unlike the earlier two studies situated in Britain (Bano, Chapter 7) and Western Europe (Larsen, Chapter 6), Internet *fatwas* situate themselves in an international, global and universal framework and context recalling the universal nature of the Muslim *ummah*. Having said that, most of the questions and responses have been framed by what we might broadly define as 'Western' Muslims or diasporic Muslims; a plausible fact due to limited access of this facility to wider 'virtual' Muslim audiences in the non-West. The websites appear to have a multiple agenda of 'Islamizing' Muslim men and women particularly in the West; hence the ethical, moral emphasis and tenor of the *fatwa* alongside the legal content of the response. Like Larsen's findings, Internet *fatwas* contain a strong pedagogical aim as they explain concepts and issues in the format of an online 'lecture'.

All three case studies suggest that emerging Muslim institutions, be they *Shari'a* Councils in Britain, the European Council for *Fatwa* and Research or Internet *fatwa*-giving websites, appear to be a manifestation of counter-hegemonic sites of Islamic sociolegal, political and religious discourse, since they challenge existing hegemonies of ethnicities, schools of juristic thought and locations. For instance, British Muslims of Asian origin or descent seek affirmation of their 'pure' and 'pristine' Islam by challenging a South Asian 'notion' of Islam in the triple divorce or in clothing and European Muslims are offered a flexible approach towards inter-faith marriages in stark contrast to the mainstream Muslim interpretation on this point. Internet *fatwas* on women and gender issues also appear counter hegemonic to the male-dominated discourse within the Islamic legal tradition by seeking 'logical', 'rational' reasons for the Muslim women's dress code, rules of contraception, and so on.

Simultaneously, these chapters suggest that these institutions are in themselves hegemonic in that they are a form of regulation of family and family formations through religion. Decisions of *Shari'a* Councils, the European Council for *Fatwa* and Research and Internet *fatwas* also highlight a counter hegemony and resistance to the dominant 'Western' discourse by ensuring that the discussions remain within the Islamic and Muslim framework and communities. Likewise, the *Shari'a* Councils reflect a resistance to the dominant legal system and what is perceived as the British state's insensitivity to engaging with Islamic law.

Cross-fertilization of ideas, opinions and arguments within a transnational framework are another common feature of the *fatwas* case studies. Thus a single *fatwa* will encapsulate and recall viewpoints of a number of *muftis* from various parts and institutions of the Muslim world as well as scholars of the Muslim diaspora. Strangely enough, Bano's empirical findings point to the fact that *Shari'a* Councils do not appear to 'cross-fertilize' their decisions. On the other hand, the discourse on human rights is pointedly invisible in its usage although claims, entitlements and obligations are addressed. This is evident from the research into the European Council for *Fatwa* and Research by Lena Larsen in this volume as well as from the Internet *fatwas*.

What is not apparent from any of the studies is whether Muslim communities in the diaspora accept and internalize these examples of Islamic living law – the decisions or recommendations from the *Shari'a* Councils or the *fatwas* from the European Council for *Fatwa* and Research and from the Internet – as the contemporary understandings of Islam, Islamic law and Muslims.

Emerging Muslim institutions are confronted with the challenge of responding to questions relating to family law, women and gender relations but from the perspective of plural identities, for example, a Muslim who is also a Pakistani and a British citizen, an American of Syrian origin who is a Muslim, and so on. The Islamic legal tradition is thus under pressure to respond to the anxieties of Muslims in Muslim majority countries as well as in the Western, predominantly non-Muslim jurisdictions and having to make decisions impacting on their lives and those of their families and communities. All three contributions reflect these anxieties.

In these studies, the discourse of international human rights and women's human rights was absent, barring a single *fatwa* 'discovered' by Ali regarding the reproductive rights of women. Even in transnational and international spaces such as these, this absence is telling of the parameters within which these institutions keep their discourse. It is also important to make the point that all three studies indicate a clear aim to remain in control of the discourse and its parameters: it is to remain within the Islamic tradition and within Muslim communities with Muslim women as the main participants or recipients of the knowledge or discussion thus generated. 'Gatekeeping' of themes, questions and knowledge is thus evident; knowledge is power and is therefore used selectively by those insiders who control the production of it.

Transnational Forms of Governance and Rule-making

Accelerating mobility of people, capital and information has led to important changes in the ways in which government is exercised. A plurality of non-state actors, such as companies, non-governmental organizations and the International Monetary Fund, are today involved in rule-making which until recently was considered the sole domain of the nation-state (F. and K. von Benda-Beckmann and

Griffiths 2009, Griffiths 2009). The plurality of regulative actors and frameworks are clearly related to globalization of governance, trade and communication. While located in an increasingly transnational setting, involving a series of non-legal institutions like the World Bank, the World Trade Organization and the Internet, the regulations of the nation-state continue to play an important role, albeit in a context which renders them only one of the factors that are taken into account in the decision-making process of the subjects of national law. Given the diversity of these institutional players and social actors, the ways in which they interact and the linkages between them, it is clear that states have had to respond to the creation and deployment of a whole range of technologies connecting multiple centres of power. Recognition of these features acknowledges the increasing variation in the functions of governing. This involves public and private dimensions (for example through privately funded public services such as hospitals) and the creation and recourse to expert knowledge derived from epistemic communities (that is communities of experts that are spread across the world).[4] These communities not only act as conduits to transport law across the globe but also establish themselves as important sources of lawmaking transnationally, for example in the regulation of financial institutions such as stock exchanges (Griffiths 2002) or in fisheries management (Wiber 2009). These characteristics have led a number of scholars (Sand 2004, Joerges 2005, Griffiths 2009) to talk in terms of 'governance' rather than 'government' in an attempt to move away from a top-down, Westphalian, hierarchical concept of government, to embrace the more multi-directional aspects of regulation that arise from the mobilization of a whole array of networks that cross-cut one another horizontally and vertically, within and beyond territorial boundaries.

The chapters by Griffiths and Kandel (Chapter 8), Papendorf (Chapter 9), Paliwala (Chapter 10) and Tharmalingam, Gaas and Eriksen (Chapter 11) in this volume directly address the relationship between regulation, governance and communication in dealing with family, market and Internet relations. The multi-faceted nature of law and plural legal norms and orders not only arises in the context of cross-border migration or transnational families but may also become evident among citizens who are not particularly mobile themselves but who encounter a diversity of conflicting values and standards that derive from international human rights jurisprudence, national law and local norms and values that are embedded in a local setting. The study by Griffiths and Kandel in this volume explores how the United Nations Convention on the Rights of the Child and the European Convention on Human Rights and Fundamental Freedoms are put into operation and interpreted in the local domain of children's hearings, often referred to as children's panels, in Glasgow. These deal with children under sixteen who are in need of compulsory measures of supervision under the Children (Scotland) Act 1995. Based on sociolegal research carried out on the children's hearings system in Glasgow,

4 This term was coined by P.M. Haas (1992) 'Introduction: epistemic communities and international policy coordination'. *International Organization* 46(1): 1–35.

they address how international and national legal standards are being integrated or resisted in terms of local actors' perspectives on their implementation. What national law embraces, namely a balance between children's welfare and rights that involves a transparent and open process, takes on another meaning for the children and families concerned that is generally one of silence and circumspection. Thus communication is not a straightforward process but embodies a range of elements that may leave participants operating at cross-purposes to one another. The study demonstrates how international concepts, such as participation, have a different salience for different people, such as panel members and the children and families that they deal with, although they all operate within the same national jurisdiction and share a common, territorial base, the city of Glasgow. Such findings raise important questions about how the 'local' is to be perceived and located in relation to national and transnational processes that embrace law. For although the actors may be said to be 'local' in that they are located within the bounded space of a city, they nonetheless find themselves situated within very different types of networks that separate them from one another in terms of power and status. These different networks reflect different life worlds that embrace differing priorities and values that have an impact on how law is perceived. In many cases what is important for children and families is the local, 'informal' law of family and neighbourhood that takes precedence for them over the international standards that panel members seek to apply in terms of national law. Thus public and private and formal and informal domains intersect in ways that make it hard for panel members to reconcile the differing norms and values that impinge on the process of creating good citizens through intervention in families.

From another perspective, Papendorf's qualitative study of Norwegian and German law firms highlights the extent to which the regulation of trade relations has been taken over by contracts drawn up by business lawyers or multilateral organizations, like the World Trade Organization, who rule through soft law. In response to the changing demands of a global market, lawyers and law firms are establishing transnational economic and legal links. In these transnational business firms it is the lawyers who develop strategies for globally-oriented, competitive corporations and generate rules needed to promote the growth in world trade. In this situation, given the need for flexible mechanisms that can respond to the rapidly changing demands of the market, it is not national legislators and judges who control the process but lawyers who regulate their business environment through contracts and their organizational practices. The growth in global lawyering has long been recognized as posing a threat to national sovereignty because it does not constrain itself to the application of the law of the nation-state (Dezelay and Garth 1996, Teubner 1997a and b, Vismann 2000). In documenting how Norwegian and German law firms adapt themselves to the needs of trade and industry through a range of administrative as well as legal practices, Papendorf points to another conception of sovereignty that may be reconceived as 'an effect of practices associated with law and other forms of regulation that construct relations between the state, its population and the market' (Perry and Maurer quoting Ong 2003:xiv).

In the 'virtual' world Paliwala explores the way cyberspace's construction of new Internet cultures also transforms economic and regulatory cultures – that is modes of production and regulation. Competition in this context not only involves capturing access to and control of the communicative resources available through the Internet but also embodies contestation over differing approaches to and perceptions of what the 'global commons' entail. On the one hand creating a new space for collaborative, non-capitalist, democratic engagement that is emancipatory for its constituents or the 'multitude' (Hart and Negri 2000) or, on the other hand, protecting state and property interests by harnessing the power of capital to develop and control new modes of regulation and production with their inclusionary and exclusionary powers. For Baxi (2006) and others (Klein 2005, Rajan 2006) it is the latter that is at stake and that represents new techno-scientific modes of production that, far from being emancipatory, stand for new modes of domination. The tensions between these perceptions are particularly pertinent when considering the North/South digital divide that raises questions about the ability to 'be empowered with the language that the box works in', as well as the resources that can be mobilized to combat the asymmetries of power that exist. These include forms of resistance to attempts to ringfence access to and control of the Internet through legal definitions of property relations, commercial market power and the architecture of code that structures cyberspace. Such resistance takes the form of file sharing; the commons movement involving organizations such as ISOC, W3C, ITEF and IRTF that support the Internet's open architecture: Free/Libre and Open Source systems (FLOSS) and Content movement (FLOSS-C), as well as the GNU/LINUX operating system and piracy. In addressing these developments Paliwala observes that 'struggles for social justice for new cyber-identities and the excluded have to take into account the complex realities of the new modes of regulation'.

Tharmalingam and Gaas examine the impact of financial regulation in Norway on the *hawala* remittance system in the wake of the September 11 attacks on the United States of America in 2001. In their chapter the authors note the importance of remittances that link diasporic communities all over the globe. Derived from a well-established historical practice by Somali pastoral nomads known as *abbaan*, the *hawala* system involves the transfer of money from immigrants to family, local communities and local businesses in the South. This is accomplished through Somali social networks located in different countries throughout the world that facilitate the transfer of money through their extensive contacts. Practised by a number of communities, including Kenyan, Ethiopian and Sudanese refugees, remittances are vital to the well-being of Somalia, providing much needed support to citizens of a country that has been plagued with civil war, loss of banking institutions and forced migration since 1991. The authors demonstrate how attempts were made to dismantle or formally regularize the *hawala* system after the September 11 attacks. What had previously been viewed as a positive development became subject to a security perspective that viewed international migration as a threat to internal and global security. One consequence of this development was the closure of the remittance company, Al-Barakaat, and its network by the United States authorities that had a negative impact on Somalia's economy and trade. Under pressure to restructure informal money transfer systems, the Financial Action Task Force (FATF), an inter-governmental body, was established. The national legislation of states that emanated from the task force recommendations varied greatly, from the more moderate regulations favoured by the United Kingdom and Sweden, to more rigorous measures employed by countries such as France and the Netherlands, and which in Norway was so draconian that it made it illegal for remittance companies to operate. Despite developments such as the Somali Finances Services Association founded to follow the guidelines and recommendations of the task force, not a single *hawala* company has been formalized in Norway. In the meantime, the need for remittances has not abated – they are estimated to account globally for more than double the official development aid. Thus Somalis continue to remit money illegally as there are no organizations enabling them to remit through formal, legally-sanctioned institutions. Such a situation, far from fostering legalization, has created insecurity among those sending and receiving money with the potentially unintended consequence of driving the system underground in a way that would render it even less accountable or transparent.

The Role Networks

These chapters, in common with other chapters in this volume, illustrate the multiplicity of laws, norms and other regulatory mechanisms that are at work in providing governance in its varying forms, whether in relation to family intervention, business lawyers, the Internet or media and communication. They exemplify the multi-directional aspects of regulation that, like other contributors' chapters, derive from differentially constituted networks. For Griffiths and Kandel these networks embody different forms of knowledge and values from those of the professionals, such as social workers, who apply their own codes and institutional imperatives in servicing panels to the more personal and social sets of relations that bind children and families in the neighbourhoods in which they live. In the case of Papendorf, the networks involve a web of relations in which lawyers, business corporations and legal firms come together in different types of constellations to create competitive commercial entities in a global market place. For Paliwala, the emancipatory aspects of cyberspace derive from the possibility of communicative collaboration that derives from a complex set of 'nodal' networks involving 'global, national state, business and non-governmental organizations'. Uncircumscribed by territorial boundaries, they permit the creation of a transcultural and 'netizen' culture that allows for new forms of hyper-cultural identity to emerge. Networks are crucial to the successful operation of the *hawala* system that Tharmalingam, Gaas and Eriksen discuss, for the transnational transfer of money or resources from Norway to Somalia and vice versa. Formal legal developments in Norway have, however, rendered these networks 'illegal' in an attempt to impose a more regularized, Western model of finance on the *hawala* system. This Western model is ill-suited to the needs of Somali immigrants and disaporic communities because it does not have the accessibility, flexibility, relative cheapness and understandings of local culture the *hawala* system offers. The imposition of such a model, in response to misleading assertions by the media about the 'informal' financing of terrorist organizations like Al Qaeda, has led to remittances taking place outside the control of state law. This has created a feeling of disenchantment among Somalis who perceive that, in rendering the current *hawala* system illegal or illegitimate, they are not being treated with the equality or respect associated with the inclusive policy of multicultural Norway.

The Role of Experts

In dealing with access to and the dissemination of various forms of information or knowledge, Papendorf and Paliwala expressly address the role of experts in this process. For Papendorf, the driving force behind the network is the desire to create an ever more specialized pool of expertise to serve the interests of the business community. This involves restructuring working relations to focus on those who can provide the necessary skills in this area and bypassing those whose legal skills do not fit the required paradigm. In Paliwala's case, expertise is necessary to construct the language of code providing for access to and use of the Internet. Such expertise can work to enhance or constrain public participation in this medium, since it can be used to provide open access and file sharing or to circumscribe it through protected access and licensing agreements. For Griffiths and Kandel, however, the role of experts, while invisible, exists in the control of what gets to be said, by whom and when, as well as how those in charge interpret the law in situ. By determining the order of proceedings, panel members, especially chairs, create the framework for participants' interactions, while other professionals, like social workers who are usually called on to speak first, create a foundational base of knowledge upon which a child and family's circumstances and behaviour are evaluated. Both shape the flow of a hearing and have an impact on the processes of communication and participation. Information and how it becomes constructed as 'knowledge' that impacts on the proceedings is central to the operation of hearings. In acknowledging the adaptations that Norwegian lawyers and law firms have made with regard to their concentration on business expertise, Papendorf raises the issue of the effects of this kind of development on the provision of legal services that are outside the commercial domain, such as social security law. He echoes Rogowski's (1995:131) concern when he asks, 'have the business lawyers of the globalized corporations not gone a bit too far when it comes to adapting the legal core sphere of activity to the economical framework?' In acknowledging how United States leadership has affected the property fencing of the global digital knowledge commons and the radical opposition to it, Paliwala acknowledges that on the global stage it is predominantly an American model of regulation that drives the global harmonization of laws and practices. Despite attempts to overcome the limitations of this approach, for example through utilizing Floss-C software, hurdles still exist. For, as Paliwala observes, implementing Floss-C 'is not merely about the software itself but the paraphernalia of systems knowledge, engineering, attitudes, consultancies and aid finance which forms obstacles to overcoming pro-Microsoft tendencies'. As a result there is a danger that progressive software may become subordinate to the interests of capital with all the implications that this has for developing countries' access to and use of the Internet. In the case of transnational remittances, the role of experts is key in restructuring financial services to accommodate a more formal model of regulation embracing licensing and registration, in their attempts to mould Somali remittance companies into a more regularized legal framework, more in keeping with Western systems. This raises questions about what forms of knowledge become privileged as 'expertise' that take precedence over other forms of knowledge. For in approaching the *hawala* system from a security rather than a development perspective, versions of local knowledge and experience associated with the system are overtaken by the demands of financial experts who form part of an epistemic community that seeks to enforce its regulatory blueprint for financial services across the globe.

Transnational Media and Freedom of Expression: Human Rights Paradoxes

Cyberspace transcends territorial space not merely in enabling inter-territorial interaction but by making territoriality irrelevant in interactions. By enabling inter-territorial communication it promotes national, cultural, religious and sexual identity based interaction. It has, as demonstrated by the chapters in this book, resulted in the growth of knowledge networks which provide space for transnational and transcultural interaction and identities. It also supports trans-border identities, for example linking diasporic communities to religious or political networks in the homeland. The growing number of websites offering online *fatwas* for Muslims in the diaspora is, as shown by Shaheen Sardar Ali, giving concrete content to Islamic principles, making it a living law. Tharmalingam, Gaas and Eriksen point out how the economic operations of the Somali *hawala* system, which for centuries has been used by migrants to transfer economic resources to their families, is facilitated by the Internet.

Facilitating trans-spacial and transcultural communication, cyberspace also reifies existing social and political divisions. The instantaneous character of contemporary communication is, as Elisabeth Eide (Chapter 12) and Thomas Hylland Eriksen (Chapter 13) point out, indicating a new world order of transnational communication that has complex effects on the construction of identities and rights at multiple levels of law and society. An unexpected outcome of a number of transnational media events is how basic human rights, like freedom of speech and gender equality, are increasingly becoming associated with standardized and static notions of cultural difference.

Eide shows the communicative power of media in a transnational context in her chapter on the twelve cartoons depicting Mohammed published by a Danish newspaper. The speed with which images can travel round the world highlights the effect that the depiction of current affairs in one country, such as Denmark, can have on other countries across the globe. In this process that not only reaches across territorial borders but also connects with diasporic communities, Eide demonstrates how universal concepts, such as freedom of speech, embodied in international conventions and national laws, take on a contextual aspect that produces variations in the comprehension and interpretation of what free speech entails. She provides apt examples of this in her discussion of how understandings of law and freedom in Norway differ substantially from those that predominate in Pakistan. An important component of her discussion is how the terms of debate around representation are framed by those generating and responding to the controversy. Their responses cluster around a North/South divide informed by an ideological persuasion driven by orientalist or occidentalist perspectives. These perspectives underpin identities that uphold a dichotomy between what is embraced as the 'self' and what constitutes the 'other'. At its most simplistic, the question for a Canadian newspaper becomes 'Will the west stand up for its customs and norms … or will Muslims impose their way of life on the west?' to other editorials that depict protestors against publication as embodying the negation of modernity and democracy. From the occidentalist perspective, what is stressed is the West's hyper-secular and superior attitude towards others. This leads an Egyptian newspaper to state: 'there is a western conspiracy against the Muslims. Freedom does not guarantee the right of blasphemy', while in Indonesia another newspaper observes: 'apart from all their material achievements, the west has this religious complex: they hate their religion. Ironically, this feeling of hatred is generalized toward all religions'. While more nuanced positions are advanced, what is clear from the debate is the differing role that is ascribed to law in this context, in upholding or delimiting freedom of speech, which creates problems for reaching consensus at an international level, as exemplified by the United Nations Conference on Racism held in Geneva in 2009.

This paradox of human rights, Thomas Hylland Eriksen argues, arises when abstract principles are given content through human agency embedded in gendered, religious or ethnic identities. In a situation where human rights provide a framework but custom and local traditions supply the substance, the latter often come into conflict with the former. Eriksen demonstrates this clash with reference to two media events: the cartoon controversy and the bookseller controversy. In the post-colonial era where individuals and groups draw on international rights discourses in order to protect their identity and dignity, the positive freedom ('freedom to') of expression is frequently used to confront the negative freedom ('freedom from') of protection from defamation by reference to customary and religious paradigms of honour and sacredness. Eriksen inquires what the way out of this paradoxical situation entails where human rights discourse, in the context of the new world order of communication, is turned into a globalized circulation of insults. He suggests we look to cosmopolitanism that in John Gray's words is '… distinct from relativism and universalism. It affirms the possibility of mutual understanding between adherents to different moralities but without holding out the promise of any ultimate consensus' (Gray 2006) for a solution. The cartoon affair, Eriksen argues, demonstrates the impossibility of legislating in favour of cosmopolitan views and practices without limiting civil rights beyond that considered acceptable in liberal societies. The most effective method for promoting cosmopolitanism is – according to Eriksen – through the same practices that also lead to frictions, namely increased contact, dialogue and interaction, but based on the principles of recognition rather than suspicion. If anything, Eriksen argues, it is the lack of practical tasks in our everyday lives that prevent cosmopolitanism in North Atlantic societies, not the lack of things to disagree or agree about in the media.

Who or What is 'In' or 'Out': Transnational Processes of Inclusion and Exclusion

Overall, the chapters in this book demonstrate the empirical complexities of plural legal constellations highlighting how transnational law becomes part of social settings in which it not only competes with and shapes state law but also competes with self-regulating mechanisms, customary and sometimes religious law. As a consequence, transnationalization of law appears to create homogeneity, fragmentation and ambiguity, creating space for some actors while silencing others. This raises questions about the nature of power and how it is accommodated, ignored or resisted by various actors through an analysis of what happens when transnational law encounters national and local law. To comprehend what is at stake, the chains of interactions connecting transnational, national and local actors in multi-sited arenas of negotiations and the power relations that structure these interactions, need to be explored.

Most of the chapters in this volume raise questions about whom within a social group or community has the power and authority to define, interpret, implement and enforce law at the multiple levels at which it operates. A crosscutting theme is how configuring networks around particular constituencies, ranging from transnational families and religious institutions to business lawyers, creates processes of inclusion and exclusion that revolve around knowledge and power. These take many forms in local, national and transnational settings through alliances that derive from diverse constellations of interest groups that operate on a number of levels.

For Griffiths and Kandel, these groups include panel members and experts who control the proceedings by defining what constitutes relevant or irrelevant information in reaching decisions about whether or not a child is in need of compulsory measures of supervision. Alliances, however, do not simply arise on the basis of perceived 'expertise' or territorial affiliation. Thus networks of cooperation can cut across social divides, as they do sometimes in the case of social workers, children and families who collude in excluding certain information from panels in order to preserve the ongoing dynamics of their working relationship that exists beyond the panel. Where this occurs, the children and families may be seen to exert some power over social workers who acquiesce in their silence on certain matters before the panel in order to ensure their ongoing relationship with them.

In Papendorf's study, it is the experts in the business world of law and commerce who form powerful, specialist networks that exclude those that do not adhere to their precepts. These networks have an impact on how the legal profession is structured, with ever changing forms to meet the demands of the market that have implications for the provision of legal services to the community at large, especially with regard to more welfare-oriented pursuits. From Paliwala's perspective, the powerful networks that operate to open up or control access to the web consist of experts who align themselves on the basis of their ideological affiliations, based on commitment to collaborative, non-capitalist democratic engagement or, alternatively, centred on more property-based and commercially-oriented considerations that underpin relations between global business and capital. In both cases these networks have access to knowledge and resources in their quest to command communicative resources for different purposes. Where these are lacking, we find those who are marginalized or excluded, whom Paliwala refers to as 'net-excluded non-netizens', that is people who are unable to participate at all or only marginally in the benefits of cyber culture. The ideological underpinnings of inclusion and exclusion are also clearly visible in Eide and Eriksen's chapters on responses to the depiction of Mohammed in cartoons. The reactions to the communicative power of media, in this case, coalesce around networks derived from orientalist or occidentalist rhetoric that is used to define their constituencies. This rhetoric that is used to create processes of inclusion and exclusion by demarcating groups in terms of 'self' or 'other' operates to enhance a North/South divide, even if the realities of alliances in practice are much more complex.

The relationship between ideology and the power of law in creating zones of inclusion and exclusion is highlighted by several chapters. How Norwegian law and policy makers use egalitarian ideas in ways that, in Marianne Gullestad's terms, '... marginalize specific groups by simultaneously creating dichotomies asking for sameness' (Gullestad 2001:54) is demonstrated in several chapters. Melhuus shows how the Norwegian Biotechnology Act excludes several contemporary family forms. Rendering women equal protection under the law, the Norwegian judiciary, like that of India and Pakistan, uses a language that relegates honour crimes to other less-civilized spaces than the law of the nation-state (Hellum, Chapter 3). Using a legal discourse clustering around a civilized/uncivilized divide, the national judiciary upholds a dichotomy between what is embraced as the 'self' and what constitutes the 'other'. To understand the way the post September 11 security paradigm was translated into Norwegian legislation, Tharmalingham, Gaas and Eriksen point to the role of the media. Contrary to Norway's high profile in development and humanitarian aid, in its regulation of the Somali *hawala* system, the Norwegian government pursued the securitization doctrine. The Norwegian government put in place regulations that were stricter than those in other European countries and in the United States. The regulations meant that none of the existing *hawala* companies were able to comply. This in turn raises questions about how the relationship between media-created stereotypes about the Somali and other forms of knowledge were constituted in the legislative process. According to Norwegian social scientists, 'being Somali is seen by the Norwegian public as being synonymous with crime, drugs, smuggling, unlawfulness, exploitation of the welfare system and having more than two spouses' (Fangen 2006). The Norwegian *hawala* controversy demonstrates the need for a more systematic exploration of the relationship between dominant cultural stereotypes, often created and upheld by the press, and the power of law in creating zones of inclusion and exclusion.

This thread of inclusion/exclusion also runs through the chapters on the Muslim diasporic sphere. On the one hand, all three contributions (Bano, Larsen and Ali) bring Islam into mainstream discussions, demonstrating its reach into public and private spheres – formal and informal institutions and dispute resolution mechanisms; law and governance; gender and family issues; citizenship and rights; autonomy and control. On the other hand, all three clearly highlight the exclusive nature of the debates, be they within the European Council for *Fatwa* and Research, the Internet *fatwas* on women and gender or the non-statutory *Shari'a* Councils in Britain. Thus, non-Muslim European compatriots are clearly excluded from the debate and the international human rights terminology is not part of the framework for discussion. A further point to note is the controlling nature of the European Council for *Fatwa* and Research's project when it comes to choosing its membership. Care is taken in keeping a certain 'balance of power' or balance of numbers when nominating Muslim scholars from the diaspora and 'Muslim' countries retain control in the hands of 'pristine, homeland scholars' rather than those born and raised in the West. Women are 'included' (read: *controlled*) by engaging them in discussion and responding to their questions by making them the subject of *fatwas*.

Bano, Larsen and Ali's chapters bring to light a whimsical inclusive/exclusive and insider/outsider game that is at play. Bano's study depicts a complete absence of any reference to the European Council for *Fatwa* and Research *fatwas* in the *Shari'a* Councils' decisions despite both institutions addressing marriage, divorce and related issues of Muslims in the diaspora. Likewise, most Norwegian Muslims of Pakistani origin adhere to their South Asian version of Islamic law despite the opposite being declared by the European Council for *Fatwa* and Research, excluding other world views of Islam and Islamic law from their understandings of 'living law'. Despite claims of the universality of the Muslim, *ummah* territory is clearly guarded within these institutions and communities and 'gatekeepers' keep a strict vigil on entry and exit.

Both religious groups and women's groups are, as demonstrated in this volume, in search of justice beyond the confines of state, customary or religious laws. The appropriation of space provided by state law to religious groups and women's groups, such as legal advice and conflict-mediation, provides a vehicle for solutions that mediate beyond the confines of the prescribed rules associated within the particular domains of state, religious or customary law. Yet the interests of the religious group and the interests of individual women within the group are, as demonstrated, often in conflict. Formalization of informal religious and customary institutions, the case studies suggest, may lead to ethnic and religious segregation and undermine women and children's access to state law and official courts.

So, are there constructive ways of promoting pluralism, choice and recognition? Pakistani and Norwegian women's rights organizations have established legal advice and individual counselling that combines a plurality of argumentation strategies, finding ways to restore justice and dignity and resist and circumvent both state and religious law, thus speaking to the potential of legal pluralism (Hellum and Taj Chapter 4). In response to a counselling process that combines Norwegian state law and Islam and where women themselves are in control, the women report that they are at ease. This way, they are able to claim their rights under Norwegian law and still be good Muslims. This process shows how people from different legal traditions can work together in response to individual problems. It suggests that Eriksen's vision of a grounded cosmopolitanism is emerging through joint engagement in practical legal problems related to everyday life. It illustrates how a 'cosmopolitan legality' is created from below (Santos and Rodiguez-Garavito 2005).

All contributions to this volume, from whatever disciplinary perspective, challenge the assumption of homogeneity that underpins so much of national legislation in relation to culture and law in Northern Europe. By depicting the plurality of formal and informal norms, invoked by different actors in various settings, that draw on international, national and local practices, norms and values, they highlight the changing nature of the sociolegal landscape. In doing so, they underline the power of 'living' law and the ways in which it operates, through processes that create relations of inequality, domination and control that are constantly being confronted and resisted. They demonstrate how differing constellations of laws and norms, including transnational elements, give rise to diverse and ambiguous outcomes for those who appeal to them in terms of gender, class and status. By exposing the pressures that national law is undergoing in Northern Europe, from both above and below, the contributors to this volume expose the advantages and disadvantages that legal pluralism poses for differentially situated actors in various contexts and settings that cannot be ignored.

References[5]

Ali, S.S. 2000. *Equal Before Allah and Unequal Before Man Gender and Human Rights in Islam and International Law*. Hague/London/Boston: Kluwer Law International.

5 Excluding literature referred to in the chapters.

An-Na'im, A. 2007. Global citizenship and human rights: from Muslims in Europe to European Muslims, in *Religious Pluralism and Human Rights in Europe: Where to draw the Line?* edited by M.L.P. Leonen and J.E. Goldschmidt. Antwerpen: Intersentia, 13–55.

Benda-Beckmann, F. von. 2002. Who is afraid of legal pluralism? *Journal of Legal Pluralism*, 47:37–82.

Benda-Beckmann, F. von and K. von. 2006. The dynamics of change and continuity in plural legal order, in *The Journal of Legal Pluralism and Unofficial Law*, 53/54:11–44.

Benda-Beckmann, F. von, Benda-Beckmann, K. von and Griffiths, A. 2005. *Mobile People, Mobile Law. Expanding Legal Relations in a Changing World.* Farnham: Ashgate.

Benda-Beckmann, F. von, Benda-Beckmann, K. von and Griffiths, A. 2009. *The Power of Law in a Transnational World.* Oxford: Berghan Books.

Ehrlich, E. 1962. *Fundamental Principles of the Sociology of Law*. New York: Russel and Russel Inc.

Fangen, K. 2006. *Identitet og praksis. Etnisitet, kjønn og klasse blant somaliere i Norge* (Identity and Practice. Ethnicity, Class and Gender among Somalis in Oslo). Oslo: Gyldendal.

Føllesdal, A. and Wind, M. 2009. Introduction – Nordic reluctance towards judicial review under siege. *Nordic Journal of Human Rights* 2. Oslo: Norwegian University Press.

Gorashi, H., Eriksen, T.H. and Algashi, S. 2009. Introduction, in *Paradoxes of Cultural Recognition. Perspectives from Northern Europe*. Farnham: Ashgate.

Griffiths, J. 1986. What is legal pluralism? *Journal of Legal Pluralism*, 24:1–55.

Griffiths, A. 2002. Legal pluralism, in *An Introduction to Law and Social Theory*, edited by R. Banakar and M. Travers. Oxford: Hart Publishing, 289–310.

Griffiths, A. 2009. 'Anthropological Perspectives on Legal Pluralism and Governance in a Transnational World' pp 164–186 in M. Freeman and D. Napier (eds), *Law and Anthropology, Current Legal Issues* 2008 Vol 12. Oxford University Press.

Gullestad, M. 2001. Imagined sameness: shifting notions of us and them in Norway, in *Forestillinger om den andre* (Images of Otherness), edited by L.A. Ytrehus. Oslo: Norwegian Academic Press.

Hardt, M. and Negri, A. 2000. *Empire*. London, England/Cambridge Mass, USA: Harvard University Press.

Haas, P.M. 1992. 'Introduction: epistemic communities and international policy coordination'. *International Organization*, 46(1): 1–35.

Hellum, A. 1999. *Women's Human Rights and Legal Pluralism in Africa. Mixed Norms and Identities in Infertility Management in Zimbabwe*. Oslo: TANO Aschehoug. Harare: Mond Books.

Hellum, A. 2006. 'Menneskerettigheter, pluralisme, kompleksitet og integrasjon' (Human rights, pluralism and complexity). *I Festskrift til Carl August Fleischer*. Oslo: Universitetsforlaget.

Hellum, A., Stewart, J., Ali, S.S. and Tsanga A. (eds) 2007. 'Paths are made by walking. Introductory thoughts', in *Human Rights, Plural Legalities and Gendered Realities. Paths are Made by Walking*, edited by A. Hellum, J. Stewart, S.S. Ali and A. Tsanga. Harare: Weaver Press.

Joerges, C. 2005. Compliance research in legal perspectives, in *Law and Governance in Postnational Europe: Compliance beyond the Nation-State*, edited by M. Zürn and C. Joerges. Cambridge: Cambridge University Press.

Moore, S.F. 1978. *Law as Process*. Oxon: Routledge.

Perry, R.W. and Maurer, B. 2003. Globalization and governmentality: an introduction, in *Globalization under Construction: Governmentality, Law and Identity*, edited by R.W. Perry and B. Maurer. Minneapolis: University of Minnesota Press, xiv.

NOU 2003:19. Makt og demokratiutredningen. (the report on the Power and Democracy study commissioned by the Norwegian government).

Petersen, H. and Zahle, H. 1995. *Legal Polycentricity. Consequences of Pluralism in Law*. Aldershot: Dartmouth.

Sand, I.J. 2004. Polycontextuality as an alternative to constitutionalism, in *Transnational Governance and Constitutionalism*, edited by Christian Joerges, Inger-Johanne Sand and Gunther Teubner. Oxford: Hart Publishing.

Santos Boaventura de, S. 1987. Law: a map of misreading. Towards a postmodern conception of law. *Journal of Law and Society*, 14(3): 279–299.

Santos Boaventura de, S. and Rodriguez-Garavito, C.A. 2005. *Law and Globalization from Below. Towards a Cosmopolitan Legality*. Cambridge Studies in Law and Society. Cambridge: Cambridge University Press.

Twining, W. 2000. *Globalization and Legal Theory*. London: Butterworths.

Wiber, M. 2009. The spatial and temporal role of law in natural resource management: the impact of state regulation of fishing spaces, in *Spatialising Law: An Anthropological Geography of Law in Society*, edited by F. and K. von Benda-Beckmann and A. Griffiths. Farnham: Ashgate Press, 121–154.

PART I
Family Relations, Transnational, National and Local Sites of Contestation

Chapter 1
Syrian Transnational Families and Family Law

Annika Rabo

Ilham is an elderly Syrian woman with seven children, five of whom are living abroad. Her daughter, Noura, married a French citizen in 1978 and moved with him to France where she had two children. Noura was widowed in 1988 and stayed on in France with her children. In 1981 Ilham's oldest son, Samir, married a woman from Sweden and moved there with her from Syria. They were divorced in Sweden in 1990 and in 1995 he married a woman from Syria who settled with him in Sweden. That year Ilham's oldest daughter, Lama, left her husband in Syria and moved with her youngest son, still a teenager, to Canada. Younis, one of Lama's older sons, married a young Swedish woman in 1996. They met when she was visiting relatives in Syria. The young couple moved to Sweden but divorced in 1999. Younis stayed in Sweden and in 2003 married a woman from Finland. They have settled in Sweden. Lama's oldest son got a work permit for Kuwait in 2003. There he met and married a Lebanese citizen. They still live in Kuwait. Ilham's youngest son, Elias, married a Syrian woman in 1992 and they had their first child in 1993. Elias's wife and child went to Canada to visit relatives in 1995 and stayed on there. In 1997 Elias was able to join his wife. Mouna, another of Ilham's daughters, applied to immigrate to Canada and was accepted. She moved there with her family in 2006 and her youngest child was born in Canada. But her husband wanted to return to Syria and Mouna has continued to go to Canada for short visits to keep her residence permit. In 2008 Lama married a Canadian man who was born in Egypt and they are thinking of settling there later on.

Through her children and grandchildren, Ilham is connected to seven countries as well as her native Syria. She has visited all her 'foreign' children. Her French and Swedish grandchildren have visited Syria a number of times. Ilham herself acquired a French residence permit when she stayed with her widowed daughter. Such geographically-spread families, like Ilham's, are not unusual in Syria or in many other parts of the world. Millions of people are now part of transnational families[1] where one, some or all its members have attachments to two or more

1 I use the term 'transnational', rather than diasporic, to underline the continuous and practical links to two or more states that members of these families maintain.

states. They are hence bound to, or influenced by, a plurality in family law,[2] as well as policies in different states and localities with various interpretations of what constitutes a 'normal family'. Currently there are complex and simultaneous processes of convergence and divergence of family law and policy in Europe and elsewhere. There is also an intricate relationship between the idealized family, the normative family, how people actually practise family-life and the way these influence and are influenced by different legal and policy arrangements. When many people maintain multi-local attachments through transnational links, this complexity increases.

Transnational families are not a new phenomenon. Many genealogically minded Syrians are able to trace links of kinship to people in many other countries of the region. This harks back to nomadic family histories and histories of other kinds of 'transnational' mobility in the periods before national borders were set up. But transnational Syrian families are also found in more recent history. In 1939, Ilham – aged thirteen at the time – was to go to Venezuela to live with some relatives who had no children. But she was suddenly married off to her second cousin. In Ilham's Syrian mountain village, all inhabitants have relatives who migrated to South America in the early twentieth century. Some never returned, others did or were able to maintain contact with the 'home-country'. But compared to Ilham's childhood and youth, transnational family connections are much more intense for her own children. There is increased international mobility on the part of citizens and increased long-distance communication in most parts of the world. Ilham does not use Skype or email so her foreign children and grandchildren talk to her on the telephone but they use more modern means of communication amongst themselves.

Although transnational connections are intense in today's world, they are also much more restricted compared to when Ilham was young. States are not always willing to let their citizens freely leave the country. Such was the case in Syria until the late 1980s. But more significant are the many restrictions and obstacles so-called 'receiver states' place on people wanting to go there. Freedom of movement across national borders is extremely unequally distributed in the contemporary world. Permanent residents and citizens of member states of the European Union are encouraged to increase their mobility within the union, partly as a means of enhancing European integration. But 'outsiders' are strongly discouraged from entry into the union. For citizens from countries in Asia and Africa, reuniting the family constitutes the legally-accepted reason, *par excellence*, for entry into the

2 The question of plurality of law or legal pluralism is a huge subject largely outside the scope of this article. Here I simply want to underline that transnational Syrians migrants have to cope with or have access to different state family laws. For important recent discussions on the links between legal pluralism, mobility, transnationalism and governance see Benda-Beckmann, Benda-Beckmann and Griffiths (2005, 2009) and Benda-Beckmann, Benda-Beckmann and Eckert (2009). For an inventory of the development of the term 'legal pluralism' itself see Dupret (2007).

European Union. The importance of 'family' has thus in no way decreased in this *age of migration*[3] and migration laws and family law have in many ways become highly intertwined. People are mobile and so are laws. Law 'operates at a global level while at the same time responding to processes of globalization' (von Benda-Beckmann, von Benda-Beckmann and Griffiths 2005:1).

The aim of this chapter is to highlight the intersection between family law and transnational families.[4] This intersection covers large and complex phenomena that can be studied, analyzed and interpreted from many different perspectives. Issues of how citizenship is interpreted and how various national laws 'meet' or 'collide' is one important phenomenon. Another important issue is how various states handle parallel or plural jurisprudence in the field of family law. But it is crucial to underline that this intersection cannot be understood only in terms of legal principles. It is equally important to look at how people actually practise family relations across national borders. Finally, questions of gender relations and family arrangements have strong symbolic value as indicators of democracy, progress or cultural authenticity. Members of transnational families may become subject to conflicting moral interests where different groups in 'sender' and 'receiver' countries can be mobilized. There are different and legitimate ways to organize family life but there are also differences that might be difficult to accept within the framework of specific legal cultures. Family conflicts that extend across national borders may also easily turn into conflicts of morality and gender and 'good family law' as will be underlined below. A scrutiny of transnational families and family law may also reveal the limits of legal universalism.

In this chapter members of transnational families with strong links to Syria will be used to illustrate a few of these complex questions.[5] Syria is interesting not only because international migration plays such an important role in the lives of many citizens – both those leaving and those staying behind – but also because family law differs according to religious affiliation.[6] Members of some minority communities follow their own religious codes that make for added complications when there are transnational family conflicts. In order to analyze cases of Syrian transnational families and their concerns, I will now take a closer look at the workings of families and family law in Syria.

3 *The Age of Migration* is the telling title of Stephen Castel and Mark J. Miller's well-known book that was first published in 1993.

4 Material in this article is based on anthropological fieldwork in Syria which started in the late 1970s and in particular on material collected within the research project *Transnational Syrians and Family Law* that has received financial support from the Swedish Research Council.

5 Some of these complex issues are discussed also in Rabo (2007a and 2007b).

6 For more discussion of this kind of legal pluralism in Syria, especially from a gender perspective, and how it may both restrict and empower citizens in various ways see Rabo (2010).

State and Family in Syria

The members of Ilham's family, outlined above, have had different reasons for their moves from Syria. Some left because of marriage rather than as part of a life-long plan. Some wanted to escape family pressures or wanted more individual freedom. Some left to give their children better educational opportunities. Only one member left for mainly economic reasons although this is the most common cause among Syrian migrants. Syria is a country with enormous complexity and variation in contemporary household and family composition and citizens manage family life in many different ways. The variation is to a large extent related to rural/urban habitation, class background and ethnic or religious affiliation. Rural, poor, Sunni Muslim Syrians, for example, tend to have larger families and be more economically independent within households than urban or better-off Syrians, or minorities (Rabo 2008).

But despite the great variation in how family practice works, Syrians – like citizens in states all over the world – are fostered into particular family-regimes. First of all families are ideologically shaped and reproduced on a national level. Many researchers (for example, Kandiyoti 1991, Rabo 1996, Charrad 2001) have demonstrated the intimate link between nationalism and nation-state building in the Middle East (and elsewhere) and the fostering of a sound and stable family as the essential building block of society. This ideal – with its local, regional or ethnic/religious variations – has been successfully inculcated in the Middle East. So states have been, and are, important in constructing the ideal family as well as in 'ordering' such families through laws, policies and bureaucratic routines. The Syrian state, for example, can be said to practise gender equality in certain domains (Rabo 1996:163). Equality between women and men is underlined in the constitution and many policies have been set in motion to liberate women from 'feudal and backward' families and kin-groups in order to enhance the development of the nation. At the same time 'family law' and many policies continue to order men and women in an unequal way.

Managing Citizens through Family Law

The so-called Personal Status Law (*qanoun al ahwaal ash-shakhsiyya*) in Syria (and elsewhere in the Middle East) covers questions of marriage, divorce, parentage, custody, legal capacity, wills and inheritance. The Personal Status Law in Syria is mainly based on Hanafi jurisprudence, one of four 'legal schools' from the classical jurisprudence. Thus unconditional divorce is the prerogative of the husband and daughters inherit only half of their brothers' share. Fathers have legal guardianship over children while mothers in the case of divorce may exercise 'care-taking' (*hadane*) until the children reach a specific age.

The concept of 'personal status' is not part of classical Islamic jurisprudence and was first used in Egypt in the 1890s by the Egyptian Minister of Justice,

Muhammad Qadri Pasha (Nasir 2002:34). Through the influence of Code Napoleon, the legislators of the late Ottoman Empire started to codify 'family issues' which became a separate legal field, rather than part of the traditionally fluid Islamic jurisprudence.[7] Codification of family law has generally taken place in the Middle East[8] and state institutions control formal family law.[9] From the late nineteenth century onwards, family matters have thus, in general, become the concern of the worldly powers in the Middle East, just as in Europe, and intimately related to debates over modernity, development and cultural authenticity and the simultaneous ordering of citizens through censuses, health programmes, education and military service.

In Syria the Personal Status Law encompasses all citizens but Christians and Druze are allowed – or obliged – to apply their own religious rules concerning betrothal, marriage and dissolution of marriage in their own religious courts.[10] This plurality of law is inherited from the Ottoman period when the imperial authorities recognized the right of various *millet* (nationalities or religious minorities) to regulate their own internal affairs. The Christian courts in Syria are dominated by clergy and the Druze by their own religious specialists. I will discuss the Christian courts more later because this particular Syrian legal pluralism has important repercussions for Christian transnational migrants. In Syria there are *Shari'a* courts that handle marriage, divorce, custody and inheritance. The courts are part of the national court system and the judges are typically not specialists in Islamic jurisprudence. Rather, they are products of the secular modern law schools where '*Shari'a*' is taught mainly in conjunction with contemporary family law.

7 In recent decades researchers with social science training have come to question the inherent goodness of the systematization of family law (c.f. Moors 1999). A fixed family law has in many Middle Eastern countries turned the earlier fluidity and flexibility into institutional gender conservatism, not least because 'family law' has become a crucial symbol of the nation.

8 Family law is still not codified in most countries on the Arab peninsula, nor in Libya or Sudan.

9 In Lebanon, however, there is no unified 'state' Personal Status Law. Instead, the many different religious communities have the exclusive right to dispense family law.

10 Syria is a multi-religious and multi-ethnic country. Partly due to the sensitivities of the ruling party where all citizens should be equal and equally Arab, there are no official statistics on religious or ethnic affiliation. The majority of the inhabitants are Sunni Muslim, but there are also various Shia groups, including Alawites as well as Druze. The Syrian Christians are split into a large number of different churches. Most Syrians classify themselves as Arabs but there are also Armenians, Kurds, Suryoye, Turkmens and Circassians. The Syrian Jews also have their own family courts. But since there are only a handful Jews left in Syria this has little practical importance in Syria today. In 2006 the Syrian Catholics amended their family codes and were at that time able to also gain jurisdiction over inheritance. Syrian female Catholics now inherit the same share as their male counterparts.

The Syrian state thus orders its citizens through the Personal Status Laws in various ways. Although the Syrian state does not register religious or ethnic affiliation in passports or on identity cards, religious affiliations come to the fore when citizens marry and have a family. Furthermore this religious affiliation affects women and men as well as the Muslim majority and the minorities in different ways. A marriage between a non-Muslim man and a Syrian Muslim woman is considered invalid, while a marriage between a Syrian Muslim man and a Christian woman is legally recognized.[11] Christians can legally convert to Islam but the opposite is not possible.

The Syrian state gives equal access to education for both boys and girls, and salaries and social benefits in the public sector are equal for men and women. But there are many other policies and routines which serve to underline the ideal patriarchal family. The Syrian family book, for example, is a document given to a married man, in which his wife – or wives – and (up to 20) children are registered. It used to be quite important in the 1970s and 1980s as a way of accessing subsidized consumer goods and it is still crucial in contacts with many bureaucracies. Polygamy is not condoned in the ideology of the Syrian ruling *Ba'ath* party but the family book actually allows for the simultaneous registration of four wives. The family book is thus a document symbolizing male adulthood and the authority of the father or husband.

Resisting State Control

The fostering of state ideologies is often complex and contradictory. In Syria there are, for example, conditions for marriages to become legally recognized by the state. All marriages have to be registered either in a state *Shari'a* court (for Muslim citizens) or in an independent religious court (for Christians and Druze). Furthermore, according to Syrian policy, a man cannot marry unless he has finished his military service. All children also have to be registered at birth. In the late 1970s villagers in the rural areas of northern Syria, however, did not always follow these rules. Many villagers thought that it was their own business how and when they got married and if and when they registered their children (Rabo 1986:88). Typically these villagers followed their own marriage traditions. The bride, for example, was not given her dower to dispose of as she saw fit but instead there was a 'bride price' which the father of the bride took as his own. There was seldom any provision for a deferred dower and if the husband divorced his wife she would return to her father's house. It was not uncommon, however, that when a woman left her husband, her father had to repay the 'bride price' he had been given. Very little stigma was attached to male or female divorcees and most

11 The children in a marriage between a Christian woman and a Muslim man will automatically be considered Muslim. There is no mutual inheritance in such a marriage and the children cannot inherit from their Christian mother.

were soon remarried. Since the splitting up typically took place in the first years of marriage, villagers said it was better to wait to register a marriage until it was clear that it would last. The Syrian authorities were always helpful in registering such marriages if they had resulted in children.[12] In these parts of Syria people still talk about the importance of their kin group and their tribe and they openly value family arrangements that more urban Syrians consider un-Islamic, uncivilized or simply against the national laws.

The marriage arrangements of these northern villagers can be characterized as *'urfi* (customary), a legal category recognized in classical Islamic jurisprudence. But contemporary states, like Syria, have been keen to suppress *'urf* and to control citizens through formal and codified state law. Lately, however, the question of new kinds of urban *'urfi* marriage has become a hot topic in Syria (c.f. Carlisle 2008). There is said to be an upsurge of young people with no common household who marry informally in order to have 'lawful' sexual relations. Sometimes there is a written marriage contract between them, sometimes there are witnesses and sometimes men of religion bless the union. *'Urfi* marriages also take place, it is said, as secret second marriages for men who are already married. According to some Syrian lawyers there is also an increase in 'tourist marriages' where rich men from the Arab Gulf countries marry young Syrian women for the summer season. In 2006 I first heard discussions in Syria about possible cases of *mut'a* marriage introduced by visiting foreigners. This is a marriage for a stipulated period which is legal among Shi'a but not among Sunni Muslims.

State employees, lawyers and Syrians at large condemn *'urfi* and *mut'a* marriages and underline that women have no legal benefits like dower and inheritance unless these unions are transformed into marriages registered by the Syrian state. It is, of course, impossible to know how common informal marriages are in Syria. But it is interesting to note that 'foreigners' are often implicated in these practices. Although these marriages have no, or few, transnational implications, these debates still highlight the state's duty to safeguard Syrian women against perils from abroad. The ideal Syrian family is a national family, from the point of view of the authorities and many ordinary citizens.

Questions of family, kinship and citizenship are closely linked in Middle Eastern states as in many other places. The nation can be seen as a family writ large. In Article 44 of the 1973 Syrian constitution it is stated that the family is the basic unit of society, that it is protected by the state, and that the state protects and encourages marriage and eliminates the material and social obstacles hindering it. According to the constitution, women and men are equal as citizen but this is not the case in practice, as discussed. In Syria – as elsewhere – citizenship is gendered (c.f. Lister *et al.* 2007, Rabo 1996:155, Fábos 2001:48).

12 'Illegitimate' children are an anomaly in Syrian legislative thinking. If there is a socially-recognized father, great pressure will be put on the couple to formally marry. In the rare cases where there fatherhood cannot be established, the child will be given a fictitious father.

Citizenship and Gender

In Syria, like in other Arab states, citizenship is basically a question of 'blood' (*jus sanguinis*) and expressed patrilineally.[13] Children inherit the citizenship of their fathers, no matter where they are born. Noura, mentioned earlier, who married a Frenchman, cannot give her children Syrian citizenship, while the children of Samir (who married a Swedish woman) are considered Syrian citizens in the eyes of the state, whether he likes it or not. But even if a Syrian woman lives in Syria with her foreign husband, neither he nor their children, can become citizens. After much debate, Egypt changed the law in 2004 and Morocco changed the law in 2007 in order to give citizenship rights to children born of foreign fathers. This has been important for women who live in their home country with foreign men. In Egypt and Morocco, such children now have equal access to state-sponsored health care and education. In Syria discussions are underway about a change in the law but the state authorities still seem unconvinced about the need for gender-equal citizenship. I have had discussions with state employees who claim that the unity of the nation could be compromised if Syrian women give citizenship to their foreign husbands. For many ordinary citizens the issue is quite different. They are concerned about the low value of Syrian citizenship in an international context. 'Who wants to become a Syrian citizen?' many ask. 'All of us would like to have another citizenship as well, to be used for travel or for entry into the European Union or other countries of the West', one woman stated.

Foreign women who marry Syrians and settle in Syria are, as stated above, allowed to acquire citizenship and in many cases they are better off as Syrian citizens.[14] A foreign woman married to a Syrian citizen needs the permission of her husband to leave the country if there are under-aged children in the family. In case of divorce or if she is widowed, she may lose her residence rights. If there are children above the age of 'care-taking' (*hadane*), custody may revert to her husband or his relatives.

Syrian Migrants and Migration

The ideology of the Syrian ruling *Ba'ath* party is based on the idea of a strong link between the national soil and the people. From such a perspective emigration is an abrogation. People should stay in the national home and contribute to its

13 Sweden, by contrast, in 1979 changed to an unconditional matrilineal link in that every child born from a mother with Swedish citizenship becomes a Swedish citizen at birth. A Swedish father may give his citizenship to his child only if the child is actually born in Sweden or if he is married to the mother of the child.

14 Until 2007 foreigners could not register real estate in their own name. Even if a foreign wife was allowed to inherit from her husband, she could not formally own property.

development. If they leave they should only do so reluctantly and come back eagerly as soon as possible. Even if they obtain another citizenship they are still considered Syrian citizens, as noted above. Sadeldine (2005:266) notes that people who emigrated more than a hundred years ago are still included in the national registration on which the annual population is calculated.

There are few reliable figures concerning Syrian migration but most labour migrants travel to Lebanon. Many of them are seasonal workers in agriculture and quite often whole families migrate together. Although the political relations between these neighbouring countries have been fraught with conflict they are also economically quite interdependent and Syrians have the easiest access to Lebanon. Many Syrians also work in Saudi Arabia, Kuwait and the United Arab Emirates, although work visas are becoming more difficult to obtain. Labour migrants with little education are seldom able to take their families to such countries. Many also prefer to leave their families behind so they can work as much as possible and save as much as possible to send back home.[15] In the Arab world there is a general tension between an ideal of pan-Arab nationalism which includes all Arabs, and a more limited nationalism. As 'Arab brothers' various countries are supposed to help and support each other, just like members in a family. But the unequal distribution of natural resources and job opportunities make the 'brothers' far from willing to share. Thus there is great pressure in the countries that are rich in people but poor in other resources for people to migrate to countries in the region where the contrary is the case.

There is a strong migratory link between Syria and France, and Syria and Germany, and the links to Australia, the United States of America and Canada are significant as well. In the early 1980s when Syria was racked by civil strife, many politically active Syrians went into exile – some in Saudi Arabia but most in Western Europe. Many of those who have left the country have for decades been unable to have their passports renewed. Even if they have acquired citizenship in the country of settlement, they are unable to visit Syria. Others, who were not regarded as political threats, still had difficulties in returning, even for a visit. But since the turn of the century there is more of an open-door policy towards the Syrian diaspora. Syrians abroad are encouraged to 'come home' for short or long periods and the policymakers set up various schemes to use their skills and their capital. A special ministry for Syrian migrants has been set up for this purpose.

Migration from Syria is gendered. Many more men than women leave the country for work, education or permanent settlement. Although there is an ideal that sons should stay close to their parents and support them in everyday life, sons are also encouraged to leave the country. 'There are no jobs here, they cannot get married and cannot set up a household of their own these days', many parents all over the country lament. 'It is better for them and for us if they can leave the country'. Although it is still politically taboo to publicly debate the lack of

15 For an excellent overview of the complexities of migration within and from the Middle East see P. Fargues (ed.) *Mediterranean Migration Report* (2005).

opportunities in the country, the Syrian authorities erect fewer and fewer obstacles for young men trying to leave.[16] But families would never urge their daughters to leave the country except as wives to migrants. Syrian families do not want to be thought of as abandoning their daughters and sisters to an unknown fate.[17]

Syrian Transnational Family Issues

Most Syrians who migrate are labour migrants and the typical labour migrant is a man leaving his parents and siblings or wife and children behind. The typical family issue in such cases of transnational migration involves the stress and strain due to the absence of the migrant. Family members left in Syria also commonly complain that migrants do not send as much money as family members at home want and expect. Typical cases of family tensions and problems due to migration commonly involve migration policies, residence and work permits in the 'receiving' countries rather than family law in Syria or in the country of migration. But when the migrant marries abroad, brings a wife to his new country of residence or migrates with his wife, family law issues often come to the fore. It is much more common for Syrian men to marry foreign women than for Syrian women to marry foreign men. Even marriage in close neighbouring countries is much more unusual for women, unless links of intermarriage and kinship are already established.[18] Probably most Syrian men who have married Western foreigners actually settle in the wife's country but some do settle in Syria. In the larger Syrian cities there are associations for German and Russian women who are married to Syrians. Most met their Syrian husbands when they studied abroad. Many Syrian women become migrants by marrying first or second generation Syrians who reside abroad and have acquired a second citizenship. In many families such a marriage may be considered advantageous if the husband is a citizen of a Western country.

16 There are, for example, ways to pay an 'exemption fee' for not doing the mandatory military service for men who reside abroad. The state gets hard currency and these men have no problem returning to Syria.

17 Sarah Gualteri (2004) is critical of the way that nineteenth-century migrants from Greater Syria to the Americas have been portrayed as (heroic) men. She brings out many interesting examples of (Christian) women who migrated on their own or who managed to support themselves and their children on their own in the United States of America. In such a perspective it seems that women are more restricted today than a 100 or 140 years ago.

18 I have no figures to corroborate these statements because no statistics are to be found. But I have worked in various parts of Syria since 1978 and only met or heard of a few Syrian women who are married to non-regional foreigners. These women were all Christians. It is, however, not uncommon that Syrian women marry Palestinian refugees who reside in Syria. These refugees have the same rights and obligations as other Syrians, except for formal citizenship, since Syrian women cannot pass on their nationality to children born with Palestinian men. This limits their freedom of movement even more than for ordinary Syrians.

Many, if not most, Syrian transnational families (or families with strong ties to Syria) prefer to manage issues like citizenship choice, inheritance and divorce without involving the Syrian authorities. When transnational family members are in agreement, Syrian authorities are typically seen as trying to control their citizens – and their foreign family members – to an excessive degree. From the point of view of a foreign woman married to a Syrian man and living in Syria, it might be advantageous, as noted above, to have Syrian citizenship. But she (and her husband) might decide that it is more advantageous for the family if she retains her original citizenship in case she is able to pass on her nationality to her children. The children may thus have easier access to higher education and employment in their mother's country of birth. Other Syrians use the possibility of having another citizenship as an insurance against political uncertainty in the region. Many Syrians actively seek opportunities to have a second citizenship in countries like France, Canada, the United States of America, Australia or Sweden. Mouna, one of Ilham's daughters, commuted to and from Canada for this purpose. In many such cases, the links to the second country of citizenship may be quite flimsy.

Many (male) Syrians have settled more or less permanently abroad but still keep strong links with their parents and extended family in Syria. If they marry abroad and never register the marriage or their children in Syria, and never bring their 'foreign' family to Syria, Syrian family law and legal policies do not come into play at all. The same goes for a divorce taking place abroad. But the Syrian authorities may force 'Syrianness' on children born abroad if they find out that their father is a Syrian (or has Syrian ancestry).

Ilham's grandchildren from her son Samir and his Swedish wife were born in Sweden. The parents chose not to register their two sons in Syria although they had married in that country.[19] Samir had managed to leave Syria without finishing the obligatory military service and this made it difficult for him to return without being immediately drafted into the military. But his wife, Monica, travelled to Syria quite frequently with the children. They entered as ordinary foreign tourists to enable them to leave Syria without any problems, since, as stated above, if the children are under-age, a non-Syrian wife cannot leave the country without the permission of her Syrian husband. This is the case even if the husband actually lives in another country. Usually Monica and the children were able to enter and leave Syria with no problem but Samir's brother in Syria was always ready to pretend to be the father or husband and once he actually had to do this.

Transnational Syrian Christians face specific disadvantages compared to Muslims. Syrian Christian citizens are not only controlled by the state authorities but also by their church authority to which the state has delegated the control of family law for its members.

---

19 They wanted to minimize the risk that the Syrian authorities in the future would draft the two sons into military service. Since 2006 it has become much simpler for Syrians working, studying or living abroad (see footnote 16) to pay a fee to avoid military service.

Christian Family Law and Transnational Family Life

A Syrian Muslim man who marries a Christian or Muslim woman in France, Sweden or the United States of America, will usually have no difficulty in registering this marriage in Syria because, under the auspices of private international law,[20] Syria normally recognizes marriages that take place in other countries.[21] If such a marriage is also dissolved abroad, the Syrian *Shari'a* court will normally recognize the foreign divorce if neither of the parties demand otherwise.[22] But for Syrian Christians and their foreign partners, the matter is much more complicated.

The various Syrian churches have the exclusive right to marry their members and all Syrian Christians are obliged to marry in church. If Christians contract a civil marriage abroad, the state will not recognize it. The couple has to marry in a church abroad or in Syria. Christians who want to dissolve their marriages have to apply to their own religious courts and not to the state *Shari'a* court. The different Syrian Catholic churches[23] – like Catholics elsewhere – do not accept divorce but marriages can be annulled if specific criteria are met. The more numerous various Orthodox churches[24] do accept divorce for a few limited reasons, like prolonged abandonment, violence or adultery on the part of one spouse. Until the 1990s annulment and divorce used to be extremely rare and very shameful among Syrian Christians. The sanctity of the Christian marriage was, according to clergy and laypeople alike, what differentiated them from Muslims. Now, instead, many complain about the difficulties couples face when they approach their religious courts, even couples that have agreed to part ways. The position of religious courts has significant repercussions on transnational Syrian Christians. The following describes a typical case.

Two Christians marry in Syria and then move to the United States of America or Sweden where they eventually divorce under the civil law of that country. This divorce will not be recognized by the Syrian state since the Christian churches

---

20 Private international law regulates legal issues of individuals connected to foreign jurisdiction. It seeks to answer which country has jurisdiction over the question, the law of which country is to be applied and if the verdict in one country will be recognized in another. Conflicts of contract are typical questions in private international law but family law is also important.

21 Recognition of a marriage made abroad is however, based on the limits of *ordre public* in Syria. Thus, for example, same-sex marriage or partnership will not be recognized.

22 This could be the case if two persons born in Syria get a divorce abroad and the man claims that this divorce did not follow the Syrian rules of *talaq* (divorce by male prerogative) or *khula* whereby a woman forfeits the economic compensation stated in the marriage contract.

23 Greek Catholics, Syrian Catholics, Armenian Catholics, Maronites and Roman Catholics are Catholic churches recognized in the Syrian Law of Personal Status.

24 The Greek Orthodox Church is the largest in Syria followed by the Armenian Orthodox and the Syrian Orthodox.

have full authority over such matters. If they want this divorce to also have legal effect in Syria, they have to go to their religious court. This court might block the case for many years or even refuse to take on the case. This means that the couple are divorced in the United States of America or Sweden but married in Syria. In such a situation it is impossible for the man or the woman to get married again to another Christian in Syria. This is what happened to Samir and Monica who were married in a Greek Orthodox Church in Syria and then moved to Sweden where they were divorced a decade later. Some years after the Swedish divorce, Samir wanted to remarry a Christian Syrian woman and had to seek a divorce in one of the Greek Orthodox religious courts in Syria. Monica cooperated in order for him to obtain this divorce. By blaming her for the problems in the marriage, the court dissolved the marriage and Samir was allowed to marry a second time. If Monica had been a Syrian citizen with a family concerned about her name and reputation in Syria, she would probably have acted differently.

Christians may also face other bureaucratic obstacles. Samir and Monica married in Syria but the Syrian church ceremony was not accepted by the Swedish authorities and they had to register their marriage in the civil court in Damascus. The only way the Syrian civil court could register the marriage was by using an Islamic marriage contract. This Islamic contract thus showed the Swedish authorities that the Syrian authorities accepted the couple's marriage. When they divorced, however, only the church marriage, and not this contract, had legal repercussions in Syria.

Transnational Migrants and Transnational Churches

Syrian Christians have migrated and settled outside Syria – especially in Europe, Australia and the Americas – to a higher degree than Syrian Muslims. In Sweden, for example, most migrants from Syria, or people born in Sweden with one or both parents from Syria, belong to the Syrian Orthodox Church. The historical 'homeland' of this church is in today's southeast Turkey but with strong links also to today's Syria and Lebanon. The first Syrian Orthodox migrants came to Sweden in 1967 as refugees from Lebanon and, within a decade, others living in the Middle East, Turkey and Europe had joined them. Today there are between 30,000 and 40,000 Syrian Orthodox Christians living in Sweden[25] and their presence is especially strong in the city of Södertälje, where they make up almost a quarter of the population. Many Syrian Orthodox Christians came to Sweden at a time when labour migration had come to an end. Instead many were granted residence permits in the late 1970s and early 1980s for 'humanitarian reasons'. Up until a decade ago many also came as partners to men and women who had already obtained permanent residence or citizenship in Sweden.

25 Cetrez (2005:29) claims that there might be 70,000–80,000 Syrian Orthodox living in Sweden.

Until 2000, Sweden had a 'state church' into which all citizens were born, unless their parents declared otherwise. Migration into Sweden has increased the presence of Catholic and various Orthodox, as well as Muslim, communities. Through increased freedom of religion, many Christian churches (and Muslim imams) have gradually obtained the right to marry their members. There are several Syrian Orthodox parishes and two bishops in Sweden but marriage in the Syrian Orthodox church is still not recognized by the Swedish state.[26] People who marry in these churches also have to have a civil marriage in order to be considered married in the eyes of the Swedish authorities. Many Syrian Orthodox do not feel married unless the ceremony is carried out in their church and, for migrants, their church is highly valued as a symbol of religious and ethnic identity (Rabo 2007b:222).

When I interviewed one of the bishops in 2005 he said he would prefer a plurality of law for Sweden, such as that in Syria (Rabo 2007b:224). That way he and his religious court could manage all family matters without involving the Swedish state. But lay people in his parish were not of the same opinion. Although they wanted their church weddings to be recognized as acts of marriage in Sweden, they did not like the church influence over divorce. A Syrian Orthodox person living permanently in Sweden can get a civil divorce. But in the eyes of the Syrian Orthodox Church in Sweden (and Syria) the couple is still married, as discussed earlier. If a couple divorce according to Swedish civil law, they can marry again in a civil marriage or in the Lutheran Church of Sweden. But unless they get a religious divorce in their own (unofficial) religious court, they will not be able to marry in a Syrian Orthodox church in Sweden or anywhere else. This divorce may, as mentioned above, take quite some time or not take place at all.

Members of Syrian Orthodox families with transnational connections to Syria who were interviewed in 2005 said that they still preferred to find Syrian Orthodox partners for themselves and their children. But they did not want these partners to come from Syria. 'To marry somebody from Syria is a second best choice', a young man said. 'Young people think that you only marry in Syria because you cannot find somebody in Sweden'. Many emphasized that it is better to marry a person who has had similar experiences and lifestyles (Rabo 2007b:220). In the 1980s and the 1990s the topic of marriage between Syrian Orthodox men living in Sweden and women living in Syria was hotly debated in Syria. Prospective grooms would visit Syria in the summer and get engaged to Christian women. Life in Sweden was painted as rosy and although many families were reluctant to have their daughters so far away, many thought they were doing them (and themselves) a service by having a link to a peaceful and rich European country.

In the 1980s and 1990s there was also considerable pressure on unmarried Syrian Orthodox girls in Sweden to marry relatives in Turkey and the Middle East in order for them to be able to migrate. 'We were not always careful enough when

26 One of the Syrian Orthodox bishops applied for the right to perform legally recognizable marriages in 2006.

Swedish Syrian Orthodox members came to get married', a priest told me in 2008 when I interviewed him in the north-eastern city of Hassake, close to the Turkish border. 'Now the church and lay people have realized that many complications may come out of hasty marriages', he continued. He was the chairman of their religious court and he stressed that the church had learned to ask Syrian Orthodox 'foreigners' for both civil and religious papers if they wanted to marry in Syria, to make sure they were not already married abroad. But no matter how careful they are, he said unforeseen problems arise and recounted the following case:

> A few years ago a man who lived in Germany came to marry a young woman in order to take her out of the country. He had all his papers in order. He was not and had not been married in Germany and the wedding took place. The day afterwards his mother came to my office with a small child to be registered. This was the child of her son, born out of wedlock in Germany. The groom had left this child in Syria to be cared for by his grandmother.

The church has no 'theological' provisions to ask previously unmarried 'foreign' grooms if they have children but now priests have learned to ask such questions in order not to be caught up in transnational custody cases.

Custody Cases as the Lynchpin of Transnational Family Law

Custody cases are clearly the most difficult to solve transnationally if there is no agreement between the mother and the father. Most of the cases concerning custody disputes in Syria are between Syrian men and non-Syrian women or two Syrians who have settled abroad. But there are exceptions. In the 1990s a Syrian Muslim man married a Russian woman in Syria where they settled and had one daughter. During a trip to Russia with the small girl, the wife decided not to come back to Syria. The husband was not able to get help from the Russian embassy. According to Russian civil law, the child of a Russian mother is Russian and she can have custody of the child. The father of the child was unable to see his daughter since he could not obtain a visa to visit her in Russia.

Syria has ratified several human rights conventions, including the Convention on the Elimination of All Forms of Discrimination against Women (CEDAW) and the Convention on the Rights of the Child (CRC) but with reservations on articles related to child custody. In 2007 I interviewed a high-ranking *mufti* – one of the leading religious officials – in Syria about Personal Status Law, legal pluralism and migration. He told me that he does not feel particularly positive about marriages between Syrian men and foreign women.[27] He recounted:

27 The *mufti* did not even discuss Syrian women who marry foreign men.

> We have lots of problematic cases in the embassies of Russia, Ukraine and Romania. Syrian men who have studied in these countries marry women and bring them back to Syria. If they end up in a socially conservative environment they will – sooner or later – have problems. Many leave and manage to take their children with them but if they leave their children behind, we have difficulties with their embassies. A foreign state cannot demand the extradition of children who are Syrian citizens, especially if the father is Muslim and the mother is not. The right of a mother to take care of younger children (*hadane*) is dependent also on her staying in Syria.

There are a number of cases where Syrian fathers who live abroad take their children to Syria and refuse to let them return to their mothers. If the children are foreign citizens the law of that country should, in principle, be applied. But, as discussed above, all children from Syrian fathers can easily be regarded as Syrian, and quickly registered in Syria. Then the mother might have great difficulty in a Syrian court, especially if the father makes accusations about her morals or if he is a Muslim and she is not.

National opinions are increasingly mobilized through mass media coverage of transnational custody disputes (Rabo 2007a: 160). A well-known and much exposed case in Syria (and elsewhere) concerns two children with a Dutch mother and a Syrian father who in 2004 took his children to Syria without the permission of the mother. In June 2006 the children – then aged 11 and 13 years – were able to get to the Dutch Embassy and asked to be returned to their mother. But in an interview the father claimed that it was the embassy people who had kidnapped his children. He stressed that he was a good father who brought them to Syria for their own good. He said he had not remarried and that he devoted his life to the children.[28] Many Syrians who heard or read about this case demanded that the Syrian authorities retrieve the children from the embassy and in the Netherlands people demanded that the children be returned to their mother. Negotiations were taking place between Syrian and Dutch authorities and they were apparently not happy about the media coverage of the case. After six months in the Dutch embassy in Damascus, the two children were able to return to their mother.

Legal Challenges

The case of the Dutch children who were stuck in their embassy for six months was probably solved by reference to private international law, the traditional legal instrument for handling such cases. The Syrian authorities decided to accept that the children were Dutch citizens and that their mother had been given sole custody of them. But private international law is becoming less useful in a world of increased transnational connections and the increased *de facto* possibilities of

28 His former wife remarried and had more children.

double citizenship (c.f. Foblets 2005). If transnational families have members in a number of countries, such as that of Ilham discussed earlier, legal complications might increase. Where do the litigants actually belong today? What law should be applied? Sweden has developed a tradition of regarding domicile as the most important criteria for judging family cases involving people who reside in Sweden but who might have strong links to another country. Germany has typically not paid the same attention to domicile.[29] Within the European Union debates, the convergence of family law can be seen as one way to address the difficulty of multiple belongings (c.f. Anatolskaia 2007).[30]

Transnational family conflicts thus pose great challenges to the states in Europe and elsewhere. But they primarily pose challenges for citizens involved in them. People do not plan to become involved in transnational family conflicts and it is not always easy for citizens or migrants to know what laws are applicable and where. In a country like Syria, knowledge of the law or legal practice is commonly spread by word of mouth. Syrians are often deeply uncertain about the correct bureaucratic or legal procedures and complain that bureaucrats and lawyers are not helpful. Rampant corruption counteracts faith in policies and the law. Legal regimes are also subject to change. What happens when changes take place in family law? In Syria it seems that family law has increasingly come under the control of the *Shari'a* and the Christian courts respectively with less scope for civil courts to handle cases with transnational connections. Transnational migration and family law with links to Syria is thus a matter not only of gender and citizenship but also, as I have pointed out, of religious affiliation.

The Good Family and the Good Law

On English-language Internet sites the case of the Dutch children in Syria and similar cases are often depicted in terms of a clash between Islam and the West, emphasizing the superior rights given to women in 'the West'.[31] The case of the Dutch children in Syria also highlights that many Muslims/Arabs are well aware that 'Westerners' regard them as inferior in terms of law and the judiciary. An

29 For an interesting shift in German legal tradition, see the following case: In Germany a verdict leaning on international private law refused to dissolve the marriage of two (Christian) Syrians residing in Germany. But a higher German court accepted the application by underlining that a refusal would be against German *ordre public* (www.internationalfamilylawfirm.com/2007/11/german-divorce). Since the 1970s domicile rather than nationality has become increasingly important in most legal traditions (Jänterä-Jareborg 1997:45).

30 Convergence of family law can of course be analyzed as an instrumental way to enhance mobility within the European Union but also as a reflection of struggles concerning the 'good' future European family.

31 See, for example: www.uslaw.com/bulletin/custody-orders-not-respected-internationally.

analysis of transnational families and family law may thus throw some light on central perceptions concerning relations between women and men, between children and their parents. 'The good family', 'the good life' and even 'good family law' come into focus.

The concern to establish policies and law for a good and gender-equal family was behind a change in the Norwegian law in 2003 whereby all people wanting to marry in Norway had to agree that both spouses have an equal right to divorce.[32] The overt aim of the law was to help Muslim women in Norway with the problem of 'limping marriages' whereby a woman might be divorced according to civil law but not according to religious law (Thorbjörnsrud 2005:10). But as Thorbjörnsrud noted, the Norwegian lawmaker had not realized that the real opposition to this law would come from representatives of the Catholic and Orthodox churches.[33] A faithful Catholic or Orthodox Christian cannot enter a marriage on the premise that it can be dissolved.

This case illustrates that the authorities in the Nordic countries with their long tradition of Lutheran state-church cohabitation may have special difficulties in understanding other Christian legal traditions. Non-Lutheran Christians may be obliged or feel obliged to follow various kinds of transnational Canon Law. Christians belonging to, for example, the Syrian Orthodox, the Armenian Orthodox or the Roman Catholic churches are part of often vast transnational organizations and many members live in countries where their religious family law may differ considerably from the law of the land.

Many of the early Syrian Orthodox migrants who came to Sweden were happy to be resettled in what they believed to be a Christian country and to escape their minority position. They became rather astonished, however, at the lack of importance of Christianity in public and family life and that Sweden accepted Muslim migrants into the country (Björklund 1981:118). In Sweden in the 1970s and the early 1980s there was some criticism of the perceived traditional and patriarchal family organization of the Syrian Orthodox immigrants and many Swedish bureaucrats saw it as their duty to help liberate women and children from the grips of male heads of families. Such memories might account for the reaction I had from one of the Syrian Orthodox priests I interviewed in Syria in 2008. He said that members of his flock come back in order to find brides or grooms who are not contaminated by Western upbringing. He insisted that Europe was not good from the point of view of family life, 'People divorce over small differences. A sick spouse is cast aside and old parents are not cared for by

32 'In 2007 a new ground for direct divorce was adopted in Norway, namely for a spouse who had been forced to marry by an unlawful act' (Lödrup 2008:24). This is another example of a law that clearly is aimed at 'liberating' female migrants.

33 Tone Linn Waerstad (2006) notes in her study of divorced Muslim women in Norway that the issue of 'limping' marriages is highly complex and that extra-legal issues were more important than the letter of the law when her informants decided to seek a Norwegian divorce.

their children'. From his point of view, a 'good' family and good family law were epitomized not by Swedes and Sweden but rather by the Middle East and Syrian Orthodox Canon Law.

Thus a stress on the superiority of the 'Swedish', the 'Syrian Orthodox' or 'the Syrian Muslim' way of organizing family life may easily turn family law into a battleground of morality. Hagelund (2008) shows how such moral accounts in Scandinavia have led to strident demands that the state intervene to save the women and children of (Middle Eastern) migrants. Liberal democracies such as the Scandinavian countries are faced with a dilemma concerning family law. How can the rights of religious minorities be safeguarded without perpetuating 'an unequal distribution of rights, duties and (ultimately) powers between men and women within the community' (Shachar 2001:6)? In Syria religious minorities are safeguarded by being obliged to follow their own family law but this solution is not what my Syrian Orthodox informants in Sweden demanded. They wanted recognition and respect for their particularity but they did not see 'Swedish' family norms as completely negative. Family relations in Sweden might be 'cold', many said, but they were 'fair', often through the help of the authorities, they said. Many Syrians with experience in Scandinavia were actually impressed by the way, for example, the interests of the child are more important than the parents' interests in cases of divorce.

Ideas about what constitutes a good and normal family and good family law are thus never static and unchangeable but the relationship between family law and policies and society are, on the contrary, always dynamic. We must acknowledge that in this equation both family and society know no state borders but are transnational in nature. Millions of people who are members of families have increasingly complex links to many localities and different states. Yet they are able – like Ilham and her family discussed earlier – to reproduce significant social relations, frequently against all odds, across often vast distances. In such a world it is a great challenge to develop legal regimes that are fair and just but which take heterogeneity and mobility into account.

References

Antokolskaia, M. (ed.) 2007. *Convergence and Divergence of Family Law in Europe*. Antwerpen: Intersentia.

Benda-Beckmann, F. von, Benda-Beckmann, K. von and Griffiths, A. 2005. Mobile people, mobile law. An introduction, in *Mobile People, Mobile Law. Expanding Legal Relations in a Contracting World*, edited by F. von Benda-Beckmann, K. von Benda-Beckmann and A. Griffiths. Aldershot: Ashgate, 1–25.

—— 2009. Introduction. The power of law, in *The Power of Law in a Transnational World*, edited by F. von Benda-Beckmann, K. von Benda-Beckmann and A. Griffiths. New York: Berghahn, 1–29.

Benda-Beckmann, F. von, Benda-Beckmann, K. von and Eckert, J. 2009. Rules of law and laws of ruling. Law and governance between past and future, in *Rules of Law and Laws of Ruling. On the Governance of Law*, edited by F. von Benda-Beckmann, K. von Benda-Beckmann and J. Eckert. Farnham: Ashgate, 1–30.

Björklund, U. 1981. *North to Another Country. The Formation of a Suryoyo Community in Sweden*. Stockholm: Stockholm Studies in Social Anthropology, University of Stockholm.

Carlisle, J. 2008. From behind the door. A Damascus court copes with an alleged out of court marriage, in *Les Métamorphoses du Mariage au Moyen-Orient*, edited by Barbara Drieskens. Beyrouth: IFPO, 59–74.

Cetrez, Ö. A. 2005. *Meaning-making Variations in Acculturation and Ritualization: A Multi-generational Study of Suroyo Migrants in Sweden*. Uppsala: Acta Universitatis Upsaliensis.

Charrad, M.M. 2001. *States and Women's Rights. The Making of Post-Colonial Tunisia, Algeria and Morocco*. Berkeley: University of California Press.

Dupret, B. 2007. Legal pluralism, plurality of laws and legal practices. Theories, critiques, and praxiological re-specification. *European Journal of Legal Studies*, 1 (1).

Fábos, A. 2001. Marriage, Sudanese-style: Transnational practices of citizenship and gender-making for Sudanese nationals in Egypt. *Northeast African Studies*, 8 (2): 47–68.

Fargues, P. (ed.) 2005. *Migrations Méditerranéennes, Rapport 2005*, Florence: European University Institute and EUROMED.

Foblets, M-C. 2005. Mobility versus law, mobility in the law? Judges in Europe are confronted with the thorny question 'Which law applies to litigants of migrant origin'?, in *Mobile People, Mobile Law. Expanding Legal Relations in a Contracting World*, edited by F. von Benda-Beckmann, K. von Benda-Beckmann and A.Griffiths. Aldershot: Ashgate, 297–315.

Gualteri, S. 2004. Gendering the chain migration thesis: Women and Syrian transatlantic migration, 1878–1924. *Comparative Studies of South Asia, Africa and the Middle East*, 24 (1), 69–81.

Hagelund, A. 2008. 'For women and children!' The family and immigration policies in Scandinavia, in *The Family in Question. Immigrant and Ethnic Minorities in Multicultural Europe*, edited by R. Grillo. Amsterdam: Amsterdam University Press, 71–88.

Jänterä-Jareborg, M. 1997. *Svensk domstol och utländsk rätt. En internationell privat och processrättslig studie*. Uppsala: Justus förlag.

Kandiyoti, D. (ed.) 1991. *Women, Islam and the State*. Basingstoke: Macmillan.

Lister, R. *et al.* 2007. *Gendering Citizenship in Western Europe. New Challenges for Citizenship Research in a Cross-National Context*. Bristol: The Policy Press.

Lödrup, P. 2008. The reharmonization of Nordic family law, in *European Challenges in Contemporary Family Law*, edited by Katharina Boele-Woelki and Tone Svendrup. Antwerp: Intersentia, 17–26.

Moors, A. 1999. Debating Islamic family law: Legal texts and social practices, in *A Social History of Women and Gender in the Modern Middle East*, edited by M.L. Meriwether and J.E. Tucker. Boulder: Westview Press, 141–175.

Nasir, J.J. 2002. *The Islamic Law of Personal Status*. The Hague: Kluwer Law International.

Rabo, A. 1986. *Change on the Euphrates, Villagers, Townsmen and Employees in Northeast Syria*. Stockholm: Stockholm Studies in Social Anthropology, University of Stockholm.

—— 1996. Gender, state and civil society in Jordan and Syria, in *Civil Society. Challenging Western Models*, edited by C. Hann and E. Dunn. London: Routledge, 155–177.

—— 2007a. Gränslösa familjer – gräns(lös) kontroll, in *Transnationella rum. Diaspora, migration och gränsöverskridande relationer*, edited by E. Olsson, C. Lundqvist, A. Rabo, L. Sawyer and Ö. Wahlbeck. Umeå: Borea, 137–164.

—— 2007b. 'Familjen betyder allt' eller 'Vi blir snart lika kalla som svenskarna': Assyrier/syrianer i Södertälje, in *Globala familjer. Transnationell migration och släktskap*, edited by M. Eastmond and L. Åkesson. Hedemora: Gidlunds, 205–229.

—— 2008. 'Doing family': Two cases in contemporary Syria. *Hawwa. Journal of Women of the Middle East and the Islamic World*, 6 (2): 129–153.

—— 2010. Legal pluralism and family law in Syria, in *Legal Pluralism and the Problem of Justice*, edited by W. Zips and M. Weilenmann. Munster: Lit-Verlag.

Sadeldine, S. 2005. Syria: the demographic and economic dimension of migration, in *Migrations Méditerranéennes, Rapport 2005*, edited by P. Fargue. Florence: European University Institute and EUROMED, 265–271.

Shachar, A. 2001. *Multicultural Jurisdictions. Cultural Differences and Women's Rights*. Cambridge: Cambridge University Press.

Thorbjörnsrud, B.S. 2005. Innledning, in *Evig din? Ekteskaps- og samlivstradisjoner i det flerreligiösa Norge*, edited by B.S. Thorjörnsrud. Oslo: Abstrakt forlag, 7–33.

Waerstad, T.L. 2006. *Retten til ikke å bli diskriminert ved skilsmisse. En rettsantropologisk studie av skilt muslimske innvandrerkvinner i Norge*. Kvinnerettslig skriftserie nr 64. Avdeling for kvinnerett, Universitetet i Oslo.

Chapter 2
Cyber-Stork Children and the Norwegian Biotechnology Act: Regulating Procreative Practice – Law and its Effects

Marit Melhuus

A Law on Display

In 2007, the Norwegian Biotechnology Advisory Board, in conjunction with the National Medical Museum, organized an open meeting in Oslo about reproductive tourism. The museum had put on a small temporary exhibition entitled 'The cyber-stork' which, according to the museum director:

> … places the Biotechnology Act in the museum … not because the act is no longer relevant to contemporary society nor because we view it as a museum piece. On the contrary. Many museums wish … also to be an arena for exploration, examination and reflection. The Cyber-Stork is our contribution. It is a so-called hotspot-exhibition: a thematic exhibition of current interest (Hamran 2008:4).[1]

In addition to a few relevant objects and a short film on Norwegians who travel abroad to 'have children', the exhibition consisted of a computer – called a 'net-kiosk' – which allowed the public to access the many different offers that exist online within the range of what can be termed 'fertility services'. The curator, Henrik Treimo, explained the exhibit:

> The Norwegian legislation in the field of biotechnology is one of the most restrictive in Europe. Only a few of the many possible alternatives are on offer and only heterosexual couples are allowed help through assisted conception.[2] The dream of having children is just as strong among those who fall outside the Act's definition of who qualifies for access to treatment, as for those who fall

1 All translations from this and other Norwegian texts are mine.

2 In 2008 (with effect from 2009), the Norwegian Marriage Act of 1991 was changed, giving same-sex couples the right to marry and to adopt; also (for lesbian couples) the right to assisted conception (Act nr 53/2008). As this book deals with transnational law, it is important to stress that laws providing for same-sex marriage are, on a global scale, exceptional, indicating the culturally-specific nature of arguments tied to this form of family formation.

> within its scope. In order to illustrate this we have placed the Act in the museum – together with some objects that each tell a story about this theme (Treimo 2008:6).[3]

As viewers of this unusual reproductive event, we are confronted with a procreative universe that is embedded in transnational space and maintained through a continual flow of people, information, knowledge and local practices – as well as legislation.

Treimo underscores two important points: the first is that the Norwegian legislation on assisted conception is one of the most restrictive in Europe. Inter alia, the law does not permit egg donation and, in the case of sperm donation, the use of known donor sperm is prescribed. The use of a surrogate is not permitted as Norwegian law states that the mother of the child is the one who gives birth to the child.[4] Secondly, he states that the desire to have children is irrespective of any legal regulation, intimating that those who fall outside the law will take matters into their own hands. By juxtaposing online fertility marketing and the Norwegian biotechnology law within the context of reproductive tourism, the organizers draw attention to what might be called a procreative interface – where law and practice meet. This interface represents a culturally significant site as it articulates a disparity between different visions of an imagined future. The exhibition is one more element in a chain of reproductive events that shape – and have shaped – public debates in Norway on assisted conception (Melhuus 2001). Thus, this small display speaks to larger issues, not only highlighting global aspects of reproductive technologies but also evoking particularities in the Norwegian Biotechnology Act and its effects. One such effect was made evident in the presentation given later in the day by Odd Jenvin, 'father of two children born by a surrogate' (as the programme notes). The title of his talk was: 'How does Norwegian bureaucracy meet the children who arrive with the cyber-stork?'

Jenvin and his partner travelled to the United States of America for the purpose of conceiving a child by a surrogate. He stresses the fact that he uses the term 'surrogate' and not 'surrogate mother'. This is because he and his partner have decided that their children will grow up with two fathers. As he says: 'In our family, there is no mother. And we do not want to give the impression that a mother exists somewhere. This does not mean that they will not have contact with the woman who gave birth but it means that she is not their mother'. He goes on to say:

3 These (and following) quotes are taken from the report from the meeting, only available online: http://www.bion.no/publikasjoner.shtml.

4 Act 2003-12-05 nr 100: Act relating to the application of biotechnology in medicine; revised in 2007: Act 2007-06-15 nr 31 (the changes pertain to pre-implantation diagnosis and research on supernumerary embryos). Children's Act 1981-04-08-7. Chapter 1A, § 2, 'Who is the mother of the child?' states: 'The woman who gives birth to the child is considered the mother'. This provision was added in 1997, with effect in 1998, as a result of the debates on reproductive technologies.

> Many politicians and experts are not used to this way of having children. But because it is uncommon does not mean it is wrong … We will most probably experience more and more that people accept this way of having children as legitimate. I think that the political processes and, in due time, the legislative processes, will be marked by this development (Jenvin 2008:32–33).

According to Jenvin there were about 100 children in Norway (in 2007) who were conceived by a surrogate.[5]

After presenting some details about the practice of surrogacy, Jenvin focuses on how children born by a surrogate abroad enter and are registered in Norway. He is especially concerned about children born to male, same-sex couples. He claims that these children, in comparison with those born through a surrogate to heterosexual couples, run into particular problems. It appears that the Norwegian bureaucracy at that time (2007) had problems with their categories: there was no way to register a child with two fathers, despite a birth certificate issued in the United States of America certifying that the two men are the parents of the child. In some cases, these couples have been asked to take a DNA test to ascertain who the biological father is so that the non-biological father can proceed to apply for step-adoption. In other cases, the child has been registered in the national register but without parents, yet given a person number (which is essential in Norway in order to be able to access all public services such as health care, kindergarten, schooling and so on). In other words, officially the tie between the parents and the children has been severed. As Jenvin says, 'We then have a child of just a few months old living alone at an address where two men also happen to live' (Jenvin 2008:36). In a few cases, same-sex couples have been able to register a child born abroad with no problem. He also notes that single fathers with a child born by a surrogate do not seem to encounter the same problems as same-sex couples. He concludes that there seems to be a somewhat arbitrary practice and that this is related to a too narrow interpretation of the Norwegian child law which says that the mother of a child is the one who gives birth. From this we can deduce, he continues, that a child can have only one father and one mother. A child cannot have two fathers (Jenvin 2008:36).[6]

The case that Jenvin presents is illustrative in several ways. In addition to demonstrating the inadequacy of state bureaucracy in confronting reality in a meaningful way (to those involved), it implicitly raises the issue of illegality and what is considered morally right. This illustrates a point Harris makes that 'laws themselves often put social actors in different moral predicaments by the fact that they forbid, or even criminalize, actions which, for the people concerned, are

5 Jenvin states that most Norwegians in need of a surrogate travel to the United States of America, where several of the states accept same-sex parenthood. He and his partner went to California.

6 See Sandberg (2009) for a discussion of the principles of equality and how they pertain to the legal status of the child.

acceptable or desirable within their own moral code' (Harris 1996:2). His case also questions the very notion of motherhood and, by implication, parenthood and what constitutes a proper family. Moreover, the example challenges the notion of infertility and what it is to be 'involuntary childless',[7] as this is perceived in Norway. In so far as infertility is based on a pathological definition, a homosexual fertile man cannot be considered infertile.[8] There are many who would argue that it is a natural fact that men cannot have babies – and that this male condition does not qualify for infertility treatment even if the man is homosexual – representatives of the Norwegian Lutheran Church are especially articulate on this but so are others.

Jenvin's case pits notions of nature (hetero-normativity and biological connectedness) against nurture, where the act of caring (Borneman 2001) is privileged over the act of begetting. Jenvin's actions challenge basic principles couched in the Norwegian Biotechnology Act while simultaneously demonstrating their effects. More than anything, perhaps, this case indicates a pervasive tension between the individual and society, between the right to choose the way one wants to procreate and society's right to impose the limits it deems proper. And Jenvin predicts that as more people choose to procreate by means of a surrogate, policies will have to change, thus indicating 'reverse' effects: those of practice on legislative processes.

I let this case stand as a backdrop to my further discussion of certain aspects of the Norwegian biotechnology law. It is this law that prompts people to travel abroad to obtain treatments not permitted in Norway, thereby entering the circuit of reproductive tourism – or what some term 'fertility tourism' (Deech 2003; Storrow 2005–2006). Thus the global (in)fertility market works to undermine national efforts to regulate procreation by means of legislation. As I have suggested elsewhere (Melhuus 2003) it could be argued that the permeability of borders – the very possibility of border crossings (be they territorial or moral) – is a precondition for the restrictions made. If that is the case then the law can also be understood as a cultural marker of national identity, placing Norway on a global bio-ethical map.

Some Points of Departure

There are two premises underpinning my argument that should be spelled out. One is related to the technologies, the other is related to my approach to law and legislative processes. Let me start with the technologies. As noted above, reproductive technologies – and their associated practices – are global phenomena that have many different local ramifications. Reproductive medicine can be, and is understood as, a globally defined field of possibility; yet technologies do not circulate unhindered. Although technologies may be recognized as the 'same',

7 This is the closest English translation of 'ufrivillig barnløs'.

8 See Johansson (2008) for a discussion on the classification of infertility in Norway.

their impact is contextually determined. For any technology to be operative, it needs a certain cultural acceptance or legitimacy. In so far as technologies and their concomitant knowledges are socially constructed and relationally embedded, they are local. In the case of reproductive technologies, it is not only the technologies that become localized once deployed, the subject of their use also has its local connotations and meanings as do the relations that the technologies are seen to create.

Reproductive technologies have become the subject of politics and policies, reflecting an interface between public and private spheres. Debates about these technologies-cum-practices converge in contested sites where fundamental values are exposed – such as the notion of motherhood, the meanings of biological connectedness and the family. These values are articulated in relation to the consequences of biotechnology and simultaneously projected in terms of hope and fear. It is what they might bring about that prompts diverse responses and spurs imaginations. The potentialities of reproductive technologies have not only produced images of possible life worlds and rekindled debates about kinship, genealogical relatedness and social and biological forms of belonging, but have also provoked strong emotional and moral reactions – from unrealistic optimism to total condemnation. A salient feature of these technologies is that they move people – morally, physically, economically and emotionally. As a contemporary, social phenomenon, biotechnology has produced effects that bring to the fore moral dilemmas that are simultaneously articulated at both individual and social levels (Melhuus 2009).

With regard to law and legislation, a premise for my argument is that these can be viewed as cultural artefacts, products of imaginations both embodying and projecting a contested morality (Melhuus 2007). A law can be read for what it evokes – in relation to what is permitted and what is prohibited. I also see legislative processes as significant social phenomena in order to grasp contemporary cultural processes. Hence, law can be seen as a system of cultural meaning where practices of law 'are productive of meaning' (Merry 1992:361). In this vein, legislative processes provide exceptionally interesting ethnography because they are normative and they reflect dominant social – and even national – concerns. They are also interesting because legislation is cumulative and therefore permits insights into changes over time. Finally, legislative processes (at least those that touch on what are perceived as significant – even ontological – issues) inevitably provoke public debates, thereby disclosing a nexus of contested values, a privileged site for exploring local moralities.[9] In the Norwegian case it is the discrepancy between the law and what the law permits and what many of those subject to the law want that is potentially interesting. Ultimately it is this relationship between the types

9 That issues of law, legislative processes and court cases yield interesting ethnographies within the field of kinship and assisted conception is exemplified through various works, for example: Fox (1997); Dolgin (1992, 1997, 1999); Dalton (2000); Simpson (2001); Kahn (2002); Strathern (2005). See also Delaisi de Parseval (2008).

of subjects the law produces and the types of subjects that produce the law that is significant. That relationship gains significance in a global context. Jenvin's case turns on this axis.

I now turn to the law and particularly to those provisions that have to do with assisted conception. More specifically, I will discuss issues related to donor gametes, with an emphasis on the differential treatment of sperm and egg donation. My focus is intentionally narrow. I wish to highlight some central aspects regarding donor gametes in order to expose some underlying trends. The analysis will primarily draw on public discourses and the ideas and values about relatedness and belonging transmitted through them. Thus, I hope to make some sense of the problems that surrogacy gives rise to in Norway. At issue are notions of maternity and paternity, kinship and fundamental ideas of belonging.

Regulations

Norway passed its first law regulating assisted conception in 1987. The immediate event prompting legislation was the birth of the first *in vitro* fertilized baby in Norway in 1984.[10] Government intervention was deemed appropriate, including by medical practitioners, 'lest matters get out of hand' (Melhuus 2005). In 1994, these regulations were incorporated into what is referred to in Norway as the 'Biotechnology Act'. With this enactment, assisted conception came under the same set of legal regulations as other medical biotechnological procedures. The Act is based on a precautionary principle: 'better safe than sorry'. At the time, it was one of the most restrictive Acts in Europe and the most restrictive within the Nordic countries. The Biotechnology Act regulates assisted conception, research on embryos, cloning, pre-implantation diagnosis, prenatal diagnosis, genetic examination of children born and genetic therapy. Since 1994, the Act was revised in 2003 and again in 2007.

These revisions indicate several things: first, the field of biotechnology is in constant flux and the problem (for legislators) is to keep pace with the new knowledge and techniques that are being developed. Second, the developments within reproductive technologies cause legislators to react so the law itself is in constant movement, adapting to the new possibilities that reproductive medicine produces. The overall thrust of these legal interventions has been to limit the local impact of such technologies. Third, the revisions also have to do with shifting political constellations, indicating the contentious nature of these technologies and

10 In 1978, Edwards and Steptoe succeeded in 'producing' Louise Brown, the world's first child to be born by in vitro fertilization. This birth represents a watershed and shifted the grounds on which procreation rested. It also triggered debates about medical ethics in this field in Norway, as elsewhere in the world. See Edwards and Steptoe (1980). In 2010 Robert Edwards was awarded the Nobel prize for medicine for his pioneering work in human in vitro fertilization.

their uses. Thus the 2003 legislation put in place by a Christian Democratic and Conservative coalition government was revised and liberalized by a centre left coalition government. There is no consensus in Norwegian society – not among law and policy makers nor among the public at large – about the application of reproductive and associated technologies. However, there is consensus about the need to regulate.

Despite revisions, one provision has remained constant – the prohibition on egg donation. It is not to be permitted which is in contrast to sperm donation. Paragraphs 2–15 in the Biotechnology Act state, 'Fertilized eggs may only be used in order to be reinserted into the woman from whom the egg cells originate'. Paragraphs 2–18 concerning the prohibition of egg donation state, 'Donation of an egg, or parts of this [egg], from one woman to another is prohibited'.[11]

Ever since the first discussions about legal regulation of artificial insemination by donor (AID) in 1953,[12] the question about the anonymity of the donor has been problematic (Melhuus 2000, 2001). With the revision and implementation of the new Biotechnology Act in 2003, the anonymity clause was abolished. Within parliament there was a large majority in favour of this move. Although the prohibition of egg donation and the rescinding of donor anonymity are not grounded in the same arguments, they nevertheless reflect aspects of the same tendencies. They cohere but perhaps in a way that is not generally recognized. This consistency has to do with two things: on the one hand, an attitude to nature – or the natural – and motherhood, which makes egg donation difficult to accept, whereas sperm donation is acceptable; and on the other hand a public discourse which increasingly tends to biologize identities and kin relatedness, in terms of rights and the best interests of the child.

By insisting on the prohibition of egg donation, Norwegian legislators recognize one dimension of reproductive disruption – that is the potential split between gestational, genetic and social motherhood – and they refuse to endorse it. In rejecting egg donation as a path to potential motherhood, the legislators deny women in need of an egg the legal means to obtain it. These women have to travel abroad to obtain one and they will also have to finance the treatment themselves. (The law does not even reflect the possibility that men may make use of a donor egg!) Obviously, the Norwegian public health care system will not cover the costs of treatments not permitted in Norway. However, within the parameters of the law, assisted conception is covered by the public health system, susceptible to certain guidelines (such as the number of cycles granted, the age of the woman, the number of fertilized eggs reinserted and so on).

11 Act 2003-12-05 nr 100. As mentioned, surrogate motherhood is not permitted in Norway. This is regulated in the Act of Children and Parents *(*the child law*);* Act 1981-04-08 nr 07 § 2. In 1997 (13 June 1997 nr 39) the following addition was made: 'An agreement to give birth to a child of another woman is not binding.'

12 See *Innstilling fra inseminasjonskomitéen*, March 1953.

Of Eggs and Sperm

At the core of European understandings of kinship is the notion of blood ties, often glossed by the expression 'blood is thicker than water'. Blood is the metaphor used to designate the biological foundation of kinship relations and to indicate that it is the sharing of substance that make people kin. To some extent in contemporary lay understandings, notions of blood, biology and genes are interchangeable: they all point to some natural, substantial aspect of kinship that is assumed to be the foundation of kin relations. However, though blood ties have been seen as a precondition for establishing kin relations, they are not sufficient for establishing legitimate kin relations. Marriage has been – and to a certain extent still is – the institution that has endorsed legitimate kinship in Europe.[13] Children born out of wedlock were considered illegitimate. Unwed mothers were stigmatized. This is in many instances no longer the case. Moreover, marriage has been by definition heterosexual, until recently. Two additional principles, embedded in Roman law, have also been central to European notions of kinship. These have to do with ascertaining legal paternity and maternity, as follows:

1. *Pater vero est quem nuptiae demonstrant* (the true father is established through marriage). Implied here is that fatherhood as a main rule is established on the basis of marriage to the mother.
2. *Mater sempre certa est* (the mother is always certain). Implied is that motherhood is established through birth.

The first principle is dependent on marriage. Recognizing the uncertainty of paternity, it stresses the significance of the conjugal tie. The second principle however, is perceived as a biological fact. No matter what the conditions of birth of a child were (whether the child was legitimate or not) – the mother is always known, as she is by definition the one who gives birth.

These principles, although not always articulated, have guided practices that concern the relationship between parents and children, that is, questions of filiation. They rest on what have been seen as undisputable biological facts: that paternity is always uncertain and that there is no doubt about the mother's identity. Although the first principle instigates marriage as the relationship that establishes legal paternity, the second principle insists on the certainty of the mother. Egg donation (and surrogacy) obviously challenge the latter; and the practice of anonymous sperm donation is in a sense inscribed in the former.

Until the 2003 amendment, the Norwegian law pertaining to assisted conception rested on these principles. However, with the rescinding of the anonymity clause

13 Legal adoption is another way of establishing legitimate relations of filiation. See Melhuus and Howell (2009) for a discussion of adoption laws in Norway in conjunction with the laws regulating assisted conception. For a discussion on the Nordic model of marriage see Melby *et al.* (2000).

in relation to sperm donation, a significant shift has occurred regarding the attitude to paternity.[14] For all intents and purposes, anonymous sperm donation collapses social and biological paternity into one father, the assumption being that the knowledge of donation is considered a private matter, a secret not revealed. Sperm donation with a known donor makes the distinction between genitor and *pater* public. Furthermore, in Norway this distinction is often framed so as to accord 'true' paternity to the biological father: he is the 'real' (*virkelig*) father. This is partially sustained by the amendments in the paternity law (see below). Nevertheless, the rescinding of the anonymity clause is not phrased in these terms. It is first and foremost grounded in a child's right to know his or her biological origins; this is considered to be in the best interests of the child. These arguments are parallel to those used in the case of adoptive children and adoption is also used as a reason to repeal anonymity in the case of donor sperm. The argument is that there should be no differential treatment of children; all children have the right to know their biological origin and reference is made to the United Nations Convention on the Rights of the Child (Article 7, ratified by Norway in 1991).

The gist of the argument is as follows: to know your biological origin is tantamount to knowing who you are; this knowledge is perceived as a right. To deny a child this right is to deny the child knowledge of who he or she is. This argument has carried much persuasive power, not only in Norway (Haimes 1998). Once it is an accepted fact that knowledge of biological origin is fundamental to identity, knowledge of biogenetic origin becomes paramount. Indeed framing the debates about donor sperm in terms of child rights and the best interests of the child has certainly been instrumental in the decision to revoke the anonymity clause.

Inviolable Motherhood: *Mater Sempre Certa Est*

The fact that the law is unequivocal regarding egg and sperm donation does not necessarily mean that there is – or has been – a consensus, either in Parliament or among people at large. Nevertheless, and in contrast to sperm donation, the question of egg donation has not generated heated debates. Moreover, the last revision of the Biotechnology Act in Norway does not include a proposal to permit egg donation. Although voices have been raised about the fact that it discriminates between infertile men and women by permitting sperm donation and not egg donation, this argument has had little purchase. This is perhaps surprising in a country that prides itself on its gender equality policies (*see* Spilker and Lie 2007; Melhuus 2003; Hellum, in this volume). Arguments based on gender discrimination and equal opportunities are more recent. They were not prominent in the earlier

14 The law grants the child upon turning 18 the right to know its biological origin. However, the law does not oblige the parents to tell the child of the way it has been conceived.

process of legislation where large sections of the women's movement saw the new reproductive technologies as a new form of control over the female body (*see* Hellum *et al.* 1990; Hellum 1993). It is only recently that the Discrimination and Equality Ombud has invoked the equality standard in debates about the legal prohibition against egg donation. However, the amendments to the Children's Act regarding new practices for ascertaining paternity (through DNA tests) have been framed in terms of a gender discourse.[15] Granting men the right to have paternity ascertained unilaterally (but within certain limits) by means of a DNA test is viewed by some as a move to recognize the true father and to rectify situations where a man has been paying support for a child that is not 'his' (the underlying assumption being that women do not necessarily acknowledge the 'real' father). It is also seen as a way of getting the facts right.[16]

Interestingly, the Centre for Equality (*Likestillingssenteret*), a publicly funded organization established in 1997 which is devoted to issues of gender equality in Norwegian society, voiced a different opinion. It stated:

> According to the opinion of the Centre for Equality the legal father is a significant person in the lives of many children. In many ways, we understand the proposed legal amendment as a displacement of rights from the legal father to the biological father without having sufficiently taken into account the consequences for the child.

Their concern was whether knowledge of biogenetic origin *per se* is good, without due consideration of the disruption such knowledge may entail for the child. They stated, 'The intention of the law must work for the child's best interest and not harm it. *Likestillingssenteret* does not see that the proposed changes ... will necessarily favour the child'. The *Likestillingsombudet* (Equality Ombud) expressed a different opinion:

> The ministry's suggestion implies that in cases where there is a doubt about paternity men are given an unconditional right to have their case tried. This means that men and women are given equal access to try paternity. The proposal implies that the consideration concerning the situation of the child is not given the same weight as in the present regulation; rather it is the significance of securing the child's right to knowledge of and possible contact with his or her biological father as early as possible which is stressed. *Ombudet* finds that this

15 See Act pertaining to children and parents – the children's act: Act 1981 04-08-7; §6. Change in paternity.

16 Another reason given for changing the paternity law is the increase in the number of children born out of wedlock. In the period of 1981–1985, 20% of all children born in Norway were born out of wedlock. In 2002, this group comprises 49.6% (*Odelsting proposisjon nr 93 (2001–2002)*).

> is a correct weighting of the various considerations to be taken in cases such as these [my translation].[17]

This last statement concurs with an underlying assumption for revising the law: that there is 'a broad agreement that the knowledge of biological origin is emotionally significant ... and that it is in the best interest of the child to know his or her biological origin as early as possible'.[18]

In the light of these contrasting public views on the significance of knowledge of biogenetic origin, it is interesting that the question of rescinding the anonymity clause with regard to sperm donation has not been framed in terms of a father's right to ascertain his biological relationship to a child. On the contrary, sperm donation, whether anonymous or not, is predicated upon an idea of a 'natural' and recurrent split between *pater* and genitor. In order to understand this inconsistency, we have to look at the combined discourses regarding egg and sperm donation.

I quote at length the Ministry of Health's arguments (put forth in 1986, when the first law to regulate assisted conception was being discussed) as these arguments are echoed later and also condense views held more generally:

> There are those who argue that egg donation is in principle not different from sperm donation ... This is a view the Ministry rejects. Women and men's reproductive functions are different – seen both from the donor's and the recipient's point of view.

The Ministry concurs with the working group's proposal that:

> In contrast to sperm donation, egg donation requires medical surgery ... Donation of an egg has more similarities to transplantation than it has with sperm donation .... In contrast to egg donation, sperm donation does not create a situation different from natural reproduction. Donor insemination does not break fundamentally with that which occurs in natural reproduction. Whether conception occurs artificially or naturally, the sperm is something that comes from the outside. This implies that there will always be some uncertainty as to who the father of the child is.

17 Both these quotes are taken from *Odelsting proposisjon nr 93(2001–2002)*, 4.2.2. Several of those heard in this process express concern about the insecurity and unrest that the suggested amendments in the law may imply for the children concerned. Yet, the argument about the significance of knowing one's biological origin had the most adherents. Moreover, the child's right to equality is coming into full force (Hellum personal communication; Sandberg (2009)), irrespective of how it has come into being.

18 *Odelsting proposisjon nr 93 (2001–2002)*. The Norwegian law grants this unilateral right to have paternity ascertained to the mother, father and child. This is in contrast to for example Spain where only the child, if he or she is over 18, can make such a request. The primacy of the best interest of the child is what presumably justifies this in Spain (Carles Salazar, personal communication).

> With natural conception it is not unusual that there is a discrepancy between legal or social paternity and biological paternity … With natural reproduction the uterus and the egg constitute a natural unity. Conception, pregnancy and birth are a unified process which occurs within the woman. With egg donation this unity is broken … with egg donation physical motherhood is split … there is reason to believe that this lack of clarity will cause insecurity with regard to the identity of the child … (*Odelsting proposisjon nr 25 (1986–1987)*, page 19).

A well-known Labour party politician, Grethe Knudsen, following this train of thought says:

> That women give birth has been so taken for granted that in Norway there are no rules of law for who the child's mother is. Conception, pregnancy, birth have been a unified process. It is not that simple any more. And this separation – that conception occurs outside the body – *implies that mother becomes more like father*. Until now we have considered mother and the unborn child as one. This has also been decisive for the right to self determination in the question of abortion [my emphasis].[19]

In a later debate, the following is stated: 'With regard to the order of nature, egg donation is a significantly larger interference than sperm donation. Egg donation would be a breach of the inviolability and unity of pregnancy'. And: 'We do not know the consequences of introducing a notion of "the strange or unknown mother" (*fremmed mor*). The feeling of belonging to mother (*morstilhørighet*) is the most fundamental of human [emotions]'. Or in the words of another female Labour Party politician:

> It is wrong that the mother of a child should be unknown. The belonging to mother (*morstilhørigheten*) is inviolable. For me this is not a question of gender equality but respect for the order of nature. To permit sperm donation is less problematical than egg donation, first and foremost because sperm is easily available and cannot be regulated by law so that we can prevent a child from having an unknown father.[20]

There are at least two things that can be drawn from this regarding the values attached to maternity. One has to do with the impossibility of imagining an

19 The debate in parliament on biotechnology, 1989. *Stortingsforhandlinger* 1988–89 nr. 41, page 4004.

20 These quotes are taken from Parliamentary debates and stated by Magnar Sortåsløkken (*male*, Socialist Left Party), Ole Johs. Brunæs (*male*, Conservative Party), and Kirsti Kolle Grøndahl (*female*, Labour Party) respectively. See *Stortingstidende* 10.6.1993: sak 1. *Stortingsforhandlinger* sesjon 1992–1993, pages 4346–4387. All translations are mine. Obviously, the question of a known egg donor is not even contemplated.

anonymous birth, a child 'without a mother'. Yet, in France, this practice is protected by law. Through the '*accouchement sous x*' a woman has the right to give birth anonymously, something which would be unthinkable in Norway. Moreover, the notion of 'mother belonging' articulated as an inviolable unity between conception, pregnancy and birth, leads to an idea that eggs belong where they come from. They should be in their proper place. The mother is given a unique status with respect to reproduction and this status determines what is right with respect to egg donation. Recognizing the implications of the technology, Knudsen acknowledges that the mother becomes more like the father. Eggs, like sperm, are now available 'outside' (the body) and this shared quality has significant implications: maternity and paternity may become equally uncertain. Where egg donation is allowed and anonymous sperm donation is upheld, this would certainly be the case. However, in Norway, the opposite is occurring – rather than rendering motherhood more like fatherhood, paternity is becoming more like maternity.

Creating Certainties

With the advent of new kin categories – such as donor father, genetic father, social father or, with regard to motherhood: genetic mother, gestational mother, birth mother, surrogate mother and social mother – both paternity and maternity are ambiguous categories. The new situation is that motherhood has been disrupted in ways that fatherhood has not and in some ways motherhood has taken on the traditional perceptions of fatherhood: it has become equally uncertain. The socio-cultural and legal responses to these new facts of life vary cross-culturally and there are disparities within Europe regarding egg donation. For example, egg donation is permitted in Spain, Denmark, Belgium and the United Kingdom, among others. In the United States of America, issues pertaining to maternity rights have been taken to court – and courts have had to adjudicate competing claims to motherhood. The most famous of these is perhaps the case of *Baby M* (Dolgin 1997; Fox 1997). However, in Norway, the situation is different.

Rather than accept these new facts as a condition of modern family formation and kinned relatedness, Norwegian legislators have opted for another path. In the face of these ambiguities about maternity and paternity, it seems that the need to establish some form of certainty is critical. This is my contention. Biogenetics serves this purpose well. In this case, certainty implies preserving the biological unity of motherhood as this is understood. It also implies standardizing biogenetic connectedness as a unique quality of each individual as this is perceived as a core element of identity. By appealing to the natural foundation of the unity of motherhood, biological relatedness is given primacy over other relationships. Moreover, by tying identity to biogenetic origins these relationships are also projected as fundamental. Therefore, it follows 'naturally' that the anonymity clause is repealed. (And also that new paternity laws, underscoring the importance of biological paternity, are passed.) By evoking a child rights discourse to ground the significance of knowing your biological origin, nature, identity, rights and knowledge all work together to produce what is projected as an ethically correct position.

Pater Vero …?

How, then, does surrogacy fit into the scheme of things? The answer is, it doesn't. Yet, as Jenvin points out, more and more people become parents through the use of a surrogate. The practice is not only being inscribed in Norwegian society, it is also becoming more public and producing effects.[21] Surrogacy sets a different agenda, not only because it challenges established notions of motherhood (egg donation does too, as we have seen) but also because it, at least potentially, allows for same-sex male parenthood that is not based on adoption. On the one hand, it follows from what I have argued above that cases of surrogacy where a donor egg is used are untenable on several counts, as such a practice defies Norwegian definitions of motherhood: the child is not related to its intended mother either genetically or by birth. On the other hand, if, as I have argued, biogenetic connectedness is paramount, the use of a surrogate to gestate a baby with the intending mother's own eggs should not be problematic. Yet, within the terms set by the law, this form of surrogacy still renders the category 'mother' equivocal.[22] In either case, then, the practice of surrogacy breaks fundamentally with Norwegian (legal) notions of motherhood as 'the mother' is evidently not known.

Significantly, surrogacy also breaks with notions of fatherhood, as these have been perceived. Let me re-state what the common assumptions have been: paternity is 'uncertain' by nature; however a child will always know who its mother is. Thus the idea of a 'fatherless' child is accepted[23] but the unknown mother is not only unthinkable, it is wrong. Yet, as we have seen in the case of Jenvin and his partner (where the sperm used issues from them),[24] the father is known but the mother is

21 That the practice of surrogacy is producing effects is evidenced in two public documents that have been published after I submitted this chapter. One is *Farskap og annen morskap. Fastsettelse og endring av foreldreskap.* NOU 2009:5. This is a commissioned report to Parliament on Fatherhood, motherhood, and the ascription and change of parenthood (there is an English summary on pages 16–18) and is, as far as I know, the first to deal with the legal aspects of surrogacy. See also *Rapport fra en interdepartemental arbeidsgruppe om håndtering av surrogat saker* (Report from an inter-ministerial working group on the handling og surrogacy cases) delivered by The Ministry of children, equality and inclusion, 28 June 2010.

22 For different takes on the notions of motherhood/surrogacy see Ragoné (1994), Dalton (2000), Dolgin (1992), and Kahn (2002).

23 However, in cases where no father has recognized a child at birth, the State has the responsibility to determine who is the father (Chapter 2 § 5, The Children's Act).

24 It is of course possible to have a child through a surrogate where both egg and sperm are donated. Such cases will inevitably turn on questions of reproductive intent.

not. They believe it is essential for them that the mother is not known as 'mother' but recognized as the woman who gave birth. Thus, Jenvin and his partner have effectively turned the tables: they deny the birth mother the status of 'mother' (they also obfuscate the egg donor), privileging fatherhood as the unique status. In many ways, their procreative act can be seen as radical, even subversive. It is an act that on one level defies Norwegian values of relatedness and nature. At another level, however, it feeds into a different trend: where paternity is becoming more like maternity. A known father is (good) enough.

Yet, still, there is a problem. And yet again the problem has to do with establishing the 'true' father through biological connectedness. If you recall, Norwegian authorities will not readily accept male same-sex parenthood. They propose a simple 'biological solution', suggesting to the couple that they each take a DNA test to ascertain biological fatherhood and then apply for permission to adopt the child of their (male) spouse – called a 'step-adoption'. This solution is unacceptable for (at least) this homosexual couple. Step-adoption undermines their mutual project of parenthood as it does not recognize that the child belongs equally to both of them, irrespective of biological ties. Authorities will accept a single father (with an unknown mother) but cannot accept two 'unknown' fathers. And the question turns on what 'known' means. To the Jenvin couple, all their children need 'to know' is that they are the sons of two fathers, born through a surrogate in the United States of America. Thus, while excluding a mother, they nevertheless confirm the traditional attitude to paternity: that it is inevitably uncertain. To the authorities, however, it is a matter of 'knowing' who the 'real' father is in order to ascribe proper filiation that can only be established by proving biogenetic connections.[25] This is another twist to the drive for certainty that a biological principle propels. (It is another effect.)

At the heart of the matter is the idea of the family and the belief that it is unnatural that two men should procreate. Family values are important in contemporary Norwegian society – so much so that for the involuntary childless, the significance of being a family, having children, overrides many other considerations. For many, being voluntarily childless is just not an option (Melhuus 2007). Thus, the desire of same-sex couples to be a family with children is congruent with values considered fundamental in Norwegian society.[26] However, the way they choose to become a family is problematic, as we have seen. Despite the new marriage law granting equal rights to same-sex couples, there is no doubt that it is the heterosexual norm that is dominant in Norway and that women are privileged when it comes to having children. The following (taken from Spilker 2008) is an apt illustration.

---

25 See Cadoret (2009) for a discussion of truth and knowing in modern kinship formation.

26 See Riksaasen (2001) for a discussion of lesbian couples in Norway and their procreative practices.

The former Christian Democratic/Conservative coalition government proposed a definition of family which *de facto* includes everyone: 'The family comprises married couples with or without children, couples co-habiting with or without children, homosexual partners with or without children, single parents who live with children ... families with foster children and single people living alone' (quoted in Spilker 2008:119).

Yet as Spilker (2008) demonstrates, the same government proceeded to clarify that some families are more 'family' than others, thereby introducing a hierarchy of values. The ideal family which serves the interests of the child is one based on a heterosexual norm and which, by implication, ensures that knowledge of biogenetic origin is known. Hence, the involuntary childless and the state agree on the significance of being a family. However, they disagree on what constitutes meaningful relatedness in family formation. In the last instance, this is what the Jenvin case demonstrates: by insisting on being recognized as a family with two 'unknown' fathers, they are creating new forms of relatedness. They are at the same time undermining central tenets in Norwegian understandings of kinship and filiation. Although their marriage is legal, their procreative practice is not. And although their parenthood is based on biogenetic relatedness, not only is this only partial (as the mother is not recognized), it is also in a sense uncertain (as they do not wish to specify who the biological father is to which child). Thus they upset the drive for certainty that appears to underpin Norwegian legislation. It is not altogether obvious whether or not this particular procreative practice also confirms the trend that fatherhood is becoming more like motherhood, although it does bring into existence a new father, placing 'father belonging' on par with 'mother belonging' (*morstilhørigheten*). What is obvious is that the children born to this marriage will, like children of many heterosexual marriages, not 'really' know who their father is. However, and more significantly, they do not 'have' a mother.

Reverse Effects?

I have stated that with regard to reproductive technologies there are two important aspects to keep in mind: that they are socially constructed and relationally embedded. This implies that the technologies gain different meanings in different contexts. This is a fact that Norwegian legislators have recognized. The Norwegian legislation seeks to restrict the application of these technologies as they can potentially create relations of kinship and family that are seen as morally wrong, threatening the natural order of things. In other words, the technologies cause some cultural confusion, as the Jenvin case amply illustrates. The use of assisted conception and surrogacy has created a new category of fatherhood that gives rise to specific problems (such as the registration of the child).

The very imaginations that reproductive technologies and assisted conception have engendered – of possible kin relations or rather rupture in these fundamental relations – moved legislators to pass a restrictive law. They have attempted to fix certain relations by explicitly making biogenetic relatedness primordial. Yet the very restrictions that are intended to immobilize certain procreative practices (by lack of access) move people to act otherwise. Moreover, biogenetic relatedness – a fact based on scientific knowledge – also assumes a truth claim about particular relationships, to the detriment of other relationships that assisted conception might create. It is this truth claim that procreative practices involving egg donation and/or surrogacy challenge. The laws that have been put in place limit people's choices as to how they wish to procreate, at least within the boundaries of the nation state. Yet people find ways to circumvent the law. Operating in a global market, they move beyond the limits established by the state in order to realize a desire – that of having a child and creating a family. Thus the transnational space within which reproductive technologies are embedded provides opportunities that some people are able to exploit. In doing so they bring these procreative practices home. This occurs not only literally, in the sense that the result of the technological intervention (if you will) – the child – is inscribed in local kin relationships, whether these are officially recognized or not. These practices also, and perhaps more significantly, produce effects that may not only confound but also actually subvert the current tendency to privilege biological forms of belonging over social ones. Thus the law which seeks to regulate access to a procreative universe by limiting people's legal options not only works to shift the limits as to what is possible, it may also, inadvertently, shift its premises as to what is permissible. Practice might, as Jenvin predicts, impinge on the law. That would indeed be a reverse effect.

Acknowledgements

This chapter is based on a paper read at a seminar I organized jointly with Enric Proqueres i Gené on *Les defies contemporains de la parenté* in Paris in November 2006. The seminar was set within the framework of a collaborative European research programme, *The Public Understanding of Genetics* (Contract QLG7-CT-2001-01668). The paper was later published in *Défis contemporain de la parenté* (2009, Paris, Éditions de EHESS, edited by Enric Porqueres i Gené). The present chapter furthers some of the arguments, with some revisions. I wish to thank the editors, and especially Anne Hellum, for insightful comments. I also wish to thank Odd Jenvin for sharing his experiences with me.

References

Borneman, J. 2001. Caring and being cared for. Displacing marriage, kinship, gender and sexuality, in *The Ethics of Kinship. Ethnographic Inquiries*, edited by J.D. Faubion. Lanban: Rowman and Littlefield, 29–46.

Cadoret, A. 2009. The contribution of homoparental families to the current debate on kinship, in *European Kinship in the Age of Biotechnology*, edited by J. Edwards and C. Salazar. Oxford: Berghahan Books, 79–96.

Dalton, S. 2000. Nonbiological mothers and the legal boundaries of motherhood: an analysis of California law, in *Ideologies and Technologies of Motherhood: Race, Class, Sexuality, Nationalism,* edited by H. Ragoné and F.W. Twine. New York: Routledge, 191–232.

Deech, R. 2003. Reproductive Tourism in Europe: Infertility and Human Rights, *Global Governance* 9, 425–432.

Delaisi de Parceval, G. 2008. *Famille à Tout Prix*. Paris: Éditions du Seuil.

Dolgin, J. 1992–1993. Just a gene: Judicial assumptions about parenthood. *UCLA Law Review* 40, 637–694.

—— 1997. *Defining the Family, Law, Technology, and Reproduction in an Uneasy Age*. New York: New York University Press.

—— 1999–2000. Choice, tradition and the new genetics: the fragmentation of the ideology of the family. *Connecticut Law Review* 32:523–566.

Edwards, R. and Steptoe, P. 1980. *A Matter of Life: The Story of a Medical Breakthrough.* London: Hutchinson.

Fox, R. 1997. *Reproduction and Succession. Studies in anthropology, Law and Society.* Paperback edition. New Brunswick: Transaction Publishers.

Haimes, E. 1998. The making of 'the DI child': changing representations of people conceived through donor insemination, in *Donor Insemination: International Social Science Perspectives,* edited by K. Daniels and E. Haimes. Cambridge: Cambridge University Press, 53–75.

Hamran, O. 2008. Velkommen, in *Åpent møte om 'reproduksjonsturisme'*, edited by O.J. Borge. Oslo: Bioteknologinemda. Accessed at: http://www.bion.no/publikasjoner.shtml.

Harris, O. 1996. Introduction: inside and outside the law, in *Inside and Outside the Law: Anthropological Studies of Authority and Ambiguity,* edited by O. Harris. London: Routledge, 1–18.

Hellum, A. (ed.) 1993. *Birth Law*. Oslo: Scandinavian University Press.

Hellum, A., Syse, A. and Aasen, H.S. (eds) 1990. *Menneske, natur og fødselsteknologi.Verdivalg og rettslig regulering*. Oslo: Ad Notam.

Jenvin, O. 2008. Hvordan møter norsk byråkrati barna som kommer med cyberstorken?, in *Åpent møte om 'reproduksjonsturisme',* edited by O.J. Borge. Oslo: Bioteknologinemda. Accessed at: http://www.bion.no/publikasjoner.shtml.

Johansson, K.A. 2008. Prioritering av ulike grupper: Bør det skilles mellom hva offentlig og private infertilitetsklinikker tilbyr? in *Åpent møte om 'reproduksjonsturisme',* edited by O.J. Borge. Oslo: Bioteknologinemda. Accessed at: http://www.bion.no/publikasjoner.shtml.

Kahn, S. 2002. Rabbis and reproduction: the uses of new reproductive technologies among ultraorthodox Jews in Israel, in *Inferitlity Around the Globe. New thinking on childlessness, gender, and reproductive technologies*, edited by M. Inhorn and F. van Balen. Berkeley: University of California Press, 283–297.

Melby, K., Pylkkännen, A., Rosenbeck, B. and Wetterberg, C. (eds) 2000. *The Nordic Model of Marriage and the Welfare State.* Copenhagen: Nordic Council of Ministers, 27.

Melhuus, M. 2000. Kultur, bytte, makt: sæd og egg på norsk. *Norsk Antropologisk Tidsskrift*, 11 (3): 161–181.

—— 2001. Kan skinnet bedra? Noen meninger om assistert befruktning in *Blod, tykkere enn vann? Betydninger av slektskap i Norge*, edited by S. Howell and M. Melhuus. Bergen: Fagbokforlaget, 45–72.

—— 2003. Exchange matters: issues of law and the flow of human substances, in *Globalization. Studies in anthropology*, edited by T.H. Eriksen. London: Pluto Press, 170–197.

—— 2005. 'Better safe than sorry'. Legislating assisted conception in Norway, in *State Formation. Anthropological Perspectives*, edited by C. Krohn-Hansen and K. Nustad. London: Pluto Press, 212–233.

—— 2007. Procreative imaginations: When experts disagree on the meanings of kinship, in *Holding Worlds Together. Ethnographies of Knowing and Belonging*, edited by M.E. Lien and M. Melhuus. Oxford: Berghahn Books, 37–56.

—— 2009. Qui a peur de la 'société de tri'? Les biotechnologies, l'individu et l'État. *Ethnologie francaise*, 39, 2:253–263.

Melhuus, M. and Howell, S. 2009. Adoption and assisted conception: One universe of unnatural conception, in *European Cultures of Kinship in the Age of Biotechnology*, edited by J. Edwards and C. Salazar. Oxford: Berghahn Books, 144–161.

Merry, S.E. 1992. Anthropology, law and transnational process. *Annual Review of Anthropology*, 21:357–379.

Ragoné, H. 1994. *Surrogate Motherhood. Conception in the Heart.* Boulder Colorado: Westview Press.

Riksaasen, G. 2001. To mammaer, går det an? En annerledes familieplanlegging, in *Blod, tykkere enn vann? Betydninger av slektskap i Norge*, edited by S. Howell and M. Melhuus. Bergen: Fagbokforlaget, 45–72.

Sandberg, K.A. 2009. Barns rettsstilling i likekjønnede parforhold, in *Arbeid og rett. Festskrift til Henning Jakhellns 70-årsdag*, edited by H. Aune, O. K. Fauchald, K. Lilleholt and D. Michalesen. Oslo: Cappelen Akademiske Forlag.

Simpson, B. 2001. Making bad deaths good: the kinship consequences of posthumous conception. *Journal of the Royal Anthropological Society*, 7, 1:1–18.

Spilker, K.H. 2008. *Assistert Slektskap: Biopolitikk i reproduksjonsteknoligiens tidsalder*, PhD thesis, NTNU, Trondheim.

Spilker, K.H. and Lie, M. 2007. Gender and bioethics intertwined: egg donation within the context of equal opportunity, *European Journal of Women's Studies*, 14, 4:327–340.

Storrow, R. 2005–2006. Quests for conception: Fertility tourists, globalization and feminist legal theory. *Hastings Law Journal* 57, 295–330.

Strathern, M. 2005. *Kinship, Law and the Unexpected. Relatives are Always a Surprise*. Cambridge: Cambridge University Press.

Treimo, H. 2008. Erfaringene med utstillingen 'Cyberstorken', *Åpent møte om 'reproduksjonsturisme'*, edited by O.J. Borge. Oslo: Bioteknologinemda. Accessed at: http://www.bion.no/publikasjoner.shtml.

Public Documents Consulted and/or Cited

Innstilling fra inseminasjonskomiteen. 1953. (Report from the Insemination Committee).

Odelsting proposisjon 25. 1986–1987. *Om lov om kunstig befruktning* (Bill to Parliament on artificial procreation).

Stortingsforhandlinger 1988–1989 (debates in Parliament).

Stortingsforhandlinger 1992–1993 (debates in Parliament).

Odelsting proposisjon 93. 2001–2002. *Om lov om endringer i lov 8. april 1981 nr 7 om barn og foreldere* (Bill to Parliament on ascription of and change in paternity).

NOU 2009:5. *Farskap og annen morskap. Fastsettelse og endring av foreldreskap* (Commissioned Report).

Rapport fra en interdepartemental arbeidsgruppe om håndtering av surrogat saker, delivered 28 June 2010, by the Ministry of Children, Equality and Inclusion.

Legal Acts

Act 1981-04-08 , nr 07. The Children's Act (amended in 1997).

Act 1991-07-04, nr 47, The Marriage Act (amended in 2008).

Act 1994-08-05, nr 56, Act Relating to the Application of Biotechnology in Medicine (Biotechnology Act).

Act 2003-12-05, nr 100. Act Relating to the Application of Biotechnology in Medicine (amended in 2007).

Chapter 3
The Global Equality Standard meets Norwegian Sameness

Anne Hellum[1]

Introduction

Embodying the right to be equal and the right to be different, human rights law has assumed prominence as one of the key global discourses on justice, equality and freedom. The international human rights system has become an arena where the balance between coexisting principles such as the right to equality and the right to culture and religion are negotiated through contestations involving individuals, civil society and government.

The emergence of the global gender equality standard, embedded in the United Nations Convention on the Elimination of All Forms of Discrimination Against Women (CEDAW) of 1979 and the two International Covenants of 1966 on Civil and Political Rights, and Economic, Social and Cultural Rights, epitomizes the complex and dynamic relationship between the right to be equal and the right to be different inherent in coexisting human rights principles. It is generally agreed that equality and difference need to be balanced to achieve substantive equality. Yet in a changing world with increased mobility of people, technologies and norms, what constitutes permissible and impermissible gender differences constitutes a site of contestation.

In post-colonial states in the South, the relationship between the equal status standard embedded in CEDAW and local norms and practices based on equal worth and complementarity is complex and contested. The equal status norm is, as demonstrated by a series of socio-legal studies in women's law, not equally beneficial for women from different classes, religions and ethnic groups (Ali 2000, Hellum 1999, Hellum, Ali, Stewart and Tsanga 2007). In the North mobility of technology and people is reflected in new contestations about permissible and impermissible gender difference. New reproductive technologies challenge established conceptions of the relationship between family, gender, sexuality and marriage. The realization that migrant women don't enjoy the same protection under the law as women from the majority population has drawn the relationship between equality and difference into attention. To achieve substantive equality

1 I would like to thank Marit Melhuus, Shaheen Sardar Ali, Thomas Hylland Eriksen and Bill Derman for insightful comments on this chapter.

the need to duly consider migrant women's disadvantages with respect to the enjoyment of basic opportunities or benefits, compared to men from their own group or to women from the majority population, has been emphasized.

In this article I explore how the equality and non-discrimination standard, embedded in international and national law, is responding to the shifting socio-legal scenario set off by transnational flows of people, norms and technology. To illustrate dilemmas and conflicts that transnational practices affecting the boundary between permissible and impermissible gender difference gives rise to at the level of national law, I use Norway as a case study. Gender equality, welfare and democracy are established national values. The Norwegian Gender Equality Act was passed in 1978. CEDAW was ratified in 1980 and incorporated in the Human Rights Act in 2009, so as to take precedence when coming into conflict with other Norwegian law.

Seeing law as a site of social and cultural contestation, the Norwegian legal discourse on gender equality and discrimination provides a well-suited case to explore how the increasing difference between women is handled in a setting where cultural 'sameness' was, to a large extent, a precondition for established values and principles like equality and welfare (Ghorahsi, Eriksen and Algahasi 2009).[2] Addressing the relationship between majorities and minorities, the Norwegian anthropologist Marianne Gullestad has argued that the Norwegian ideal of equality is premised on the notion that '... people have to be more or less the same to get along' (Gullestad 2001:37). Egalitarian ideas, in her view, are often '... used to marginalize specific groups by simultaneously creating dichotomies asking for sameness' (Gullestad 2001:54). To explore whether and to what extent these cultural perceptions of difference as a shortcoming of some kind are reflected in contemporary Norwegian discrimination law I focus on three sets of transnational practices that disturb established notions of 'treating like cases alike' and at the same time permit 'unalike' cases to be treated differently. These are the use of assisted procreation offered in a global market, the wearing of headscarves in schools and workplaces, and the use of cultural defense in criminal cases.

Equality and Difference – Shifting Sites of Contestation

CEDAW is ratified by 186 states. It is embedded in the Aristotelian notion of justice prescribing that like cases be treated alike while permitting 'unalike' cases to be treated differently. While laying the foundation for an equal status approach, the preamble to the Convention also includes the notion of gender complementarity and equal worth. In the preamble the parties bear in mind that

2 This is one of the theoretical propositions of the interdisciplinary and comparative research conducted in the research project 'Cultural Complexity in the New Norway' at the University of Oslo, compiled in the *Paradoxes of Cultural Recognition. Perspectives from Northern Europe* (Gorashi, Eriksen and Algashi 2009).

'the great contribution of women to the welfare of the family and the development of the society' is so far not fully recognized. The relationship between equal status and equal worth has been at the core of the discussion of how 'justified' and 'unjustified' distinctions between the sexes should be drawn without succumbing to either homogenizing universalism or paralyzing cultural relativism since the Convention's reception in 1979.

The sameness/difference approach informing CEDAW was criticized in its initial phase for its underlying male and Western normative biases. Many scholars within the emerging feminist jurisprudence saw the sameness/difference approach as problematic for women because their social, cultural and economic reality systematically differed from men's. The Canadian legal scholar, Kathleen Mahoney, argued that '… it does not allow for any questioning about the extent to which the law is male-defined and built on male conceptions of problems and of harms' (Mahoney 1994:442). Taking the work women do in society, in terms of caring for children and the elderly, the Norwegian Professor of Woman's Law, Tove Stang Dahl, argued that, 'Equal status favours manliness. The equal status policy has its qualitative basis in male life contexts as guiding norms for the organization of society, and the result of equal status measured by counting heads with male and female bodies' (Dahl 1993:1). Whether the notion of equal worth – embedded in Norwegian marriage law that sees care, subsistence and cash as different but equal means of fulfilling the spouses' mutual duty to support each other – should be abolished so as to comply with the equal status norm was the object of fierce debate in Norway in the 1980s (Hellum 1986).

Scholars in the Global South were concerned about the equal rights project's Eurocentric bias. The Nigerian legal scholar, Adetoun Illumoka, pointed to the unequal power relations between women in the North and the South that informed CEDAW. In her view:

> The international women's rights movement, like the international human rights movement, largely projects the concerns of privileged women who are able to make their voices heard. The voices of middle class European and American women, because of their cultural affinity with and the access to power from where the dominant discourse emanates, often is loudest (Illumoka 1995:320).

Recognizing that human rights can never be an abstract neutral position, scholars like Abdullahi An-Na'im, the Islamic reformist, and the Ugandan Professor of Law, Sylvia Tamale, set out a middle ground position, emphasizing the need to develop a united set of principles, without losing focus on difference, through a sustained intra-cultural and cross-cultural dialogue (An-Na'im 1995, Tamale 1995).

Recognizing the human rights project's historical biases in terms of gender, religion, culture and race, most scholars within African, Asian and Western feminist jurisprudence agreed on the need for a space to represent women's different voices and interests in international law (Cook 1994, Knop 1994). The quest for an international space can be seen as rooted in two interrelated sets of critique – firstly, the critique of the inherently patriarchal character of national law and national political institutions, and secondly, the critique of the equal rights project's Eurocentric historical and political bias.

With the increased mobility of people and norms and the subsequent growth in social and normative communities that transcend the territorial and legal boundaries of nation-states in the South and the North, the terrain of these theoretical debates is shifting. In Africa the ratification of the Protocol on the Rights of Women to the African Charter on Human Rights has prompted claims to equality and non-discrimination that counter the nationalist notion of gender equality as a Western feminist phenomenon (Banda 2005). In a similar vein, a growing body of Islamic feminist scholarship is seeking a harmonization between gender equality and gender complementarity through a dynamic interpretation of Islam (Ali 2000, Barals 2002, Mir-Hosseini 2006).

In Europe, migration from the South has unleashed an accelerating stream of claims invoking cultural and religious rights and in some instances a quest to formalize religious and customary norms. Addressing the relationship between cultural diversity, collective identity and individual rights, the feminist philosopher, Susan Moller Okin, in her provocative essay, 'Is multiculturalism bad for women?', launched political and legal debates about feminism and multiculturalism that pit group rights against individual rights and gender against ethnicity (Okin 1999). Seeking an approach that speaks to women's multiple identities as individual citizens and members of social minority groups, one strand of feminist jurisprudence has, along the lines suggested by the African American legal scholar, Kimberlé Crenshaw, approached gender discrimination as a result of intersecting racial, ethnic or social factors (Crenshaw 2004). Emphasizing how sex, race, class, ethnicity and religion interact to the disadvantage of migrant women, this position is in turn giving new life to old questions about how equal status and equal worth should be balanced.

Local Footprints in International Equality and Discrimination Law

The diverse and shifting terrain of equality and difference in feminist jurisprudence illustrates how human rights standards in general and the gender equality standard in particular constitutes what the anthropologist Thomas Hylland Eriksen in his book, *Globalization*, termed 'a set of shared benchmarks, or a shared language of comparison whereby people can frame their differences' (Eriksen 2007:65). We now turn to how the CEDAW committee has struck a balance between permissible and impermissible difference in its interpretation of the equality and non-discrimination norm through a jurisprudence involving communication with state parties, non-governmental organizations and individuals in different social, economic, cultural and legal contexts.

Through an interactive and dynamic jurisprudence the CEDAW committee, like other human rights treaty bodies, has adopted the equality and non-discrimination standard in response to current challenges and developments in different parts of the world. A stream of particular incidents are breathing life into this standard through the state reporting procedure and the individual complaint mechanism. A set of general recommendations entailing an increasingly complex and nuanced concept of equality and non-discrimination reflects how the boundary between justified and unjustified difference is changing. This is a result of the Committee's context-sensitive mode of interpretation. The four dimensions of discrimination – direct, indirect, structural and multiple – embedded in Article 1 of the Convention, bespeak and reflect the diverse and complex relationships in which women are involved. How the Committee is responding to this diversity so as to promote substantive, as opposed to formal, equality, is illustrated by its interpretation of the object and purpose of the Convention:

> In the Committee's view, a purely formal legal or programmatic approach is not sufficient to achieve women's *de facto* equality with men, which the Committee interprets as substantive equality. In addition, the Convention requires that women are given an equal start and that they be empowered by an enabling environment to achieve equality of result. It is not enough to guarantee women treatment identical to that of men. Rather, biological as well as socially and culturally constructed differences between women and men must be taken into account.[3]

In line with this overarching concern, the Committee has moved beyond both the formalized and individualized notion of discrimination. It defines 'direct discrimination' as occurring when a difference in treatment relies directly and explicitly on distinctions based exclusively on the basis of sex and characteristics of men or of women, which cannot be justified objectively. 'Indirect discrimination', according to the Committee, occurs where laws, policies and programmes – based on apparently gender-neutral criteria – fail to take into account social, economic and cultural gender differences.[4] They may 'be inadvertently modelled on male lifestyles and thus fail to take into account aspects of women's life experiences that may differ from men's'. Indirect discrimination can occur when women are disadvantaged compared to men with respect to the enjoyment of a particular opportunity or benefit due to pre-existing inequalities.

Recognizing the social and cultural structures that often underlie acts of discrimination, Article 5(a) in the Convention addresses 'structural discrimination'. Understanding direct and indirect discrimination as informed by gender stereotypes that have no objective justification, this article obliges state parties to take all appropriate measures to:

---

3 CEDAW Committee General Recommendation No. 25 on Article 4, paragraph 1:11.

4 CEDAW Committee General Recommendation No. 25 on Article 4, paragraph 1, note 1.

> … modify the social and cultural patterns of conduct of men and women, with a view to achieving the elimination of prejudices and customary and all other practices which are based on the idea of the inferiority or superiority of either of the sexes or on stereotyped roles for men and women …

Gender stereotypes, according to Rebecca Cook and Simone Cusak, degrade women when they assign them subservient roles in society (Cook and Cusak 2010:1). Prejudices about women's inferiority generate disrespect and devalue women. When societies fail to recognize and eliminate stereotypes they are, according to Cook and Cusak, 'exacerbating a climate of impunity with respect to women's rights'.

The Committee sees 'multiple discrimination' as being based on a combination of women's identity as women and their belonging to a group which is discriminated against on grounds such as ethnicity, race, age, disability, and so on. The Committee on Economic, Social and Cultural Rights defines multiple discrimination as a situation when: 'some individuals or groups of individuals face discrimination on more than one of the prohibited grounds, for example, women belonging to an ethnic or religious minority'.[5] A recurrent concern in the CEDAW committee's concluding comments on European state reports is the multiple discrimination faced by migrant, refugee and minority women in relation to education, employment and health care, and exposure to violence. According to the CEDAW committee:

> … Women migrant workers often experience intersecting forms of discrimination suffering not only from gender-based discrimination but also xenophobia and racism. Discrimination based on race, ethnicity, cultural particularities, language, religion or other status may be expressed in sex and gender specific ways.[6]

The concept of direct, indirect and structural discrimination protects the right to individual identity and, as such, the right to be different. At the core of the equality and non-discrimination norm is the protection of the individual against gender stereotypes that lack an objective justification. In this regard the non-discrimination norm often comes to a head-on collision with religious and cultural prescriptions that limit women's right to freedom and equality compared to men's. Yet the concept of indirect and multiple discrimination also frames the relationship between equality and difference and equal status and equal worth in a way that responds to the critique of the equality standard's male and Western normative bias. It is, however, an uneasy relationship between the concept of indirect discrimination that calls for consideration of social and cultural difference and

5 Committee on Economic, Social and Cultural Rights, General Recommendation No. 20 'Non-discrimination in Economic, Social and Cultural Rights' (Article 2, paragraph 2).

6 CEDAW committee's General Recommendation No. 26 on Women Migrant Workers, paragraph 14.

the concept of structural discrimination that, in terms of Article 5(a), calls for elimination of social and cultural patterns of conduct that are based on stereotyped roles for men and women.

The CEDAW committee's inconsistent consideration of the '*mahr*' illustrates the unsettled relationship between equal status and equal worth.[7] The *mahr* is, for the purpose of this chapter, defined as 'the property or cash the groom is obliged to give to the bride as part of a Muslim marriage contract'. Whether this gendered contractual construction can be reconciled with Article 16 of CEDAW, which requires that men and women have the same rights and obligations to enter marriage, during marriage and at the dissolution of marriage, has been a site of contestation. The practice of the Committee is inconsistent. In its comment on the Tunis periodic report to the 27th session, the Committee saw the *mahr* as 'a practice that gave the impression that the bride was bought and could be managed like a chattel'.[8] On the 38th session, on the other hand, the Committee asked Syria to 'review its existing laws and policies to ensure that women who go to shelters do not forgo other legal rights, such as rights to maintenance and dower'.[9] The comment on Syria's report indicates the Committee's concern that a gender-neutral divorce law may mean that women fall between two legal stools, namely the equal status approach seeing the spouses as two equal individuals and the equal worth approach seeking to compensate women for existing social and economic differences. The Committee's comment on Syria's report indicates that it acknowledges the need to take the gendered social and legal construction of the Muslim marriage contract into consideration to achieve substantive, as opposed to formal, equality. Pursuing this path the Committee is balancing equality and difference, and equality and equal worth within the broad notion of substantive equality, calling for consideration of socially and culturally constructed differences between women and men.

Ambiguities of Human Rights, Gender Equality and National Identity

To illustrate the complex process whereby these internationally-shared benchmarks are translated into national law and local practice, I use Norway as a case study. The Norwegian national identity is associated with overarching values like equality, welfare and democracy. But what happens when new

7 An account of how the *mahr* is adjudicated in Scandinavian, English and French courts is given in Lene Løvdahl's Masters thesis: *Private International Law, Muslim Laws and Gender Equality*, Studies in Women's Law No.79/2009, Institute of Women's Law, University of Oslo.

8 http://daccessdds.un.org/doc/UNDOC/GEN/N02/426/33/PDF/N0242633.pdf?OpenElement, accessed on 10 September 2008.

9 http://daccessdds.un.org/doc/UNDOC/GEN/N07/375/96/PDF/N0737596.pdf?OpenElement, accessed on 10 September 2008.

and different gender constructions, gender values and gender practices enter Norwegian law and society?

Faced with accumulating international legal obligations, unprecedented cultural diversity and increasing transnationalism, a revitalization of traditional nationalism is taking place in Norway, as elsewhere in Europe (Ghorashi, Eriksen and Algashi 2009:283). These social, political and legal processes are reflected in contemporary Norway in a highly ambiguous relationship between human rights and national law. In Norway there is an increasing worry about the prospect of the dynamic interpretation of international and regional human rights treaty bodies challenging national laws, policies and practices. A recent 'Power and Democracy Study' in Norway expressed concerns that the incorporation of international conventions in Norwegian law would undermine national sovereignty (NOU 2003:19). One of the hypotheses purporting to explain the growing state resistance to human rights in Norway and other Nordic countries is the prevalence of communitarian narratives of the Nordic states as ethnically and culturally homogenous and egalitarian nations with a strong emphasis on grassroots movement and participatory local democracy (Føllesdal and Wind 2009:132).

The controversy surrounding CEDAW's status in Norwegian law epitomizes the tense relationship between national sovereignty on the one hand and Norway's national identity as a champion of human rights and gender equality on the other. Gender equality is an established national value embedded in the Norwegian Gender Equality Act of 1978. CEDAW was ratified in 1980 and incorporated into the Human Rights Act in 2009, so as to take precedence when coming into conflict with other Norwegian laws. At the level of Norwegian foreign policy, CEDAW is a powerful symbol of Norway's self image as a world champion of human rights and gender equality. According to the Norwegian Ministry of Foreign Affairs' *Action Plan for Women's Rights and Gender Equality in Development Cooperation* (2007–2009):

> The government wants Norway to be a fearless champion of women's rights and gender equality. Accordingly, the rights, participation and influence of women will be at the core of Norway's development cooperation efforts. Our aim is to ensure the realization of the rights of women that are set out in international human rights conventions.[10]

International human rights conventions' contested status in Norwegian law in general and CEDAW's contested status in particular stands in stark contrast to its key position in Norwegian development policy.[11] Norwegian development policy is based on a rights approach seeing the relationship between gender

10 Foreword, Action Plan for Women's Rights and Gender Equality in Development Cooperation (2007–2009), Norwegian Ministry of Foreign Affairs.

11 A. Hellum points this out in *Politisk spydspiss med sviktende legitimitet, Kronikk i Dagbladet* 8 March 2007.

equality, human rights, democracy and development as mutually constitutive. At the national level the rights-based approach has met with resistance from legal bureaucrats and politicians who have seen the increasing inflow of international law as a threat to national sovereignty. To protect Norwegian self-determination and democracy, legal experts in the Ministry of Justice and the Government Legal Counsel have argued that the Norwegian state should avoid incorporation models, like the Human Rights Act, that give international law precedence when coming into conflict with Norwegian law.[12] According to this view, incorporating CEDAW in the Human Rights Act would undermine national sovereignty.

When presenting the Government's proposal to incorporate CEDAW into the Human Rights Act in 2009, the Minister of Justice, Knut Storberget, assured parliament that preserving national sovereignty was an overall political concern and that CEDAW was the very last international convention that would be incorporated into the Human Rights Act.[13] A series of conventions, such as The Convention on the Elimination of All Forms of Racial Discrimination, would not be given the same status under national law, in order to preserve national sovereignty and national legal culture.[14]

The ambiguous relationship between the principle of gender equality as a marker of national identity and gender equality as an international human right is also manifest in more specific debates about the content and outreach of the Norwegian Gender Equality Act. Seeing legal discourse as a site of socio-cultural contestation, I will show how changing notions of permissible and impermissible gender difference embedded in international law and transnational practices are adopted or resisted in Norwegian law. Towards this end I look into three sites of legal contestation: access to assisted procreation, wearing headscarves in schools and workplaces, and using a cultural defence in criminal cases. These examples have been chosen because they epitomize the contested relationship between different gender values. They provide a window into the process whereby the boundary between permissible and impermissible gender difference is renegotiated and show how the idea of cultural 'sameness' was to a large extent a precondition for the Norwegian Gender Equality Act.

---

12 The State Legal Counsel has argued on these grounds against the enactment of the Human Rights Act and the incorporation of the Convention on the Rights of the Child, CEDAW, the International Convention on the Elimination of All Forms of Racial Discrimination and other treaties into the Human Rights Act. For the same reasons, the Counsel is against ratifying Protocol 12 to the European Convention on Human Rights and the Optional Protocol to the International Covenant on Economic, Social and Cultural Rights.

13 Article by Minister of Justice, Knut Storberget, and Minister of Equality and Children's Affairs, Anniken Huitfeldt, in *Dagbladet*, 7 May 2009.

14 See H. Skjeie (2009) 'Policy views on the incorporation of human rights conventions – CEDAW in Norwegian Law'.

Contested Notions of Permissible Difference – Assisted Procreation

How transnational practices, movements and networks prompt negotiations about the boundary between permissible and impermissible difference is illustrated by childless Norwegian men and women's use of reproductive services offered on the global market. A major issue in the Norwegian legislative debate is what kind of reproductive technologies should be made accessible and to what groups of women and men? Whether the Norwegian Biotechnology Act that prohibits access to egg donation should be changed, so as to be in consonance with transnational procreative practices and the international equality and non-discrimination norm, is a highly controversial issue.

As access to procreative technologies grows, their different uses are, as demonstrated by Marit Melhuus' chapter in this volume, giving rise to new forms of parenthood that challenge established cultural and legal conceptions of permissible and impermissible gender difference. Melhuus' research shows how efforts to circumscribe people's procreative choices by means of national legislation so as to preserve established notions of motherhood and fatherhood, is failing in a situation where these technologies are available on the global market.

Whether and to what extent a state, out of a desire to preserve traditional gender and family values, can restrict access to procreative technologies, is a site of political and legal contestation. At the United Nations conferences in Cairo and Beijing, Catholic and Islamic states wanted to replace the term 'gender' with the term 'sex' in United Nations terminology to make it clear that the heterosexual married couple constitutes the natural unit of human procreation. Seeing gender as a social – as opposed to a biological, natural and God-given – construction, human rights treaty bodies, like the CEDAW and the Economic, Social and Cultural Rights Covenant committees, have by and large turned down biological justifications for differential treatment of women and men. Giving content to the right to non-discriminatory access to health services, both committees have emphasized that biological factors that differentiate women from men, such as their reproductive functions, cannot justify differential treatment.

To be in tune with new procreative practices, many countries have changed their legislation. The Norwegian Biotechnology Act is, as Marit Melhuus points out, an attempt to preserve established notions of gender, family, fatherhood and motherhood. In the 1980s, where the medical and social consequences of egg donation were unclear, the Norwegian Ministry of Health suggested a restrictive approach which parliament followed up. The Artificial Procreation Act of 1987 thus allowed access to sperm donation but did not permit access to egg donation. The argument that egg donation should be treated differently from sperm donation was based on the argument of gender difference:

> In contrast to sperm donation, egg donation requires medical surgery … Donation of eggs has more similarities with transplantation than it has with sperm donation … In contrast to egg donation, sperm donation does not create

> a situation different from natural reproduction. Donor insemination does not break fundamentally with that which occurs in natural reproduction. Whether conception occurs artificially or naturally, the sperm is something which comes from the outside. This implies that there will always be some uncertainty as to who is the father of the child. With natural conception it is not unusual that there is a discrepancy between legal/social paternity and biological paternity … With natural reproduction the uterus and the egg constitute a natural unity. Conception, pregnancy and birth is a unified process which occurs within the woman. With egg donation this unity is broken … with egg donation, physical motherhood is split … there is reason to believe that this lack of clarity will cause insecurity with regard to the identity of the child … (Ot. prp. nr 25:19; 1986–87).

Whether these considerations have any relevance in contemporary Norway is highly contested. The Norwegian Equality and Anti-Discrimination Ombud, who monitors the Gender Equality Act, believes that the prohibition against egg donation constitutes a contravention of the Norwegian Gender Equality Act. The Ombud has argued that there is no objective reason to limit assisted procreation to donor insemination under the Biotechnology Act. Rejecting the construction of maternity and paternity as fundamentally different, she is of the view that male and female reproductive tissue should be treated equally. Dealing with this matter, the Equality and Anti-Discrimination Tribunal disagreed. The Tribunal held that the ban on the donation of eggs in section 2–8 of the Biotechnology Act is not in breach of section 3 of the Gender Equality Act. The Biotechnology Act, according to the Tribunal, should take precedence because it is a newer Act than the Gender Equality Act. According to the Tribunal, the preparatory work of the Biotechnology Act was an expression of the democratic will of parliament and, as such, should take precedence.[15]

The Norwegian political and legal reluctance to make existing reproductive technologies available on a non-discriminatory basis epitomizes the tension between the notion of equality based on cultural sameness and equality based on social and cultural difference. By limiting access to certain technologies (allowing sperm donation and prohibiting egg donation) and certain family forms (allowing married and cohabiting heterosexual and lesbian couples but prohibiting single women and male homosexual couples), the Biotechnology Act defines the dominant ideal of cultural sameness whereby other family forms are judged and deemed inferior.[16] It is thus not surprising that a core controversy related to Norway's incorporation of CEDAW into the Human Rights Act was whether Norway, by implication, would have to change the Biotechnology Act so as to permit access to egg donation. An argument against incorporating CEDAW into the Human Rights Act was that it would undermine national sovereignty with a view to what should be regarded as permissible and impermissible gender difference.

---

15 The Ombud's recommendation was appealed before the Tribunal, LKN 9/2006.

16 Pertaining to revision of the Marriage Act and the Biotechnology Act in 2009 married lesbian women are entitled to assisted procreation.

Contested Notions of Difference: Headscarves and Cultural Defence

The idea of cultural sameness underlying the Norwegian Gender Equality Act has been challenged on a number of occasions by the quest for a conception of equality and non-discrimination that moves beyond the concerns of ethnic Norwegian women. This quest has come from both immigrant organizations and international human rights treaty bodies. In 2001 the MIRA Resource Centre for Immigrant and Refugee Women expressed concern that the Norwegian Gender Equality Act did not take their life experience and problems into account. In their comment to the Government's proposed revision of the Act they stated:

> We are of the view that the new proposal to the Gender Equality Act does not represent the multiplicity of diversity that exists in contemporary Norway. We wish that the Ministry of Children and Family would take the living conditions of immigrant and refugee women in Norway into account so as to enhance equality for women from the minority population.[17]

With regard to the situation of migrant women, the CEDAW committee has asked state parties to pay attention to how differences between women and men within immigrant communities and between immigrant women and women from the majority population are played out in relation to the rights to participation, education and work, and equal protection under the law.[18] In its comment on Norway's seventh periodical report in 2005, the CEDAW committee urged:

> … the state party to take effective measures to eliminate discrimination against migrant, refugee and minority women and to further strengthen its efforts to combat xenophobia and racism. It also urges the state party to be proactive in its measures to prevent discrimination against these women, both within their communities and in society at large.[19]

In the following I use legal controversies about headscarves and cultural defence to illustrate the messy interface between permissible and impermissible differences in the area of equality and non-discrimination law in the changing socio-cultural context of Norway.

---

17 MIRA Resource Centre, comment to Ot. prp. nr. 77 2001–2002.

18 See the CEDAW committee's General Recommendation No. 26 on Women Migrant Workers.

19 CEDAW/C/2003/CRP.3/Add.2/Rev.1 paragraph 25.

Headscarves

Resistance to national laws prohibiting headscarves in workplaces and schools has been framed in multiple ways. Legal restrictions have been seen as a contravention of the right to religious freedom, as ethnic discrimination and as gender discrimination. The outcomes of cases where the gender discrimination argument has been invoked differ. Departing from the notion of cultural sameness the European Court of Human Rights in the case *Layla Sahin v Turkey* upheld the prohibition against the headscarf with reference to the principle of gender equality.[20]

Addressing the complex situations that women's multiple identities give rise to, the CEDAW committee has on a number of occasions urged state parties to carefully consider both intended and unintended consequences of new laws that are introduced to abolish practices and beliefs that are informed by stereotypical gender roles, such as the headscarf. In its comment on Turkey's periodic report it expressed concern about how the ban on headscarves negatively affected women and girls' right to education: 'The Committee is also concerned about the impact on girls and women of the ban on wearing headscarves in schools and universities'.[21] A similar concern was expressed by the Child Rights committee when dealing with France's country report. Both Turkey and France have been asked to account for the ban's impact on women and girls' right to education. Both the CEDAW and the Child Right's committees have expressed concern that a prohibition against wearing headscarves in schools may negatively affect women and girls' right to education and participation.

In Norway, the main site of legal resistance to prohibitions against wearing headscarves has been the gender equality principle embedded in the Gender Equality Act.[22] In the Oslo Plaza Hotel case, the Norwegian Equality and Anti-discrimination Tribunal concluded that the banning of headscarves by the hotel constituted an outright breach of the prohibition against gender discrimination in the Gender Equality Act.[23] The background of the case was the dismissal of a woman working as a room hostess at the Oslo Plaza Hotel because she was wearing the *hijab*. The woman was, with reference to the hotel's dress code, asked to stop wearing the *hijab*. When she refused to conform she lost her job and made a complaint to the Equality and Anti-discrimination Ombud. The Gender Equality Ombud and later the Equality and Anti-discrimination Tribunal concluded that the gender-neutral dress code – which prohibited use of religious attire for both women and men – did not have the same adversarial effects for women and men.

20 2005, *Leyla Sahin v Turkey.*

21 UN DOC. A/60/38 (Turkey), paragraph 371 and 372.

22 In Denmark attempts to challenge prohibitions against the use of headscarfs in supermarkets on the basis of ethnic discrimination have not been successful, see Ketscher 2007.

23 LDN 8/2001.

Since the majority of immigrants in Oslo wearing religious attire are Muslims, such a prohibition would, according to the Ombud and the Tribunal, mainly affect women. The Ombud and the Tribunal were both of the view that Muslim women's personal integrity was so closely linked to wearing the *hijab* that a prohibition would mean that they could be barred from work. This would entail significant disadvantages for these women so the Ombud and the Tribunal concluded that the prohibition constituted indirect sex discrimination. Furthermore, the Ombud and the Tribunal considered that demanding that the hotel design a uniform that was acceptable for women wearing the *hijab* for religious reasons would not be unreasonable.

The CEDAW committee's concluding comment to Turkey and the Norwegian Equality Tribunal's way of balancing sameness and difference opens up a space to reconcile women's multiple identities as citizens and members of an ethnic and religious group. Departing from the notion of the need to take cultural difference into account this is in tune with liberal philosophers like Martha Nussbaum who argue that wearing headscarves should be accepted so as to facilitate equal access to education and work for women with different cultural and religious backgrounds (Nussbaum 2000). A similar approach is advocated by Shaheen Sardar Ali who suggests we enter women's human rights discourse through a route that has legitimacy in Islamic principles, such as the uncontested right to survival, development and participation all of which opens up women's empowerment by claiming equal access to health, education and work (Ali 2000:278–279). This differs from the European Court of Human Rights' approach which sees the rights to equality and to religion as irreconcilable (Skjeie 2008). In the case of *Layla Sahin v Turkey*, the Grand Chamber of the European Court of Human Rights reiterated the view as follows:

> In the *Dahlab* case, which concerned the teacher of a class of small children, the Court stressed among other matters the 'powerful external symbol' which her wearing a headscarf represented and questioned whether it might have some kind of proselytising effect that appeared to be imposed on women by a religious precept that was hard to reconcile with the principle of gender equality. It also noted that wearing the Islamic headscarf could not easily be reconciled with the message of tolerance, respect for others and, above all, equality and non-discrimination that all teachers in a democratic society should convey to their pupils.[24]

Cultural Defence

In Europe the increased mobility of people and norms and the subsequent growth in social and normative communities that transcend the territorial and legal boundaries of nation-states in the South has set off an accelerating stream of claims invoking cultural and religious rights and, in some instances, a quest for

24 *Sahin*, supra note 1, 111.

formalizing religious and customary norms. In Norway, as elsewhere in the world, such claims have in turn sparked controversies as to how freedom of religion and protection of culture should be balanced against women's right to equality and non-discrimination.

The CEDAW committee, in its General Recommendation No. 26 on Women Migrant Workers, addresses the gendered character of the relationship between the individual's right to equal protection under the law, cultural diversity and collective identity. Emphasizing how migrant women are more vulnerable to sexual abuse, sexual harassment and physical violence than women from the majority population, the Committee states: 'Women migrant workers who migrate as spouses of male migrant workers or as family members, face an added risk of domestic violence from their spouses or relatives when they come from a culture that values the submissive role of women in the family'.[25] This recommendation resonates the international equality standard that, according to the Human Rights committee, obliges 'state parties to ensure that traditional, historical, religious or cultural attitudes are not used to justify violations of women's right to equality before the law and to equal enjoyment of all Covenant rights'.[26] Underlining the need for measures to ensure equal protection under the law for women from the majority and minority population, the CEDAW committee in its comments on Norway's seventh periodic report called upon the Norwegian state party to '... ensure the collection of comprehensive statistical data disaggregated by sex, age and ethnicity, and by type of violence and the relationship of the perpetrator to the victim'.[27]

The changing consideration of claims invoking cultural and religious rights to justify violation of women's right to freedom and integrity illustrates how the boundary between permissible and impermissible gender difference is renegotiated at the international, national and local level of law. Since the 1970s Norwegian courts have dealt with a series of criminal cases where men have argued that violence against wives, daughters or sisters was motivated by their duty to restore the family honour embedded in customary or religious norms from their country of origin. The following case law from Norwegian, Indian and Pakistani appellate courts illustrates how courts in different parts of the world are responding to pressure from both human rights treaty bodies and women's rights movements to protect women's right to equality and free choice in matters of sexuality and marriage.

In 1984, dealing with a case where a Turkish father had killed his daughter to restore family honour, the Norwegian Supreme Court, referring to the testimony of the anthropologist Reidar Grønhaug, took the honour code from the father's

25 The CEDAW committee's General Recommendation No. 26 paragraph 20.

26 Human Rights Committee, General Comment No. 28: Equality of Rights between Men and Women Article 3.

27 CEDAW/C/NOR/CO/7 paragraph 20.

home area into consideration as a mitigating circumstance.[28] Stressing cultural difference, the Norwegian Supreme Court condoned family punishment of women who freely choose their partners. The Court emphasized in its reasoning that:

> Immigrants must as a main rule adjust to the laws of this country. In this case, the accused's actions are, however, influenced and motivated by expectations, both in the home country and in the immigrant community in Norway, to such a degree that it puts them in a position they would otherwise not find themselves, that I find it should be taken into account as a mitigating circumstance. The conflict that forms the background of the murder had its background in moral views and traditions which exist in the country of origin, that are different from this country's. The tradition in the home country with its norms and expectations are in my view putting the accused in a particular position.

The case, which undermined immigrant women's right to autonomy and equal protection under the law, was the object of fierce criticism from both anthropologists and lawyers.[29] In 1989 the Norwegian Supreme Court took the opposite stand in a case where a Pakistani man, who had murdered his wife, argued that his act was motivated by the existing honour code in his country of origin. In this case the Norwegian Supreme Court pursued an 'equal under the law' approach.[30] Without any investigation of the legal situation in Pakistan, the Court stated that, 'in this case, I find also that those immigrants who change their way of life in a way that is accepted in this country, but constitutes a breach of prevailing norms in their country of origin, have a right to full legal protection'. Taking this line of argument further, Norwegian lower courts have in recent years sharpened their symbolic language to make it clear that breaching the equality norm is a serious offence. In a recent case, which was dealt with by Oslo city court, a woman who had been subject to severe violence and held in isolation was granted compensation from her husband because he had barred her integration into Norwegian society.[31] Criminal law is an arena where national gender values that distinguish between permissible and impermissible differences are communicated to immigrants.

While including migrant women as citizens that are entitled to the same protection under Norwegian law as ethnic Norwegian women, the judiciary is also using a language suggesting that Islamic and Pakistani law is inferior. The messages that these judgments communicate are highly ambiguous. While on the one hand the Norwegian Supreme Court is reversing its own practice, on the other hand it is disassociating itself from the male code of honour by placing it in the realm of 'prevailing norms in the country of origin'. Judicial discourse, in

28 Rt 1984, 1146.

29 The anthropologist, Tordis Borchgrevink, argued that women, regardless of culture, should have the same protection under the law as men (Borchgrevink 1997).

30 Rt 1989:445.

31 Oslo Tingrett's judgment of 8 October 2003 (03-05791 M/46).

other words, is constructing Norwegian law as being in opposition to the law in Pakistan. A similar line of argument was pursued in the Sujit Kumar case from Allahabad High Court in India where the Court constructed opposition between the laws of the secular and liberal Indian state and the Pakistani state that was based on a feudal and communal ideology:

> The barbaric practice of 'honour killings' that is, killing of young women by their relatives or caste or community members for bringing dishonour to the family or caste or community by marrying or wanting to marry a man of another caste, community or someone whom the family disapproves of, is frequently reported to take place in Pakistan which is a state based on feudal and communal ideology. However, this Court has been shocked to note that in our country also, which boasts of being a secular and liberal country, 'honour killings' have been taking place from time to time, and what is deeply disturbing is that the police and other authorities do not seem to take steps to check these disgraceful and barbaric acts (Quoted from Baxi, Ali and Rai 2006:52).

Turning to Pakistani appellate courts, we find similar responses to pressure from the international human rights community and women's rights groups to protect women's right to exercise choice in matters of sexuality and marriage. In the case *Muhammad Siddique v the State*, the High Court upheld the conviction against a father who had murdered his daughter because she married according to her own choice, stating:

> … there is nothing religious about it and honourable either. It is male chauvinism and gender bias at its worst. These prejudices are not country specific. The roots are rather old and violence against women has been a recurrent phenomenon in human history.

In this case and a series of other cases, Islamic law is reconstituted with reference to international human rights conventions and also the Cairo Declaration of Human Rights and constructed in opposition to custom and colonial law (Baxi, Ali and Ray 2006:50–51).

While responding to international law's quest for equal protection under the law, it is interesting to note how appellate courts in Norway, India and Pakistan are simultaneously resorting to discourses refashioning the national legal realm, by displacing the honour crimes to other spaces less civilized than the law of the nation-state. This demonstrates how the adoption of principles like equal protection under the law acquires multiple symbolic meanings when entering the national judicial realm. Resorting to a language of national cultural sameness involving displacement and 'othering', the judiciary, as suggested by Baxi, Rai and Ali, may reinforce nationalist sentiments (2006). The multiple symbolic meanings of judicial practice in Norway, India and Pakistan thus portray how porous judicial reasoning may be to external norms and environments such as popular nationalist ideas of cultural sameness.

These observations beg the question of whether the judiciary, by adopting a less offensive and insulting language, would increase its social and cultural legitimacy among the immigrant population. The potential for a comparative legal approach that also pays attention to commonalities between Norwegian law and Islam is emphasized by Professor Shaheen Sardar Ali, as cited in the chapter by Farhat Taj and Anne Hellum in this volume. Rather than widening the gap between us and them, she suggests that actors in the national legal arena should seek consensus through a mutual understanding. Instead of relegating Islam to an uncivilized space she suggests legal discourse should also pay attention to existing commonalities between Islam and international and national law.

Navigating Sameness and Difference through Substantive Equality

The accelerating mobility of people, technologies and norms is, as discussed, making its mark on international and national gender equality debates about how to strike a balance between permissible and impermissible difference. In a situation of unprecedented cultural diversity and widespread transnationalism, it is a tense and unresolved relationship between sameness and difference.

Challenging narrow, legal, cultural or religious paradigms underlying established national and local interpretations of the principle that like cases be treated alike, the global equality standard protects the right to individual identity for women with different nationalities, sexualities or ethnicities and, as such, the right to be different. It constitutes an important mechanism for including individuals and groups that in national and local contexts have been excluded from participation and access to resources on the basis of legal, social and religious paradigms that depend on stereotypical perceptions of gender, sexuality or ethnicity.

When translated into national law, the global equality standard often takes on new and different meanings. In their adoption of the principle of equal protection under the law, appellate courts in Norway, India and Pakistan all use language that relegates honour crimes to other, less-civilized spaces unrelated to the law of the nation-state. Resorting to a language of national cultural sameness involving displacement and 'othering', national judiciaries thus reinforce popular nationalist sentiments that assume cultural sameness.

The global equality standard is often met with outright national resistance due to its recognition of cultural differences that fall outside the scope of dominant national values. The Norwegian political and legal reluctance to make existing reproductive technologies, like egg donation, available on a non-discriminatory basis epitomizes the tension between the notion of equality based on cultural sameness and equality based on cultural difference.

International human rights law's overall consideration of substantive equality is, as suggested earlier, given content through a context-sensitive jurisprudence that takes social, cultural and economic differences into account. International human rights treaty bodies' increasing concern about socially, culturally and linguistically appropriate measures to prevent discrimination, speaks to the fluid borderline between equality and difference and equal status and equal worth. Examples are the CEDAW committee's contextual approach to the headscarf and the *mahr*. This engagement with difference speaks to a process whereby the equal status norm is re-embedded in social relationships so as to prevent women from being excluded from the national equality project. This was clearly the intention of the Norwegian Gender Equality Appeals Board when concluding that a prohibition against the *hijab* in the workplace constituted indirect gender discrimination under Norwegian law.

Yet the attempt to include women from different ethnic, religious or social backgrounds through an increasingly difference-oriented jurisprudence is also a contradictory project. The *hijab* or separate social and legal services for women do not sit well with the equal status norm and the prohibition against gender stereotypes. Yet, as the CEDAW committee's definition of substantive equality points out, historical, social and cultural differences constitute an entry point for equal access to basic human rights, such as the rights to work, education and protection against violence. The Committee's call for socially and culturally appropriate measures to make migrant women's right to equality real require a constructive engagement with difference as a means of achieving substantive equality.

References

Ali, S.S. 2000. *Gender and Human Rights in Islam and International Law*. Hague/London/Boston: Kluwer Law International.

—— 2007a. Interpretative strategies for women's human rights in plural legal frameworks: Exploring judicial and state responses to Hudood laws in Pakistan, in *Human Rights, Plural Legalities and Gendered Realities. Paths are Made by Walking*, edited by Anne Hellum, Julie Stewart, Shaheen Sardar Ali and Amy Tsanga. Harare: Weaver Press.

—— 2007b. Religious pluralism, human rights and Muslim citizenship in Europe: Some preliminary reflections on an evolving methodology for consensus, in *Religious Pluralism and Human Rights in Europe*, edited by T. Loenen and J. Goldschmidt. Utrecht: Intersentia, 57–79.

An-Na'im, A. 1995. State responsibility under international human rights law to change religious and customary laws, in *Human Rights of Women. National and International Perspectives*, edited by R. Cook. Pennsylvania: University of Pennsylvania Press.

Banda, F. 2005. *Women, Law and Human Rights: An African Perspective*. Oxford: Hart.

Barlas, A. 2002. *Believing Women in Islam: Unreading Patriarchal Interpretations of the Qur'an*. Texas: Texas University Press.

Baxi, P., Rai, S.M. and Ali, S.S. 2006. Legacies of common law: Crimes of honour in India and Pakistan. *Third World Quarterly* 27 (7)1239–1253.

Bentzon, A.W., Hellum, A., Stewart, J., Ncube, W. and Agersnap, T. 1998. *Pursuing Grounded Theory In Law. South-North Experiences in Developing Women's Law*. Oslo: TANO Aschehoug. Harare: Mond Books.

Borchgrevink, T. 1997. Et ubehag i antropologien. *Norsk Antropologisk Tidsskrift* 8:26–36.

Cook, R. (ed.) 1995. *Human Rights of Women. National and International Perspectives*. Pennsylvania: University of Pennsylvania Press.

Cook, R. and Cusak, S. 2010. *Gender Stereotyping*. Pennsylvania: University of Pennsylvania Press.

Coomaraswamy, R. 2005. Preface: Violence against women and crimes of honour, in *'Honour' Crimes, Paradigms and Violence Against Women*, edited by L. Welchman and S. Hossain. London: Zed Books.

Crenshaw, K. 2004. Demarginalizing the intersection of race and sex: A black feminist critique of anti-discrimination doctrine, feminist theory and anti-racist politics, in *Anti-Discrimination Law, International Library of Essays in Law and Legal Theory, Second Series*, edited by C. McCrudden. Dartmouth: Ashgate.

Dahl, T.S. 1986. *Women's Law. An Introduction to Feminist Jurisprudence*. Oslo: Norwegian University Press.

—— 1993. Birth law and equality, in *Birth Law*, edited by A. Hellum. Oslo: Norwegian University Press.

Eriksen, T.H. 2007. *Globalization: Key Issues*. Oxford: Berg.

Føllesdal, A. and Wind, M. 2009. Introduction – Nordic reluctance towards judicial review under siege. *Nordic Journal of Human Rights* 2 Oslo: Norwegian University Press.

Gorashi, H., Eriksen, T.H. and Algashi, S. 2009. Introduction, in *Paradoxes of Cultural Recognition. Perspectives from Northern Europe*. Farnham: Ashgate.

Griffiths, J. 1986. What is legal pluralism? *Journal of Legal Pluralism* 24:1–55.

Gullestad, M. 2001. Imagined sameness: Shifting notions of us and them in Norway, in *Forestillinger om den andre. Images of Otherness*, edited by L.A. Ytrehus. Oslo: Norwegian Academic Press.

Hellum, A. 1988. Money and Dignity in Section 1 of the Spouses Property Relations Act, in M. Fastvold and A. Hellum, Money and Work in Marriage, *Studies in Women's Law No. 26*, University of Oslo.

—— 1999. *Women's Human Rights and Legal Pluralism in Africa. Mixed Norms and Identities in Infertility Management in Zimbabwe*. Oslo: TANO Aschehoug. Harare: Mond Books.

—— 2006. Menneskerettigheter, pluralisme, kompleksitet og integrasjon (Human rights, pluralism and complexity). I *Festskrift til Carl August Fleischer*. Oslo: Universitetsforlaget.

—— (ed.) 2003. *Birth Law*. Oslo: Norwegian University Press.

Hellum, A., Stewart, J., Ali, S.S. and Tsanga, A. (eds) 2007. Paths are made by walking. Introductory thoughts, in *Human Rights, Plural Legalities and Gendered Realities. Paths are Made by Walking*, edited by A. Hellum, J. Stewart, S.S. Ali and A. Tsanga. Harare: Weaver Press.

Ilumoka, A. 1994. African women's economic, social and cultural rights – Toward a relevant theory of practice, in *Human Rights of Women. National and International Perspectives*, edited by R. Cook. Pennsylvania: University of Pennsylvania Press.

Ketscher, K. 2007. Cultural rights and religious rights, in T. Loenen and J. Goldschmidt (ed.), *Religious Pluralism and Human Rights in Europe: Where to Draw the Line?* Utrecht: Intersentia.

Knop, K. 1994. Why rethinking the sovereign state is important for women's human rights law, in *Human Rights of Women. National and International Perspectives*, edited by R. Cook. Pennsylvania: University of Pennsylvania Press.

Løvdahl, L. 2009. *Private International Law, Muslim Laws and Gender Equality*. Masters thesis, Faculty of Law. Studies in Women's Law No 79. Oslo: University of Oslo.

Mahoney, K.E. 1994. Canadian approaches to equality, rights and gender equity in the courts, in *Human Rights of Women. National and International Perspectives*, edited by R. Cook. Pennsylvania: University of Pennsylvania Press.

Mir-Hosseini, Z. 2006. Muslim women's quest for equality: Between Islamic law and feminism. *Critical Inquiry* 32:629–645.

Norwegian Ministry of Children and Equality 2008. *Action Plan against Forced Marriages (2008–2011)*. Oslo: Government of Norway.

Norwegian Ministry of Foreign Affairs 2007. *Action Plan for Women's Rights and Gender Equality in Development Cooperation (2007–2009)*. Oslo: Government of Norway.

NOU 2003:19. *Makt og demokratiutredningen* (The power and democracy report). Oslo: Government of Norway.

Nussbaum, M. 2000. *Women and Human Development*. Cambridge: Cambridge University Press.

Okin, S.M. 1999. Is multiculturalism bad for women? in *Is Multiculturalism Bad for Women?*, edited by S.M. Okin with J. Cohen, M. Howard and M.C. Nusbaum. Princetown: Princetown University Press.

Skjeie, H. 2009. Policy views on the incorporation of human rights conventions – CEDAW in Norwegian Law. *Nordic Journal of Human Rights* 2:2009. Oslo: Norwegian University Press.

—— 2007. Headscarves in schools. European comparisons, in *Religious Pluralism and Human Rights in Europe*, edited by T. Leonon and J. Goldschmidt. Utrecht: Intersentia, 57–79.

Tamale, S. and Oloko Onyango, J. 1995. The personal is political, or why women's rights are indeed human rights: An African perspective on international feminism. *Human Rights Quarterly* 17:691–773.

Tsanga, A. 2003. *Taking Law to the People. Gender, Law Reform and Community Legal Education in Zimbabwe*. Harare: Weaver Press.

Chapter 4

Taking What Law Where and to Whom? Legal Literacy as Transcultural 'Law-Making' in Oslo

Anne Hellum and Farhat Taj[1]

Introduction

In its concluding comments on Norway's fifth and sixth periodic reports, the Committee on the Elimination of All Forms of Discrimination Against Women (the CEDAW Committee) urged the Norwegian state to take steps to increase awareness of the availability of social services and legal remedies for migrant women.[2] An area of increasing concern for the CEDAW Committee, who monitors state compliance with the Convention, is migrant women's vulnerability to intersecting forms of gender, race and class discrimination. To provide access to law and prevent these intersecting forms of discrimination, the Committee emphasizes that 'state parties should ensure that linguistically and culturally appropriate gender-sensitive services for women migrant workers are available'.[3]

Pointing out the need for a context-sensitive approach to legal literacy, advice and counselling, the CEDAW Committee's recommendation speaks to the complex relationship between protection against discrimination, cultural diversity, collective identity and individual rights. A top-down legalistic 'one size fits all' approach is, as observed by the Committee, not capable of delivering justice to immigrant women embedded in a multiplicity of social and legal ties. To situate legal literacy in the diverse and complex socio-cultural contexts in which law operates poses challenges for law and policy-makers, human rights activists and socio-legal scholars. Towards this end in this chapter we are taking as our starting

---

1 We would like to thank Professor Shaheen Sardar Ali for her contribution to this chapter. Her delivery of information about Islam and Pakistani state-law to women in the Norwegian/Pakistani community in Oslo is an integrated part of the action research described in this chapter. We would also like to thank Abdul Paliwala for valuable comments.

2 CEDAW/C/2003/CRP.3/Add.2/Rev.1 para 25.

3 CEDAW Committee, General Recommendation No. 26, para 24 b.

point the lived experiences of women from the Pakistani community in Oslo and their search for dignity and justice through engagement with the law.[4]

In this chapter we describe how a pluralist legal literacy approach is evolving on the ground, in response to individual women's mixed identities, as Norwegian citizens and members of social and religious communities. Our point of departure is the work of a Pakistani women's organization in Oslo and its interaction with Norwegian organizations that provide legal information and legal advice. The overall focus of our chapter is their way of taking law to women, embedded in transnational relationships, where a multiplicity of norms and expectations deriving from relatives, religious networks and authorities in Norway and Pakistan are at work.

Migrant women's engagement with law thus serves as a window into the relationship between citizenship and religion in the increasingly multicultural Norway.[5] Focusing on the use of rights, we show how immigrant women exercise citizenship in the context of their multiple belonging – as Norwegian citizens, family members and Muslims. Through a perspective from below and within we uncover practices and discourses that constitute resistance to dominant Western and Islamic discourses that pit group rights against individual rights and gender equality against religion.[6] By highlighting the transnational 'law-making' that is taking place on the ground, we aim to provide law and policy makers with food for thought.

Our chapter is divided into seven parts. After this introduction, in the second part we situate legal literacy within the broader human rights framework, with reference to the state obligation to make law available, acceptable and accessible for all its citizens. A context-based framework for the analysis of migrant women's access to legal resources is presented in the third part. How the right to legal information is translated into Norwegian laws, policies and practices is addressed in the fourth part. The fifth part describes how law is made available and acceptable through engagement with the multiplicity of norms that are at work in the lives of women from the Pakistani community in Oslo. In the sixth part we discuss two individual case studies which draw attention to the options and limits of the evolving pluralist approach. The conclusion, in part seven, draws attention to the empowering aspect of a space where women are free to discuss and consider the multiple normative forces that shape their lives.

---

4 We are standing on the shoulders of Tove Stang Dahl's feminist jurisprudence suggesting taking women as a starting point through a combination of doctrinal, ethical and empirical sources (Dahl 1986). The approach is further developed in Bentzon, Hellum, Stewart, Ncube and Agersnap who uses grounded theory (1998).

5 The relationship between citizenship, women's movements and religion in muliticultural Norway is dealt with by Beatrice Halsaa in the paper 'Religious citizenship? The Complex relations between women's movements and women's religious identities', which is as part of the FEMCIT project (Gendered Citizenship in Multicultural Europe: The Impact of the Contemporary Women's Movement).

6 The debate about feminism and multiculturalism was set off by Susan Moller Okin in the essay 'Is multiculturalism bad for women? (Okin 1999). A critique of this dichotomous approach is found in Anne Phillips *Multiculturalism without Culture* (Phillips 2007).

The Right to Equal Access in a Diverse and Unequal Context

Equal access to law and the right to legal information is a human right that, in principle, applies to all individuals regardless of time and place. In practice, the availability of legal information and subsequently the access to law is highly dependent on people's class, gender and race. Addressing mechanisms of legal exclusion, the United Nations Commission on Legal Empowerment of the Poor, in their report, 'Making the law work for everyone', estimates that at least four billion people are excluded from the rule of law. The Commission understands legal empowerment as 'a process of systemic change through which the poor and excluded become able to use the law, the legal system and legal services to protect and advance their rights and interests as citizens and economic actors' (Commission on Legal Empowerment of the Poor 2008:3).

The jurisprudence of international human rights treaty bodies constitutes a dynamic attempt to facilitate access to law for the poor and marginalized through increased attention on the right to legal information. The Human Rights Committee sees the duty to provide legal information as an inherent part of the state obligation embedded in Article 2 in the International Covenant on Civil and Political Rights. To fulfil this obligation, states parties, according to the Human Rights Committee, are required to adopt legislative, judicial, administrative, educative and other appropriate measures.[7] The Human Rights Committee believes it is important to raise awareness about the Covenant, not only among public officials and state agents but also among the population at large. Following suit, the Committee on Economic, Social and Cultural Rights has outlined a set of criteria that also apply to legal education: 'Fundamental education included the elements of availability, accessibility, acceptability and adaptability which are common to education in all its forms and at all levels'.[8] Contributing to the contextualization of the right to legal information, the CEDAW Committee has, with a view to women migrant workers, emphasized the need for context-specific education programmes ensuring 'that linguistically and culturally appropriate gender-sensitive services for women migrant workers are available'.[9]

International human rights treaty bodies are, as these examples show, gradually leaning towards a pluralist and contextual approach. The shortcomings of the legal centralist approach, assuming that state law is the single regulatory force at work, have been addressed by the Special Rapporteur on Violence against Women. Discussing how to take legal action against honour killing she emphasizes women's wariness of the 'arrogant gaze of critical outsiders' who

7 Human Rights Committee, General Comment No. 31. The nature of the general legal obligation imposed on state parties to the Covenant.

8 The Committee on Economic, Social and Cultural Rights General Recommendation No. 13. The Right to Education.

9 CEDAW Committee, General Recommendation No. 26 on Women Migrant Workers, para 24 b.

suggest simplistic legalistic solutions. Rights must, in her view, be asserted in a manner which takes cognisance of the social embeddedness of women's identity. According to the Special Rapporteur: 'Where international attention and leverage are rooted in culturally-sensitive strategies and locally supported, they can give strong underpinning to our situation-specific approaches and interventions on the ground' (Coomaraswamy 2005:xiii).

The Special Rapporteur's critique of legal centralism, which assumes that state law is the only regulatory force, resonates post-colonial feminist legal scholarship's engagement with legal pluralism. In a situation where inherited colonial systems of Western law, religious laws and customary laws are gradually replaced by formally unified and gender-neutral legal systems, in response to human rights standards, post-colonial women's law scholars are turning their attention to the complex interaction with people's living customs and practices (Bentzon *et al.* 1998, Griffiths 1997, Hellum 1999, Ali 2000, Hellum, Stewart, Ali and Tsanga 2007). Innovative legal education methods that respond to women's complex legal needs have been pioneered by action-oriented researchers in Asia and Africa (Shaheed 1997, Tsanga 2003, 2007). The Pakistani sociologist and activist, Fareda Shaheed, addressed the interface of human rights and local activism in the light of her experiences from a legal awareness programme run by Shirkat Gah in Lahore. She described how supporting the rights of individual women 'entails a constant shifting back and forth from strategies for intervening in legal arenas to those that address custom and religion' (Shaheed 1997:59).[10] According to Shaheed, interventions aiming to change women's lives and empower them to determine the choices available must 'first consciously work to free women from the preconceptions emanating from either custom or law and certainly the culture that permeates both' (Shaheed 1997:62).

Towards a Trans-cultural Legal Literacy Approach

A key question is how we can draw on these approaches to understand the experiences of Muslim women's engagement with law in a Western socio-liberal democracy like Norway. Assuming that legal pluralism is not a post-colonial phenomenon but a feature of all modern nation states, we turn to the grounded pluralist approach employed by socio-legal women's law studies in the South (Griffiths 1986, Moore 1978, Bentzon *et al.* 1998). Our starting point is the experiences of a Pakistan women's organization that, in an effort to make law available to women, collaborate with both Norwegian and Pakistani institutions in Oslo. The practices of the women in this organization serve as a window to the shifting back and forth from legal strategies aiming to change women's lives to engagement with religious and cultural constraints.

---

10 Shirkat Gah is a branch of the global network, 'Women living under Muslim Law'.

Through the research project, 'From Formal to Real Rights', located at the Institute of Women's Law at the University of Oslo, we have been engaged in an action-oriented research project involving dissemination of legal information to women from the Norwegian/Pakistani community in Oslo.[11] The research has involved cooperation between Norwegian and Pakistani researchers at the Institute of Women's Law and the NGO Free Legal Advice for Women (JURK) who provides legal literacy and legal advice.[12] JURK is a charity based at the Faculty of Law at the University of Oslo and the research project has been able to study how it provides legal literacy for members of a Norwegian/Pakistani women's organization, PAKWOM. In response to the challenges that the coexisting and sometimes conflicting norms at work in Norwegian/Pakistani women's lives poses for legal literacy two of the researchers, Anne Hellum and Shaheen Sardar Ali, initiated a pilot programme that engaged with both Norwegian law and Islam. As researchers, our engagement with the non-governmental organizations JURK and PAKWOM, thus involved both observation and participation in the process of delivering law to women from the Norwegian/Pakistani community.[13]

Over the last two years Farhat Taj has been studying how PAKWOM, which has integrated a legal awareness component into its work, makes law available, acceptable and accessible to women in the Norwegian/Pakistani community.[14] She has observed how PAKWOM navigates the multiplicity of norms and expectations that derive from relatives, religious networks and Norwegian and Pakistani authorities in its work. Her study is based on participating in the day to day work of the organization, their meetings and social events. Information about individual counselling has been obtained through in-depth interviews with the organization's caseworkers, the women clients and, in one instance, with the lawyer who was involved in an ongoing court case.

At the theoretical level this chapter drew inspiration from the legal scholar Abdullahi An-Na'im's cross-cultural dialogue approach (An-Na'im 1994). To deal with a situation where conflicting international, national and religious norms are at work he emphasizes the need for both an internal and an external cross-

---

11 An introduction to the research project From Formal to Real Rights, conducted at the Institute of Women's Law at the University of Oslo and led by professor Anne Hellum is available at: http://www.jus.uio.no/forskning/grupper/riks/prosjekter/IMER/Fra%20formelle%20til%20reelle%20rettigheter.html.

12 Tina Nordstrøm's Masters thesis *Minority Women's Right to Legal Information* describes and analyzes the offers that exist in the Oslo region in the light of Norwegian legislation and international human rights standards. It provides an in-depth study of the methods employed by JURK (Free Legal Advice for Women) (Nordstrøm 2009).

13 On legal advice as research method see 'Legal advice as research method' (Hellum 1990, 1999).

14 The fieldwork is a part of Farhat Taj's PhD project at the Centre for Interdisciplinary Gender Studies at the University of Oslo, titled 'Legal pluralism, gender and Islam in Norway'. An introduction to Farhat Taj's doctoral project is available at: http://www.stk.uio.no/English/researcher_farhat.html.

cultural dialogue. At the crux of An-Na'im's theory on law and social change is that human rights need to be transmitted through the lens of existing religious and customary concepts if they are to be accepted and adopted. He sees human rights lawyers providing the external discourse while members of the social or religious community provide the internal discourse and considers these two aspects as mutually interdependent and constitutive. As the cases presented below show, this approach is taking root through cooperation between Pakistani and Norwegian actionists, educationalists and researchers in Oslo.

While a cross-cultural approach may make information about women's equal rights acceptable, it may also, as demonstrated by the case studies below, repackage the principles of justice, dignity and choice to the extent that they resonate patriarchal versions of Islam.

Activist scholars within the global network, 'Women Living Under Muslim Laws' (WLUML), have emphasized the limits of an approach that redefines equality so that it fits difference, promotes cultural relativism and justifies practices that are not accepted for women from the majority, all in the name of respect for 'the other' (Helie-Lucas 2004:34). To distinguish between processes where human rights are adapted to local circumstances and situations where human rights are made resonant with dominant cultural or religious norms, the legal anthropologist, Sally Engle Merry, uses the terms 'vernacularization' and 'indigenization' (Merry 2006:216). This pair of concepts provides a valuable analytical tool, adding a normative dimension to John Griffiths' descriptive approach to legal pluralism as 'that state of affairs, for any social field, in which behaviour pursuant to more than one legal order occurs' (Griffiths 1986:2) and An-Na'im's division between external and internal discourse.

Access to Legal Information: Norwegian Laws, Policies and Practices

Immigrants account for 8 per cent of the Norwegian population and 25 per cent of the population in Oslo has a minority background. With the increased mobility of people and norms and the subsequent growth in social and normative communities that transcend territorial and legal boundaries, Norway, like other nation-states in Northern Europe, is in the throes of rapid and uneven change (Algashi, Eriksen and Gorashi 2009). The shift from a relatively homogenous to an increasingly diverse and culturally complex society has subsequently challenged the notion of law as a unified system of norms and state law as the single regulatory force (Hellum 2006).

To address the multiple discriminations associated with migrant women's complex social and legal situation, the CEDAW Committee has urged Norway to make these women more aware of the social services and legal remedies available.[15] Norway has incorporated the International Covenants on Civil and Political Rights and on Social, Economic and Cultural Rights and the

15 CEDAW/C/2003/CRP.3/Add.2/Rev.1 para 25.

Convention on the Elimination of All Forms of Discrimination Against Women into their Human Rights Act. This implies that the obligation to provide legal literacy in a manner that makes law available, accessible and acceptable through linguistically and culturally appropriate, gender-sensitive methods is part and parcel of national law.

Access to law is in Norway, as elsewhere in the world, highly dependent on people's class, gender, ethnicity, race or immigrant status (Mathiesen 2005). The few measures that the Norwegian government has taken so far to ensure equal access to legal information have been piecemeal and fragmented. They have lacked any systematic analysis of the complex relationship between gender, law, society and culture in the new Norway (Nordstrøm 2009). National information campaigns directed at migrant women and their families have focused exclusively on female genital mutilation, forced marriages and honour killings. So far, not a single campaign has been carried out to inform migrant women about the laws that protect them against discrimination on the basis of gender and ethnicity. So the inequalities between majorities and minorities in Norway appear to be ascribed to the migrant's own culture and not to any discrimination related to the majority's stereotypical perception of migrant women. Law and policy makers in this field use egalitarian ideas in ways that, in Marianne Gullestad's terms, '... marginalize specific groups by simultaneously creating dichotomies asking for sameness' (ibid. s.54).

Dissemination of legal information to immigrants has by and large been carried out on a voluntary basis. Committed legal scholars at the faculties of law at the universities of Oslo, Bergen and Tromsø have set up programmes for vulnerable groups, including women, prisoners and immigrants, with funding from national and local government. These university clinics, that provide information and advice in areas like refugee law, immigration law, housing law and women's rights, lean towards a legal centralist approach.[16] Since its formation in 1974, JURK (Free Legal Advice for Women) at the University of Oslo has given priority to disseminating legal information to women. Realizing that their service fell short of non-Western women's needs, JURK started an outreach programme for immigrant women in 1997. They offer this programme at language classes for newly-arrived women with different national, ethnic and religious backgrounds. Covering immigration law, family law, inheritance law and violence against women, it deals with Norwegian state law and, to a certain extent, international private law.

A number of non-governmental organizations in the Oslo region have integrated a socio-legal component in their practical work on family, health and education issues, in response to immigrant women's quest for legal information.[17] Many of these initiatives are premised on the assumption that information about

16 In Oslo these programmes are two student schemes at the Faculty of Law at the University of Oslo, Juss Buss and JURK (Free Legal Advice for Women).

17 An example is *Primærmedisinsk Verksted* (Primary Medical Workshop) PMV (Thune 2007).

Norwegian society and law must be transmitted through a socio-cultural lens if it is to be seen as relevant and acceptable.[18] Emphasizing the importance of dialogue and cooperation, the Norwegian government is funding an increasing number of non-governmental organizations where immigrant women of the same national background assist each other.[19] 'Natural helpers' or 'cultural assistants' who have the confidence and trust of the communities lead the work in these organizations. Their task is to establish an enabling environment where people can speak out about practical problems related to health, sex, personal relations, marriage or childbirth that, in turn, give rise to human rights problems (Thune 2007:363). A characteristic feature of these organizations' engagement with law is that information about rights is not dealt with in isolation but in response to concrete problems.

Taking the Law to Women in the Pakistani Community in Oslo

Addressing challenges involved in making legal education available, accessible and acceptable we now turn to the experiences of a Pakistani women's organization and its interaction with JURK, a Norwegian non-governmental organization.[20]

Locating the Case Study

The complex socio-legal situation of first generation Pakistani women in Norway illustrates the need to contextualize Norwegian law in its gendered and multicultural context. Pakistanis are the second largest immigrant group in Norway with 29,000 people. The highly gendered migration patterns reflect strong trans-boundary family and marriage networks.[21] Most Pakistani male and female immigrants marry a spouse from the country of origin.[22] The majority of the male migrants are workers who migrate independently while most of the women join their spouses or other members of their families who have formal employment. These patterns

18 An example is *Regnbueprosjektet*.

19 See 'Turning Point', the action plan against domestic violence (2008–2011), Ministry of Justice and Police. Government of Norway and Action Plan against force marriages (2008–2011), Ministry of Children and Equality, Government of Norway.

20 The sessions which took place in Oslo in April 2008 and April 2009 were attended by Anne Hellum and Farhat Taj. Both sessions were videotaped with the permission of the leader of the non-governmental organization and transcribed by Farhat Taj.

21 Available statistics show that immigrants from Sri Lanka, Somalia and Pakistan keep close economic ties through regular remittances to family members in the home country. *Samfunnsspeilet* nr. 6, 2004.

22 Of the 11,000 Pakistani immigrants who were married and living in Norway, only 200 married a Norwegian spouse. *Samfunnsspeilet* nr. 3, 2004.

are reflected in occupational gender segregation and unequal language skills, particularly for first generation immigrants.[23]

While in principle Norwegian law applies to all migrants, in practice it is often overruled by the formal or informal norms and practices of the country of origin. Most Norwegian-Pakistanis are followers of Hanafi Islam which contains personal and family law within its teaching that categorizes women as people in need of protective rights rather than equal rights with men (Ali 2000:138). This school of Islamic thought does not sit well with the gender equality principle embedded in CEDAW and in Norwegian family law.

PAKWOM, a non-governmental organization that receives state support, arranges social events, classes and discussion groups to support women from the Pakistani community in Oslo and to promote gender equality. External resource persons are invited to give talks on topics ranging from religion and literature to politics and law. PAKWOM is a membership organization with about 150 members who come from different parts of Punjab. Most of them belong to *Jatt* and *Butt biradries* (sub-clans or extended families). Their period of residence in Norway varies greatly – some members have been living in Norway for 25 years, others for 20 or 10 years while some only arrived in 2007.

PAKWOM, according to its leader, strives for women's rights at two levels.[24] On one level it seeks to protect women's rights and on the other, it strives to not be seen as violating religious and cultural limits. Towards this end the organization keeps close contact with the *imam* in one of the Oslo mosques. According to the caseworkers, this contact carries the symbolic message to the wider community that the organization's work is not violating Islam. Explaining the rationale behind this approach, the caseworker said:

> We have a perception problem within the local community. It is often assumed that we are out there to instigate divorces and break up marriages. Wanting to promote women's rights we are walking a tight rope. Some families do not allow women to contact us. We try to send out a message to the wider community that we accord due respect to our religion and culture. This makes it easier for the women to contact us and for us to promote women's rights in a less hostile environment. At least this is our aim.

There is no interaction with women's non-governmental organizations in Pakistan. The leader reports that most of her clients' problems are related to the legal system in Norway, not in Pakistan. Furthermore, Pakistani women in non-governmental organizations are regarded as 'bad women' both in Norway and in Pakistan.

---

23 Gender differences regarding occupation and language are greatest among immigrants from Pakistan, Irak, Serbia and Montengero. *Statistisk sentralbyrå, Levekår blant innvandrere*, 2005/2006.

24 Interview conducted by Farhat Taj with the caseworker at her office in Oslo on 15 March 2007.

When issues pertaining to Pakistani law arise the leader accesses help through her personal contacts in Pakistan or through the friends and relatives of the women concerned.

Making Law Available

To make law available to their members, PAKWOM has included legal literacy awareness in its social programme. The Norwegian organization, JURK, has on a number of occasions been invited to disseminate information about women's rights under Norwegian law. By adding a legal awareness component to social events for women, information about what the law is and where it can be accessed is made available for women whose course of action is often restricted by husbands and in-laws.

In two of the sessions we observed, Norwegian state law relating to marriage, divorce, domestic violence and inheritance law was presented by two female Norwegian students from JURK. Their presentation was translated into Urdu by one of the leaders of the organization. The introduction was based on practical cases and actively engaged the women in a discussion about their legal rights in different situations.

The strength of this method of taking law to the women is that it situates legal information in an environment where women feel confident, in a language they understand and it gives concrete content to abstract principles, encouraging engagement and discussion about real life issues. In the course of the discussion the women in the audience talked about problems they themselves or women they knew were facing. Several of them reported that the Norwegian legal system had not rendered them justice in their encounters with it. Most queries related to the division of matrimonial property and matters relating to the children in connection with divorce. During the informal discussion over lunch several women complained that they had lost out due to lack of information about their rights. One woman complained that she did not know that she had the right to stay in the matrimonial home since she had custody of the children. She said her in-laws had demanded that the house be sold and she had had to move.

Making Law Acceptable

Rights awareness does not automatically translate into legal action. While women are becoming aware of their rights under Norwegian law they are often held back by moral and religious constraints. Responding to women's concerns about religious constraints related to how Islam is understood in the community, Anne Hellum suggested that Professor Shaheen Sardar Ali join JURK's legal literacy programme to add a comparative component. To reconcile the women's identities as Norwegian citizens with their identity as Muslims, Professor Ali set out to make the information on women's rights under Norwegian law comparable with Islam and Pakistani law.[25]

Professor Ali addressed the ambiguities many of the women experienced in relation to their identity as Norwegian citizens and as Muslims. In the two presentations of women's rights under Muslim family law that we observed, she focused on issues related to the acceptability of women's rights under Norwegian law. Her presentations started out with the relationship between Norwegian civil law and religious norms from the perspective of Islamic international law:

> Islam believes in universality of humanity and is not tied down to a specific country or place. Yet Islam sees us as duty bound to obey the laws of the country that has offered us citizenship, this is what Islam demands of us. So long as the laws of our acquired countries do not contradict the main pillars of our faith, such as saying prayers, fasting during Ramadan, *haj*, *zakat* and so on.

Addressing forced marriages she emphasized the similarities between Islam and Norwegian law:

> Forced marriages as we all know are completely unIslamic and illegal in Pakistan as well as Norway. In Islam marriage is a civil contract and both parties must freely consent to it. So we have a rather sophisticated Islamic position on this issue. Forcing girls and boys into marriage against their will is to my mind a greedy, economic ploy because we feel that if we get someone over from Pakistan, we are fulfilling an economic promise made to some relative some years ago. There are other ways of helping relatives and loved ones than to make your own child a sacrificial lamb! So please let us take this message to the men in our families.

Addressing inheritance law, which is an area of conflict between the equality principle in Norwegian law and Islamic law, she sought ways of negotiating the two:

> While Norwegian law does not discriminate between girls and boys, Islamic law gives half of a share to the girl and a full one to a boy. How do we deal with that? While there are points of flexibility in Norwegian law there is nothing stopping you if you as a Muslim feel that you want your boy to get more. But with regard to equal opportunities, resources, access to education, health, food, shelter and so on, there is no discrimination in Islam. That Islamic principles of justice demand equality in all these to boys and girls and that if we did just that with our children, when they become adults, they would have substantive equality …

25 Professor Shaheen Sardar Ali is professor II at the Institute of Women's Law. These classes have been observed by Anne Hellum as part of the research project 'From formal to real rights'.

Addressing marriage issues she underlined the importance of registering a marriage under Norwegian law. In response, women often brought up problems related to the situation of women who for various reasons had contracted a *Nikah* marriage without registering it in accordance with Norwegian law. According to one woman, 'some people do not register marriage because then they may lose social benefits or concessions in tax'. According to another woman the problem is that '… men say the paperwork on marriage is a new thing. When Islam came there was no paperwork and just two witnesses were enough for *Nikah*'. Underlining similarities between Norwegian law and Islam Professor Ali responded:

> Okay, fine, but where does Islam go in such a situation? We claim we are good Muslims. This abuse of the social system is clearly unethical in Islam. So we are showing this kind of Islam to the world. But most important is that if the marriage is not registered, how do you go to the government and claim social and legal assistance if the husband leaves you? Women must take it very seriously and secure their own and their children's future by registering the marriage with the authorities. They must put the condition to the man that she will not perform *Nikah* with him if the marriage is not registered with the authorities.

Many of the women are deeply concerned about the man's right to divorce his wife by pronouncing *talaq* three times. They refer to incidents where women have been sent back to Pakistan on the basis of a triple *talaq* divorce. Many women insist that: 'The point is that *talaq* must be said three times. The time does not matter. The effect is the same in both cases (over a long time or in one go): the marriage is dissolved'. This led to a long debate where different interpretations of Islam were employed. Disagreeing with this version of Islam Professor Ali stated:

> No again and again. Three pronouncements in three different sittings and then the marriage will be dissolved. What I want to say is that Islam is a logical religion. Islam is justice. Three instant verbal *talaq* is not justice to women. I want to tell you this method of *talaq* is nowhere in the *Qur'an*. I request all you sisters to please read the *Qur'an* carefully so that you know that this method of divorce is not in *Qur'an*. It came much later which is why it is called *Talaq-e-Bidda*. The law of scholars can change but the words of Allah cannot. What Allah told us in the *Qur'an* is justice. Tell me how is it justice that a woman is thrown out of a marriage in seconds? Where could she go? Who will feed her? What if she is pregnant? Is this Islam? Is this justice?

The women also brought up incidents where, for example, a woman had been granted a divorce in the state courts but her relatives, in-laws or neighbours maintained that she was still married to the man. Responding to such problems Professor Ali referred to basic principles of justice underlying Islam, Pakistani law and Norwegian law alike:

> Denying a woman that right is denial of justice, which is a violation of Islam. So in this case a woman takes her right – divorce – it does not matter at all whether the right came to her through the Norwegian authorities or some other authorities. It is her right to take it anyway. Five years ago I met a woman here in Norway. She cried to me and said she had a divorce certificate from the Norwegian court but the husband was saying she was not divorced because he had not said with his tongue 'I divorce you'. I want to tell you ladies that there is nothing in Islamic *fiqh* that demands that a man should utter the word divorce for a woman to be divorced. In the Islamic *fiqh* a judge has a right to pronounce divorce. A Norwegian judge pronouncing divorce is what a Muslim judge would do. If there is violence, it is right for the woman to get divorced. It does not matter whether the judge is Muslim or non-Muslim.

Emphasizing basic principles underlying Norwegian law, Pakistani law and different versions of Islam in terms of justice and integrity, a comparative approach helps to build a conceptual bridge. The following statement from one of the women who participated in the comparative legal literacy sessions speaks to the potential of this approach:

> As Muslims we believe we have to be accountable and answerable to God on the Day of Judgement about what we do in this world. We follow the Norwegian law to get social benefits or some relief, like divorce or having our human rights protected. But it would be psychologically very difficult to follow the law if we know that the law violates Islam. We think we get benefits from the Norwegian law, but at the same time make our life hereafter very difficult. We then think it is better to not follow the Norwegian law because Norwegian law is only for this worldly life which is short and rather make sure to protect ourselves from perpetual punishments on the Day of Judgement. Dr Shaheen's lectures and our discussions with her beautifully convince us that going by the Norwegian law is not a violation of Islam. This is such a relief in terms of concerns about the life hereafter.[26]

Considering both similarities and differences among the plurality of norms at work in women's lives, opens up a space for active and inclusive engagement with core issues related to the acceptability of law. The comparative approach constitutes a mixture of what Abdullahi An-Na'im has termed external and internal discourse. Through the discussion about equal right in marriage, human rights law was adapted to Islam and local circumstances and as such 'vernacularized', in Sally Engle Merry's terms.

26 Reseach notes, Farhat Taj, 24 March 2009.

Making Law Accessible: Individual Counselling

Through individual counselling PAKWOM seeks to enable women to act on the knowledge they have gained through legal literacy.[27] To make law accessible, women are offered multiple forms of assistance ranging from referral to a lawyer or a social welfare officer to help finding a place to live or a job. Dealing with family problems, the non-governmental organization takes recourse to Norwegian lawyers, police and state courts on one hand and Muslim religious institutions on the other.[28]

The first step in a family dispute resolution process is for the woman and the non-governmental organization worker to discuss the problems. Depending on the circumstances of a case and subject to the consent of the woman concerned, the case may be referred to an *imam* for religious counselling or to a lawyer to be pleaded in a court of law or to both. The woman and the caseworker deliberate on the advice given by the *imam* and/or lawyer in order to take further appropriate action. At every stage the woman is free to turn down the advice of the caseworker, the *imam* or the lawyer.

The aim is to facilitate women's access to their rights under Norwegian state law. According to JURK's leader, they promote women's equal rights and, towards this end, they seek ways to overcome the constraints posed by different versions of Islamic law at work in the family network and in the different religious communities in Oslo.

Two cases follow that demonstrate the selective use of Norwegian and Islamic norms and institutions in Oslo. In the first, a polygamy case, Norwegian law was invoked without any engagement with the *imam*. In the second, a marital dispute case, the woman invoked Islamic norms against the wishes of her husband who maintained that Norwegian law applied.

Restoration of Dignity through Norwegian Law

Asma married her first cousin under Pakistani law before she came to Norway. Her husband, who had become interested in another woman, divorced her after a few years. After the divorce her parental family and the husband's family married her off to her husband's younger brother in Oslo. Some years later he married another woman in Pakistan. He had applied for a divorce under Norwegian law but it had not yet been granted. After a quarrel Asma was thrown out of their home in Oslo by her husband and her in-laws.

---

27 This part of the chapter is based on Farhat Taj's fieldwork notes and her paper presented at two conferences: Transnational Law and Transnational relations in Oslo in June 2007 and American Anthropologists Association in Washington in December 2007.

28 In 2006 six women were assisted with problems related to domestic violence and three of these women wanted help to obtain a divorce. The organization was approached with ten instances on matters related to forced marriage.

One of Asma's acquaintances took her to the Pakistani women's organization and they accompanied her to the social welfare office which arranged for accommodation and financial help. Asma had been subjected to violence, sexual abuse and humiliation and wanted assistance from a lawyer to sue her husband for bigamy in a Norwegian court of law. She and her husband had contracted a marriage under Norwegian law which makes bigamy a criminal offence. On the advice of the lawyer, the organization collected video clips of her husband's marriage and marriage documents from Pakistan to substantiate her case in court. The Norwegian court heard the evidence, found the husband guilty of bigamy and handed down a penalty of 21 days in jail and a fine of 7,000 kroner. A mitigating circumstance was, according to the court, that the husband had not intended to be polygamous since he had already applied for divorce.

The interviews with Asma and the caseworker at the organization revealed Asma's strong desire to restore the self-respect she felt she had lost in the humiliation inflicted on her by her in-laws and former husband:

> They (the in-laws and the husband) battered me. They tortured me, physically and mentally. They used to say I was a good for nothing, useless, mindless creature. I descended into having an inferiority complex. I have lost my self-esteem. I feel everyone in the world is better than me. I am good for nothing. I have no children, not much formal schooling and I can't speak the Norwegian language. I live alone. The only thing that will restore my self-respect is to get him behind bars. This will re-establish confidence in myself. It will prove them wrong – with their repeated assertion that I am good for nothing. It will prove to them and to the extended family that I can set goals and achieve them single-handedly.[29]

One reason she sought the assistance of the organization and the Norwegian court to reassert her dignity was that there was no family who could assist her:

> My brother in Denmark has almost no time to care for me. The only person who cares is my ailing mother who lives alone thousands of miles away in Pakistan. I have no children to turn to. My husband married my cousin and this alienated me from the family of that cousin. So I had no relatives in Norway to turn to for help. I felt I stood humiliated in the eyes of my relatives both in Pakistan and in Norway. There was no one to avenge my humiliation. It befell on me to stand up and reassert myself.[30]

An important reason for turning to Norwegian state law was that both Asma and the caseworker who assisted her believed there was no point in asking the *imam* to reconcile the case. According to the caseworker, the *imam* that the organization

29 Farhat Taj, interview with Asma in September 2006.

30 Farhat Taj, interview with Asma in September 2006.

regularly turns to in matters of dispute resolution did not consider polygamy illegal:

> We knew what the *imam* would say. He would say what the problem is. Polygamy is legal in Islam. There is no violation of God's law. There can be no punishment for polygamy. Keeping in view Asma's strong wish, I and she agreed to keep the *imams* out of the issue.[31]

Yet Asma's decision to pursue Norwegian law was also grounded in Islam:

> Islam may permit it. But the Norwegian law does not. He is a citizen of Norway and lives in Norway. He must not violate the law of Norway. But he did. Any citizen of this country who violates the law of this country must face the law and so must he. The religion of Islam that I understand does not obligate its followers to violate the law of a country that they have freely chosen to live in.[32]

Asma's argument that Islam does not require Muslims to violate the laws of their freely chosen host country goes to the heart of the debate initiated by contemporary Muslim legal scholars in Europe, like Professor Ali. She argues that for the Muslim immigrants Europe is *dar-al-sulh* (the land of peace) and implies that they are subject to all the laws of their respective states of domicile (Ali 2007). Asma had picked up this information through a Western website on issues of Muslim women's rights. By linking Islam with Norwegian state law and responsibilities of citizenship, Asma felt she could answer any criticism of her decision. When Asma and the caseworker decided to keep the *imam* out of the case, they knew that polygamy was a disputed issue and that there are different interpretations of the *Qur'anic* verses regarding polygamy. Notwithstanding the local Oslo *imam's* view on polygamy, women members of the organization continue to question polygamy in their group discussions and seminars. Some women members also surf the Internet to look for Islamic arguments against polygamy.

The *imams* are not the only 'experts' that the organization consults on family disputes. They also hold seminars with liberal Muslim legal scholars, like Professor Ali, who argue against polygamy from an Islamic perspective. Thus the organization provides a milieu where Muslim personal law, as upheld by the *imams,* is debated and questioned. This is in line with the inbuilt pluralism of the Muslim legal tradition and this milieu provides the conceptual potential within the framework of Islam to extend the limits of Muslim personal law, as shown by Asma's case. According to the leader of the organization, this case was '[their] contribution towards the elimination of gender discrimination in the Norwegian-Pakistani community'.

31 Farhat Taj, interview with the non-governmental organization caseworker in November 2006.

32 Farhat Taj, interview with Asma in September 2006.

Restoration of Women's Honour through Islam?

Ayesha's case shows how archaic patriarchal interpretations of Islam may be mobilized to reinstate women's honour while simultaneously upholding the very understanding of Islam that is at the root of her oppression. This case shows how human rights through engagement with Islam can become 'indigenized' rather than 'vernacularized'.

Ayesha lived in a violent marriage. Angry and under the influence of alcohol her husband had divorced her through 'triple *talaq*' at least five times since 1998. Their youngest son was conceived and borne after his pronouncement of the third 'triple *talaq*'. According to Ayesha the in-laws argued that the child was a 'bastard' child. The consultations with the caseworker made it clear that Ayesha wanted to maintain her marriage but at the same time, she wanted her husband and her in-laws to respect her. Towards this end they agreed to seek religious advice from an *imam*. The *imam*, with reference to Hanafi Islam, upheld the husband's unilateral right to terminate the marriage through 'triple *talaq*'. In Pakistan this type of divorce is curtailed by the Muslim Family Law Ordinance which lays down a procedure for divorce involving the local marriage authorities. Yet in diasporic communities in Norway or the United Kingdom, marriages are often terminated unilaterally through 'triple *talaq*'. The Oslo *imam* who was contacted reaffirmed the validity of the triple *talaq* with reference to Verse 230 of Chapter 2 of the *Qur'an*:

> If a man divorces her again (a third time). She becomes unlawful for him (and cannot remarry her) until she has married another man.

The *imam* maintained that Ayesha could not legitimize her relationship through remarriage without *hilala* – a second marriage. The second marriage (*hilala*) is an intervening marriage which is contracted with the intention of dissolving it by divorce. However, according to the *imam*:

> It is unIslamic to perform *hilala* marriage as a formality to remarry the first husband. It is forbidden for a woman to marry a second man with the intention to be divorced by him and remarried by the first husband.[33]

The outcome of the consultations with the non-governmental organization and the *imam* was that Ayesha wanted her husband to concede to *hilala* but he opposed this solution. Her 'public' reason for the *hilala* was that it would legitimize her son in the eyes of her in-laws who called him a 'bastard'. Her personal reason was that she wanted to punish her husband through the humiliation of *hilala*. During an interview she stated:

33 Interview with the *imam* in October 2006.

> I want to torture my husband through *hilala*. I want him to feel how much I suffered because of him, first due to his violence and now because I have to pass through the humiliation of *hilala*. He does not want *hilala* and I wish to make him accept what he is not ready to accept. It is only through the humiliation of *hilala* tha he will feel the equivalent torture he put me through.[34]

The caseworker explained how her client felt that this would make a difference in her life:

> She wants *hilala* to make her husband realize what he has done to her. That she had been with another man without his consent. She wants to make him realize that he always brought torture on her, including the torture of *hilala*. She wants to hurt his male honour for the miseries he had been inflicting on her in the past.[35]

In this case the standards of equality and freedom that PAKWOM sets out to promote were 'indigenized' to resonate a version of Islam that has been used to invoke female submission and inequality (Merry 2006:216). This case demonstrates the multiple outcomes of a pluralist approach. Considering the long-term provision of emotional and material support, the woman however, in the final analysis decided to opt for divorce.

Real change, these examples show, calls for sustained support and commitment at multiple levels of life and law, over a long period of time.

Legal Literacy as a Counter-hegemonic Discursive Practice

To reconfigure socio-legal relationships that constrain their courses of action, individual women and women's organizations in the Pakistani community in Oslo are, as we have seen, mobilizing a multiplicity of norms and institutions ranging from *imams* to legal aid schemes to Norwegian courts. The outcome of this process is an innovative and responsive legal literacy approach that invokes both Norwegian and Islamic law to make basic human rights available, acceptable and accessible. In response to women's quest for justice, dignity and choice, these practices and discourses transgress the boundaries between Norwegian law and Islam, to resonate the mixed identities and mixed norms on the ground.[36] It is a contextual and situated approach that mediates the contested relationship between individual and group rights.

34 Interview with Ayesha in August 2006.

35 Interview with the caseworker in August 2006.

36 On the ambiguities underlying women's mixed identities and mixed norms in post-colonial Zimbabwe and diasporic muslim communities in the United Kingdom, see Hellum (1999) and Bano (2004).

The trans-cultural counter-hegemonic discourses that the women are developing reflect the coinciding and conflicting norms and expectations derived from the different relationships in which they are embedded. The law they are developing is, in Boaventura de Sousa Santos' terms, a porous legality constituted in a situation with 'multiple networks of legal orders forcing us to constant transitions or trespassing' (Boaventura de Sousa Santos 1987:208). It is characterized by interlegality as defined by Sousa Santos as 'an intersection of different legal orders that is, by interlegality'.

Drawing on multiple sources and networks both within the local Pakistani community and the Norwegian legal community, PAKWOM provides an enabling environment that facilitates choice and empowerment. They have constructed a space where women are assisted by women in the spirit of free and informed choice so as to define a place for themselves in the context of the conflicting expectations and pressures deriving from husbands, in-laws, religious institutions and Norwegian authorities. Established customary and religious paradigms that restrict women's opportunities and choices are challenged by demonstrating the multiple normative avenues that are available.

The different outcomes of this process speak to the options and limits of an engagement with legal pluralism. When women, in response to Professor Ali, say they feel at ease because she enables them to claim their rights under Norwegian law and still be good Muslims, human rights are 'vernacularized'. Yet engagement with Islamic norms and institutions also poses a risk that human rights are 'indigenized' so as to reinforce the very structures that limit women's right to freedom and justice.

How to translate the steps that are taken by individual women into collective action is a question that calls for further consideration. To challenge dominant perceptions of Muslim womanhood and related customs is a delicate balancing act. The fear of being pushed beyond the collectivity of the Pakistani community in Oslo constrains the non-governmental organization's course of collective action. While the religious leaders in Oslo, through religious dialogue funded by the Norwegian state, maintain close ties with mosques in Pakistan, women are hesitant to form partnerships with women's rights organizations in Pakistan because they, according to PAKWOM's leader, are regarded as 'bad women'. Yet by sharing information about the strategies that women individually have pursued, they are expanding their space and inspiring each other by example and insight and are, as such, agents of legal change (Shaheed 2006:16).

References

Algashi, S., Eriksen, T.H. and Gorashi, H. 2009. Introduction, in *Paradoxes of Cultural Recognition. Perspectives from Northern Europe*. Farnham:Ashgate.

Ali, S.S. 2000. *Gender and Human Rights in Islam and International Law*. Hague/London/Boston: Kluwer Law International.

—— 2007a. Interpretative strategies for women's human rights in a plural legal framework: Exploring judicial and state responses to *Hudood* laws in Pakistan, in *Human Rights, Plural Legalities and Gendered Realities. Paths are Made by Walking,* edited by A. Hellum, J. Stewart, S.S. Ali and A. Tsanga. Harare: Weaver Press.

—— 2007b. Religious pluralism, human rights and Muslim citizenship in Europe: Some preliminary reflections on an evolving methodology for consensus, in *Religious Pluralism and Human Rights in Europe,* edited by T. Loenon and J. Goldschmidt. Utrecht: Intersentia, 57–79.

An-Na'im, A. 1995. State responsibility under international human rights law to change religious and customary laws, in *Human Rights of Women. National and International Perspectives*, edited by R. Cook. Pennsylvania: University of Pennsylvania Press.

—— 2009. A theory of Islam, state and society, in *New Directions in Islamic Thought. Exploring Reform and Muslim Tradition*, edited by K. Vogt, L. Larsen and C. Moe. London: I.B. Tauris.

Bano, S. 2004. *Complexity, Difference and Muslim Personal Law: Rethinking the Relationship between Shariah Councils and South Asian Muslim Women in Britain.* PhD thesis. Warwick: Warwick University.

Bentzon, A.W., Hellum, A., Stewart, J., Ncube, W. and Agersnap, T. 1998. *Pursuing Grounded Theory In Law. South-North Experiences in Developing Women's Law.* Oslo and Harare: TANO Aschehoug and Mond Books.

Boaventura de Sousa Santos. 1987. Law: A map of misreading. Towards a postmodern conception of law. *Journal of Law and Society*, Vol 14(3): 279–99.

Boaventura de Sousa Santos and Rodriguez-Garavito, C.A. 2005. *Law and Globalization from Below. Towards a Cosmopolitan Legality.* Cambridge studies in Law and Society. Cambridge: Cambridge University Press.

Commission on Legal Empowerment of the Poor 2008. *Making the Law Work for Everyone Volume 1.* Report. New York: United Nations Development Programme.

Coomaraswamy, R. 2005. Preface: Violence against women and crimes of honour, in *'Honour' Crimes, Paradigms, and Violence against Women*, edited by L. Welchman and S. Hossain. London: Zed Books.

Dahl. T.S. 1986. *Feminist Jurisprudence.* Oslo: Norwegian University Press.

Griffiths, A. 1997. Gendering culture: Towards a plural perspective on Kwena women's rights, in *Culture and Rights. Anthropological Perspectives,* edited by J.K. Cowan, M. Dembour and R.A. Wilson. Cambridge: Cambridge University Press.

Griffiths, J. 1986. What is Legal Pluralism? *Journal of Legal Pluralism* 24:1–55.

Gullestad, M. 2001. Imagined sameness: Shifting notions of us and them in Norway, in *Forestillinger om den andre. Images of Otherness*, edited by L.A. Ytrehus (ed.). Oslo: Norwegian Academic Press.

Helie-Lucas, M. 2004. What is your tribe? Women's struggles and the construction of Muslimness, in *Dossier 26 Identity Politics*. London: Women Living Under Muslim Laws.

Hellum, A. 1990. Legal advice as research method, in *Perspectives on Research Methodologies*, Harare: Women and Law in Southern Africa Research Project.

—— 1999. *Women's Human Rights and Legal Pluralism in Africa. Mixed Norms and Identities in Infertility Management in Zimbabwe*. Oslo and Harare: TANO Aschehoug and Mond Books.

—— 2006. Menneskerettigheter, pluralisme, kompleksitet og integrasjon, (Human rights, pluralism, complexity and integration) I *Festskrift* til Carl August Fleischer (Syse, A. *et al.* eds) Oslo: Universitetsforlaget.

Hellum, A., Stewart, J., Ali, S.S. and Tsanga A. 2007. Paths are made by walking. Introductory thoughts, in *Human Rights, Plural Legalities and Gendered Realities. Paths are Made by Walking,* edited by A. Hellum, J. Stewart, S.S. Ali and A. Tsanga. Harare: Weaver Press.

Mathiesen, T. 2005. *Retten i samfunnet. En innføring i rettssosiologi* (Law in Society: an Introduction to Sociology of Law). Oslo: Pax Forlag.

Mehdi, R. and Shaheed, F. (eds) 1997. *Women's Law and Legal Education Practice in Pakistan. North-South Cooperation.* Copenhagen: New Social Science Monographs.

Merry, S.E. 2006. *Human Rights and Gender Violence*. Chicago: University of Chicago Press.

Ministry of Children and Equality 2007. *Action Plan Against Forced Marriages 2008–2011*. Oslo: Government of Norway.

—— 2008. *Action Plan for Combating Female Genital Mutilation.* Oslo: Government of Norway.

Moore, S.F. 1978. *Law as Process*. London: Routledge.

Nordstrøm, T. 2009. *Immigrant Women's Right to Legal Information.* Masters thesis. Studies in Women's Law No. 81. Oslo: Faculty of Law, University of Oslo.

Okin, S.M. 1999. Is Multiculturalism bad for women?, in *Is Multiculturalism Bad for Women?*, edited by S.M. Okin with J. Cohen, M. Howard and M.C. Nusbaum. Princeton: Princeton University Press.

Phillips, A. 2007. *Multculturalism Without Culture*. Princeton: Princeton University Press.

Shaheed, F. 1997. The interface of culture, custom and law – implications for women and activism, in *Women's Law and Legal Education and Practice in Pakistan. North-South Cooperation*, edited by R. Mehdi and F. Shaheed. Copenhagen: New Social Science Monographs.

—— 2006. Constructing identities – culture, women's agency, and the Muslim world, in *Dossier 26 Identity Politics*. London: Women Living Under Muslim Laws.

Thune, H.G. 2007. New fellow citizens – challenges and possibilities; Implementing human rights among immigrants, the case of female circumcision in Norway, in *Human Rights, Plural Legalities and Gendered Realities, Paths are Made by Walking,* edited by A. Hellum, J. Stewart, S.S. Ali and A. Tsanga. Harare: Weaver.

Tsanga, A. 2003. *Taking the Law to the People. Gender, Law Reform and Community Legal Education in Zimbabwe.* Harare: Weaver.

—— 2007. Legal literacy in plural legal contexts, in *Human Rights, Plural Legalities and Gendered Realities, Paths are Made by Walking,* edited by A. Hellum, J. Stewart, S.S. Ali and A. Tsanga. Harare: Weaver.

Woodman, G. 2008. The possibilities of co-existance of religious laws with other laws, in *Law and Religion in Multicultural Societies*, edited by R. Mehdi, H. Petersen, E.R. Sand and G.R. Woodman. Copenhagen: DJØF Publishing.

PART II
Transnational Religious Rule: Muslims in the European Diaspora

Chapter 5

Behind the Cyberspace Veil: Online *Fatawa* on Women's Family Rights

Shaheen Sardar Ali[1]

Introduction

This chapter seeks to explore the discourse of Internet *fatwas*[2] relating to women and gender relations and its potential implications for international family law norms within a plural Islamic legal tradition.[3] It will engage with selected *fatwas* (on women and gender) drawn from three Internet sites[4] posing the question whether this burgeoning field of communication reflects emerging discursive sites for Muslim women within a counter-hegemonic[5] transnational and global 'virtual' space. Who are the actors in this field, where are they located and who controls the 'script' – the websites, questions and responses? What constituency (of Muslim women) do these '*fatwa*-seekers' represent, which countries are they based in and to what extent do the questions posed have relevance beyond the country of the

1 Professor of Law, University of Warwick, Professor II, University of Oslo, Norway and Vice-Chair of the United Nations Working Group on Arbitrary Detention. Formerly, Professor of Law, University of Peshawar, Pakistan. I gratefully acknowledge feedback and comments from Professor Anne Hellum on earlier drafts and the research assistance provided by Shahbaz Cheema for this chapter. I benefited hugely from comments from colleagues at the CULCOM (Cultural Complexity in the New Norway) Research Group on Transnationality workshop to discuss draft chapters, organized by Professor Hellum, University of Oslo, 1–2 April 2009 and thank all colleagues present for their observations and suggestions.

2 *Fatwas* is the anglicized version of the plural form of *fatwa* but *fatawa* is strictly the correct plural form.

3 It is not within the scope of this chapter to engage in detailed discussion and analysis of Islamic law and focus is on how one of the mechanisms of norm making in the Islamic legal tradition – *fatwa* – has been used for this purpose by contemporary Muslims through the worldwide web.

4 Available at: www.islamtoday.com; www.islamonline.net; www.islamonline.com.

5 Counter-hegemonic to the dominant discourse within the Islamic legal tradition or within Muslim communities. I also use the term to imply counter-hegemonic to ethnic formulations of identity and religious understandings of women and gender issues in the Muslim diaspora. For instance, Muslims of Arab, South Asian or African descent, and so on.

questioners? What is the profile of the Internet *muftis*[6] and what schools of juristic thought (*madhab*)[7] do they follow when handing down *fatwas*? What sorts of questions are being posed and what areas of life are these most focused on? Are new communication systems (such as the Internet) essentially an enabling and empowering mechanism for Muslim women, who are often unable to articulate challenging and private questions in 'public' or at face to face meetings? Or, is the *fatwa* site proliferation tantamount to yet another regulatory process to channel Muslim women towards a particular understanding and interpretation of Islam?

This chapter argues that increasing access to the Internet challenges historical conceptions of legitimacy surrounding the legislative prerogative of state and governments as well as regulatory norms (policy frameworks, legislation and so on) arising from governmental and governance functions, particularly those enacted in the name of Islam. Further, that these 'new' cyberspace regulatory mechanisms serve as a global Muslim space. They generate an international discourse encompassing a wide spectrum of (legal) interacting norms exploring which set of rules to apply to a certain situation in issues relating to women and gender, and why. It also highlights the 'irrepressible' plurality of the Islamic tradition which is not lost even in the most contemporary communication systems as each website analyzed adopts a distinctive approach towards similar questions posed. Finally, that '*fatwa* sites' have enabled Muslim women, in particular from diasporic communities in the West, to raise questions and issues surrounding their lives which they would not have been able to frame in a 'face to face' encounter due to the sensitive, private and at times challenging nature of the enquiry.[8]

Contextualizing *Fatwas* on Women and Gender Issues in a Globalized World

Bearing in mind the focus of this chapter, I propose to situate and contextualize Internet *fatwas* within the Islamic legal tradition with a view to assessing and evaluating its normative status across territorial borders and boundaries and its influence on the 'Islamic law of nations' or *siyar*. What constitutes 'Islamic law' or, more broadly, the Islamic legal tradition, is an extremely complex web and hierarchy of sources and juristic techniques developed over time and space. These

6 Persons qualified to give *fatwas*.

7 Plural: *madahab*.

8 For instance, questions regarding dress code, mixing with members of the opposite sex, sexual relations with ones' spouse, women's right to abortion, masturbation, husband's obligation to provide sexual satisfaction, and so on.

include the *Qur'an*[9] and *hadith*[10] (primary sources) and *ijma*,[11] *qiyas*[12] and *ijtihad*[13] (secondary sources). Alongside these, a host of juristic techniques operate: *taqlid, ikhtilaf, talfiq, maslaha, darura, istishab, istihsan, sadd al-dharai.* These have been developed by the various schools in Islam – Hanafi, Maliki, Shafi'i and Hanbali among Sunnis and Athna-Ashari, Zaidi and Ismaili among the Shia sect. Last but not least are people and communities' customs or practices, known as *'urf, ta-amul* or *adah.* The tension between doctrinal law from 'above' (through formalized procedures of state and legislature) and 'living law' from 'below' (through consistent practices of peoples and communities) are not unknown in the Islamic legal tradition, particularly in the institution of *ifta*, when *muftis* have reflected custom through their *fatwa.* It is therefore important to note the connection and interface, both juristic and historical, as well as the nuanced distinction between *ijtihad, 'urf* and *ifta.*

The *fatwa* is a non-binding advisory opinion given to an individual questioner (Masud, Messick and Powers 2005). Hallaq defines a *fatwa* as, '... consisting of a question (*sua-al, istifta*) addressed to a jurisconsult (*mufti*), together with an answer (*jawab*) provided by that jurisconsult' (Hallaq 1994). It is a *mufti's* non-binding opinion given in response to a question (posed by a *qadi*, a private person or an institution). The *fatwa* is perceived by many as the 'meeting point between legal theory and social practice' (Caeiro 2006) and serves a number of functions. These include employing *fatwas* as a legal tool,[14] a social instrument,[15] as inputs to the political discourse[16] or as a device for reform.[17] It has historically 'formed the vital link between academic theories of pure scholarship and the influences of practical life, and through them the dictates of the doctrine were gradually adapted to the changing needs of Muslim society' (Coulson 2001:142). *Fatwa* as a socio-legal advisory process has therefore undergone transformation due to its wider reach to the ordinary Muslim. As demonstrated below, from its departure point as

9 Believed by Muslims to be the word of God, revealed to the Prophet Muhammad through the Angel Gibrael.

10 Record of the words and deeds of the Prophet Muhammad.

11 Consensus of opinion or agreement among Muslim jurists in a particular age on a question of law.

12 Analogy.

13 Independent juristic reasoning; a person qualified to undertake *ijtihad* is known as *mujtahid.*

14 In assisting the adjudication process at the behest of a *qadi.*

15 In the form of questions from private persons in the community.

16 Seeking a *fatwa* in relation to an act of state or government either within the state or to another state or states.

17 Where a *mufti*, in response to a question, presents his viewpoint for reform in existing practice.

a response by an individual *mufti* to an individual questioner, it appears to have acquired a collective and public nature and deeper normative influence.[18]

Internet Fatwas on Women and Gender: A Brief Methodological Overview

The phenomenal proliferation of *fatwa* websites, Internet *muftis* and increasing access to the worldwide web led to the present exploratory study. It does not purport to be either a comprehensive survey of Internet *fatwas* on women and gender issues; neither is the sample representative or exhaustive of the rich body of *fatwas* available on various websites. The aim, however, was to explore the nature of questions posed by Muslims – mostly Muslim women in the diasporic and increasingly globalized world – and responses offered on these websites. The conclusions and inferences therefore take into account these limitations of the study.[19]

After an initial research of websites giving *fatwas*, I chose three Internet sites: www.islamonline.net, www.islamonline.com and www.islamtoday.com, whose main objective is information dissemination on Islam and Muslims, including a dedicated section for *fatwas*. These websites offer users the option of reading their contents in Arabic or English and of identifying the theme on which the user wishes to seek guidance. Accessing the Internet and being computer-literate as well as being able to communicate in Arabic or English are serious limiting factors ruling out a large percentage of Muslims who are unable to read and write these two languages and/or unable to gain access to the Internet.

The next step in the research methodology consisted of two weeks of surfing the selected websites to develop a list of approximately 100 *fatwas* relating to women and gender issues. I then proceeded to re-read these *fatwas* with a view to summarizing issues raised, ascertaining similarities between questions and highlighting trends and patterns of questioning and the *fatwas*. I wanted to see what countries the questions were coming from and, finally, what the most 'burning' questions were for these women. Due to limited information – the name and place of questioner only – it was not possible to either develop a detailed profile of the questioners or ascertain their socio-economic, political or educational levels. Whilst it is not possible to be completely sure of the transnational and international nature of the forum and discourse due to its virtual nature, I did try to include a wide spread of questions and responses from different countries, including Australia, Canada, Egypt, France, the United Kingdom, the United

18 This view is advanced bearing in mind the ordinary Muslim's increased media access and the input of non-governmental organizations, regional and international organizations into the norm-making and law-making processes of Muslim states and governments.

19 The present study and its methodology is inspired by positive feedback and comments on an earlier study of Internet *fatwas* on the obligations of Muslims as a result of the Iraq war and its occupation by foreign forces. See: Ali (2009).

States of America, Kuwait, Nigeria, the Maldives, India and Saudi Arabia, to name a few. The questions and their responses encompass a rich spectrum of subjects and themes,[20] including: Muslim women's dress code; interactions with *mahram* and non-*mahram*; etiquettes of social interaction of men and women; women's education; women's employment in a mixed environment; chatting and interacting with the opposite sex through Internet whether engaged or not; love between opposite sexes and its parameters; pre-marital relationships between engaged couples; pre-consummation relationships between those who have been married (*nikah*); the domain of girls and women's activities and their overall status within the family; resolving or negotiating conflicts between outdoor activities and responsibilities within the home; the marital rights of husband and wife; the right to divorce in different circumstances, such as when the wife refuses to wear *hijab* or *nikaab*; the triple divorce; the wife's right to seek divorce if a husband does not observe religious dictates; women's consent and a guardian's authority in matters of marriage; women's participation in religious ceremonies; women's role in politics; personal bodily matters including menstruation and its effect on sexual and religious matters; women's right to abortion; spacing between children; women's involvement in sexual practices such as fornication and masturbation; female circumcision and its validity in the Islamic legal tradition; women employing artificial or medical means to enhance beauty; and the difference in legal status between men and women.

The *fatwas* selected revealed three broad thematic streams. The first consisted of women requiring responses to matters of dress code as well as questions relating to their body and sexual and intimate relations. The second stream included questions and *fatwas* impacting on family life, relationships with their spouses as well as the families of their spouses. The third stream consisted of *fatwas* where the questions could fall into both streams one and two. The present chapter has chosen a selection of *fatwas* for discussion and analysis from each stream to highlight the diversity of issues, line of questioning and responses from Internet *muftis*.

At the Intersection of Gender, Culture, Religion and Women's Rights: An Overview of Muslim Women's Position through the Lens of Internet *Fatwas*

Muslim women and their position within the Islamic legal tradition is a fascinating canvas of complex and diverse understandings of the primary and secondary sources of Islamic law discussed above. The gap between the rhetoric and reality of Muslim women's lives and the status and rights they enjoy are informed by plural normative frameworks based upon cultural, traditional, socio-economic and political practices. In recent decades a further element has been added to this – that of life in a non-Muslim diaspora and membership of transnational families and

20 These are not presented in order of priority or number of *fatwas* pronounced but randomly as they were being read from the websites that formed the research universe.

communities. This places interpretative demands on the Islamic legal tradition regarding Muslim women's status and entitlements. The position of Muslim women ranges from complete equality and dignity when it comes to the ethical, moral and reward and punishment paradigm, to being placed at the lower level of the socio-economic, political and family-life hierarchy. I have elsewhere presented a detailed categorization and hierarchisation of women's human rights in Islam arguing that these categories are fluid and evolving and not set in watertight compartments (the corrective, protective, non-discriminatory and discriminatory formulation of women's entitlements) (Ali 2000:42–88). The *fatwas* discussed in this chapter bring this fluidity into relief by using language and terminology that may be interpreted as discriminatory by some and protective and/or corrective by others (see analysis below).

Two areas of the Islamic legal tradition appear to be foremost in the minds of the questioners seeking *fatwas*: norms regulating Muslim women's dress and demeanour, and her rights and entitlements in family life (mostly *vis-à-vis* their spouses). This is hardly surprising as both areas are fertile ground for an interpretative discourse, placed as they are at the intersection of culture, tradition and religion. Muslim women's status and entitlements and how she conducts herself draws upon six of the 6,666 verses of the *Qur'an* and the focus of contestation arising from literal, patriarchal and historical understandings of *Shari'a* arguably creating and upholding a hierarchy on the basis of sex (Ali 2000:43).[21] A number of scholars have challenged these restrictive interpretations, adopting the position that the verses in question, which have become the only benchmark for women's position and rights in Islam, are susceptible to multiple interpretations and are hence contested terrain.[22] The questioning and clarifications linked to these verses continue unabated across Muslim communities in transnational and international settings as evident from the Internet *fatwas* presented below.

Dress Code

The dress code for Muslim women attracts the most questions on all the websites studied and they range from whether a Muslim woman may uncover her head in public, to whether she must cover her face (*niqab*), hands and feet. In the present study, elements of an appropriate dress code for Muslim women living in the non-Muslim diaspora, was quite significant.

The first *fatwa* selected from www.islamonline.net raises complex issues of multiple identities, divided loyalties and legal obligations to the country of residence or nationality. The question (posed by a Muslim from the United States of America) and response in the form of a *fatwa* are presented opposite:

21 These six verses include 2:228; 2:282; 24:30-31; 4:3; 4:34.

22 Fazlur Rehman, An-Na'im, Riffat Hassan, Amina Wadud, Fatima Mernissi, Asma Barlas, Ziba Mir-Hoseini, Aziza al-Hibri, Leila Ahmed, Haleh Afshar, Shahla Haeri, Shaheen Sardar Ali.

Question:

As-Salamu 'alaykum. I was watching a TV programme that broadcasts some court cases. When I tuned to this channel, it was about a Muslim woman who is suing the State of Florida's Vehicle and License Department because it asked her to remove her face veil (*niqab*) so that an ID photo could be taken. One of the Muslim leaders in that state was in the cross-examination and argued that the woman can remove her *niqab* only in case of death!

What would you say to Muslim women who live in the West generally, and in the United States particularly, about the issue of *niqab*? Is it so difficult to remove the *niqab* that she must file a case against the State, which doesn't even require her to uncover her hair, as some states do require for the drivers' license?

Answer:

Wa 'alaykum As-Salamu wa Rahmatullahi wa Barakatuh.

In the Name of Allah, Most Gracious, Most Merciful.

All praise and thanks are due to Allah, and peace and blessings be upon His Messenger.

Dear brother, we commend your eagerness to become well acquainted with the teachings of Islam, which is the way Allah has chosen for the welfare of His servants.

As for your question, bear in mind that the majority of *imams* – including those of the four schools of *fiqh* as well as others – hold the opinion that a woman is not obliged to cover her face and hands. However, a group of scholars, the majority of whom belong to the Hanbali School, teach that a woman must cover her face and hands as well.

It goes without saying that Muslims precede others in keeping the public interest and security of the nation. Therefore, if the law governing a given country requires uncovering the face of the woman for genuine reasons, such as identification, the Muslim woman, like all other women, abides by the law.

In response to your question, the prominent Muslim scholar, *Sheikh Muhammad Iqbal Nadvi*, Imam of Calgary Mosque, Alberta, Canada, and former Professor at King Saud University, Riyadh, Saudi Arabia, states:

The issue of *niqab* (covering the whole body including the face and hands) is a basic condition of *hijab* (Muslim woman's dress) in one school of *fiqh*, while it

> is a recommended part of *hijab* in other schools. *But what is agreed upon in all schools is to remove the niqab [to uncover the face] for some genuine reasons such as identification or medical purposes.*
>
> The case you mentioned may be a reason to remove the *niqab* if the police officer is in need to do so and there is a legal requirement by the law to show the face, regardless of the faith and this applies to all faiths.
>
> However, this should not be a way of discrimination against a veiled woman just to tease her. Therefore, the sister has to insist on her right to use *niqab* and fight for this right IF she is targeted for discrimination and the law does not require showing the face.

Dr Rifat Fawzi, professor of *Shari'a* at Cairo University, adds:

> It is permissible, as far as *Shari'a* is concerned, to remove the *niqab* (face cover) for some genuine reasons such as identification or to get a photo for an ID or driving license. Therefore, if a Muslim woman is asked to remove the face cover to get a photo for such genuine reasons, then she is permitted to do so and Almighty Allah will forgive such matters. Added to that, she will keep the photo and such matters are pardoned for the facilitation of the affairs of people. If you are still in need of more information, don't hesitate to contact us. Do keep in touch. May Allah guide us all to the straight path![23]

This *fatwa* raises multiple issues, not only regarding the dress code for Muslim women generally but also in a transnational and international environment, especially within the Muslim diaspora where laws are being adopted to prohibit Muslim women from covering their heads. The *muftis* in the instant *fatwas* lay out the plurality of interpretations regarding *niqab* (where some schools of juristic thought in Islam declare it as mandatory; others discretionary). They then proceed to locate the question within the specific minority setting arguing that Muslims must abide by the law of the land they live in and therefore the Muslim woman ought to remove her face covering for identification in accordance with the law. Finally, *fiqh al aqalliyat* is invoked (minority *fiqh*) where necessity (*darura*) may make the prohibited permissible (in this case, a Muslim woman is permitted to uncover her face in the best interest of the law and in her position as a law-abiding citizen).

In the Islamic tradition, veiling represents the ultimate dichotomy into the public and private spheres of life through a pronounced dress code for Muslim women. What usually does not come across in describing this practice is the *Qur'anic* emphasis on 'recognition' and visibility of identity through dress

---

23 Available at:http://www.islamonline.net/servlet/Satellite?pagename=IslamOnline-English Ask_Scholar/FatwaE/FatwaE&cid=1119503547012.

as a protective measure in a politically and socially hostile and unfriendly environment. Were this aspect of the context highlighted, it would be clear that time and place, context and situation inform the dress code as much as the text. For instance, in a politically-hostile environment where, after September 11, 2001, Muslim women wearing headscarves were harassed in public places, some scholars questioned the 'protective' nature of this dress code, calling for Muslim women to be cautious and conscious of their safety. For instance, a questioner from the United States of America sought a *fatwa* on 1 October 2003 on whether his wife could take off her *hijab* due to the anti-Muslim sentiments following September 2001. He asked:

> Following what happened in the United States of America lately on 11 September, my wife can't go outside because she is scared. Can she take off her *hijab* when she goes out or not?[24]

In response the *fatwa* stated that while covering the hair is non-controversial and all schools of thought agree that a woman must cover her hair, yet only in cases of a threat to her life, may she remove it (and then, too, only temporarily).

Another *fatwa* presented below reflects some of the confusion regarding the parameters of appropriate dress for Muslim women in the public space. The questioner is a woman named Asma from Saudi Arabia who asks Sheikh Ahmed Kutty the following question:

> Dear scholar, *As-Salamu 'Alaykum*, *hijab* (as a dress code) for women in Islam, does it concern women only? Do men have nothing to bear in this? Secondly, I hear a lot of confusing things about *hijab*. While some say one does not need to cover the hair, others say that one must also cover one's face and hands besides the rest of the body. If a person refuses to cover the head, can others call her a non-Muslim simply for baring her head?

The response by the *mufti* repeats the position in an earlier *fatwa* regarding the diverse positions adopted by various scholars ranging from mandatory covering of the face as well as the head and body to only covering the head, stating that 'covering the head, however, is not at all a disputed issue among them – they all agree that this is a necessary part of *hijab*'.

It may be argued that the Internet *fatwas* on dress code for Muslim women reflect the divergence of opinion among scholars of Islam regarding this institution due to the interpretation of general and vaguely phrased *Qur'anic* verses regarding modesty in behaviour for men and women. See for instance, the *Qur'anic* injunction in Verses 24:30–31, as follows:

24 Available at: www.islamonline.net

> [Prophet], tell believing men to lower their glances and guard their private parts: that is purer for them. God is aware of everything they do. And tell believing women that they should lower their glances, guard their private parts, and not display their charms beyond what [it is acceptable] to reveal; they should let their headscarves fall to cover their necklines and not reveal their charms except to their husbands, their fathers, their husbands' fathers, their sons, their husbands' sons, their brothers, their brothers' sons, their sisters' sons, their womenfolk, their slaves, such men as attend them who have no sexual desire, or children who are not yet aware of women's nakedness; they should not stamp their feet so as to draw attention to any hidden charms. Believers, all of you, turn to God so that you may prosper (Abdel Haleem 2004:222).

As may be gleaned from the translation of the verses of the *Qur'an* cited above, the objective is to set out a code of conduct and dress for Muslims (male and female) as well as adding specific rules for Muslim women in vulnerable social and political environments.[25] The first rule relates to lowering of the gaze in interaction with members of the opposite sex which leads one to extrapolate the possibility of a gender desegregated environment and women's role in the public space. Second, Muslim women have the added responsibility of covering their bodies except 'what is apparent' or what 'is acceptable'. Here is where the multiple interpretations of this verse are generated leading to a controversy that continues to this day and beyond as evidenced from the focus of *fatwas* in the present study. Thus the *fatwa* mentioned above states that while all schools of thought in the Islamic legal tradition accept that covering the head is mandatory for Muslim women, covering the face is not. Yet despite these differences, scholars also agree that in times of necessity, covering the hair can also be dispensed with. (See *fatwa* where the *mufti* advises the questioner to remove the headscarf as required by the law but use a wig instead.)

International Human Rights Law and Women's Reproductive Rights

The second *fatwa* presented here raises important issues about international law. What is the relevance of international institutions, declarations and conventions on human rights to similar norms within the Islamic legal tradition, particularly with reference to those issues considered as 'Islamic'? What is the trend within the *fatwas* discourse regarding reconciling human rights in Islam and international law

25 For instance, in the early days of Islam there were incidents of harassment against Muslim women; the Prophet Mohammed asked women to identify themselves in the public space by wearing an outer garment. But, where socio-political compulsions demand that Muslim women 'blend' with the wider population, this is advisable. Finally, where covering the head, face and so on is against the law of the country where Muslim women reside, and adhering to the *hijab/nikaab* endangers access to basic education, health, employment and so on, a judgement has to be made whether it is advisable to confront the law and to what end.

and does this discourse resonate within local and national contexts? Reproduced below is one such *fatwa*:

Question:

Dear scholars, *As-salamu'alaykum*. What is the view of *Shari'a* on the issue of reproductive health in the 1995 Beijing Platform for Action, which was recently reaffirmed at the 49th Session of the United Nations Commission on the Status of Women? First, it calls for reproductive health services to be made available to individuals and couples – including adolescents and unmarried people. This includes counselling and access to sexual and reproductive health information and services; and information on sexuality, reproduction and sexually transmitted diseases, including HIV/AIDS, to be spread through public health campaigns, the media, counselling and the education system. The Platform for Action has also been interpreted to promote the legalization of abortion.

Second, the Platform for Action seeks to eliminate all distinctions between men and women; it sees the differences between women and men's achievements and activities to be 'the consequences of socially-constructed gender roles rather than immutable biological differences'. This is done on the plea of promoting woman's status and ensuring that she receives her rights. Jazakum Allahu Khayran

Answer:

Wa 'alaykum As-Salamu wa Rahmatullahi wa Barakatuh.

In the Name of Allah, Most Gracious, Most Merciful.

All praise and thanks are due to Allah, and peace and blessings be upon His Messenger.

Dear questioner, we would like to thank you for the great confidence you place in us, and we implore Allah Almighty to help us serve His cause and render our work for His sake.

The Beijing Platform for Action is a policy statement, not a binding convention, which does have good points, for it aims to give women rights to equal pay for equal work, equal education, health care, nutrition, social benefits, right to own property and inherit, and so on. It also aims to protect them from violence and exploitation.

However, the Platform for Action also contains items that promote immorality. To begin with, Islam prohibits any premarital or extramarital sex and all means that could lead to it. As for the immorality that the Beijing document promotes, Islam rejects it totally and fights it resolutely. As for the equality of men and women, they are equal in rights and duties, but not in their functions. In this concern, *Dr. 'Ali Jum'ah, Mufti of Egypt*, states:

Among the blessings with which Allah has endowed Muslims is the prohibition of adultery and fornication, immoral acts and practices. Allah Almighty says, (And come not near unto adultery. Lo! It is an abomination and an evil way) (Al-Isra' 17:32). In this noble verse, the Almighty forbids us even from drawing near to whatever could lead us to such a grievous sin as adultery or fornication. That is why Allah has commanded us to lower our gaze by saying, (Tell the believing men to lower their gaze and be modest. That is purer for them. Lo! Allah is Aware of what they do) (An-Nur 24:30). Thus, Muslims have been interested in clarifying the legal rulings pertaining to the sexual aspect of human life, and this clarification is the basis of sex education at any stage in life, up to the stage right before marriage and to those who will be married soon. Hence, if this international declaration asks Muslims and others to apply a programme for sex education, then we will apply what our righteous predecessors used to follow and according to the rulings of our religion. This will be done by educating Muslims on the juristic rulings related to sex.

According to the above, we should teach our children that practising sex outside marriage is prohibited and that there are rulings pertaining to adultery/fornication concerning the young, the old, the married (or previously married) and the unmarried. Moreover, teaching children and teenagers in schools and by mass media how to practise sex 'safely' and suchlike topics is prohibited; it contradicts the principles of Islam. Thus, it is also prohibited to distribute contraceptives among children and teens (as the document calls for), for this leads to sexual chaos.

As for abortion, it is basically prohibited according to the consensus of Muslim scholars. However, abortion can be resorted to in exceptional cases when there is a medical necessity [that is, when the pregnancy will inevitably endanger the life of the mother].

When it comes to the similarity of the genders, Islam rejects and prohibits it, for man and woman are equal in Islam in rights, duties, obligations and humanity, but those rights and duties are not necessarily identical due to the biological differences of the sexes.[26]

---

26 Available at: http://www.islamonline.net/servlet/Satellite?pagename=IslamOnline-English-Ask_Scholar/FatwaE/FatwaE&cid=1119503549624.

The *fatwa* presented above is a most interesting and valuable 'find' on a number of counts. This was the only *fatwa* I was able to access on any of the 'Islamic' websites studied that actively engaged with human rights conventions and treaties emanating from the 'West'. The question appears to have been posed by someone who has knowledge of international human rights law and would like guidance on how to develop her or his understanding from a comparative perspective. The *fatwa* delivered in response is given by a *mufti* equally knowledgeable about comparative human rights and Islamic law on the subject and able to highlight points of convergence and divergence between international human rights law and Islamic law. The *fatwa* is also important in the way in which it summarizes various positions of the Islamic tradition in the area of reproductive rights, duties and entitlements.

The *fatwa* adopts a clear position regarding complete prohibition of pre-marital sexual relations for Muslim women and men and thus limits information on the subject to married couples. Convergence with human rights law appears in situations where, due to the mother's ill health and threat to her life, abortion is permissible under Islamic law.

Having 'discovered' the above *fatwa*, I set about searching for similar *fatwas* but was intrigued to find that none engaged with human rights law, the Beijing Platform for Action or reproductive health issues using the rights terminology. What was fascinating, however, was that this sole *fatwa* was reported on multiple websites.[27] What I did come across during this research were numerous *fatwas* on contraception, the Islamic views on birth control, breastfeeding as a birth control mechanism, and so on. For instance, one *fatwa* states in response to a question of whether 'permanent prevention from conception' is permitted due to the ill health of the woman: 'Permanent prevention of procreation by inactivating related body organs is unequivocally forbidden …'[28] Temporary contraception including coitus interruptus, as practised during the times of the Prophet Mohammed, is stated to be the recommended method of birth control. Drawing upon this as an example of permissibility, various *fatwas* argue for birth control as permissible within the Islamic tradition. 'In our time, new methods of contraception are available which realize the objective intended by the Prophet (peace and blessings be upon him) that of protecting the suckling infant from any possible harm?'

'Halala' Marriage

The third set of *fatwas* presented here address an area of Islamic family law where there is constant debate among the Muslim communities around the world and this

27 See: http://infad.usim.edu.my/modules.php?op=modload&name=News&file=article&sid=4515. The Islamic Science University of Malaysia under the *Fatwa* Management System, World *Fatwa* Management and Research Institute.

28 See: http://www.islamonline.net/servlet/Satellite?cid=1251021156172pagename=IslamOnline-English-Ask_Scholar%2FFatwaE%2FFatwaEAskTheScholar.

has found its way into the Internet *fatwa* debates. This is the *tahleel* marriage, also known as the *halala* marriage, entered into by a divorced woman where she and her former husband wish to remarry and must have an intervening marriage enabling them to marry their previous spouse. There is confusion around the validity of this intervening marriage and the *fatwa* is being sought to clarify this ambiguity.

Question:

My friend has divorced his wife the third and final divorce. Is it permissible that I marry her then divorce her so that she can return to her first husband?

Answer:

Praise be to Allaah. If a man divorces his wife for the third time, then she is not permissible for him to marry until she has married another man, because Allaah says (interpretation of the meaning): And if he has divorced her (the third time), then she is not lawful unto him thereafter until she has married another husband (al-Baqarah 2:230).

It is stipulated that this marriage which will make her permissible for her first husband should be a valid marriage. Temporary marriage (*muta* marriage) or marriage for the purpose of making her permissible for her first husband then divorcing her (*tahleel* marriage) are both *haraam* and invalid according to the vast majority of scholars, and it does not make the woman permissible for her first husband.

See: al-Mughni (10/49-55).

There are *saheeh ahaadeeth* from the Prophet (peace and blessings of Allaah be upon him) which show that *tahleel* marriage is *haraam.*

Abu Dawood (2076) narrated that the Prophet (peace and blessings of Allaah be upon him) said: Allaah has cursed the *muhallil* and the *muhallal lahu*. This was classed as *saheeh* by al-Albaani in Sunan Abi Dawood.

The *muhallil* is the one who marries a woman and divorces her so that she can go back to her first husband, and the *muhallal lahu* is the first husband.

Ibn Majaah (1936) narrated from Uqbah ibn Aamir (may Allaah be pleased with him) that the Prophet (peace and blessings of Allaah be upon him) said: Shall I not tell you of a borrowed billy goat. They said, Yes, O Messenger of Allaah. He said, He is *al-muhallil.* May Allaah curse *al-muhallil* and *al-muhallal lahu.* Classed as *hasan* by al-Albaani in Saheeh Sunan Ibn Maajah.

Abd al-Razzaaq (6/2650 narrated that Umar ibn al-Khattaab (may Allaah be pleased with him) said whilst addressing the people: By Allaah, no *muhallil* or *muhallal lahu* will be brought to me but I will stone them. …

This applies whether he states his intention clearly when doing the marriage contract and they stipulate that when he has made her permissible for her first husband he will divorce her, or they do not stipulate that and he intends it to himself only.

Al-Haakim narrated from Naafiâ that a man said to Ibn Umar: I married a woman and made her permissible for her first husband, and he did not tell me to do that and he did not know. He said: No, marriage should be based on genuine intentions; if you like her then keep her, and if you do not like her then leave her. He said: At the time of the Messenger of Allaah (peace and blessings of Allaah be upon him) we would regard that as *zina*. And he said: They will still be adulterers, even if they remain for twenty years.

Imam Ahmad was asked about a man who married a woman intending thereby in his heart to make her permissible for her first husband, but the woman did not know about that. He said: He is a *muhallil*, and if he intends thereby to make her permissible for her first husband, then he is cursed.

Based on that, it is not permissible for you to marry this woman if you intend thereby to make her permissible for her first husband. Doing that is a major sin, and the marriage will not be valid, rather it is *zina*. Allaah forbids it.[29]

Similar *fatwas* were issued from other websites included in the present study (islamonline.net) which also categorically denounced *halala* marriages as prohibited in Islam and *haram*.[30]

Halala or *tahleel* marriages are a highly sensitive issue in Muslim communities and its discussion is avoided at all costs. *Fatwas* are sought by couples who believe that they have been irrevocably divorced but are truly repentant and wish to reconcile but believe that without the wife marrying another husband, consummating the marriage and being divorced by this man, they cannot legally remarry. The issue has always caught the popular imagination and as a Muslim woman growing up in Pakistan, I saw a number of films where this view of Islamic family law forms the theme and the wife is portrayed as the victim. As a legal

29 Available at: http://islamonline.com/news/articles/3/Tahleel_marriage_is_haraam_and_invalid.html.

30 See: http://www.islamonline.net/servlet/Satellite?pagename=IslamOnline-English-Ask_Scholar%2FFatwaE%2FFatwaEAskTheScholar&cid=1245159042160 and http://www.islamonline.net/servlet/Satellite?cid=1119503543092&pagename=IslamOnline-English-Ask_Scholar%2FFatwaE%2FFatwaEAskTheScholar.

academic, when I had occasion to research into the subject, I realized that a woman marrying another man simply to 'tick the box' of an intervening marriage is illegal and *haram* and one that has no roots in *usul ul fiqh*. It has to be said though, that the predominant view in South Asian Muslim communities is that a *halala* marriage is in accordance with the *Qur'anic* injunction. Divorced parties end up requesting the *mulla* of the neighbourhood mosque to act as the 'intervening' husband who often obliges the desperate couple in what is an illegal and immoral act according to Islamic law (cross reference here to Taj-Andersen and Hellum in this book). Challenging this dominant approach to remarriage of divorced Muslim couples through *halala*, all *fatwas* accessed on the websites in this study, were of the unanimous opinion that this practice was evil and not permitted in Islamic law. Yet one wonders how and where this practice originated and how it has travelled to the diaspora where Muslim communities hold fast to it.

Fatwas as Counter-hegemonic Discursive Sites: Some Reflections and Tentative Conclusions in the Light of 'Internet *Fatwas*' on Women and Gender

This exploratory study on Internet *fatwas* relating to women and gender issues from selected websites dedicated to information on Islamic law offers fascinating insights into the area. In view of the limited nature of the sample and scope of the study, concluding reflections are few, preliminary and tentative. At the outset, it is obvious that the websites studied (as well as others not forming the subject of this study), have situated themselves in a global and universal framework and context recalling the universal nature of the Muslim *ummah*. Having said that, most of the questions and responses have been framed by what we might broadly define as 'Western' Muslims or diasporic Muslims; a plausible fact due to limited access of this facility to wider 'virtual' Muslim audiences in the non-West. The websites appear to have a multiple agenda of 'Islamizing' Muslim men and women, particularly in the West; hence the ethical, moral emphasis and tenor of the *fatwa* alongside the legal content of the response. Finally, there is a strong pedagogical aim to the *fatwas* as they explain concepts and issues in the format of an online 'lecture'.

An interesting aspect of Internet *fatwas* is that they meticulously follow the traditional prototype of the *fatwa*. The *mufti* recites the name of Allah and His Prophet indicating that this opinion is delivered from an Islamic perspective, drawing upon Islamic sources and to the best of his knowledge and competence (I did not come across any female *muftis* in this sample). The *fatwa* closes with the acknowledgement that this opinion is in no way a claim to the only truth or opinion, as only Allah knows best. This apparently religious invocation may also be construed as the *mufti's* disclaimer that he has done his best within the realm of human reason and that there may be other truths that he has not been able to extract from his knowledge of the Islamic legal sources.

As to the substance of the *fatwa*, it draws upon opinions of other jurists and also offers evidence of the plural norms operating within the Islamic legal tradition. For example, it is the requirement of Islamic law that one should follow the law of the country where one happens to be, if that law does not grossly violate one's personal beliefs. There also appears to be an acknowledgement of changing realities and exigencies of time, space and regulation, as well as necessity. Based on the range of themes, questions posed and responses received from *muftis* in the present sample of *fatwas*, I suggest that Internet *fatwas* websites are a manifestation of counter-hegemonic sites of Islamic socio-legal, political and religious discourse since they challenge existing hegemonies of ethnicities, schools of juristic thought and locations. For instance, British Muslims of Asian origin or descent seek affirmation of their 'pure' and 'pristine' Islam by challenging a South Asian 'notion' of Islam in, say, the triple divorce, clothing (see *fatwa* where a bride-to-be seeks to break away from the traditional bridal outfit to be more 'Islamically dressed'. Internet *fatwas* on women and gender issues also appear counter-hegemonic to the male-dominated discourse within the Islamic legal tradition by seeking 'logical', 'rational' reasons for the Muslim women's dress code, rules of contraception and so on. Simultaneously, these Internet sites are in themselves hegemonic in that they are a form of regulation of family and family formations through religion. The *fatwas* in the study also highlight a counter-hegemony and resistance to the dominant 'Western' discourse by ensuring that the discussion remains within the Islamic and Muslim framework and communities.

Cross-fertilization of ideas, opinions and arguments are another common feature of the *fatwas* studied. Thus a single *fatwa* will encapsulate and recall viewpoints of a number of *muftis* from various parts and institutions of the Muslim world as well as scholars of the Muslim diaspora (cf. Samia Bano's empirical findings in this volume where *Shari'a* Councils do not appear to 'cross-fertilize' their decisions). On the other hand, the discourse on human rights is pointedly invisible in its usage although claims, entitlements and obligations are addressed. This is evident from the research of the European Council on *Fatwa* and Research by Lena Larsen in this volume as well as the Internet *fatwas*.

Internet-based *fatwas* have also provided Muslim women with opportunities to inquire about issues that are not posed due to the societal environment's dictates of what may or may not be discussed in public. For instance, a Muslim woman has asked whether it is permitted to go for breast augmentation surgery to please her husband; the nature of her relationship with her fiancé, whether a Muslim woman can have a belly button ring, and so on.

It is not apparent from this study whether questions addressed through *fatwas* invoking the *Shari'a* are becoming part of an evolving discourse embedded within these *fatwas* with the potential of moving beyond websites impacting on the broader stage of globalized Muslim communities and Muslim state practice. Or, is this an academic, Internet based exercise likely to remain within the confines of a cyber Islamic environment?

Fatwas are opinions of individual *muftis* or groups of *muftis* that vary in the position and approach adopted regarding the questions posed to them. The range of opinions offered on the same subject is potentially infinite and one that in the context of our present study gives cause for concern and confusion. For instance, in the case of the dress code for Muslim women, the advice ranges from *niqab* to a headscarf and to covering hands as well as feet. The plurality of opinions reflects the diverse opinions of scholars and commentators of the *Qur'an* and *hadith.* Legal implications of the approach adopted regarding dress code also vary. In Iran, for instance, it is legally binding for women to cover their head in the public space and disregarding this rule is an offence. Following the recent surge of the so-called Taliban in the North West frontier province of Pakistan, the University of Peshawar has had to put in place a dress code for female students consisting of an outer garment and a veil to cover the head. The autumn term (September 2009) in some private universities in the North West frontier province of Pakistan saw an institutionally imposed 'uniform for female students'.

Despite the limitations of the present study, it is submitted that the *fatwas* provide some useful insights into the use of this interpretative tool within the Islamic legal tradition. Muslims globally appear to refer to it to raise questions and address issues affecting their lives, communities, countries and the world they live in. In particular, we have focused on *fatwas* that have generated a discourse on the Islamic legal tradition, relating to women and gender issues and, more broadly, family law in contemporary transnational settings. The sample analyzed raises a number of important points in informing our understandingMuslim views on norms and principles impacting on the status of Muslim women and the role and obligations of Muslims, individually and at a collective level. But the study also alerts us to dangers of cyberspace engagement with 'faceless', 'voiceless', 'shadowy' figures and entities whose credentials we do not know. We have no way of knowing whether the questioners and the *muftis* are 'real' persons. Or, are Muslim women caught in a controlling mechanism in the garb of autonomy to seek knowledge and responses to their most intimate and critical dilemmas?

Following on from this point is another concern the present study raises that in the absence of a uniform, agreed, global, authoritative voice across the Muslim world, regarding the accuracy or otherwise of a *fatwa*, what or how might *fatwa* pronouncements be regulated, if at all? What are the implications of these *fatwas* on law and policy making in Muslim countries as well as on regulatory norms for Muslims living in non-Muslim countries? Further research is required to address some of these questions and concerns.

Historically, questions relating to family law were formulated within the confines of particular communities and *muftis* were rarely called upon to address and develop comprehensive norms and guidance regarding plural identities, for example, a Muslim also being a Pakistani and a British citizen, an American of Syrian origin and a Muslim, and so on. The Islamic legal tradition is thus under pressure to respond to the anxieties of Muslims in Muslim majority countries as well as in 'Western', predominantly non-Muslim jurisdictions, and their need to make decisions impacting on their lives and those of their families and communities. This discourse has found a variety of contemporary manifestations, of which the use of Internet discussions, chat rooms, email and *fatwas* is one.

Finally, what is the role of these *fatwa*-giving websites in the evolution and development of transnational and international on laws, norms and regulatory mechanisms on women and gender? This is where the need for further research is required. For instance, have Muslims in France decided to adhere to the *fatwa* that requires them to register their marriages within the mainstream French legal system? Have Muslim women in Norway accepted the un-'Islamicness' of the triple *talaq* and acknowledged that the Muslim Family Laws Ordinance 1961 Pakistan (the country of origin of many Norwegian Muslims), prohibiting this mode of divorce, is an 'Islamically' valid one? And, have Muslim women reading these *fatwas* refused to enter into *halala* marriages on the basis of their illegality in Islamic law? These and many other questions remain unanswered.

References

Abdel Haleem, M.A.S. (translator) 2004. The *Qu'ran*. Oxford: Oxford University Press, 222.

Ali, S.S. 2000. *Gender and Human Rights in Islam and International Law. Equal Before Allah, Unequal before Man?* The Hague: Kluwer Law International.

—— 2007a. Religious pluralism, human rights and Muslim citizenship in Europe: Some preliminary reflections on an evolving methodology for consensus, in *Religious Pluralism and Human Rights in Europe*, edited by T. Leonon and J. Goldschmidt. Antwerp: Intersentia, 57–79.

—— 2007b. 'The twain doth meet!' A preliminary exploration of the theory and practice of *as-Siyar* and international law in the contemporary world, in *Religion, Human Rights and International Law: A Critical Examination of Islamic State Practices,* edited by J. Rehman and S. Breau. Leiden: Martinus Nijhoff Publishers, 95–136.

—— 2009. Resurrecting *Siyar* through *fatwas*? (Re)constructing Islamic international law in a Post–(Iraq) invasion world. *Journal of Conflict and Security Law* 1–30.

Allot, A. 1980. *Limits of Law*. London: Butterworths.

An-Na'im, A.A. 1990. *Towards an Islamic Reformation.* Syracuse: Syracuse University Press.

—— (ed.) 2002. *Islamic Family Law in a Changing World: A Global Resource Book*. London: Zed Press.

Arabi, O. 2001. *Studies in Modern Islamic Law and Jurisprudence.* The Hague: Kluwer Law International.

Awan, A.N. 2008. Antecedents of Islamic political radicalism among Muslim communities in Europe. *PS: Political Science and Politics* 41:1:13–17 Cambridge University Press. Available at http://journals.cambridge.org/download.php? file=%2FPSC%2FPSC41_01%2FS1049096508080013a.pdf &code=a98db3cd9b19125d3592b187924f0996. Accessed 2 August 2008.

Bowen, J. 2003. *Islam, Law, and Equality in Indonesia: An Anthropology of Public Reasoning* (American title: *Entangled Commands*). Cambridge: Cambridge University Press.

Bunt, G.R. 2000. *Virtually Islamic: Computer-mediated Communication and Cyber Islamic Environments.* Cardiff: University of Wales Press.

—— 2003. Islam interactive: Mediterranean Islamic expression on the world wide web, in *Shaping the Current Islamic Reformation,* edited by B.A. Robertson. London and Portland, Oregon: Frank Cass, 164–186.

Caeiro, A. 2006. The shifting moral universes of the Islamic tradition of *ifta*: A diachronic study of four *Adab al-Fatwa* manuals. *The Muslim World* 96 (4):661.

Coulson, J. 1857. The state and the individual in Islamic law. *International and Comparative Law Quarterly* 6:57.

Coulson, N.J. 1994. *A History of Islamic Law.* Edinburgh: Edinburgh University Press.

Fyzee, A.A.A. 1974. *Outlines of Muhammadan Law*. Fourth edition. Delhi: Oxford University Press.

Haddad, Y.Y. 2005. Operation Desert Storm and the war of *fatwas*, in *Islamic Legal Interpretation Muftis and their Fatwas*, edited by M.K. Masud, B. Messick and D.S. Powers. Oxford: Oxford University Press.

Hallaq, W.B. 1994. From *fatwas* to *furu*: Growth and change in Islamic substantive law. *Islamic Law and Society* 1:29.

Kamali, M.H. 2003. *Principles of Islamic Jurisprudence.* Third edition. Cambridge: Islamic Texts Society.

Masud, M.H., Messick, B. and Powers, D.S. 2005. *Muftis, fatwas*, and Islamic legal interpretation, in *Islamic Legal Interpretation. Muftis and their Fatwas*, edited by M.H. Masud, B. Messick, D.S. Powers. Karachi: Oxford University Press, 3–32, 4.

Pearl, D. and Menski, W. 1998. *Muslim Family Law.* Third edition. London: Sweet and Maxwell.

Rahim, A. 1995. *Muhammadan Jurisprudence*. Lahore: Mansoor Book House.

Rehman, F. 1979. *Islam*. Second edition. Chicago: University of Chicago Press.

Schacht, J. 1959. *Origins of Muhammadan Jurisprudence*. Oxford: Oxford University Press.

—— 1964. *An Introduction to Islamic Law*. Oxford: Clarendon Press.

Vasey-Fitzgerald, S.G. 1955. Nature and sources of the *Sharia*, in *Law in the Middle East*, edited by M. Khadduri and H.J. Liebesny. Washington DC: The Middle East Institute.

Wax, E. 1999. The *mufti* in the chat room: Islamic legal advisers are just a click away from ancient customs. *Washington Post* (31 July 1999) C01. Available at: http://www.ijtihad.org/Mufti.htm accessed 2 August 2008.

Three Main Websites Consulted for the Study

Islam Online.net, numerous news articles and *fatwas* (questions and responses), available at http://www.islamonline.net.

Islam Online.com, numerous articles and *fatwas* (questions and responses), available at: http://islamonline.com.

Islam Today.net, numerous articles and *fatwas* (questions and responses), available at: http://www.islamtoday.net.

Chapter 6

Islamic Jurisprudence and Transnational Flows: Exploring the European Council for *Fatwa* and Research[1]

Lena Larsen

This chapter analyzes the working of the European Council for *Fatwa* and Research (referred to as the Council in this chapter), and its attempt to serve Muslims in Europe by guidance in matters of Islamic Law in the form of *fatwas*.[2] Despite its claim of being a local authority, the Council is an example of transnational flows with regard to its legal heritage, membership, *fatwas* and resolutions, as well as the manner in which these are disseminated. I will explore these elements and present three women-related *fatwas*, authoritative legal opinions,[3] to see in what way they are included in the field of Islamic reference and debate, described as an underestimated dimension of a 'transnational Islam' (Bowen 2004:880).[4]

Bowen argues that transnational Islam creates and implies the existence and legitimacy of a global public space of normative reference and debate (Bowen 2004:882). This transnational public space of Islam is embedded in the imagination of a worldwide community (*umma*) transcending specific boundaries and borders, and based on a set of extra-national social norms – the many interpretations of *Shari'a* and 'God's plans and commands' (Bowen 2004:883). 'This consciousness,' writes Bowen, 'supports the legitimacy and indeed the imperative of searching anywhere in the world for the highest authority on Islamic matters. This imperative creates specific networks of authority, learning and communication that are more historically and sociologically specific than the general sense of global *ummahood*' (Bowen 2004:882–883).

1 This chapter is based on research related to current work on my PhD dissertation '*Fiqh* facing Everyday Challenges: *Fatwas* as Solutions for Muslim Women in Western Europe' at University of Oslo, Norway.

2 *Fatwas* is the popular anglicised plural form of *fatwa* but *fatawa* is the more strictly correct plural form.

3 I deliberately use the term 'women-related' and not 'gender-related', taking into consideration the strong emphasis on 'women's issues' in the current Islamic debate.

4 Bowen emphasizes three dimensions of 'transnational Islam': demographic movements, transnational institutions and the field of Islamic reference and debate.

The relatively new Muslim presence in Western Europe represents a challenge for Muslims themselves. How are they going to practise Islam in a new social context? Western Europe is like a new and open field, without previous established (Muslim) authority structures and therefore represents a possibility for new claims of authority for religious scholars. Key questions are: Who is speaking on behalf of the Muslims? How is the claim of authority formulated? Which interpretation of *Shari'a* principles is argued? In what way do the actors belong to the field of Islamic reference and debate?

The Council promotes the term *fiqh al-aqalliyat,* 'minority jurisprudence', both as a *raison d'être* among prominent *fatwa* bodies in the Muslim world, such as the Egyptian Dar al-fatwa and the International *Fiqh* Academy of the Muslim World League, and as a methodology framework for deducing norms. I will look at the Council and its attempt to define Western Europe as a new local 'jurisdiction' with its own Islamic legal doctrine (*fiqh al-aqalliyat*) as a strategy for authority on European soil. In other words how orthodoxy is argued and hence becomes an integral part of the field of Islamic reference and debate.

Fatwa

A *fatwa* is an authoritative legal opinion given by a jurisconsult (*mufti*) in response to a question. It is not legally binding and thus differs from the domain of legal procedure, including binding judgements and state enforcement, which belongs to the judge (*qadi*). The practice of giving *fatwas* (*ifta'*) within the Muslim tradition is considered to be as old as Islam itself. In the Islamic legal literature, reference is made to the *Qur'an* and Muhammad is considered to be the first *mufti*.The question could be about almost any subject, including matters Westerners would not consider to be related to the legal field. No question is too small to be asked about. Skovgaard-Petersen gives some examples: '... detailed rules are set up for proper conduct in all walks of life, including civil and religious matters, but also such areas as personal hygiene' (Skovgaard-Petersen 1997:2). He then makes the following important point: '... *fatwas* not only helped regulate and Islamize people's conduct, but also brought all sorts of action into the sphere of *fiqh.* The *fatwa* and the *mufti*, then, are situated at the interface between worldly dealings and theorizing about them' (Skovgaard-Petersen 1997:2). The Islamic legal expert, Wael Hallaq, ascribes the *muftis* a central role in relation to the development and change of the Islamic legal doctrines within the law schools:

> ... the juridical genre of the *fatwa* was chiefly responsible for the growth and change of legal doctrine in the schools, and [...] our current perception of Islamic law as a jurists' law must now be further defined as a *mufti's* law (Hallaq 1994:65).[5]

5 'Schools' refers to *madhahib* (singular: *madhhab*), schools of legal thought within the Islamic legal tradition.

The Islamic legal tradition insists on the availability of *muftis* for the person who needs to ask a question. In the legal literature this availability is formulated in the requirement of a *mufti* for about every 80 kilometres.[6] This also could mean that every geographical area could be defined as a 'jurisdiction'.

The Muslim religious scholars, (*al-'ulama'*) who are giving *fatwas*, have a privileged position within the Islamic legal tradition. The Islamic scholar Ibn Qayyim (who died in 1350) compares a *mufti* with a minister who signs on behalf of the King. 'If this is high rank status, how much higher is not the status of the *mufti*, because he signs on behalf of Lord of the worlds, *al-rabb al-'alamin*'.[7] This rank is ascribed to the *mufti* because he or she, by issuing *fatwas*, is considered to be formulating *Shari'a* in terms of specific rules and norms on the basis of the textual sources. This requires knowledge, as well as morals and manners. The institutional conditions that regulate the practice of *ifta'* are spelt out in detail in the *adab al-mufti* literature.[8] One of the conditions is knowledge of the social context in which the question has been posed and hence the *fatwa* is to be given. Imam al-Nawawi (who died in 1278), the leading scholar of the Shafi'i school of thought and author of one such *adab al-mufti* manual, formulates this requirement in the following way: 'It is not allowed to give a *fatwa* concerning oaths and similar things (with regard to ways of expression) without having one's origin in that particular place (country), or having acquired experience [at the same level as the natives] with regard to ways of expression and traditions, *'urf*, in them' (al-Nawawi undated 1:104).[9]

A *fatwa* is not a static normative statement but changes according to place and time. As a result of the massive Muslim immigration to Western Europe after the Second World War, more than 20 million Muslims are living on Western European soil and are now considered to be a new Muslim minority.[10] This new situation has resulted in the Muslims finding themselves facing a new social and cultural reality, many looking for religious advice, taking the local context into consideration. *Fatwas* aimed at this relatively new context would, according to the believer's mind, be important as guidance on how to live as a Muslim in Western Europe. The Mauretanian scholar, Abdullah bin Bayyah (2002), claims that the *fatwa* institution is a vital Islamic institution in the West, to solve issues that are causing disruption.

6 *al-Mawsu'at al-fiqhiyya* 32:22. The term used is *masafat qasr* [*salah*], in other words, the distance which permits shortening the prayer, calculated to be approximately 80 kilometres.

7 Ibn Qayyim referred to in *Mawsu'at al-fiqhiyya*, 32:23.

8 The *adab al-fatwa* literature deals in detail with the requirements for the *mufti* as well as etiquette for the petitioner.

9 Translation from Arabic mine.

10 Muslims living as minorities in countries with a non-Muslim majority population is not new. We find 'old' Muslim minorities in India, Eastern Europe and China, among others.

Among Muslims in Western Europe the position of women is subject to an intense debate and women's questions play a central role regarding Islamic identity. Muslim women themselves are torn between two competing sets of norms based upon the notion of *qiwama* (guardianship) and complementarity, with the focus on obedience and duties, and the equality–rights paradigm. The challenge for many Muslim women is to keep their Islamic identity while maneuvering between these two concepts. Asking for *fatwas* is a way of trying to find what they consider to be religiously acceptable solutions to the challenges they are facing, and indeed the majority of questions are posed by women.[11] Three women-related *fatwas* will be presented in this chapter.

The European Council for *Fatwa* and Research (ECFR)

The year 1992 represents a watershed in the history of Muslims in Western Europe. Until then the main focus of the Muslim community was the institutionalization of Islam by opening mosques and Islamic centres, and establishing Islamic umbrella organizations.

'Care for the needs of Muslims in their new environments' was the reason that Union Organisations Islamiques de France (UOIF) invited Muslim scholars to the seminar 'Muslims in the West: A *Fiqh* Seminar' (held 13–15 July 1992). The objective was '... to tackle the pressing *Shari'a* questions facing those who are trying to preserve the identity of the Muslim communities in Western society' (Darsh undated: 4). The seminar was the first event where Muslim scholars were dealing with specific *fiqh* challenges that Muslims in Europe were facing. It was reported from the seminar:

> It was a good start in building up a *Fiqh* tradition dealing with situations that are new in the life of the Muslim communities in Western societies. [...] It was felt too, that such seminars should continue to find Islamic legal answers to many new developments faced by Muslims in the West (Darsh undated: 21).

The next seminar took place in 1994 and was a further step towards founding the European Council for *Fatwa* and Research, *al-majlis al-urubi lil-ifta' wal-buhuth*, an initiative of Yusuf al-Qaradawi in cooperation with the Union Organisations Islamiques de France.

The European Council for *Fatwa* and Research was established in London in 1997 to serve Muslims in Europe, on the initiative of the Federation of Islamic Organizations in Europe (FIOE).[12] 'The main objectives of the Council, according to its constitution, are to bring together European scholars and to aim to unite legal

11 According to findings in my empirical material.

12 The Federation of Islamic Organizations in Europe (FIOE) is an umbrella organization for mostly Muslim Brotherhood inspired associations.

injunctions on various issues, thus providing both legal injunctions suitable for Muslims in Europe and research for general, public *fatwas*' (Izzi Dien 2004:146). A central concept, which is the basis for the work of the Council, is *fiqh al-aqalliyat* (minority jurisprudence) and it is claimed to be a distinct field within Islamic substantive law (*furu' al-fiqh*).[13] The use of the concept is partly due to the fact that Muslims in Europe are a minority and it partly serves to define Europe as a 'jurisdiction' on its own, and hence the legitimacy of the Council in relation to already existing *fatwa* institutions in the Muslim world, such as the Egyptian State *Fatwa* Office, the *dar al-ifta'*, and the Organization of Islamic Conference's International *Fiqh* Academy in Saudi-Arabia.[14]

Membership of the Council

Participants at the *fiqh* seminars in France represented a pool from which to invite members to the Council.[15] Fifteen people were present at the founding meeting and adopted the 'draft constitution of the ECFR' in London in 1997.[16] The aims were ambitious: '*Nous souhaitons que ce Conceil devienne une référence incontournable pour les musulmans européens, les représentant et portant leurs aspirations au niveau des institutions religieuses et officielles sur l'ensemble du territoire européen*' (Caeiro 2002:16). A description of objectives and methodology below provides an insight into how these may be achieved:[17]

1. Achieving proximity and bringing together the scholars who live in Europe, and attempting to unify the jurisprudence views between them with regard to the main *Fiqh* issues.
2. Issuing collective *fatwas* which meet the needs of Muslims in Europe, solve their problems and regulate their interaction with the European communities, all within the regulations and objectives of *Shari'a*.
3. Publishing legal studies and research, which resolve issues arising in Europe in a manner which realizes the objectives of *Shari'a* and interests of people.
4. Guiding Muslims in Europe generally and those working for Islam particularly, through spreading the proper Islamic concepts and decisive legal *fatwas*.

---

13 See for example al-Qaradawi 2001:32 and al-'Alwani 2003:viii.

14 *Fatwas of European Council for Fatwa and Research*: X.

15 Six participants, including al-Qaradawi, are members of the Council. The other five are Faysal Mawlawi, 'Isam al-Bashir, and Nasir al-Mayman, who live outside Europe, and Ahmad Jaballah and Ounis Guergah from France. The latter is a member and director of the Dar Al-fatwa of the Union des Organisations Islamiques de France (UOIF).

16 *Fatwas of European Council for Fatwa and Research*: 1.

17 *Fatwas of European Council for Fatwa and Research:* 1ff.

Who could become a member of the Council? The conditions for membership are indicated in the statutes of the council:[18]

5. To be of appropriate legal (*Shar'i*) qualification at university level, or to have been committed to the meetings and circles of scholars and subsequently licensed by them, and to have sound knowledge of the Arabic language.
6. To be of good conduct and commitment to the regulations and manners of Islamic *Shari'a.*
7. To be a resident of the European continent.
8. To enjoy the knowledge of legal jurisprudence (*fiqh*) as well as awareness of current environment.
9. To be approved by the absolute majority of the members.

The last condition is, according to Alexandre Caeiro, decisive with regard to the acceptance of a new member (Caeiro 2002:21).

In spite of the aim of the Council to be established by and for Muslims in Europe, the Federation of Islamic Organizations in Europe decided that certain people outside Europe should also be invited to become members. Several considerations seemed to have been in mind: Caeiro mentions the *mufti's authority* (Caeiro 2002:24). Personalities such as Yusuf al-Qaradawi (living in Qatar), Faysal Mawlawi (living in Lebanon) and Abdullah bin Bayyah (living in Saudi-Arabia) provide necessary *legitimacy* to the Council. They are considered to be *mujtahid* (one who exercises independent reasoning), which would be of relevance when new topics related to Muslims' life in Europe are discussed.[19] But it could also imply an attempt to control the development of Islamic thought on European soil. The percentage of members from outside Europe should, according to the statutes, not exceed 25 of the total number of members.[20] However, out of 38 members, 14 (more than 30 per cent) are living in the Muslim world. Twenty-two members are living in Europe, while two are living in North America.

The Annual Sessions

Before 2000 the Council met for one session a year; from 2000 to 2005, the Council met twice a year and has reverted to annual sessions since 2006. Before 2006, sessions were held in cities around Europe. After 2006, the sessions have

18 *Fatwas of European Council for Fatwa and Research*: 5.

19 The term *mujtahid* is in Sunni Islam, according to *The Oxford Dictionary of Islam*, reserved for the founders of the four official schools of Islamic law, although modern Islamic reformers call for the revival of *ijtihad* as a means of accommodating new ideas and conditions (Esposito 2003:214).

20 *Fatwas of European Council for Fatwa and Research*: 5.

taken place in Istanbul and Sarajevo.[21] A huge apparatus is in motion before and during each session:[22] The secretariat of the Council prepares the meeting, including booking flights, and cooperates with a local body in the town where the session takes place, which is in charge of the local logistics, such as transport to and from the airport, hotels, meals and setting up a meeting for the local Muslim community. Members are also dependent on being able to obtain visas for the country where the session is to take place. These challenges and efforts made on the part of the organizers may be gleaned from the final statements read at the conclusion of each session.[23] The final statement of the nineteenth session, which took place in Istanbul (30 June to 4 July 2009), illustrates this point. The Turkish government is thanked 'sincerely' for facilitating convening the session on its soil, not least with regard to permitting Council members into Turkey. Local organizations are mentioned for their cooperation with regard to setting up the session. Lastly the Council's Board is mentioned in addition to brothers and sisters who 'have contributed to the success of the session'.

The Meetings

The Council sessions normally start on a Tuesday night and end at noon on Sunday. Administrative issues are dealt with in a closed meeting and then a number of meetings take place where studies, prepared on a topic previously decided upon, are presented. The studies are discussed with the aim of agreeing on resolutions (*qararat*). A resolution is a decision made as a result of research papers that are discussed at the annual sessions of the Council. The resolution is not a response to a particular question but to initiatives taken by the members about issues they consider to be important for Muslims in Europe. Saturdays normally include a *fatwa* session. *Fatwas* are issued as the result of a question posed by a petitioner that has often been dealt with by one member or a small group of members in advance. As the Council tries to issue consensual *fatwas*, the wording of the texts are modified in order to accommodate a range of individual sensibilities. Both *qararat* and *fatwas* are considered by the Council to be *fatwas*.[24] The session ends

---

21 This could be ascribed to difficulties obtaining visas for the members living outside Europe.

22 I have attended five sessions of the ECFR (2002, 2003, 2004, 2005 and 2006) as a part of my research, and have been witness to these efforts.

23 Final statements are published at the Council's website www.e-cfr.org.

24 Personal communication with Ounis Guergah, member of the Council and chair of the Dar al-fatwa (Fatwa House) in Paris, France, May 2008. The term '*fatwa*' is not only used when it addresses specific questions and answers to them, in the introduction to the book *Islamic Legal Interpretation* a usage specific to Central Asia and India is mentioned, where '… a work was characterized as a "*fatwa*" collection if it concentrated on issues that arise in practice' (Masud 1996:15).

with reading of the final statement, where the two types of legal opinions, *fatwas* and resolutions (*qararat*) are included.

The existence of *fatwas* is dependent upon the public and dissemination becomes a central issue for the *mufti* or body of *muftis* who have issued the responses. The *fatwas* and resolutions of the Council are disseminated through different channels. They are included in the final statements from each session of the Council, and in the *Scientific Review of the European Council for Fatwa and Research* (*al-Majalla al-'ilmiyya*) (printed in Lebanon), published once a year. *Fatwas* and resolutions from the first seven sessions of the Council are also published as a two-part *fatwa* collection.[25] The *fatwas* are also published on the European Council for *Fatwa* and Research website. Some of them can also be found on Islamonline.net, where they are often included as part of *fatwas* on the same topic.[26] The target of the *fatwas* and resolutions is the 'Muslim reader', according to Caeiro, the paradigmatic figure of the public imagined by the Council – an individual who engages in silent and solitary practice and finds a measure of rational interest and/or spiritual comfort in the *mufti's* responses to the dilemmas faced by fellow Muslims residing in Europe (Caeiro 2010:439). Furthermore Caeiro claims that:

> This public appears as a distinctively transnational space, crucially enabled by the proliferation of modern mass media. Although its international orientation draws in part on an older social imagery – the 'global space of normative reference and debate' that has characterized Muslim *fiqh* through the ages – the public at hand functions through a reflexive discourse that arguably goes beyond the expectations underlying traditional *fatwa*-giving (Caeiro 2010:483).

The Legal Heritage of the European Council for *Fatwa* and Research: An Historical Overview

The legal heritage for the *fatwa* activity in the Council as well as the importance given to women's issues can be traced back to Cairo, harking back to the end of the nineteenth century. In 1899 the Egyptian jurist, Qasim Amin, published a small book, *Tahrir al-mar'a* ('The Liberation of Women') – a document on the history of Egyptian feminism. According to Samiha Sidhom Peterson, who translated the book into English, it 'continues to be a source of controversy and debate in the Arab world'. It is also analyzed in academic literature.[27]

25 The first collection has been translated into French. The second collection was translated, but was never published.

26 *Fatwas* on IslamOnline.net could safely be described as edited *fatwas*, according to a certain template developed by members of the *fatwa* team at IslamOnline.net (visit to the *fatwa* desk at IOL in Cairo, March 2007).

27 See, for example, Leila Ahmed's *Women and Gender in Islam* (1993).

Amin's book could be seen as a part of a nationalist project. (Egypt was at the time both under Ottoman domination and threatened by Western colonialism.) The premise of his book was that the liberation of women was a prerequisite for the liberation of Egyptian society from its inferior position. Amin's requests for reform are as follows: mandatory education for girls, at least up to elementary level; abolishing face covering and segregation; giving women the right to decide for themselves with regard to marriage; prohibiting polygamy; and delegating *talaq* (the man's unilateral right to repudiation) to the court. These issues were linked to the liberation of the Muslim woman: to be counted as an equal human being, born with the same faculties and entitled to the same rights as the male. This implied a new interpretation of *Shari'a* and reform of the woman's legal status in family law. Amin also criticized the use of *taqlid* (imitation) as an argument for rejecting the demand for reforms. Improving women's conditions, Amin claimed, was in the interests of the whole Egyptian society. Amin was heavily criticised, not least due to his opinion on *hijab*, but the agenda was set with regard to women's issues, and the Islamic debate has been turning around this agenda since then.

Muhammad Abduh – The Founder of Modern Salafiyya

Qasim Amin's arguments for promoting women's liberation were based on the Egyptian state *mufti* Muhammad Abduh's project of reform, *tajdid*.[28] Abduh is regarded as the architect of Islamic modernism, '... the reform of Islamic tradition through emphasis on the *Qur'an* and *Sunnah* to meet the demands of modern society, including its institutions and technology ...'[29] Abduh made a distinction between *'ibadat* (worship) and *mu'amalat* (social relations and transactions), which in turn made *ijtihad* (independent reasoning) both legitimate and necessary to find 'new answers to new questions'. With regard to methodology of interpretation,

28 Here: 'The attempt by Islamic modernizers and Salafiyya advocates to introduce more Islamic influences into the lives of Muslims who have been subject to Western currents of thought and practice particularly in the wake of the Napoleonic invasion of Egypt. [...] A distinction should be made here between the strict and orthodox Salafiyah trend and the reformist trend championed by people such as Muhammad Abduh'. 'Revival and renewal' in the *Oxford Encyclopedia of the Modern Islamic World* (Esposito 1995, 3:431).

The term 'modernism' is often used interchangeably with '*salafiya*'. The word *salafiya* is derived from the Arabic root *salaf*, to 'precede'. In Arabic lexicons, the *salaf* are the virtuous forefathers (*al-salaf al-salih*), and the *salafi* is the one who draws on the *Qur'an* and *sunna* as the only sources for religious rulings. Most Muslim scholars agree that the *salaf* comprise the first three generations of Muslims. In addition, other prominent scholars and independent figures are recognized as *salaf*. Relevant for our purpose is Abu Hamid al-Ghazali, Ibn Taymiyya, and Ibn Qayyim al-Jawsiyya, since they serve as references for the actors in the field of 'Islam and women' in today's Europe.

29 Modernism. *The Oxford Dictionary of Islam* (Esposito 2003:204f).

Abduh adopted two concepts in order to legitimate change: *maslaha 'amma* (public interest) and *talfiq* ('piecing together'). He defined *maslaha 'amma* as 'a jurist using his own reason ... [to] interpret the law in the light of public interest' (Esposito in Laading 1986:58) – with regard to *mu'amalat* and in cases where there are no explicit texts covering the matter. The concept of *talfiq* he defined as 'not simply borrowing of a specific point from some other code, but a systematic comparison of all four *madhahib*, schools, and even of the doctrines of the independent jurists who accepted none of them, with a view to producing a "synthesis" which could combine the good points of all' (Hourani 1987:152). Once the legitimacy of *ijtihad,* as well as of the use of the concepts of *maslaha* and *talfiq*, is granted, it is possible to implement and justify law reforms which could meet the changing needs of the society (Laading 1986:59).

The teaching of the *Salafiya* was further developed and put into writing by Muhammad Rashid Rida,[30] and continued to inspire later generations of Muslim activists. In the 1930s, new Islamic movements emerged sharing many of the ideas of the *Salafiya.* The most influential were the Muslim Brothers in Egypt and *Jama'at-i Islami* in Pakistan. They did not attempt to build on the intellectual venture the modern *Salafiya* had undertaken in legal, political and educational reform. '[... Instead] these movements focused on reforming the morality and beliefs of the Muslim individual ...' (Esposito 1995, 3:467). *Khuluq al-muslim* ('A Muslim's Character'), authored by Muhammad al-Ghazali (1917–2000) would illustrate this point quite well.[31]

Muhammad al-Ghazali

Muhammad al-Ghazali may be seen as a continuation of scholars such as Muhammad Abduh and Muhammad Rashid Rida. He developed methodological principles related to the interpretation of Islamic law further, for example, he criticized traditional scholars who insisted on a literal interpretation of *hadith.* This argument is elaborated in perhaps his most famous book, *al-Sunna al-nabawiyya bayna ahl al-fiqh wa ahl al-hadith* ('The Prophet's *sunna* between the people of *fiqh* and the people of *hadith*'), which presents his thoughts and ideas (Izzi Dien 2004:131). According to Izzi Dien, al-Ghazali's methodology was particularly important with regard to reforming the social position of women. In his book he rejects the claim that a woman's blood money or indemnity for bodily injury (*diya*) should be only half a man's, he disputes the practice of face covering, providing a new definition for female garb (*al-sufur al-mubah*), and he supports female education and employment as well as women's rights to leadership and managerial posts and the public office as governor (Izzi Dien 2004:131f). Al-Ghazali considered the objectives and means in order to understand Islamic law

30 In his magazine *al-Manar.*

31 The book is translated into English and is widely distributed in the West by International Islamic Federation of Student Organizations (IIFSO).

properly, and he did not preclude the experience of non-Muslim societies as inspiration for Muslim societies (Esposito 1995, 2:64). We see that some of the cases dealt with by Muhammad al-Ghazali add to the field of women's issues initiated by Qasim Amin and the range of methodological tools of the modernists is further broadened.

What then is the thread that leads us to the Islamic discourse on women in Western Europe? Let us turn to Yusuf al-Qaradawi, a great admirer of al-Ghazali.

Yusuf al-Qaradawi (1926–)

The year is 1960 and a book titled *al-Halal wal-haram fil-islam* ('The permitted and the prohibited in Islam') is published. The book is the result of a request to Qaradawi by the Institute of Islamic Culture of al-Azhar to:

> ... participate in an academic project of writing easily understandable books or pamphlets which, when translated into the English language, would introduce Islam and its teachings to Europe and America, educating the Muslims who reside there and attracting the non-Muslims toward Islam [...] since many Muslims in Europe and America have very little knowledge of Islam ...[32]

The reason for the project was questions coming from Muslims in the West, through the Egyptian embassies. At al-Azhar it was considered that the Muslims in the West were in need of knowledge and guidance on how to practise Islam in Western non-Muslim countries.

In the introduction, Qaradawi clearly presents his principles and methodology: The middle way *(wasatiyya)* between those 'who have been blinded by the Western civilisation' and those who have 'fixed opinions concerning questions about the *halal* and the *haram*' tending to forget the principle that things Allah has created are permissible except what is prohibited by 'a sound *nass* [text]' (al-Qaradawi 1960:3). Qaradawi's concept of *wasatiyya* is based upon the principle of 'application of law and understanding Islam' (Izzi Dien 2004:133).

According to Izzi Dien many of the issues raised by Muhammad al-Ghazali were also raised by Yusuf al-Qaradawi, women's issues being one of them. In *al-Halal wal-haram* almost one third is dedicated to *halal* and *haram* in marriage and family life, focusing directly or indirectly on women's issues. With regard to the question of *hijab*, he continues the argument of al-Ghazali as well as presenting 'new' issues: One of the examples discussed in the book, namely plucking eyebrows, has become a symbolic reference of morality of Muslim women in the West. In the chapter mentioned we can also see the 'image of the virtuous woman' reflected, as constructed by the Islamists in Egypt. The image implies the use of the *hijab* in order to facilitate female participation; the sexual division of labour

32 Translation of the author's introduction to the Arabic Edition in 1960, as presented by al-Birr Foundation's English edition of *al-Halal wal-haram fil-islam.*

and public space; idealized female roles in correspondence with a woman's life cycle; and expressed core notions of femininity (Zuhur 1992:87).

Qaradawi's effort resulted in a *fiqh* book in the language of *fatwa*.[33] It has become a classical guide for individual morality and it laid the base for his fame worldwide, but it was only the beginning.[34] Muslims in the West have obviously been a main concern in his life and work for almost five decades. In his book *Fi fiqh al-aqalliyat al-muslima,* Qaradawi describes his engagement with questions related to Muslims in the West. After the *al-Halal wal-haram* he visited Europe as well as the United States of America and included *fatwas* aimed at Muslims in the West in his four-volume *Fatwas mu'asira* ('Contemporary *fatwas*'), which is partly a result of his television programme from a Qatari channel. His engagement in the media also includes his own programme from an Abu Dhabi channel, as well as the more famous *al-Jazeera* (al-Qaradawi 2001:7). During his programme, *Shari'a wal-hayya*, which is shown once a week from *al-Jazeera*, Muslims in the West are given plenty of opportunities to ask questions.[35] The Norwegian religious historian, Anne Sofie Roald, describes Yusuf al-Qaradawi's approach to *fiqh* questions as follows:

> The socio-political message conveyed by al-Qaradawi in his programme [...] is to a great extent built on a pragmatic approach. Instead of looking at matters from an ideal point of view, al-Qaradawi tries to find the best solution to the problem. What seems obvious is that his perspective coincides with Western democratic ideals and human rights' ideas such as [...] women's right to education even at the cost of not wearing headscarves, a matter he regards as a fundamental Islamic principle (Roald 2001:43).

Yusuf al-Qaradawi also has his own website (www.qaradawi.net) and is one of the founders behind the website www.IslamOnline.net (referred to by Ali in this book) which has focused on minority issues and offered the visitor an archive of *fatwas*, some of them with reference to *fatwas* from the European Council for *Fatwa* and Research. After an editorial change in 2010 this archive is not longer available.

---

33 Wael Hallaq describes the structure of a *fiqh* book as consisting of four major fields: 'rituals, sales, marriage and injuries'. Each of these terms stands for a variety of subjects that belongs to a single quarter. Treaties on *fiqh* tend to differ from each other, depending on school affiliation, or in diachronic developments within one and the same school (Hallaq 2009:551f). Al-Qaradawi's book is divided into four parts and the topics dealt with are, according to the author himself, the result of the task he was given from al-Azhar in writing a book aimed at Muslims in the West.

34 The book is even sold in Iran, where the majority are Shia Muslims. I came across the book in the Islamic propaganda bookshop in Tehran when I visited Iran in 2002.

35 According to Anne Sofie Roald, calls from Western countries are given priority over calls from Arab countries. *Encounters* 7:1 (2001:39).

Fiqh al-aqalliyat

Fiqh al-aqalliyat is, according to the Islamic legal scholar, Muhammad Khalid Masud, a fast growing new subject that will impact quite significantly on the future of Muslims living in the West.[36] Core questions are at stake. Muslim minorities are considered to be an integral part of the Muslim *umma* and most Muslims insist that they should be governed by Islamic law. Living outside the *dar al-islam* is considered by many Muslim scholars as temporary. In the meantime they should protect their religious and cultural identity.[37] Masud comments on this position as follows: These jurists are obviously restrained by the methodology as well as the worldview of the old laws; to the extent that they still use the term 'enemy countries' for the abode of the Muslim minorities.[38] Other Muslim scholars are approaching the challenges of Muslim minorities in the West in terms of expediency, considering it acceptable for Muslims who have come to the West, to stay. This includes another categorization of the world. Taha Jabir al-Alwani claims that any country is *dar al-islam* by virtue of Muslims having freedom to practise their religion. Furthermore relations should be based upon the golden rule, *fiqh al-aqalliyat*, presented as a *fiqh* of co-existence (al-Alwani 2003:26).[39] The main basis of the European Council for *Fatwa* and Research's understanding of the concept of *fiqh al-aqalliyat* is formulated by Yusuf al-Qaradawi, the chair of the Council, in his book *Fiqh al-aqalliyat*, published in 2001. The book is divided into two parts: the first part presents the theory while the second part consists of cases where this theory is applied.

Qaradawi's starting point is that Muslims in the West are finding themselves in a new situation and facing challenges due to living in societies with non-Muslim legislations, where nothing automatically supports the individual with regard to socialization into Islamic practice. Many of these challenges are related to *fiqh*.[40]

---

36 www.maruf.org/frames/Articles/article-10.htm (accessed on 1 December 2008).

37 Masud refers to *Muslim Minorities, Fatwa regarding Muslims as Minorities* by the late Saudi Shaykh Ibn Baz and Shaykh Uthaymeen, to illustrate this position.

38 www.maruf.org/frames/Articles/article-10.htm (accessed on 1 December 2008).

39 Andre March argues that present in many contemporary works on the 'jurisprudence of Muslim minorities' is an attempt to provide an Islamic foundation for a relatively thick and rich relationship of moral obligation and solidarity with non-Muslims (March 2009, 16, 1:34).

40 Some of the questions al-Qaradawi poses could give an impression of where he considers the shoe pinches: What is the norm for a Muslim settling down permanently in a non-Muslim land if he fears for his and his children's religion? What about citizenship? What is the norm with regard to jelly, cheese and meat? What is the norm regarding working in a restaurant where pork and alcohol are served? What is the norm if a Muslim is invited to a wedding where pork and alcohol are served? What is the norm with regard to buying a house with an ordinary bank mortgage? (2001:25–28).

With regard to women's questions, al-Qaradawi presents the following questions:[41] What is the status of a civil conducted marriage in Islam? What about divorce granted by a non-Muslim judge? What is the norm with regard to marrying a second wife in a non-registered marriage when the national legislation does not permit more than one spouse? Which rights does the second wife have in case of conflict? And is an *imam* in an Islamic centre permitted to marry the man to a second wife under these conditions? What about entering into marriage without a guardian? What is the norm of a married woman converting to Islam and her husband does not? Should she divorce her husband? (al-Qaradawi 2001:27).

Fiqh al-aqalliyat, according to al-Qaradawi, looks at the Islamic heritage with one eye and the social and cultural reality with the other. It binds together Islam's global character with different social realities, represents a balance between detailed *Shari'a* texts and overall objectives (*maqasid al-shari'a*), it refers the detailed norms back to sources in light of a *fiqh* of priorities, it changes according to custom, *'urf* – all the while keeping an Islamic identity while being integrated into the majority society (al-Qaradawi 2001:35ff). The basis of this *fiqh* is to be 'correct', *ijtihad*. Al-Qaradawi presents it technically as a set of Islamic norms to be eclectically reconstructed from the traditional *fiqh* heritage (*ijtihad intiqa'i*) or discovered through new interpretative efforts (*ijtihad insha'i*), which he considers to be most important, whereupon he presents and argues for the use of concepts and methodology that should be applied when doing independent reasoning (*ijtihad*).[42] The recognition of the orthodoxy of the norm expressed is not only due to the actual opinion expressed in the *fatwa* but is also dependent upon recognition of the methodology and concepts applied. 'In traditional Islamic law it was the use of recognized juristic methods of interpretation that guaranteed the orthodoxy of results …' (Meyer 1990:194).

Al-Qaradawi claims this type of *ijtihad* is a part of the renewal (*tajdid*) that the Prophet is supposed to have said will come in every century, hence claiming recognition of *fiqh al-aqalliyat* as an integrated part of the *fiqh* tradition. This enterprise, however, is considered to be performed by a collective body, which then has the central role of being a *mujaddid* in this century.[43] Al-Qaradawi's book therefore seems to have a double agenda: being a part of the Islamic scholars'

---

41 Two of these questions will be presented later in this chapter because they have been responded to by the Council.

42 The sources for *ijtihad* are the *Qu'ran*, the Prophet's *sunna* (example), *ijma'* (consensus) which are agreed upon by the majority of Muslim scholars. Al-Qaradawi then adds what he calls controversial sources, such as public interest (*maslaha mursala*), juristic preference, 'blocking the means to evil' (*sadd al-dhar'i*), tradition or custom (*'urf*), 'revealed laws preceding the *Shari'a* of Islam' (*shar'u min qablina*), *fatwas* of Companions of the Prophet (*fatwas sahabi*) (al-Qaradawi 2001:39). The sources mentioned are almost identical to the sources mentioned in the statutes of the Council. However the Council has also included presumption of continuity (*istishab*) (*Fatwas of European Council for Fatwa and Research*: 3).

43 'Renewal' is, according to the *Oxford Dictionary of Islam*, typically used in the context of modern Islamic movements, although it has pre-modern roots. Pre-modern renewal was usually associated with a designated renewer (*mujaddid*) who, according to

debate, arguing for authority 'among equals', as well as applying his way of reasoning to disclose norms in the examples presented in the second part of the book.[44]

This double target strategy is also reflected in the European Council for *Fatwa* and Research. Challenges related to being a Muslim minority in the West have been debated and dealt with, and published in the Council's scientific review,[45] which obviously has *fiqh* specialists with knowledge of Arabic as a target group, while two collections of *fatwas* have been published with an obviously more general readership in mind.[46]

Some *Fatwas* from the European Council for *Fatwa* and Research

Fatwas and resolutions on women's issues form a considerable proportion of the total number of answers and resolutions issued by the Council. The reason for this is two-fold. Firstly, a much higher percentage of women contact the Council than men.[47] Secondly, members of the Council consider women's issues to be *the* most important issue with regard to Islamic identity.[48] According to Alexandre Caeiro, the Muslim woman's body functions as a barometer of people's 'Islamicness' (*islamité*) (Caeiro 2002:118). Furthermore it serves as a symbol of the border to an image of the non-Muslim West. Kate Zebiri explains it in the following way:

> It is not hard to ascertain the reason for this; on the one hand, it is the area in which Muslims have felt themselves most under attack, and on the other, it represents a sort of last bastion of Islamic law and civilization. Many Muslims see the woman as the repository of Islamic Culture and values, and family law or personal status is the area of traditional Islamic law which has been least eroded in modern times (Zebiri 1993:61).

---

hadith, would come in the beginning of each century to renew Muslim faith and practice (Esposito 2003:265).

44 *Fiqh al-aqalliyat* has been translated from Arabic into English and published with the title *Fiqh of Muslim Minorities. Contentious Issues and Recommended Solutions.* Interestingly, the first part, which deals with the theory of *fiqh al-aqaliyyat*, has been translated in an abridged version, while the second part is presented in full text. It could mean that the English version targets ordinary Muslims in the West, while the specialized legal arguments are reserved for the legal scholars who all are fluent in Arabic. But of course, this is speculation from my side.

45 See, for example, *al-Majalla al-'ilmiyya lil-majlis al-urubi lil-ifta' wal-buhuth* 1:17–80, and 3:67–136.

46 The collections of *fatwas* have been translated into English and French. Only the first of the two has been published in French.

47 In interviews I had with members of the Council, I was informed that 70 per cent of the petitioners are women.

48 Conversation with a number of members of the Council.

The *fatwas* and resolutions cover various topics, both legal and non-legal in a Western legal sense. Some of the following questions illustrate this point: What is the ruling of Islam on a man attending his wife's delivery of a baby? (Yes). What is the ruling of the *Shari'a* regarding what is called a marriage of convenience? (Not permitted). May a newly-wed man divorce his wife if he discovers that she had lost her hymen? (No). Can a husband prevent his wife from attending Islamic women's gatherings? (No).

Three *fatwas* will be presented below. They have been chosen to show different aspects of transnational Islam. The texts are unabridged, to show the reader the format, argumentation and style of language, hence opening the door to a world view of Islamic reference and debate.

Example 1:

> Question:
>
> If a woman wanted to cut her hair, should she seek the permission of the husband?[49]
>
> Answer:
>
> There are types of hair trimming which the woman does from time to time and which a husband may not even notice due to the very slight alteration being made. Women usually do this so that their hair does not become as lengthy as to become difficult to manage. This form of hair shortening does not usually require the permission of the husband. However there are forms of hair shortening and alteration, which completely change the appearance of the woman, which may surprise the husband if he was not consulted. This form of alteration requires the agreement of the husband and wife so that their relationship is not affected by this radical change in the woman's appearance. Due to the fact that a Muslim woman does not show her hair in public nor in front of foreign (*sic!*) men, it becomes true that the husband has the foremost right to enjoy his wife's hair. A wise woman would make sure to pursue all means of maintaining love and affection between herself and her husband, ultimately leading to good Muslim households becoming the real basis of good Muslim societies.

Example 2:

> Ruling on a divorce issued by a non-Muslim judge.[50]

49 *Fatwas of European Council for Fatwa and Research*: 62.
50 *Fatwas of European Council for Fatwa and Research*: 145.

Resolution:

The principle is that a Muslim only resorts to a Muslim judge or any suitable deputy in the event of a conflict. However, and due to the absence of an Islamic judicial system in non-Muslim countries, it is imperative that a Muslim who conducted his marriage by virtue of those countries' respective laws, complies with the rulings of a non-Muslim judge in the event of divorce. Since the laws were accepted as governing the marriage contract, then it is as though one has implicitly accepted all consequences, including that the marriage may not be terminated without the consent of a judge. This case is similar to that in which the husband gives the authority to the judge to do so, even if he did it implicitly, and which is considered acceptable by the vast majority of scholars. The juristic principle applicable in this case is that whatever is normal practice is similar to a contractual agreement. Also implementing the rulings of a non-Muslim judiciary is an acceptable matter, as it falls under the bringing about what is considered to be of interest and to deter what is considered to be of harm and may cause chaos, as stipulated by more than one of the most prominent Islamic scholars, such as Al-'Izz ibn 'Abdul Salam, Ibn Taymiyah and al-Shatibi.

Example 3:

A woman embraces Islam and her husband does not.[51]

Resolution:

On this issue, the Council issued the following:

Having considered the numerous papers and studies submitted for its attention over three consecutive sessions, and which carried a variety of perspectives and opinions all dealing with this problem in detail and length, observing the objectives of *Sharia* and relating those to principles of *Fiqh*. The Council also recognises and acknowledges the conditions in which the new Muslim sisters in the West find themselves when their husbands choose to remain on their religion.

The Council affirms and repeats that it is forbidden for a Muslim female to establish marriage to a non-Muslim male. This has been an issue of consensus throughout the history of this nation. However, in the case of marriage being established prior to the female entering Islam, the Council has decided the following:

First: If both husband and wife revert to Islam and there is no *Sharia* objection to their marriage in the first place, such as particular blood relations or relations

51 http://www.e-cfr.org/en/index.php?ArticleID=281.

established as a result of breast-feeding, which deems the very establishment of marriage unlawful, the marriage shall be deemed valid and correct.

Second: If the husband reverts to Islam alone, and no objection to the establishment of marriage exists and the woman is a Jew or a Christian, then the marriage shall be deemed valid and correct.

Third: If the wife reverts to Islam and her husband remains on his religion, the Council sees the following:

One) If her reversion to Islam occurred and the marriage is yet to be consummated, then they must immediately separate.

Two) If her reversion to Islam occurred after the consummation of marriage, and the husband also embraced Islam before the expiry of her period of waiting, then the marriage is deemed valid and correct.

Three) If her reversion to Islam occurred after the consummation of marriage, and the period of waiting expired, she is allowed to wait for him to embrace Islam even if that period was a lengthy one. Once he does so and reverts to Islam, then their marriage is deemed valid and correct.

Four) If the wife chose to marry another man after the expiration of the period of waiting, she must first request a dissolution of marriage through legal channels.

Fourth: According to the four main schools of jurisprudence, it is forbidden for the wife to remain with her husband, or indeed to allow him conjugal rights, once her period of waiting has expired. However, some scholars see that it is for her to remain with him, allowing him and enjoying full conjugal rights, if he does not prevent her from exercising her religion and she has hope in him reverting in Islam. The reason for this is for women not to reject entering into Islam if they realise that they are to separate from their husbands and desert their families by doing so. Those scholars based their view upon the ruling of Omar ibn Al-Khattab, may Allah be pleased with him, in the case of the woman from Al-Heera who reverted to Islam while her husband remained on his religion. According to the authentic narration of Yazeed ibn Abdullah Al-Khatmi, Omar ibn Al-Khattab gave the woman the choice: 'If she wishes to leave him, or if she wishes to stay with him'. These scholars also base their opinion upon the view of Ali ibn Abi Talib concerning the Christian woman who reverts to Islam and is married to a Christian or a Jew; that her husband is more deserving of his conjugal rights, as he has a contract. This is also an authentic narration. It is also known that Ibraheem Al-Nakha'i, Al-Shi'bi and Hammad ibn Abi Sulayman had the same views.

Discussion

According to *al-Mawsu'at al-fiqhiyya* ('Encyclopedia of *fiqh*') a *fatwa* clarifies the legal norm based upon proof. A *fatwa* can be very short: 'permitted' (*halal*) or 'prohibited' (*haram*). The *fatwas* presented here are longer, have a far more complex style of argumentation and could not be easily reduced to these two categories.[52] The language and style of argumentation used in the respective texts indicates the target audience, as well as focusing on the relation between the petitioner and the *mufti*. Each of the *fatwas* are, in one way or another, an example of transnational Islam.

According to Yusuf al-Qaradawi, the president of the Council, Muslims around the world have some common as well as specific local challenges (al-Qaradawi 2001:5). Cutting hair could safely be said to be a common human issue and this *fatwa* is not limited to Europe but could be issued anywhere. The question itself, however, clearly indicates a certain cultural perception of the relation between husband and wife that is of an origin other than Western Europe in the twenty-first century. This impression is strengthened through the advice given to the woman: 'A wise woman would make sure to pursue all means of maintaining love and affection between herself and her husband, ultimately leading to good Muslim households becoming the real basis of good Muslim societies'. Making the woman responsible for the happiness and stability of the family is a common topic in the Islamic apologetic literature. It is based upon the notion of the biological differences between men and women, with different sexualities. The woman has the responsibility of being a source of pleasure and joy for her husband. This notion of a 'virtuous Muslim woman' (mar'a *saliha*) which also implies wearing hijab, idealized woman's roles according to her life cycle and a certain type of femininity (Zuhur 1992:87), is similar to the female ideal in the West in the 1950s, linked to a certain type of gender relations.[53]

It is interesting that the argument is a purely personal opinion and not legal, presented as an expression of taste. The argument is emotional, playing on perceived women's experiences ('long hair that could be difficult to manage' and 'the husband not noticing ...'), as well as on her making the husband happy by covering her hair in public and letting him be the only one to enjoy her hair. By this intimacy established between the petitioner and the *mufti*, the *fatwa* is given. The authority behind the *fatwa* lies in the perceived understanding of the woman's experience. When the *mufti* clearly understands her situation – the husband has

52 This observation is also made by A. Caeiro (2002:79).

53 One example is Sanna Sarromaa, research fellow at Lillehammer University college, Norway, who is doing research on an agony aunt column in the women's magazine 'Det Nye' from 1958, 1968 and 1977, looking at young girls' roles, expectations and possibilities. In the 1950s the answers stated that men and women have different sexualities and that the woman has the responsibility, through her femininity, for the husband not being unfaithful (http://kilden.forskningsradet.no/c16880/artikkel/vis.html?tid=62029).

probably not – it is logical that the woman will accept the *mufti* as an authority. This is also due to the kindness that is indirectly shown to the woman, a traditional way Muslim scholars have of dealing with women, in a gentle and generous way, taking her emotions into consideration.[54]

The *fatwa* is clearly transnational with regard to topic and argumentation, as well as the image of the ideal Muslim woman and a certain type of gender relations, in the sense that it has crossed geographical boundaries and is presented as relevant for Muslims in Europe.

The second *fatwa* deals with divorce and has a very different style of argumentation. It contains layers of norms and *fatwas*. The basis is the concept of *talaq*, the husband's unilateral right to repudiation. It is a well-established principle in traditional Islamic jurisprudence that a Muslim only resorts to a Muslim judge, or any other suitable deputy, in the case of a conflict, in this case, divorce. The *fatwa* does not contradict this principle by limiting the *fatwa* text to dealing with civil marriage conducted in a Western country. In the text, civil marriage is considered to be valid, an opinion which in itself is the result of a resolution in the Council. Furthermore the question about accepting the law of the land when living in a country is dealt with. What is considered to be a normal practice is similar to a contractual agreement between the Muslim and the state, hence implying respect for the law.[55] To respect the law does not mean to pick and choose but to accept it all. The text is arguing for the divorce that has to be given by a non-Muslim judge in order to be valid because it is the law of the land. The question is sensitive. One may claim, on the basis of traditional Muslim jurisprudence, that divorce is a man's privilege and the woman's 'headache'.[56] To make the man accept and swallow this 'bitter pill', it refers to the majority of the scholars that accept that a man can give his authority to *talaq* to the judge.[57] The next argument, supporting the authority of the non-Muslim judge, is interesting. Implementing the rulings of a non-Muslim judge is accepted due to the public interest, a core objective of *Shari'a* (*maqsad al-shari'a*) (Masud 1995:viii). Obeying the law of the land has, according to this argument, become a part of *Shari'a*.

The *fatwa* is an example of the transnational flow of concepts and methodology, used by the *mufti* in an interpretational reasoning (*ijtihad*) to clarify a norm, which

54 I came across this ideal of Muslim manhood in my fieldwork as well as in interview situations with *muftis* in relation to my PhD dissertation.

55 The Council holds the position that settling down in a non-Muslim country is like a contract and following the law of the land becomes mandatory.

56 Mir Hosseini's film *Divorce Iranian Style* is one example. It describes the restrictions imposed upon women who want a divorce and how they are using the legal framework to find their way and obtain a divorce within a system that is clearly in men's favour. The divorce question is an important point on women's rights agendas and in the reforms of Muslim family laws.

57 As we have seen earlier in this chapter, this proposal was put forward by Muhammad Abduh in Qasim Amin's book *Tahrir al-mar'a* in 1899 as a part of a reform project to improve Muslim women's conditions.

clearly limits itself to Muslims in Europe in a local sense. The argument seems to be cautious and to clearly limit the validity of the *fatwa* to Muslims living as a minority in Western Europe, to not enter the jurisdiction of *fatwa* councils in the Muslim world. At the same time, the *fatwa* has a transnational character due to its crossing borders, on its way from the Council to the Muslims in each European country.

The third example is a resolution on a question that is considered to be most sensitive within traditional Islamic jurisprudence, namely a Muslim woman being married to a non-Muslim man, which is considered to be prohibited. This resolution is interesting in the way that it is the result of a question from a petitioner but acquires the status of a topic of research and papers in order to get to a resolution. Normally resolutions are not the result of one particular question. This could be related to the sensitivity of the question. The source for the resolution was a question from a woman who converted to Islam while her husband did not. The woman found herself in a situation where following traditional *Shari'a* would mean breaking up the family and letting her husband down. The woman was facing an ethical dilemma (Caeiro 2002:121).

The text of the resolution differs radically from the text of the first *fatwa* presented, firstly disclosing the legal argument in detail in addition to then describing the topic to have been dealt with thoroughly 'during three consecutive sessions', taking a number of perspectives into consideration as well as mentioning two legal terms, objectives of *Shari'a* (*maqasid al-shari'a*) and social and cultural reality (*waqi'*). All this is presented in the first short paragraph. It seems obvious that the target Muslim reader is the Islamic scholar and the detailed argument which is to follow serves to claim authority among the scholars. Firstly the Council declares itself part of the consensus of Islamic scholars who hold the opinion that it is forbidden for a Muslim female to establish a marriage to a non-Muslim male. Then a new element is introduced: what about marriage prior to Islam? Three scenarios are described: if they both convert to Islam, if just the husband converts and if just the wife converts. The interesting point in question is the third scenario, which is described in detail. The resolution presents different norms according to different situations. The relevant resolution in the case of the petitioner who caused this lengthy process of reflection by the Council is that '… she is allowed to wait for him to embrace Islam even if that period was a lengthy one'. This position is argued by the use of concepts and methodology described in the statutes of the Council.[58] The Council goes outside the abode of the four legal schools, using the legal aims of *Shari'a,* which includes the principle of the protection of religion ('if he does not prevent her from exercising her religion') at the top of its hierarchy, together with protection of life, private property, mind and offspring (Hallaq 2003:112). Then a missionary argument is included. Marriage and family before becoming a Muslim should not be a hindrance against converting to Islam. Two references are

58 Mentioned earlier in this chapter.

given to support the Council's position: Umar ibn al-Khattab and Ali ibn Ali Talib, two of the companions of the Prophet, declared to be a source for *ijtihad*.

This resolution has borrowed literally from the *fatwa* text of Qaradawi on the same question as presented in his book *Fiqh al-aqalliyat*. Caeiro ascribes this to the measure of Qaradawi's charisma as chairman of the Council. Qaradawi's text is longer and more detailed, and includes a subchapter on the permissibility of issuing a *fatwa* based upon the sayings of the companions and *tabi'un* (their successors). He also refers to the scholar Abdullah al-Judai, also a member of the Council, whose argument goes along the same lines as al-Qaradawi's argument.[59] This strengthens our assumption that the Islamic scholar is the target reader for the text. It is also worth mentioning that the woman who asked the question was happy about the resolution and, according to Caeiro, expressed her thanks to the Council (Caeiro 2002:124).

The concept of the *fiqh al-aqalliyat* framework is contested by traditional scholars belonging to the legal schools. It is defended by the members of the Council and was held up by a member of the Council as making this resolution possible. 'It could never have been given in a Muslim country'.[60] The decision made in the resolution was aimed only at Muslims in the West, but has been making a 'world tour' and ascribing the European Council for *Fatwa* and Research a name on an international level – for better or for worse.

Conclusion

Despite the ideal of Europe being a jurisdiction and the use of the *fiqh al-aqalliyat* concept to legitimize the European Council for *Fatwa* and Research aiming to be an authority for Muslims in Europe, the Council could clearly be distinguished by its transnational character. This goes for the legal history, members of the Council and their activities, their *fatwas* and resolutions and the way they are disseminated.

The concept of *fiqh al-aqalliyat* serves as the legitimacy of the European Council for *Fatwa* and Research versus other *fiqh* councils, in the competition for authority that takes place with regard to this 'new jurisdiction', and is used as a tool to include Europe as part of Islamic reference and debate – described by John Bowen (2004) as a neglected aspect of transnational Islam.

59 According to al-Qaradawi, Judai presented his argument on the topic as a paper for the Jordanian Council for *Fatwa* and Research. It seems that Judai's work could have been initiated by a question from Batool al-Toma, in charge of the New Muslim Project at the Islamic Foundation, Leicester, United Kingdom. In a conversation with her she informed me that, based upon experience with a number of converts, she had urged Judai to deal with this question (conversation with Batool al-Toma, Brussels, 1 November 2009).

60 Conversation with Ahmad Jaballah, Cairo, March 2007.

The *fatwas* presented in this chapter provide us with far more information than just knowledge about the particular norm. They give us an insight into the mental universe of the *muftis* and the elements they take into consideration when *fatwas* are given. Each *fatwa* contains a message. In the first *fatwa* the importance of the 'wise woman' is underlined, both as a model *of* and model *for* an ideal reality, as presented in the *fatwa* (Geertz 1993). She is thereby invited into a project that is greater than just making an agreement about cutting her hair. The second *fatwa* is that the religious specialist keeps his authority in relation to the common believer living in Europe, even when the *fatwa* states that the Muslim should obey the law of the land, even in a non-Muslim country. This is done by discarding detailed norms of practice in Muslim countries and by performing *ijtihad* in light of overall principles. The third *fatwa* represents reform, not only with regard to the answer but also with regard to the reasoning behind the *fatwa*. It could be characterized as a direct claim of authority over a new geographical area, as well as an argument for recognition by '*ulama*' in the Muslim world. This should be understood in the light of the importance of 'correct' use of method and concepts for the orthodoxy of the norms.

Meanwhile, Muslim women continue to face the dilemma of different expectations, based upon the two competing sets of norms, the notion of *qiwama* (guardianship) and complementarity with a focus on obedience and duties, and the equality–rights paradigm. The 'settling down' of a tradition in a new social and cultural context is a slow process. In this chapter the European Council for *Fatwa* and Research has been used as a case study illustrating some considerations in this process, or in other words 'the politics of *fatwas*' as a part of Islamic reference and debate.

References

Ahmed, L. 1992. *Women and Gender in Islam*. New Haven: Yale University Press.

al-Alwani, T.J. 2003. *Towards a Fiqh for Minorities. Some Basic Reflections.* London/Washington: The International Institute of Islamic Thought.

Amin, Q. 1992. *The Liberation of Women: A Document in the History of Egyptian Feminism.* Translated by Samiha Sidhom Peterson. Cairo: The American University Cairo Press.

bin Bayyah A. 2002. Muslims living in non-Muslim lands. Available at: http://www.witness-pioneer.org/vil/Articles/shariah/muslims_in_non_muslim_land.htm, accessed 10 December 2009.

Bowen, J.R. 2004. Beyond migration: Islam as a transnational public space. *Journal of Ethnic and Migration Studies* 30:5, 879–894.

Caeiro, A. 2002. *La Normativité Islamique á L'épreuve de l'Occident. Le Cas du Conceil Européen de la Fatwa et de la Recherché.* Paris: DEA, Ecole des Hautes Etudes en Sciences Sociales.

—— 2010. Interpellation the European Muslim Subject: The minority *fiqh* project and the making of an Islamic counterpublic. *Int. J. Middle East Studies* 42 (2010), 435–449.

Darsh, S. Undated. Muslims in the West: A *Fiqh* Seminar in France. Unpublished.

—— Esposito, J.L. 1995. *The Oxford Ecyclopedia of the Modern Islamic World.* Volumes 1–4. Oxford: Oxford University Press.

—— (ed.) 2003. *The Oxford Dictionary of Islam*. Oxford: Oxford University Press.

European Council for *Fatwa* and Research. 2010. *Fatwas of European Council for Fatwa and Research.* Cairo: Islamic Inc. Publishing and Distribution.

—— 2003. *al-Majalla al-'ilmiya lil-majlis al-urubi lil-ifta' wal-buhuth*. Dublin: European Council for *Fatwa* and Research Volume 1:2002, Volume 3.

Geertz, C. 1993. *The Interpretation of Cultures: Selected Essays*. London: Fontana.

Hallaq, W. 1994. From *fatwas* to *furu'*. *Islamic Law and Society* 1, 1:29–65.

—— 2003. *A History of Islamic Legal Theories: An Introduction to Sunni usul al-fiqh.* Cambridge: Cambridge University Press.

—— 2009. *Shari'a. Theory-Practice-Tranformations.* Cambridge: Cambridge University Press.

Hourani. 1987. *Arabic Thought in the Liberal Age 1798–1939*. Cambridge: Cambridge University Press.

Izzi Dien, M. 2004. *Islamic Law: From Historical Foundations to Contemporary Practice.* Edinburgh: Edinburgh University Press.

Laading, L. 1986. *Fra harem til kvinnebevegelse: En historisk oversikt over utviklingen i Egypt (1800–1924), med vekt på Qasim Amins diskusjon og nytolkning av kvinnens tradisjonelle status i islam.* Oslo: Magister artium dissertation, University of Oslo.

March, A.F. 2009. Sources of moral obligations to non-Muslims in the 'jurisprudence of Muslim minorities' (*Fiqh al-aqalliyat*) discourse. *Islamic Law and Society* 16, 1:34–94.

Masud, M.K. 1995. *Shatibi's Philosophy of Islamic Law.* Islamabad: International Islamic University, Islamic Research Institute.

Masud, M.K., Messick, B. and Powers D.S. (eds) 1996. *Islamic Legal Interpretation. Muftis and their Fatwas.* Cambridge, Massachusetts: Harvard University Press.

Meyer A.E. 1990 The *Shari'ah*: A methodology or a body of substantive rules, in *Islamic Law and Jurisprudence*, edited by N. Heer. Seattle: University of Washington Press, 177–198.

al-Mawsu'at al-fiqhiyya. Al-Kuwayt: Wizarat al-Awqaf wal-Shu'un al-Islamiyya, 1994.

al-Nawawi, Muhiyddin Abu Zakariya bin Sharaf. Undated. Adab al-fatwa wal-mufti wal-mustafti. *Kitab Majmu': Sharh al-Muhadhdhab lil-Shirazi.* Volume 1. Beirut: Dar Ihya al-Turath al-'Arabi.

al-Qaradawi, Y. 1960. *The Lawful and the Prohibited in Islam* (*al-Halal wal haram filislam*). London: al-Birr Foundation.
——2001. *Fi fiqh al-'aqalliyat al-muslima. Hayat al-muslimin wast al-mujtama'at al-ukhra.* ('On Muslim minority jurisprudence. The life of Muslims in other societies') Cairo: Dar al-Shuruq.
Roald, A.S. 2001. The wise men: Democratization and gender equalization in the Islamic message: Yusuf al-Qaradawi and Ahmad al-Kubaisi on the Air. *Encounters* 7(1), 29–55.
Skovgaard-Petersen, J. 1997. *Defining Islam for the Egyptian State: Muftis and Fatwas of the Dar al-Ifta.* Leiden: Brill.
Zebiri, K. 1993. *Mahmud Shaltut and Islamic Modernism.* Oxford: Clarendon Press.
Zuhur, S. 1992. *Revealing Reveiling: Islamist Gender Ideology in Contemporary Egypt.* Albany: State University of New York Press.

Personal Communications

Ahmad Jaballah, Cairo, March 2007.
Ounis Guergah, Paris, May 2008.
Batool al-Toma, Brussels, 1 November 2009.

Chapter 7

Cultural Translations and Legal Conflict: Muslim Women and the *Shari'a* Councils in Britain

Samia Bano

Introduction

In November 2009 a new crisis concerning the visible presence of Muslims in Europe erupted when an estimated 57.5 per cent of Swiss voters voted in favour of a ban on building minarets in Switzerland.[1] This result was all the more remarkable considering that Switzerland currently has only four minarets and Swiss Muslims are described as being extremely well integrated into Swiss society. Although this result itself produced widespread condemnation both from religious and secular authorities (including the Vatican and various human rights organizations) it also reflects the continuing and strained relationship in Western European societies over the management of ethnic diversity and the regulation of religious communities. Over the past decade in particular, Muslim claims over the recognition and accommodation of faith-based practices has been characterized by a perception of a 'cultural clash' whereby demands from Western Muslims are deemed to encroach on civic society which is characterized by the values of secularism, human rights and equality. As Levey (2009:3) points out, this raises a number of pressing questions: How should liberal democracies respond to their growing Muslim communities? What is the appropriate liberal response to a girl wearing a face veil to a French school, to an Islamic organization requesting public funding in the United Kingdom or to a request that images of the Prophet Muhammad not be published in newspapers? Should these cases be seen as instances of 'multiculturalism' and 'diversity' which contemporary liberalism should defend and celebrate? Or are they rather examples of a dangerously theocratic impulse, which threatens the social peace and the liberal separation of religion and the state? Should places like France, Germany and the United Kingdom adjust their legal codes to accommodate a religious tradition that was not party to the original peace compacts and that may not accept some of the limiting terms of modern liberalism? Such questions not only capture perfectly the polemical nature of

1 See, 'Swiss voters back ban on minarets', BBC News, Sunday 29 November 2009. A copy of this report can be accessed at www.news.bbc/minarets.

debates surrounding the presence of Muslims in Europe but raise a set of interesting issues regarding the conflicts generated by the possible recognition of rights of minority religious groups.

Against this backdrop we now have an emerging body of scholarship which seeks to better understand the relationship between religion and multicultural citizenship while reconceptualizing our understanding of notions of equality, religious belief and state law relations. For example, in Britain, scholars (see Sayyid 2006, Modood 2007, 2009, Malik 2006) document and explore the tensions inherent in much of Western liberal political theory on the normative values that underpin the liberal political state, with the social and legal regulation of minority communities and conflicts generated by claims for the recognition of cultural and religious practices. For many it seems blindingly obvious that Western states are simply unable to cope with the pluralism generated by the diversity of migration patterns and the emergence of plural and heterogeneous multicultural societies.[2]

This chapter draws on this scholarship to consider debates on the practice of Muslim family law in Britain and traces the emergence of *Shari'a* councils as alternative dispute resolution mechanisms. The purpose of this chapter is to tease out some of the complexities to better understand the dialogical relations between Muslim communities and state law processes and to consider whether such processes produce specific outcomes for Muslim women in Britain, as primary users of *Shari'a* councils. The chapter begins with an analysis of the debates concerning the emergence of 'multicultural legalism' in English law. It considers whether the demands for 'justice-sensitive' outcomes have potentially led to conflictual situations with Muslim communities living in Britain. It goes on to question whether dominant discourses of formal law-making and the emergence of multicultural legal environments are based on the embodiment of certain prescribed values of 'otherness' and 'illiberal practices' which lead to the framing of Muslim identities in Britain. The second part of the chapter draws on empirical fieldwork to discuss one particular issue in Britain: the emergence of Muslim family law frameworks to resolve matrimonial disputes for Muslims. In particular, I specifically draw upon the experiences of a group of Muslim women using *Shari'a* councils to resolve matrimonial disputes in order to better understand how such socio-legal processes take shape.

2 In Britain, for example, efforts to ensure the successful integration of minority groups into mainstream society (described more generally as multiculturalism) have been accompanied by ill-defined conceptions of what is understood as British identity, most vividly illustrated by the various commissions on integration and citizenship tests introduced to define national identity. Yet it remains unclear what values nationality should include (see Jacobson 1997).

Multicultural Legalism

In recent debates on multiculturalism in Britain, the relationship between minority ethnic groups and the responsibility of the state to ensure the successful integration of all ethnic groups into mainstream society has come under sustained attack from all sides of the political spectrum (Goodhart 2004). The multicultural project has largely been articulated around questions of identity and the forging of a national British identity. Yet both the meanings and representations of these identities have been appropriated and contested by the various groups in question. In her work Avtah Brah has traced the emergence of an Asian group identity not as 'a singular but rather a multi-faceted and context-specific construct' (2005:60). This identity fractures along many lines – notwithstanding religion, caste and language differences. Thus the focus on new ethnicities and cultural hybrid identities shifts the focus from all previous dominant categories of identity such as 'Black' or 'Asian' to new identities and their manufacture and communication provides the emphasis on new forms of political agency (Hall 1997). Tariq Modood takes this up and documents one such fracture in Britain – the development and emergence of a specific Muslim identity in the United Kingdom and Europe – and in doing so challenges the commonly held idea that Muslims more than other groups are demanding rights that are 'particularly intractable and uncooperative' (2009:166). Modood argues that one way of better understanding this renewed assertion of a religious identity is to understand the emergence of a Muslim political agency which allows it to be reconceptualized in the same way as race and gender equality debates.

Indeed the diversity of religious belief systems in Britain and in many other European states has long raised critical questions regarding the limits of accommodating diverse religious practices in the public spheres and the extent to which state and religion should be separated and, if so, in whose interests this separation is best served? Levey points out that Western democracies today are being challenged by religion along three intersecting fault-lines namely, 'religion–politics, religion–multiculturalism and Islam/Muslims–multiculturalism' (2009:3). The rights of citizens as members of a wider social and political community are realized via a relationship with the state – which endows us with a legal status. However, as individuals, as Charles Taylor points out, our identities and conceptions of ourselves as free and individual beings are also and most importantly perhaps forged as part of a dialogical process with ourselves and others, using certain given 'cultural scripts' (Taylor 1994:25). In this way culture becomes an important part of us all and reflects how we see the world, how we participate and how we evaluate it for ourselves. Ayelet Shachar (1999) points out that this has led to extensive discussions on the type of multicultural citizenship model adopted in Western democratic societies and the ability to deal with the complexities of culturally diverse communities, 'The multicultural understanding of citizenship therefore departs from the perception of all citizens as individuals who are merely members of a larger political community, and instead views them as *simultaneously* having equal rights as individuals and differentiated rights as members of identity groups' (1999:89). The establishment of the multicultural citizenship model takes shape in the sphere of legal relations where a legal rationale is worked out by state law processes which aim to protect the rights of minority communities without violating human rights norms.

The transnational nature of migration has led to much discussion on the plurality of legal systems in Europe (see von Benda-Beckmann *et al.* 2005). There are various explanations as to both the process and evidence of this change and its location within a transnational global context. As regards Western Europe, the focus has been on the impact that 'mass migrations from the South, particularly to Europe, but also to other parts of the global "North"' (Shah and Menski 2006:2) have had on the apparent uniformity of state law (see also Shah 2005, Estin 2008). There is now a strong body of scholarship which analyzes the ways in which migration has led directly to structural adjustments in various legal systems and, in particular, in the ways in which European legal systems have to grapple with a renewed assertion of religious identities. This literature is usually situated within the context of international law with the result that the legitimacy of domestic institutional structures is open to critique. The term 'multicultural legalism' pays particular attention to the 'constellations of plural legal orders' (von Benda-Beckmann *et al.* 2005:6) and local concerns. Yet the complex and variable configurations of law operating in a multicultural setting means that the term 'multicultural legalism' is itself open to criticism as it can ignore the interconnectedness to the nature of state law and civic relations and its power-brokers. As Mathias Roe points out, 'Only the state can decide whether and to what extent "foreign" law can be applied and foreign customs can be practised on its territory. Thus the legal system is not "multicultural" as far as it concerns the decisive exercise of legal power' (2006:57). In this way the emergence of multicultural legalism merely reinstates law in very specific liberal forms which continues to be based on a formal rational sense of law which neither accepts nor permits alternative interpretations. And at the heart of these discussions lie the fundamental questions regarding the historical legal development of legal theory and the significance and nature of law in an increasingly complex and global world. For legal anthropologists, discussion has focused on the different types of model legal systems that can be adopted in order to reflect the plural and culturally diverse nature of Western democratic societies (see Twining 2000).

The *effects* of a plural and multicultural society on the development of English law have been extensively documented over the past 20 years – by anthropologists, sociologists and, increasingly, legal scholars. The debate over the nature of this interaction is often characterized by a clash of a given set of values, identity and interest claims by state law and the demands of minority religious communities. The question therefore rests on the level and type of legal accommodation.

Ayelet Shachar discusses the normative arguments in support of both 'soft and hard multiculturalism' while discussing the extent to which cultural and religious norms and practices should be accommodated in the public spheres (Shachar 2005).

However there remains a deep mistrust and suspicion as to whether the liberal-democratic constitutions 'that guarantee freedoms of political communication and anti-paternalist decision-making' (Bader 2009:115) can withstand conditions of strong or deep cultural and religious pluralism.

The 'framing' of minority ethnic groups as 'the other' in conflicts seems to lie at the heart of policy and decision-making. What is clear however is that the fundamental questions regarding freedom of religion and the right to religious practice currently lie at the fore of contemporary debates on national and international security and human rights. As Samantha Knights points out:

> While the freedom privately to hold particular religious or philosophical views is unlikely to give rise to practical difficulties, the extent to which manifestations of religious belief are considered acceptable in society is a vexed issue. The diversity of views on substantive beliefs, on the position of religion in the public sphere, and the balance between the right to express and manifest religious views on the one hand, and the legitimate restrictions that may be imposed by the state on the other, all create considerable challenges for society today (Knights 2007:19).

Muslims and State/Law Relations

As discussed above the twin goals of promoting social cohesion and political solidarity underpin the values and ideals of Western liberal-democratic states and the crucial issue of cultural pluralism underpins discussions of legitimacy and justice. More recently, and in particular over the past two decades, political theorists have with some increased urgency and renewed vigour addressed these questions in relation to the conflicts generated by cultural and religious differences. Moreover the focus on Muslim communities and individual demands to practise the Muslim faith in the public sphere has taken centre stage. It seems that in most Western European states the emergence of 'difference-sensitive' laws and policies (Shabani 2007) have accompanied increasing concerns relating to the impact of cultural diversity and religious pluralism on the stability and cohesion of society as a whole. Critics point to the disintegration of political stability and solidarity within and between groups which leads to inconsistent understandings of justice, equality and stability. As Shabani (2007:1) points out, 'The classic challenge of how to operationalize the tension between the permanence of difference in politics and the goal of solidarity has become acute once again, but this time on a qualitatively new level; that of post-recognition'. So what is the role of law in this process of change, adaptation and recognition in relation to Muslim identities? Can law recognize and accommodate diversity while preserving individual autonomy, agency and identity?

Muslim Family Law Debates

In contrast to the early twentieth century, legal practitioners now readily recognize the plural systems of laws operating within different societies. Menski (2006) refers to the emergence of a 'plurality conscious jurisprudence' which draws upon concepts such as legal pluralism and hybrid legal cultures to better understand the limitations of single legal uniformity. It also raises questions of what we understand as the relationship between law and society. Menski argues that Western law must take account of inter-legality pluralism that needs to be conceived as 'a universal phenomenon covering both Western and non-Western societies, and at the same time appearing in not only the dual structure of state law and minor customary law but also the triple of customary law, national law and international law' (2006:83).

Legal pluralists often turn to the work of the Austrian jurist, Eugen Ehrlich, to better understand the relationship between law and society. Law, he argued, derived from social facts and thus could only be understood in relation to the historical and social context in which it was situated. He described this as 'living law' which becomes an important tool in understanding how law evolves and takes shape and its relationship to power and compulsion.

In this way state law is never the only source of law – people look to other forms of rules and sources of authority as part of their understanding of law and legal relations. Ehrlich and his concept of 'living law' is a useful way of understanding how Islamic law operates in a multicultural setting. As Menski points out:

> … Muslim law, too, is in reality a family of legal systems with immense internal diversities, rather than one uniform law. All that is common to all branches of this great tree are the basic conceptual roots, evidently of a religious nature, presenting an alternative vision of a natural law system, since Muslim law is not primarily made by the state (2006:20).

Muslim Family Law in Britain

Western legal scholars have long recognized the social fact that the existence of different and varied social and legal orders operating within the context of the liberal legal framework can challenge the assumed legal centrality upon which Western law is based. In Britain this critique of legal positivism also reveals a tension between the norms and values that underpin English law and the challenges arising from cultural and religious pluralism in multicultural Britain. One theoretical challenge to the concept of law comes from 're-evaluating the concept of law in a culturally diverse, plural society' (Shah 2005:1). This approach draws upon a postmodern conception of law to explore the relationship between cultural diversity, legal pluralism and the state response to conflicts generated by settled diasporic communities. These diasporic communities' continued practice of cultural or religious norms and values can produce conflicts with official state law rules and norms. This body of literature conceptualizes contemporary legal conflict as a clash between systems of law (both formal and informal) and draws upon the origins and migration patterns of specific ethnic minority communities in Britain. In particular the family and wider kin groups are presented as the two key sites upon which such legal conflicts are based. As Shah argues:

> … family and wider kin groups are the primary location of self-regulation, which also gives rise to conflict and negotiation in the wider British social order. Since Asian and African laws emphasize self-regulated societies rather than positivist top-down regulation as the British state law does there is a fundamental clash of basic values … (2005:19).

This critical reassessment not only challenges the ontological premises which frame the formalist definitions of law but in doing so also reframes the discourse on settlement patterns of diasporic communities living in the West. More recently still, discussion has centred on the relations between law and religious identity and the move from individual notions of identity towards a communitarian identity (and the possible consequences for undermining the legal principles of 'equality before the law' and 'common citizenship'). These issues are discussed in more depth later in this chapter but this shift in the terms of the debate provides us with new understandings of the relationship between pluralism, multiculturalism and legal pluralism and how they co-exist and manifest in Britain. However this body of literature is, to some extent limiting. Little attention is paid to the relationship between law and power and pluralism, in this context, remains dependent upon reified definitions of cultural norms and values and religious practice. Hence the problematic interaction between state law and cultural and religious customs posits a commitment and a loyalty to a community based upon immutable markers of religious and cultural difference. In this way there is an underlying assumption that the spaces inhabited by diasporic communities are based upon and can be identified by fixed and discrete notions of culture and religious practices which in essence define the communities as a whole. Clearly, as with the pluralism inherent in legal diversity, cultural diversity and identity must also be understood as historically fragmented, unstable and contradictory and in Britain this situation is well illustrated by the heterogeneity of Muslim communities and the multiplicity of meanings of Islam and Islamic jurisprudence and practice. Yet current scholarship continues to posit Islam as in opposition to the values of Western human rights and pays insufficient attention to the fact that 'religious communities are internally contested, heterogeneous, and constantly evolving over time through internal debate and interaction with outsiders' (Sunder 2003:1403).

In Britain, *Shari'a* councils operate as unofficial legal bodies specializing in providing advice and assistance to Muslim communities on Muslim family law matters. They are neither unified nor represent a single school of thought but instead are made up of various bodies representing the different schools of thought in Islam.[3] Many *Shari'a* councils are closely affiliated to mosques and this reflects developments in Islamic religious practice in Britain.[4] In his study of Muslims in Bradford, Lewis argues that the socio-political establishment of Muslims in Britain via mosques and community organizations such as *Shari'a* councils indicates a shift 'within the migrants' self-perception, from being sojourners to settlers' (1996:56). Indeed there has been much academic discussion and contributions to our understanding of citizenship and identity and national belonging within minority ethnic communities.[5] In essence, a *Shari'a* council has three main functions: issuing Muslim divorce certificates, reconciling and mediating between parties and producing expert opinion reports on matters of Muslim family law and custom to the Muslim community,[6] solicitors and the courts. It is also significant that in addition to providing advice and assistance on matters of Muslim family law, *Shari'a* councils have been set up to promote and preserve Islam within British society (Bunt 1998:103). Subsequently the socio-legal reality of Muslim communities in Britain is presented as a complex scenario of state law and personal laws which challenges the assumed uniformity of state law (as superior, monolithic and homogeneous) and instead points to a postmodern analysis of law and legal relations which highlights 'a diversity of laws'.[7]

---

3 The four ancient Islamic schools of Sunni thought can be broadly categorized as Hanafi, Maliki, Shafi'i and Hanabali. For an in-depth analysis on the historical development of these schools see Coulson (1969) and Schacht (1964).

4 Many are based within mosques but have their own distinctive approach to dispute resolution. Mosques are classified as charitable organizations and are essentially free to develop their own policies within the framework of existing legislation. In particular mosques play a significant role in *Shari'a* councils by reinforcing the significance of Islamic religious practice, a significance often underpinned by the role of *imams* who act as a link between mosques and *Shari'a* councils. For example, *imams* often lead religious prayer at mosques and also act as mediators in resolving marital disputes within *Shari'a* councils. This relationship is clearly important in its emphasis upon Islamic beliefs and morality and identification to a wider global Islamic culture (Ahmed and Donnan 1994).

5 On the demands made by the 'new generation' of South Asians (Amin 2002) in Britain and debates on social cohesion, poverty and deprivation and how the concept of citizenship is articulated within South Asian communities (Bagguley and Hussain 2003; Cantle 2001; Denham 2002; Kalra 2002).

6 There are no known precise figures on the number of *Shari'a* councils in Britain but a recent estimate put this figure in the range of between 60–70 councils across the country. *Shari'a* councils also issue *fatwas* which can simply be translated as rulings from a religious scholar to members of the Muslim community over a contested issue. Observation research reveals that at some *Shari'a* councils the scholars spend considerable time deliberating on issuing *fatwas*. The outcomes of these *fatwas* are not known but this certainly raises interesting questions on how the community attempts to deal with local conflicts within the boundaries of the 'Muslim community' and the extent to which these processes may conflict with state law.

7 Menski (1998) was one of the first scholars to look at this and describes a complex process whereupon British Muslims combine Islamic law and English law to create a new

The Experience of Muslim Women using *Shari'a* Councils

This section draws upon data from interviews with a group of British Muslim women who have used *Shari'a* councils to obtain a Muslim divorce certificate.[8]

In his study of Muslim legal pluralism, Menski points to what he describes as 'the legal de-recognition of Muslim divorces … in the United Kingdom' (1998:382). By this he means the lack of provisions in English law to recognize religious law as an official form of divorce. In the current, revised English family law there is only one way to obtain a divorce, on the grounds that the marriage has irretrievably broken down, after a two-year separation where the decree is made absolute. Muslim divorces granted through a 'non-judicial process' (*talaq*) in Britain are generally not recognized as valid, a situation which has led to the creation of 'limping marriages' (Menski and Pearl 1998:383). This has meant that women who may have been divorced through civil procedure continue to be married under Muslim religious law and those who may have been divorced abroad may not be legally recognized as divorced in this country and thus continue to be legally married. Consequently this has led to a conflict of laws scenario and when husbands refuse to grant a unilateral divorce to Muslim women, they contact a *Shari'a* council.

In this study obtaining a Muslim divorce was important to all the women. Given that the issue of divorce is fraught with difficulties and tension for women within South Asian Muslim communities, many questions can be raised about the processes involved in obtaining a divorce. These relate to issues concerning negotiations, conflict and decision-making, both within the family or community and via such unofficial dispute resolution bodies. So how did this sample of women negotiate issues of marriage breakdown and divorce within the family, home and community?

The reasons for marriage breaking down were cited as forced marriage, family interference, 'clash of upbringing', adultery and domestic violence. A staggering eighteen women reported that they had experienced some form of emotional, sexual and/or physical abuse during their marriages and a small percentage of women continued to face this threat. The reasons for the breakdown in marriages were premised upon inter-family inequalities with discussion focusing on issues of power, negotiation and struggle. In relation to 'family pressure' the women described relationships with in-laws as being particularly difficult and fraught. Those who opposed or challenged their authority were ostracized and alienated from other members of the family. For other women, the control of their physical movements meant they were given very little space to assert their independence

form of hybrid laws which he identifies as 'Angrezi *Shari'a*'– a form of dynamic Muslim legal pluralism.

8 Part of a PhD study entitled, 'Complexity, difference and Muslim personal law: Rethinking the relationship between *Shari'a* councils and South Asian Muslim women in Britain', completed in 2005. This is to be published by Palgrave Macmillan in 2010.

within the family context. In three cases this had led to increased levels of domestic violence. The extracts below provide a brief snapshot of the effects on the women:

> It wasn't that bad in the beginning but over time he became very violent and by the end I wasn't allowed to go out by myself (Mina, London).

> My dad was never on my side, when he found out about the problems he always used to shout at me saying that I must do everything they tell me to do. He only said that 'cause he was scared that I was going to end up divorced and he kept saying don't get divorced, don't get divorced (Zareena, Bradford).

The Decision to Leave

Unsurprisingly perhaps, there was a close link between the decision to leave the marriage and financial independence. Those women financially dependent on their husbands were more likely to remain in the marriage for a longer period of time than those who were not. These findings confirm the work of feminist analysts who have explored the conditions that facilitate or impede the decision to leave the marriage and household. Salma drew attention to the 'assumed link between tradition and being backward':

> I am traditional and that's important to me. I like to wear Asian clothes and, you know, do Asian things but people make assumptions. Like my in-laws, they thought that my parents would never want me back if they treated me badly and if I wanted to leave, just because of my religion and the way I was. I felt as though I was tricked into the marriage and when I told his family they said, well, so what? As if I would just stay in the marriage.

She left to return to her parents' home. It is also useful to highlight that those women educated to university level, mentioned education as a contributory factor in the breakdown of their marriage. Parveen described how the difficulties in the marriage were compounded by the fact that she was perceived as being too educated and hence 'too independent':

> I did everything they wanted me to do, I cooked, I cleaned I looked after them as well as my husband but still it was never enough. Just the fact that I'd been to college, that I had an education, was a problem for them.

At the same time, the interviews revealed that the women experienced specific problems relating to 'being too Westernized'. Interestingly these views did not transcend class and education differences and a number of the interviewees were keen to discuss familial expectations.

> I could never win in the eyes of my in-laws, never. I could never do right, that's how it always felt … I wasn't traditional enough, I just didn't fit the mould of a traditional girl and that's what my mother-in-law really wanted (Shabana, London).

> He started imposing things on me like you have to wear a scarf and I'm not really comfortable with it, you know, and I told him well I'm not really comfortable with it and I don't believe I should do something that someone is making me do, Islam is within myself, I do it because I want to do it. I'm not saying I don't have any intention of it, I will do it but not just yet and he was more worried about his dad than himself. The impression I got was that he wasn't really that bothered himself he was more bothered about his family (Nighat, London).

Prior to this decision to leave, many women embarked upon alternative strategies to save the marriage, such as reconciliation and family mediation. This gives rise to a more sophisticated analysis of matrimonial dispute resolution and provides a clearer understanding of the conditions upon which such dispute resolution is based. As well as arranging the marriage, the family plays a vital role in organizing and facilitating attempts to reconcile the parties. Of the sample, 20 women explained that they had been involved in lengthy discussions with their families on reconciling with their husbands prior to any contact with a *Shari'a* council. Shah-Kazemi (2000) points out that family mediation takes on particular significance for minority ethnic communities and this was confirmed in this study as the importance of this intervention seems to be closely associated with the families arranging the marriage. Apparently this gives rise to a set of obligations and responsibilities for both parties. It is also clear that women operate within a gendered environment (Griffiths 2005:129) and often occupy less powerful positions in the disputing process.

> The thing with arranged marriages is that when it breaks down you're not really left alone. It's the family that arranges it so when it breaks down they go into this motion of trying to sort things out (Shazia, London).

> Yes I did expect my family to help me and yeah I do think it was because I had an arranged marriage. I suppose the way I got married was different from how my English friends get married and they probably don't expect the kind of help that I got (Humeira, London).

In their management of the marital dispute the interviewees were involved in a complex and shifting process of fulfilling social and cultural expectations while negotiating their terms for reconciliation. This demonstrates the dilemmas and conflicts that women's identities as individuals and as members of the family group may give rise to (see Hellum 1999:88).

> Well initially I told no-one 'cause I didn't want my parents to get involved and then you know for things to get worse, the more people that get involved then things can get out of hand. I was a bit scared anyway because I hadn't been married that long and if I say I've got problems, they'd be really really worried about it … It was too difficult I was expected to make it work so it really had to get bad before I could tell them (Farhana, Birmingham).

> Well not my side of the family but his side of the family did get involved. His eldest sister did give me a lot of support. She said this is not right something has to be done and then she told her husband and they talked within the family and they told me they did speak to him but I don't know what was said (Shaheen, London).

The dilemma of preserving the 'family honour' can limit the women's ability to make decisions within the home and family. Thus the issue of 'leaving' the marriage was neither easily resolved nor uncritically accepted and some women grappled with the pressures of maintaining the '*izzat* of the family' (family honour) while others expressed ambivalence:

> I couldn't tell my parents straight away 'cause of the *izzat* thing. They were always saying that my marriage had kept the *izzat* of the family, so when things started to go wrong it was difficult for me to explain to them how I was feeling and what I wanted to do about the situation (Nasima, London).

> My parents aren't educated and we're not middle-class … But we're Muslims and they understand right from wrong. I wanted their help to sort things out and in Islam they have a duty to support me in my time of need. We discussed things together and only when they came to the conclusion that things wouldn't change did I make up my mind that it was time to go (Zareena, Bradford).

These findings suggest that some women were able to challenge the notion of family honour, reconceptualize its meaning, reject its imposition in determining their decision to leave and were able to transfer this 'responsibility' to their husbands. In this way family honour was characterized as an obligation to fulfil social and cultural expectations during the process of marriage and, in some cases, this shift challenges the potency of the argument that women are reluctant to leave, due to concerns of preserving the family honour. Yet the interview data also revealed the close connection between family intervention and the decision to reconcile. The failure of the family to resolve the marital difficulties was then, for some, a source of regret.

Thus at one level the women engaged in complex negotiations with parents and wider family to either justify their decision to leave or to establish the grounds on which divorce should be sought. In addition, the support generated by female members of the family was of particular importance and this, for many women, had been a significant factor in their decision to leave. In this way the women were able to create alliances with mothers and sisters, highlighting the importance of interwoven solidarity between them and thus challenging the dynamics of patriarchal power inherent within the family (Bhopal 1997). Notwithstanding the obvious value of these relationships, at the same time this 'collective approach' reveals a number of ambiguities and contradictions, as this form of 'strategic essentialism' is imbued with possibilities and limitations. It is true that the women were able to gain support and strength but in doing so many reported they had to respond with an axiomatic acceptance of arranged marriages. Even though ostensibly opposed to remarrying, some women accepted a new marriage to be arranged on their behalf by parents in exchange for exit out of the present marriage. What at first seems like a new space of dialogue and autonomy in the family can in some cases rely on the traditional framework of power (Anthias 2002). For some, therefore, the impact of family mediation was a distressing experience. Nabila complained that her parents had been unwilling to accept that her marriage was over and her subsequent refusal for family mediation was met with stern opposition. This had led to a deterioration of relations with her husband and family, culminating in her parents blaming her for the breakdown of the marriage. Regrettably in this sample, pressure to return to the family home led to the increased risk of physical and emotional abuse for some women.

This form of family mediation is legitimated under the public/private distinction (see Roberts 1997). Eekelaar describes this in terms of the relationship between social and legal norms:

> ... there exists within society a network of social norms which is formally independent of the legal system, but which is in constant interaction with it. Formal law sometimes seeks to strengthen the social norms. Sometimes it allows them to serve its purposes without the necessity of direct intervention; sometimes it tries to weaken or destroy them and sometimes it withdraws from enforcement, not in an attempt to subvert them, but because countervailing values make conflicts better resolved outside the legal arena (2000:8).

Feminists have extensively critiqued this tenuous relationship between family and state intervention across a wide spectrum of disciplines (see for example Thiara and Gill 2010). In particular the criminalization of domestic violence has to some extent shaped the nature of state intervention over the past decade and these sites continue to be contested in debates recognizing cultural autonomy for minority groups. Thornton also points out that unofficial family mediation ensures the state is absolved of responsibility. She explains, 'In mediating interests which appear to be irreconcilable, the task of the liberal state is made easier if there are some areas conceptualized as "private" with which it does not have to grapple' (1991:167).

Yet proposals to develop family mediation to suit the specific needs of minority ethnic communities are rendered problematic due precisely to these divergent experiences (see Shah Kazemi 2000, 2001). There is an inherent conflict in recognizing identities as multiple and fluid and formulating social policy initiatives that are based on specific cultural practices. Cultural and religious practices are open to change, contestation and interpretation. At the very least we must put mechanisms in place to ensure that those who do not wish to take part in such processes are not compelled to do so. It is within this context that concerns have been raised about such proposals leading to communities being delegated the rights in regulating family law matters, effectively a move towards some form of cultural autonomy. Maclean rightly questions, 'What are the implications for family justice of this move towards private ordering? Is this form of "privatization" safe?' (2001:137). Undoubtedly in this context formal law provides protection against abuse in the 'private' sphere in which this legal ordering operates. Maclean questions,

> … is it dangerous to remove disputes from the legal system with the advantage of due process, plus protection of those at the wrong end of the far from level playing field, and visible negotiation and settlement which takes place if not in court then in the shadow of the law? (2001:136).

Contact with *Shari'a* Councils

With the exception of one interviewee all the women had contacted a *Shari'a* council voluntarily, notwithstanding guidance from family, friends and the local *imam*. In most cases initial contact had been made via telephone and this was followed up with an application form citing the reasons for seeking a religious dissolution of marriage. The most obvious question for us concerns the autonomy and independence of the women during this process. In particular we are interested in assessing the effectiveness of mediation and evaluating the women's response to these reconciliation practices. Existing literature does not present consistent evidence to support the view that women are marginalized and denied equal bargaining power during official mediation processes (Davis and Roberts 1988). On the other hand there is evidence which runs flatly counter to this view and reveals a deep anxiety of all women at the prospect at and during official and unofficial mediation (Bottomley 1983, Roberts 1997).

Thus for some women the initial advice given was described as helpful and sympathetic which enabled them to pursue the divorce whilst others were critical of the initial perception formed by the scholars at these bodies. Sameena explained:

> I rang the number of this *Shari'a* council that our Maulvi had given to us. I told them what had happened to me and that I wanted to divorce my husband but that he wasn't happy with it and wouldn't agree to it. They were very helpful, they

> explained that divorce was wrong but that in Islam in some circumstances it was allowed ... they took my address and contact details and told me they would send me some forms to fill in and then decide whether it would be possible.

Fauzia explained:

> They sent me some forms to fill in. They wanted to have copies of my marriage certificate, my *nikah* certificate, copies of petition and a copy of the decree absolute and a cheque for £50. I also had to fill in some of their forms which stated why I wanted to have a divorce, what were my reasons.

In cases where documents such as proof of marriage (a copy of the *nikah* or civil marriage certificate) were unavailable the women were required to provide an affidavit to confirm that the marriage had taken place. Notably most women did not have a copy of the *nikah* certificate and in these cases they did provide an affidavit. Unsurprisingly, perhaps, what we ascertain quickly from the interview data is the desire of all the women to complete the process with minimal disruption and conflict. Despite this, 23 women complained of the process being inchoate, time-consuming and at odds with *Shari'a* council claims of being sympathetic to the women's needs.

> I got a letter back from them saying they were looking into the case and in the meantime I think they had met with my husband and heard his side of the story. But I'm not sure, every time I asked what was going on I never got an answer (Rabia, Birmingham).

Reconciliation and Mediation

For all the *Shari'a* councils, the reconciliation and/or mediation process is principally an investigation into the possibility of reconciling the parties. It is by no means an uncomplicated process and gives rise to an interesting set of overlapping cultural and religious practices that are, at times, in conflict. What becomes clear is the centrality of gender relations that frame the terms of the discussion seeking a basis for reconciliation. These 'common understandings' regarding the position and representation of Muslim women are crucial to the outcome of the dispute.

Interviews with religious scholars revealed the importance attached to reconciling the parties. In this context, reconciliation is understood both as a moral duty (to preserve the sanctity of the Muslim family) and a religious obligation (a divorce cannot be pronounced without reconciliation). Mohammed Raza, at the Muslim Law *Shari'a* Council, explained:

> We do not just distribute divorces on a footpath ... we are not encouraging divorce, that's not our role. When a woman rings here to find out about divorce

> or to request an application form, we are initially reluctant to issue a divorce application. We ask that you should try to rethink your position because divorce is something that is considered a stigma in society and divorce is nothing good for you and if they have children that will be another problem after divorce so we discourage it.

With the exception of one *Shari'a* council, all female applicants are expected to participate in the reconciliation and/or mediation process. One imporant question is whether the characteristics and parameters of this alternative dispute resolution process can determine specific outcomes for Muslim women? While associated with sources which derive authority from the divine, interview research also revealed that religious scholars were keen to promote the idea of the *Shari'a* council alternative dispute resolution framework as a system whose authority, legitimacy and validity can mirror that of state law. To this end religious scholars were keen to distance themselves from persuading female applicants to reconcile with estranged husbands:

> They wanted me to meet with my husband. In fact they said that I couldn't have a divorce unless we both met with the *imam*. But it wasn't as bad as I thought. My husband took it very seriously … what the *imam* was saying. I think he needed a religious person to explain to him where he was going wrong and why I was leaving him (Sabia, London).

> I needed to explore the possibility of us getting back together from an Islamic perspective. I'm a Muslim so it helps if you can get advice and assistance from another Muslim. I think a Muslim woman would have been able to understand where I was coming from (Humeira, London).

> Well at the end of the day we had the responsibility to make it work so I can't blame those who were trying to help us. Besides by that stage it was too late to get back together we'd been through too much and our families weren't even speaking to each other (Noreen, Birmingham).

Feminist scholars have warned of the dangers of resolving marital disputes away from the protection of formal law. This may include situations where 'cultural norms deny women decision-making authority' (Roberts 1997:129) and where the mediator is not neutral and provides the 'normative framework for discussion' (Roberts 1983:549) which can transform the nature of the discussion and curtail the autonomy of the disputant. Brunch raises concerns that negotiations occur in private 'without the presence of partisan lawyers and without access to appeal' (Bruch 1988:120). Numerous studies point to the fact that official mediation places women in a weak bargaining position where they are encouraged to accept a settlement considerably less than if they had they gone through the adversarial process. In their study of mediation and divorce, Greatbach and Dingwall found that mediators do not act in a neutral way and enter the mediation process to guide the participants to particular outcomes (1993:208). There is a strong imbalance of power and the parties are not equal and do not respond in a fair way. Furthermore Bottomley reminds us that conciliation 'has not arisen in a vacuum and is not practised in one' and we need to explore the dynamics of power, which underpin this process (1984:45). Hence mediation promotes a particular familial ideology that is based on social control and patriarchal norms and values. Thus, in operation, it is a subliminal covert form of power and coercion. In this context formal law provides protection against abuse in the private sphere. In response to the move towards private legal ordering, critics argue that mediation fails to deliver on the key issue of 'justice'.

Concluding Remarks

The practice of Muslim marriage and divorce in Britain encapsulates an interesting set of cultural and religious formations. Existing literature seems to promise heterogeneity but clearly marks this practice of Muslim personal law in Britain as homogeneous, a narrow particularism, which ignores the subjective experiences of women. This approach attempts to make the experience and outcome of the process as one approach for all and as unified in the Muslim community. Clearly this is not the case and what this argument has succeeded in doing is privileging a particular religious practice as part of a specific Muslim identity. The problem with this approach is that it tends to ignore the possibility of alternative narratives. Clearly in this sample, for example, there was a sense of belonging to a Muslim community which the women expressed. Yet these descriptions of belonging and community were articulated in different ways. Some women had been marginalized, others occupied a closer position to the acceptable dictates of community expectations.

Empirical research in this study reveals that management of the marital dispute in the sphere of privatized religious arbitration gives rise to a different set of responsibilities and obligations. Women who participated in the *Shari'a* councils' process viewed themselves as not only individuals but also as members of families and communities. In a situation where notions of religious identity, belonging and familial norms and values interact with the values of individual choice and consent, some women were successfully able to negotiate between the plurality of norms and values that exist within the context of family, home and *Shari'a* councils. An important aspect of such findings, therefore, is to challenge the perceived inherent marginality of Muslim women in this process of dispute resolution. For example, it is interesting to note that several women reported that they were aware that the meanings and interpretations of some Islamic perspectives put forward by religious scholars were contested and therefore open to change. In this way they were able to disregard them and were fully aware of the need to use state law for their protection and entitlement of rights. For this reason they were able to challenge their weak bargaining position in the marriage within the family context and occupy a more 'open' space at the *Shari'a* council as a basis for entering into negotiation, dialogue and possible change. In such a situation some women participated in the reconciliation process as a strategic manoeuvre to challenge conflicting interests. Yet this shift of dispute resolution from the public to the private sphere also raises serious concerns about how power is effectively reconfigured from the state to the family and community. From such a perspective the differential treatment of women in the process of marriage and divorce can lead to a conflict between equality and autonomy and the conflicting interests of the protection of family, culture and religion as enshrined by the norms and values of *Shari'a* councils.

The challenge of diversity and the goal of social cohesion reflected in law and policies have also had the effect of influencing the law-making process in very particular and specific ways. The institutions of liberal democracy and individual rights to uphold the values of justice, equality and tolerance are continually engaged via a dialogical process and struggles over the recognition of difference. The social anxieties about Muslim bodies is two-fold: the Muslim male is constructed as a dangerous threat in the battle with the 'war on terror' and the Muslim female is deemed a victim, without autonomy, choice and personal subjectivity against the patriarchal customs of Islam and especially Muslim fathers, brothers and uncles who are deemed the custodians of this culture. The recent controversy generated by the Archbishop of Canterbury's comments cannot be seen in isolation. The centrality of gender to the debates is crucial. There is an interesting continuum to the debates that all point in the same direction, for example, in France the banning of the *burqa* and religious symbols in public, in Britain the conflicts over the *hijab*, *jilbab* or *niqab* and now the possibility of recognition of parallel legal systems in Britain. These support the idea that Muslim women need to be protected from fathers and brothers and from Islam itself, and we can only understand their motivations for subjecting themselves to such oppression in relation to the opposing frameworks of social coercion versus free will and false consciousness – West and non-West. The agency, autonomy and choice of Muslim women as active agents of their families and communities are lost and we see a resurgence of the frameworks of secularism versus religious practice.

References

Afshar, H. 1994. Muslim women in West Yorkshire: Growing up with real and imaginary values amidst conflicting views of self and society, in *The Dynamics of 'Race' and 'Gender'*, edited by H. Afshar and M. Maynard. London: Taylor and Francis.

Ali, S.S. and Rehman, J. 2003. Freedom of religion vs equality in international human rights law: Conflicting norms or hierarchical human rights? (A case study of Pakistan). *Nordic Journal for Human Rights* 404–429.

Anthias, F. 2002. Beyond feminism and mutliculturalism: Locating difference and the politics of location. *Women's Studies International Forum* 25 (3):275–286.

Anwar, M. 1998. *Between Cultures: Community and Change in the Lives of Young Asians*. Oxford: Routledge.

Badawi, Z. 1995. Muslim justice in a secular state, in *God's Law versus State Law*, edited by M. King. London: Grey Seal.

Bader, V. 2009. Secularism, public reason or moderately agonistic democracy?, in *Secularism, Religion and Multicultural Citizenship*, edited by G.B. Levey and T. Modood. Cambridge: Cambridge University Press.

Ballard, R. 1994. The emergence of Desh Pardesh, in *Desh Pardesh: The South Asian Presence in Britain*, edited by R. Ballard. London: C. Hurst and Co. Ltd.

Bano, S. 2005. 'Standpoint', 'difference' and feminist research, in *Theory and Method in Socio-Legal Research*, edited by R. Banakar and M. Travers. Oxford: Hart Publishing.

Benda-Beckmann, F. von, Benda-Beckmann, K. von and Griffiths, A. 2005. Expanding legal relations, in *Mobile People, Mobile Law: Expanding Legal Relations in a Contracting World (Law, Justice and Power)*, edited by F. von Benda-Beckmann, K. von Benda-Beckmann and A. Griffiths. Aldershot: Ashgate Publishing, 1–26.

Bhopal, K. 1999. South Asian Women and Arranged Marriages in East London, in *Ethnicity, Gender and Social Change*, edited by R. Barrot, H. Bradley and S. Fenton. New York: St. Martin's Press.

Bottomley, A. 1984. Resolving Family disputes: a critical view, in *State, Law and the Family: Critical Perspective*, edited by M.D.A. Freeman. London: Sweet and Maxwell.

Bousetta, H. and Jacobs, D. 2006. Multiculturalism, citizenship and Islam in problematic encounters in Belgium, in *Multiculturalism, Muslims and Citizenship,* edited by T. Modood, A. Triandafyllidou and R. Zapata-Barrero. Oxford: Routledge.

Brah, A. 1996. *Cartographies of Diaspora and Contesting Identities*. Oxford: Routledge.

Bruch, C.S. 1988. And how are the children? The effects of ideology and mediation on child custody law and children's well-being in the United States. *International Journal of Law and Family* 2(1):106–126.

Bunt, G. 1998. Decision-making concerns in British Islamic environments. *Islam and Christian–Muslim Relations* 19(1):103–113.

Burlet, S. and Reid, H. 1998. A gendered uprising: Political representation and minority ethnic communities. *Ethnic and Racial Studies* 21(2):271–287.

Collier, F.J. and Starr, J. 1989. *History and Power in the study of Law: New Directions in Legal Anthropology*. Ithaca and London: Cornell University Press.

Crenshaw, K. 1989. Demarginalizing the intersection of race and sex: A black feminist critique of antidiscrimination doctrine. Feminist theory and antiracist politics. *The University of Chicago Legal Forum* 1989:139.

Eastin, A.L. 2008. T*oward a Multicultural Family Law in The Multicultural Family*, Aldershot: Ashgate Publishing.

Geaves, R.R. 1996. Cult, charisma, community: The arrival of sufi pirs and their impact on Muslims in Britain. *Journal of Muslim Minority Affairs*, 16(2):169–192.

Gilliat-Ray, S. 1998. Multiculturalism and identity: Their relationship for British Muslims. *Journal of Muslim Minority Affairs*, 18(2):347–354.

Goodhart, D. 2004. Discomfort of strangers. *The Guardian*: 24 February.

Griffiths, A. 2001. Gendering culture: Towards a plural perspective on Kwena women's rights, in *Culture and Rights: Anthropological Perspectives*, edited by J. Cowan, M.-B. Dembour and R. Wilson. Cambridge: Cambridge University Press, pp. 102–126.

Hall, S. 2000. The multi-cultural question, in *Un/settled Multiculturalisms*, edited by B. Hesse. London: Zed Books.

Hellum, A. 1999. Women's human rights and African customary laws: Between universalism and realitivism – Individualism, in *Development and Human Rights: Negotiating Justice in Changing Societies*, edited by C. Lund. London and Portland, Oregon: Frank Cass Publishers.

Hirsch, F.S. 1998. *Pronouncing and Persevering: Gender and the Discourses of Disputing in an African Islamic Court*, Chicago: University of Chicago Press.

Jacobson, J. 1997. Perceptions of Britishness. *Nations and Nationalism* 3 (2):181–99.

Knights, S. 2007. *Freedom of Religion, Minorities and the Law.* Oxford: Oxford University Press.

Levey, G.B. and Modood, T. (eds) 2009. *Secularism, Religion and Multicultural Citizenship*. Cambridge: Cambridge University Press.

Lewis, P. 2002. *Islamic Britain: Religion, Politics and Identity among British Muslims*. London: I.B. Tauris.

Maclean, M. 1997. Delegalized family obligations, in *Family Law and Family Policy in New Europe,* edited by J. Kurczewski and M. Maclean. The Onati International Institute for the Sociology of Law. Sudbury: Dartmouth Publishing.

—— (ed.) 2000. *Making Law for Families*. Onati International Series in Law and Society. Oxford/Portland: Hart Publishing.

Malik, M. 2000. Faith and state jurisprudence in *Faith in Law, Essays in Legal Theory*, edited P. Oliver, S. Douglas Scoot and V. Tadros. Hart Publishing, pp. 129–150.

Mayer, E. 1990. The *Shari'ah*: A methodology or a body of substantive rules?, in *Islamic Law and Jursiprudence*, edited by N. Heer. Washington: University of Washington Press.

Menski, W. 2006. *Comparative Law in a Global Context, Legal Systems of Asia and Africa*. Cambridge: Cambridge University Press.

Mirza, Q. 2000. Islam, hybridity and the laws of marriage. *Australian Feminist Law Journal* (14) 1–22.

Modood, T. 2006. British Muslims and the politics of multiculturalism, in *Multiculturalism, Muslims and Citizenship*, edited by T. Modood, A. Triandafyllidou and R. Zapata-Barrero. Oxford: Routledge.

Nielsen, J.S. 1992. Emerging claims of Muslim populations in matters of family law in Europe. *Research Papers: Muslims in Europe* 13:64.

Okin, S. 1999. *Is Multiculturalism Bad for Women*? Princeton: Princeton University Press.

Parekh, B. 2000. *Rethinking Multiculturalism: Cultural Diversity and Political Theory*. Basingstoke: Macmillan Press.

Pearl, D. and Menski, W. 1998. *Muslim Family Law*. Andover: Sweet and Maxwell.

Pieterse, J.N. 1997. Travelling Islam: Mosques without minarets, in *Space Culture and Power*, edited by A. Oncii and P. Weyland. London: Zed Books.

Roberts, M. 1997. *Mediation in Family Disputes: Principles of Practice*. London: Arena.

Rohe, M. 2006. The migration and settlement of Muslims: The challenges for European legal systems. in *Migration, Diasporas and Legal Systems in Europe*, edited by P. Shah and W.F. Menski. London: Routledge-Cavendish, pp. 57–72.

Sayyid, S. 2000. Beyond Westphalia: Nations and diasporas – The case of the Muslim Umma, in *Unsettled Multiculturalisms: Diasporas, Entanglements, Transruptions*, edited by B. Hesse. London: Zed Books.

Shachar, A. 2005. *Multicultural Jurisdictions*. Cambridge: Cambridge University Press.

Shadid, W. and Konindsveld, V.S. 1996. Loyalty to a non-Muslim government: An analysis of Islamic normative discussions and of the views of some contemporary Islamicists, in *Political Participation and Identities of Muslims in Non-Muslim States*, edited by W. Shadid and V.S. Konindsveld. Kampen, Netherlands: Kok Pharos, 84–114.

Shah, P. 2005. *Legal Pluralism in Conflict*. London and Portland: Glass House Press.

Shah, P. and Menski, W.F. 2006. *Migration, Diasporas and Legal Systems in Europe*. London: Routledge-Cavendish.

Shah-Kazemi, N.S. 2001. *Untying the Knot: Muslim Women, Divorce and the Shari'a*. London: The Nuffield Foundation.

Sunder, M. 2005. Enlightened constitutionalism. *Conneticut Law Review* Vol 37:89.

Taylor, C. 2005. What is Secularism? in *Secularism, Religion and Multicultural Citizenship*, edited by G.B. Levy and T. Modood. Cambridge: Cambridge University Press, p. xv.

Thiara, R. and Gill, A. 2010. *Violence Against South Asian Women: Issues for Policy and Practice*. London: Jessica Kingsley Publishers.

Twining, W. 2000. *Globalization and Legal Theory*. Cambridge: Cambridge University Press.

Woodman, G.R. 1998. Ideological combat and social observation: Recent debate about legal pluralism. *Journal of Legal Pluralism and Unoffocial Law* (42): 21–59.

Yilmaz, I. 2001. Muslim law in Britain: Reflections in the socio-legal sphere and differential legal treatment. *Journal of Muslim Minority Affairs* 20(2): 353–360.

PART III
Transnational Modes of Governance: Family, Market and Media

Chapter 8
Local Responses to National and Transnational Law: A View from the Scottish Children's Hearings System

Anne Griffiths and Randy F. Kandel

Introduction

In recent years attention has focused on transnational relations and transnational laws, fuelled by the mobility of persons and of knowledge and concepts that cross national frontiers. This may come about through economic migration, involving a whole range of actors from transnational corporations and corporate executives or non-governmental organizations, at one end of the scale, to undocumented migrants whose existence is often precarious due to their 'illegal' status in the host country. It may also involve the displacement of large numbers of the population due to war or conflict resulting in streams of refugees or asylum seekers who bring their way of life and laws with them to their new countries of residence. Alternatively, the process may embrace states' attempts to incorporate international standards, such as those set down in the European Convention on Human Rights and Fundamental Freedoms (European Right's Convention) or the United Nations Convention on the Rights of the Child (Children's Convention), into national law for the benefit of their citizens.

Our chapter focuses on attempts made to incorporate international concepts of participation and transparency through a study of local children's hearings in Glasgow. It highlights how local actors respond to these developments in diverse ways, documenting the range of localized sets of meanings and practices that impinge on the process and that challenge any notion of 'the local as a sphere that is simply acted upon through the imposition of external institutions, interests or market forces that derive from national, regional or international agencies that are brought to bear on its domain' (Griffiths 2002:305). This perspective is important because it fills a gap in legal scholarship on globalization and the transnational domain that has tended to focus on the relationship between the legal systems of nation states and international and transnational law. What is lacking is an account of how international norms and national laws operate at a local level in terms of individuals' acceptance, appropriation or resistance to them. We seek to redress the balance by demonstrating the complex array of factors that are at work in a local arena that undermine any simple categorization of the 'global' and the 'local' in terms of essentialist, homogenizing characteristics, and that reveal that 'state law is not the only source of power' (Benda-Beckmann and Griffiths 2005:14) that operates in this process.

An Overview of Children's Hearings in Scotland

Hearings exist to deal with children under16 who are in need of compulsory measures of supervision. Implemented in 1971,[1] on the recommendations of the Kilbrandon Committee (Kilbrandon 1964), children's hearings in Scotland represented a novel form of juvenile justice that permitted state intervention in the lives of children across a broad spectrum of circumstances. These include neglected or abused children, as well as those children who have committed offences or who are 'beyond the control of a relevant person' or who fail 'to attend school regularly without reasonable excuse' under section 52 (2) of the Children (Scotland) Act 1995. The system's underlying rationale was, and continues to be, that of a welfare perspective based on the best interests of the child. Currently regulated by Part II of the Children (Scotland) Act 1995, the system has attempted to implement a more rights-based orientation based on international norms brought about in part by lobbying from non-governmental organizations like the Child Law Centre and Childcare Scotland (Griffiths and Kandel 2004).

Children's hearings take the form of lay panels, consisting of three members who are unpaid volunteers and not required to have legal qualifications. Referrals are made by a reporter who is employed by the Scottish Children's Reporter Administration (SCRA), a national body charged with the management and deployment of reporters throughout Scotland. Decisions, however, are made by panel members who must assess whether a child is in need of compulsory measures of supervision and, if so, what conditions, if any, should be imposed. In doing so they must adhere to three overriding principles. The first is that the welfare of the child is paramount (s.16 [1]). This reflects a focus on welfare under Article 3(1) of the Children's Convention that is enhanced under Scottish legislation by making it a 'paramount' and not just 'a primary consideration'. The second principle, that reinforces Article 12(1) of the Children's Convention dealing with children's participation, provides that children must be able to express their views and have them taken into account, where sufficiently mature (s.16 [2]), with a presumption in favour of children aged 12 or over having sufficient age and maturity (s.11 [10]). This is not only in keeping with Article 12 but is also in keeping with Article 5 of the Children's Convention that requires states to take account of the child's evolving development and capacity. Finally, the third principle states that there should be minimum intervention, that is, that a hearing should only make an order if it is better for the child that such an order is made than to make no order at all (s.16 [3]). This is in keeping with the idea of family autonomy in decision-making

1 Under the Social Work (Scotland) Act 1968.

and with Article 8 of the European Right's Convention dealing with respect for private and family life, in other words that there should be no interference in family life unless absolutely necessary.

In cases of dispute, where children and families reject the grounds for referral, the hearing must either discharge the referral or refer the matter to the sheriff court for a finding as to whether the disputed grounds are established.[2] This approach, premised on consensus as the starting point for discussion, seeks to avoid the adversarial nature of legal proceedings. Those present at hearings include the three panel members and a reporter, together with, usually, the child or young person, at least one parent or carer and a social worker.

When the hearing ends, a decision is made and communicated immediately to the child and family. This is in keeping with its ethos of transparency. The decision is based on a majority vote[3] which is reached by each panel member making a recommendation (without consultation) as to whether compulsory measures of supervision are necessary and the reasons for it. The child and family are informed that, if dissatisfied with the decision, they have three weeks to appeal to a sheriff.[4] The reporter then forwards the decision, the reasons for it and a notice of the right to appeal in writing, to the child and any relevant person.[5] The formal process at the beginning and end of the hearings stands in marked contrast to the rest of the proceedings which attempt to foster a more relaxed conversational form. However, it is important to note that although relatively informal in comparison with courts, panel members wield wide-ranging powers under Section 70, including the power to make a residential supervision requirement placing the child in a foster or local authority home or even in secure accommodation.

Our Study

It was just after the implementation of the 1995 Act and prior to the introduction of the Human Rights Act 1998 that we commenced our research on children's hearings in Glasgow.[6] At that time it was clear that hearings personnel were aware of the need to take account of transnational standards in their daily practice. Our

2 Section 65(7)(a).

3 There is no statutory provision to this effect but it has been the universal and accepted practice since 1971.

4 Section 51(1)(a).

5 1996 Rules, r.21(1).

6 This formed part of a comparative research project from 1997–2000 on 'The Child's Voice in Legal Proceedings' in Scotland and the United States of America, funded by the Annenberg Foundation and the British Academy. It involved interviews with 40 of the 400 active panel members in the Glasgow area, 25 social workers, 25 safeguarders, 65 young people with experience of panels and 67 without (who were interviewed individually and in groups), 25 parents and the observation of 34 hearings.

interviews with 40 panel members together with attendance at initial and follow up training sessions revealed that they were conscious of the international standards outlined above and their potential effects on the system through changes brought about by the 'new' Act (as panel members referred to the 1995 Act). They were also aware of changes that were imminent due to legislation contained in the Human Rights Act 1998 (incorporating provisions of the European Right's Convention) that was about to become part of national law (Griffiths and Kandel 2009b).[7]

Participation and Transparency: Panel Members' Perspectives

All panel members agree that their role is to reach a decision that is in the child's 'best interests'. In this process, which they view as being open and transparent – a positive space in which to communicate with the child and his or her family and that involves reaching consensus on the way forward – they consider it 'essential' to hear the child's story directly from the child. This is important because the hearings are, for the panel, a means of forming an independent assessment about the disposal of the case, measured against recommendations made by various professionals in reports circulated to the panel and family members or other relevant persons[8] prior to the hearing. For while most panel members agree that they form a preliminary view of a child and his or her family from the reports, all are of the view that this may alter radically during the hearing when they are able to observe firsthand the kind of interactions that take place between family members and the professionals. They stress the importance of body language and non-verbal communication in providing valuable information about family relationships (for example, how a child acts with his or her mother) as well as the family's attitude towards the various professionals that are involved (for example, the degree of rapport with the social worker). These factors may be at odds with information provided in the reports and assist panel members to form an independent view of family dynamics that may afford a check on the professionals' recommendations. However, all panel members admitted that getting a child to speak is often 'an uphill struggle' (Griffiths and Kandel 2000, 2001), for although 'it's important all the time, every day, every hearing, to hear the child's story right from the child. Whether you do or not is a different matter' (Griffiths and Kandel 2006:136).

7 The current system is in the process of being restructured under the draft Children's Hearings (Scotland) Bill 2009 that is beyond the scope of this study which was based on findings compiled between 1997 and 2000.

8 Such persons include those with parental responsibilities and rights under Part I of the 1995 Act, as well as anyone who ordinarily (other than by reason of employment) has charge of, or control over, the child: see section 93(2)(b).

Social Workers' Perspectives on Children's and Families' Participation

Part of the problem is that although panel members view a hearing as a forum for open communication that is not judgmental (because the grounds of referral must be accepted before the hearing can proceed thereby taking the emphasis away from 'deeds' and placing it on 'needs'), this is not the way in which it is perceived by most children and families who attend. For however egalitarian panels attempt to be they can never quite escape from the fact that there is generally a class divide between the panel members and the children and families that inhibits discussion (Hallett and Hazel 1998, Waterhouse *et al.* 2000, Waterhouse and McGhee 2002). While all the panel members we interviewed were in employment or were in receipt of a pension having taken early retirement and most came from professional or management backgrounds (except for one taxi driver and one secretary), only five out of the twenty-five parents we interviewed were employed. Out of those who were unemployed, a number had been so for a substantial period of time. This is not surprising given the areas of Glasgow in which they lived. The 25 social workers that we interviewed, who came from 11 different areas in Glasgow,[9] all described the areas they work in as involving high levels of deprivation, low employment, poverty, low educational attainment and high levels of drug and alcohol abuse. In this situation, as a social worker from Castlemilk remarked, the majority of children get little support from their parents who 'put the responsibility on the social worker' to deal with them. A social worker from Maryhill observed that many children are initially referred for not going to school 'but when you dig deeper there're family problems here and that's just a symptom'.

While the children and families attending panels come from all over Glasgow, the localities in which they live share many characteristics in common. In contrast, panel members and social workers we interviewed generally live in more affluent parts of the city. Only two panel members and two social workers still live in the kind of neighbourhood that the children come from. Given these disparities in employment, education[10] and living conditions it is hardly surprising that children and families feel at a disadvantage in hearings. In this setting power cannot be ignored for it is not only the panel members' social and economic standing that is at issue but their capacity to remove children from their homes. Although such power is rarely exercised, children and families remain fearful of this outcome. This fear is hard to allay. Three of the young people who had experience of panels expressed the view that 'they're just there tae put you in a residential home'. Even those who had no experience of panels expressed the view that they existed to deal with 'wee neds', or 'hard men' or children who were in some way 'bad'.

9 These are Drumchapel, Easterhouse, Castlemilk, Royston, Maryhill, Partick, Pollock, Possil, Priesthill, Ruchizie and Bridgeton.

10 All the social workers we interviewed had a university qualification of some sort.

Children and Families' Perspectives on Hearings: Fear Inducing

Despite all that panel members do to try to put parties at their ease, they have to contend with the parties' fear of the process's outcome as well as their perception of the hearing as a form of 'trial' involving a punitive role for those who have been at fault in some way. All 50 of the young people interviewed found panels 'scary' because:

- 'It's frightening to have to go and talk in front of lots of people' (13 year old boy).
- 'They're all strangers. I don't know them. But they know all about you' (13 year old girl).

Over time with exposure to the system it may become less nerve-wracking. As one 14 year old boy explained, 'the first and second time I found it hard to speak. Then I found it easier [at panels after that]'.

Of the 38 young people commenting on the process:

- Seven saw it as having a regulatory or punitive role –'Tae deal with those in the wrong' (14 year old boy).
- Two viewed it as a court – 'A court for young people' (15 year old girl).
- Three viewed it as deciding whether or not to remove you from home – 'They're just there tae put you in a residential home' (14 year old boy).

Seven out of the 25 parents interviewed reported negative experiences with the panel. One parent commented 'they don't have respect for me because I walk the streets … I just feel as if they think I'm just a bit of shite'. Another felt they were judgmental 'like my lifestyle, sort of thing … they could sit there an' judge me like that … how they can judge you by sittin' talking tae yi, an takin' a few notes is beyond me'.

A number of the social workers supported these perceptions and commented that in their experience 'panel members can be judgmental' especially where they are dealing with children who have committed offences or with parents whose children are before the panel on the grounds of care and protection. Nine of the social workers who commented on young people's perception of hearings noted that despite all the panel's efforts the young people still view it as a form of court where they or their parents are being judged. As one social worker explained, 'The children are very loyal and they're afraid that they're going to be asked to say things that might injure their parents'. Several social workers we interviewed saw class as being a 'huge issue' because 'the majority of panel members do seem to be very middle class'. Their clients see the panel as being from 'a different class' or 'snooty' or 'on a different wave length'. One panel member acknowledged this. Now a computer sales manager, he grew up in a poor area and joined the panel at 18 because, 'I felt that I probably had a better understanding of what some kids were going through'.

Implications for Participation

Given the anxiety that hearings produce in both children and families it is not surprising that their participation is very guarded. All young people observed that they had been very frightened at their first hearing and that this had affected their ability to participate.[11] Six commented that while they had had difficulty speaking initially they had learned to do so over time.[12] They explained:

- 'When I first went [to a hearing] I never spoke. Now, I just talk straight away [but doesn't have any sense of whether adults listen]' (15 year old boy).
- 'The first time I didnae speak 'cos I was scared. The second time I was a bit shy and then I started talking' (15 year old boy).
- Initially 'I just didnae care about the panel, I just agreed with them and aw that but see now I've realized that ye canny just sit, ye need to ask questions an aw that' (14 year old girl).

Out of the 25 parents interviewed, only five observed that their child could talk at a panel, albeit in basic terms. One parent commented that her son just went 'aye' and nodded his head. He never expanded on anything further. In six cases parents noted their child felt able to speak sometimes, but in three cases this was just to answer 'yes' or 'no' to questions. This made one parent feel 'embarrassed for those people and sorry for the panel members'. She did try to get her adolescent daughter to 'speak up a bit' but she just sat 'with her head down'. In only one case did the parent state that one of her children 'will say his piece' but he is unusual.

Fifteen of the young people interviewed expressly stated that they kept quiet for the following reasons:[13]

- 'I hardly talk at panels. I get a wee bit nervous' (14 year old girl).
- 'I'm worried what is gonnae happen to me' (12 year old boy).
- 'Depends a lot on what kind of panel it is and who's on the panel. I prefer to just get it done quick, get it over as quick as I can so I can get hame' (14 year old boy).
- 'Too many strangers in the room' (14 year old girl).

In some cases the young person not only declined to participate but was openly hostile. One 14 year old girl in a residential home explained '[I used to say] fuck

11 Lack of participation in hearings was also found in a field study conducted by researchers at the University of Stirling. See Hallett *et al.* (1998). See also Marshall (1997:50).

12 Two girls and four boys.

13 Seven girls and eight boys.

the system before it fucks you, but now I'm saying you've got to work with the system or you're not going to get anywhere'. However, although she speaks up now 'there are times when I've just sat and shut my gob [mouth]'.

Parents may fare better with participation as was the case with 13 out of 25 parents interviewed. Only three expressed negative views and only one stated that she could participate sometimes but not always. Social workers generally regarded parents as being more vocal because they are older and more mature. Nonetheless, they do 'have difficulty participating' because even 'for adults these situations are difficult'. A social worker explained that he has had parents who say they are going to make their views known at the hearing but when they get there 'you can see that they get embarrassed and they say nothing'. Social workers put constraints on participation down to lack of parents' self-esteem and confidence. As one social worker commented, 'A lot of my caseload is parents who are fairly limited intellectually and they feel very, very threatened'.

Even a parent with experience like a mother who is a care worker, who regularly attends panels in the course of her work, finds herself intimidated when attending panels with her son because she feels 'disempowered'. Parents and social workers report the anxiety threshold is very high. One social worker observed 'they're just uptight about the whole thing'. He has not had many parents who have felt able to disagree with a panel's decision and say 'no, they're wrong'. This is because they view panel members from a different class background as being judgmental about them as 'good' or 'bad' parents. As a result they are very defensive. One social worker explained that, in his experience, families 'feel totally inadequate when they go into a hearing … they don't have the confidence'. It's painful for them because, as another social worker commented, it is very hard for them in this public arena 'even though they know what's being said, to hear it being read out again and to hear themselves being discussed is a painful experience'. Those parents that participate tend to have experienced the system themselves or been cared for by social workers as a child. They know the system and have a good relationship with their social worker.

In the case of children, social workers' perceptions support what they and their parents have to say, that is that they do not generally participate or speak up at hearings.[14] They may do so 'occasionally' or 'sometimes' but the overall perception is 'there are not many children who do it' or 'the majority don't for whatever reason'. The overall sense is that they 'do not put across their own views' and that 'nine times out of ten' most just give one word answers like 'yes' or 'no'. Those children who speak are apt to be extroverts who 'enjoy talking' and who are 'very, very verbal' but these children are in the minority. Some social workers observe that younger children find it easier to participate because panel members are more comfortable with them and cajole them into talking. Others claim young

14 For details on how panel members attempt to improve participation which is beyond the scope of this chapter, see Griffiths and Kandel (2006, 2009a). For details on children's views on participation through representation see Griffiths and Kandel (2004).

children find it harder to speak than adolescents do, although they note that older children always 'hold back in some kind of way'. Where young people do speak up, they 'tend to be a bit more aggressive'. This is because 'they don't know what to say or how to say it'. As one worker put it, 'I think there're very, very few young people who have the confidence and the verbal skill to speak out in a children's hearing'.

According to social workers there are a range of factors that constrain young people's participation in hearings. These include: fear and intimidation (for example that they will be taken away from home, will feel uncomfortable in an unfamiliar environment, have to face strangers and that the setting is so formal, despite attempts to make it more user-friendly); concern about doing what parents have told them to do before the hearing (and fear of repercussions); and lack confidence, self-esteem and verbal skills. Even those children who are articulate outside panels may be rendered 'inarticulate' within the forum. For children view panel members as 'officials', however friendly they are. They fear making things worse for themselves or for their parents by speaking up. Social workers see children as 'carrying the weight of the world on their shoulders'. They don't find it easy to speak out 'in front of mum or dad' (especially in cases involving abuse). As adolescents they may be embarrassed and self-conscious. They may also feel that adults don't listen to them so why should the panel be any different.

Understanding Language, Grounds and the Decision-making Process

Added to these concerns are difficulties that children and families encounter in understanding the language, the grounds and the decision-making process. Only four out of the 50 young people interviewed stated they had had no difficulty in understanding the language that was used. In one case, a 15 year old girl explained this was due to her parents' assistance. In contrast, 17 out of 50 claimed they had difficulty in understanding the language of referral and the language used by panel members.[15] Another eight noted that, while they had come to understand what was being said, they still had difficulties sometimes.[16] In six of these cases the young people attributed their understanding to help given by parents, relatives and social or care workers. Some of the young people's observations were:

- 'They use too big words I think. When you're only young, I mean 12 or 13 … I would sit and go through my report, I would be sitting in the children's panel and I would say what does that mean. What did this mean? I didnae have a clue what half the words meant 'cause its social work language' (16 year old girl).

15 Nine girls and eight boys.

16 Four girls and four boys.

- 'I didn't really understand what panels were about when I first started going' (girl, unrecorded age). She would advise panel members to, 'Break all their big long words down into their [young people's] kind of speech so that young people can understand it better'.
- 'I only understood a wee bit' but 'didnae ask them [panel members] nuthin' 'cos yer shy when yer talking tae other people' (12 year old boy).
- 'I wisnae listening when they read out the Acts and all that rubbish I didnae have a clue' (16 year old girl).

Fourteen out of the 25 parents interviewed also observed that they found the language difficult because 'some of the jargon is ... whew it's very hard to pick up'. Out of these parents, five said that they did generally understand but got caught out by language such as references to sections of the 1995 Act and to schedule offences. One parent explained, 'I understood to a certain extent' but 'I'm not really intelligent enough as far as the law is concerned', although in this case she understood enough to dispute one of the grounds of referral. Only five claimed to understand the language and the process. In three of these cases the parents had had extensive experience of panels as social workers (two of these were former social workers, one of whom was now unemployed because she was an alcoholic) and a care worker. In a number of cases parents were helped to understand by the panel or by a social worker who 'put it into layman's terms'. In one case a parent understood the grounds because they were explained by her social worker before the panel. This parent had difficulty following the process because, 'I was losing my temper. I didnae understand nothing [in the hearing] due to all those big words'. Getting angry at a panel is not uncommon. As one social worker explained, he had a client who just 'mouths off [at panels] because it's the only way she knows how to communicate'.

Social workers acknowledge that children and parents have problems with comprehension. Twelve observed that children did not understand the language because there's 'too much jargon' and because it is 'quite a formal system'. While some recognize panel members do a good job of paraphrasing and 'are pretty good at saying what this actually means', others reported that panel members do not translate the grounds into user-friendly language. Four social workers stated that children sometimes understand the language 'if the grounds are straightforward' but not where the grounds are 'quite lengthy' and 'quite legalistic'. This is particularly the case when dealing with timing around child care and protection orders involving a second day hearing or an eighth day hearing with a case conference in between. In these circumstances children want to know why they are going back to a hearing and 'I think it can be quite confusing [for the child]'. One social worker observed that panels members find it difficult to deal with grounds because 'they are hemmed in by this document that they must read' with the result that 'some children get lost'. Only three social workers expressed the view that children do understand the grounds and this was put down to panel members' attempts to employ user-friendly language or to assistance from social workers in explaining the grounds either before the panel or through intervention at it. Even when a child appears to understand this is not always so. As one social worker explained, 'I've been surprised myself with things children have said to me after an event [panel] like, "Why was I there?" You think it's been clear because you've been talking about truancy or whatever but something's going amiss'.

Where children did comprehend, this depended to a large extent on the person's age, whether or not this was his or her first time before a hearing and panel members' abilities to translate from technical legal language (which forms the basis for the remit) or on social workers' interventions to get panel members to translate grounds into ordinary, age-appropriate language. For example, in one case a 13 year old girl found her social worker intervening to get the panel chair to explain what they meant when they referred to an 'interdict'.[17] Almost all the young people interviewed found the language very hard to follow at times because of its formality. Those with the greatest comprehension were those who had been through the system for years, usually ending up in residential homes or in secure units. By 15 they had acquired an understanding of the system through experience. Ironically, the formal legal language of referral was introduced to bolster the rights component of the system to protect children and families from the dangers of 'informalism' that may lead to coercive state intervention under the guise of welfare. The use of formal, technical language is especially prevalent at the start of the hearing where the grounds for referral are read out and at the end of the hearing where rights to appeal are set out.

The use of language directly correlates with an understanding of the grounds of referral that are central to the hearing's process. For unless the grounds are accepted, the hearing cannot proceed. Twenty-one out of the 50 interviewed stated that they had had some difficulty in understanding the grounds presented to them. These broke down as follows:

- Four stated that they did not understand the grounds.[18]
- Thirteen stated that they generally understood the basis for their referral but not always.[19]
- Four stated that they did not initially understand the grounds but had come to do so as they gained more experience of the system.[20]

Sixteen expressly stated that they did understand the grounds as presented to them, but in five cases this was only through the intervention of a third party, such as a parent or social worker. Sixteen[21] reported accepting grounds that were unclear to them or that they did not understand or that they disagreed with, while

17 An interdict is the Scottish equivalent to an English injunction.

18 One girl and three boys.

19 Five girls and eight boys.

20 One girl and three boys.

21 Ten girls and six boys.

only 14[22] stated that they had never accepted grounds in these circumstances. Although some young people (especially those with experience) felt they could ask for an explanation where they were unclear about grounds for referral, these were in the minority. Most felt they should just let matters ride, because:

- they had a general idea why they were there (often because their social worker had discussed the panel with them beforehand);[23]
- they felt asking for an explanation was not worth the effort – three had the attitude that: 'I could'nae be bothered' (14 year old boy);
- they were afraid of appearing stupid – two expressed the same opinion that: 'I just said aye to everything they [panel members] said because I didn't know what they were talking about so I thought if I just said 'aye' they wouldn't think I was stupid or something' (15 year old girl);
- they wanted to get the panel over with as quickly as possible – five had views like this, for example, 'To make it quicker' (15 year old boy);
- they felt if most of the grounds were applicable it was easier to admit to them all and get on with the hearing;[24]
- one was embarrassed and said, 'I couldn't do that' [ask what it meant and show ignorance] (14 year old girl);
- one wanted to say as little as possible – ''cos if I said no I would have to speak more [and I hate to talk]' (15 year old girl).

One parent commented that his 12 year old son understands what his social worker tells him but does not understand the legal jargon at panels. When spoken to 'He tends to go "aye, aye" because he doesnae know [and doesn't want to admit to this] ... the kid's not got a clue what's happening'.

Even children with understanding note that others may have difficulty. One 14 year old girl understood the process:

> ... because I'm dead bright. Just because I'm in a place like this [residential school] doesn't mean I'm not bright.

However, she conceded that other young people may need help because:

> They [panel members] use all these big words and all that and a lot of people can't understand them and you're like 'Oh god, what's going to happen at the panel' and you're too scared to ask anybody.

22 Three girls and eleven boys.

23 Those in focus groups strongly expressed this view.

24 This reasoning that one should accept all the grounds if most of them applied was most strongly expressed in focus groups.

However, panels' decisions are clearly understood and only a few require clarification from a social worker after the hearing. Only four out of 50 young people did not understand the hearing's decision,[25] in contrast with 27[26] who acknowledged understanding. Twelve[27] maintained they generally understood but sometimes had not, especially when younger. Of the 14 parents reporting on this issue, eleven understood the decision reached. Only three said 'not really' and that they had had to turn to their social workers for clarification. Young people did generally know what a right of appeal was. There were only eight who did not.[28] Twenty-four generally understood what it meant (but not the technicalities of it)[29] and six[30] had not known when they first came into the system (aged five or six) but had learned from experience. The same was true for parents. Of the 14 parents expressing views, 12 understood they could appeal, although two stated that they did not know how to go about this. Only two stated that they did not know what an appeal was.

None of the 50 children interviewed individually had ever appealed. Only three of the parents interviewed had appealed but were unsuccessful. Panel members expressed the view that the low rate of appeals was due to a high degree of consensus reached in the panel and acceptance of the panel's decision. However, one social worker observed that in his experience families 'very rarely agree with what's been said yet when you say to them they can request [a review] or get a decision appealed, they tend not to and just accept the decision that's been given, despite the fact that they're very angry afterwards'. Eight[31] young people did not appeal because they were satisfied with the panel's decision but a number put forward other reasons, such as that it was not worth the effort or that it was pointless.[32] One 16 year old girl observed, 'Most times I just can't be bothered appealing because I don't think I'd get anything out of it anyway'. In two cases the social workers advised against it. These views were based on perceptions that adults don't really listen or pay attention to young people. Although a number of young people and their parents acknowledged that panel members try their best they may not succeed because of the language, generation and/or class barriers.[33]

25 Three girls and one boy.
26 Seven girls and twenty boys.
27 Six girls and six boys.
28 Two girls and six boys.
29 Two girls and six boys.
30 Four girls and two boys.
31 Four girls and four boys.
32 Fifteen expressed this view, six girls and nine boys.
33 A study of 1,155 children referred to in the hearings system in Scotland in 1995 found that children primarily came from households characterized by social and economic disadvantage. See Waterhouse and McGhee (2002:279). Of the 40 panel members interviewed in our study out of around 400 members serving Glasgow in 1997–1998 nearly all came from professional or management backgrounds. Only one panel member was a taxi driver (who owned his own business) and one was a secretary.

Interpreting the Landscape: Differing Perceptions of the Local and Priorities

Understanding the context that leads to children being brought before a hearing is very important. Yet the ways in which panel members and children and families view them is often at odds. We put three scenarios that reflected the kinds of cases that we observed in hearings to 50 young people with some experience of the system and to the 25 parents we interviewed to explore their responses to the situation before the panel. We did this because our research constraints prevented us from questioning young people or families at the hearings we observed. The scenarios were drawn from hearings that we had observed. The first scenario involved an eleven year old boy who is living with his granny and who is not attending school. He stays at home to look after her. The young people were asked 'Do you think an eleven year old boy would tell the panel why he is not going to school?' The second scenario involved a 13 year old who has not been to school for a year because of bullying. The young people were asked if the 13 year old would tell the panel what was going on. The third scenario involved a 15 year old girl who goes to school but disappears at the weekend without her parents' consent because her stepfather, who drinks at weekends, gets aggressive and abusive. The young people were asked if she would tell the panel the real reason for her absence at weekends. A detailed account of these young peoples' responses can be found in Griffiths and Kandel (2005).

As noted in our chapter, these young people's responses

> … clearly brought out the issues and options – such as whether the panel would be a help or hindrance, whether to treat the panel members as friend or foe, whether to make a statement of autonomy or yield to state authority, whether to be loyal and protective of family and friends or to protect oneself, whether to be silenced by fear of shame, and young people's knowledge of resources or lack of them (Griffiths and Kandel 2005:288).

It is clear that young people's strategies for dealing with these issues fall into three broad responses, namely: 1) silence or saying as little as possible, 2) apparent compliance where necessary and 3) autonomy and defiance. Those parents who responded to the scenarios were roughly in agreement with what the young people had to say for the reasons outlined above. Making an open declaration of what is going on in their lives requires careful consideration. For although panel members view a hearing as an open space for dialogue, children and families often see it as an arena that is fraught with danger and that demands circumspection. For children and families must assess their participation in the light of the local informal law of loyalty and strong discipline that shapes their lives outside the hearing (Griffiths and Kandel 2009c). As a result, the strategies that they employ in handling this space puts panel members at a disadvantage because they are unable to acquire all the information they would like to have in order to make the best possible decision for the child. The priorities of panel members may not be those of the children and families they deal with.

Getting children to go to school, to stop hanging around with older children who may lead them into trouble, or to stop undertaking activities that may lead them into offending behaviour (such as hanging around on the street) are in children's best interests from the perspective of panel members, especially with regard to keeping them on the right side of the law. This may, however, clash with the children and their families' perceptions of the need to stay home to care for a parent, not to 'grass' on one's mates, or to put on a good show in order not to let oneself or one's family down. These considerations may well outweigh panel members' priorities. A number of social workers observed that parents' attention may wander at hearings because they are worrying about where the next meal for the family is coming from or how to pay pressing bills. Understanding the context in which events occur that bring children before a hearing is important as the way the parties view the events may vary. Just as the 11 year old boy in the first scenario did not go to school because he was looking after his granny, so one social worker commented as follows about a case where a thirteen year old girl's mother had a serious drug problem and so the girl was not going to school:

> … and the panel were honing in on her not going to school rather than listening to why she is not going to school. That her whole family life is chaotic. Her mother doesn't get her up in the morning and instead of focusing on mum, they were focusing on her. Why are you not going to school?

Another social worker acknowledged, 'It's important to tell kids to go to school' but sometimes the panel 'don't do this the right way'. Yet another commented, 'there are a lot of circumstances that I don't think are taken on board [at panels]', for example, accepting a ground of referral in order to take the blame 'for something a mate did'.

Similarly, when it comes to the issue of bullying, panel members are aware that this goes on both in and out of school but they often see this as an excuse that is put forward for not going to school, as was the case in the truancy hearing B set out in Griffiths and Kandel (2005:281–283). This may be due to this featuring in training exercises where panel members are encouraged to be wary of such allegations. While bullying is not an acceptable legal ground for non-attendance at school, like ill health, nonetheless it does have a real impact on children's lives. Four of the parents we interviewed expressly stated that they had to deal with this issue because their children were being bullied at school or in their neighbourhood. In the hearing we outline, the panel members do not take the young man, Steve's account of bullying seriously, despite his social worker and school's recognition of the bullying. In this case the panel members declined to take account of local knowledge about the existence of gangs and their effects although social workers are well aware of what is going on.

As one worker from Priesthill noted, in his area 'children are very territorial'. This means that if a child from one area enters another, she or he may risk getting into a fight. Understanding the local context is something that eludes most panel members. As one panel member, who was an exception to this, explained, 'I know the streets in Drumchapel, Easterhouse, Possil' this means that he can tell when children are genuinely talking about problems they face and when they are making excuses 'so sometimes ye sae tae them well if you're talking about no going tae school because of the bullying well how come you're going from Drumchapel or Easterhouse or Baillieston into Parkhead Forge to meet other gang members there?' In his view, 'local knowledge does help'. Another panel member supported this view and was of the opinion that panel members could benefit from having a better understanding of the areas in which children live. As he explained, through working in the Post Office:

> … you got to know the rough areas where the postman wouldn't go up the stairs because of the drug addiction, the needles lying about the place and this is what some of these kids are coming down, to go to school or whatever. It's horrifying. I had to get my drivers fitted with thick gloves, because of the needles going into the post boxes … I feel as if some of the panel members could, it wouldn't do them any harm to visit these places.

When it comes to children's behaviour, how this is perceived by panel members may have an important effect on the decision-making process. In the truancy hearing B (Griffiths and Kandel 2005:281–283) the panel view Steve's behaviour as uncooperative. They listen to what he has to say but they do not hear, or rather they interpret, what he has to say as the product of being 'outwith' control. One mother explained how her son's behaviour at a panel was all bravado but that it was in danger of being misinterpreted. 'Simon would come out with things like "oh it's rubbish, I don't want to be here" or he wouldn't answer when a question was put to him or he would answer cheekily because he was nervous'. However, rather than understanding his behaviour for what it represented 'people would see him as being a naughty little boy'.

A number of young people we interviewed in schools complained about the way adults took issue with them for hanging about in the street. For many young people this is the only kind of social space that they can access in their neighbourhoods but adults tend to view this behaviour as putting them at risk because of the potential for mixing with their peers and getting into trouble through drinking or taking drugs. This leads to situations where young people sometimes find themselves picked on unfairly. As one social worker commented, the young people in his area all hang out at Pollock because there is a 'shopping centre up there'. He complained that:

> … for ages we were just getting silly referrals [from the reporter], you know, for breach of the peace. They [young people] were just walking down the road, and its about, kind of, are the police trying to get their figures up or are the police scapegoating young people … But I think panels have great difficulty in accepting the police may victimize young people.

Accounting for Difference: Varying Local Responses to National and Transnational Law

It is clear that transnational concepts, such as participation, promoted by Article 12 of the Children's Convention, have a different salience for different people, such as panel members and the children and families that they deal with, although they all share a common, territorial base – the city of Glasgow. What national law embraces in the form of the Children (Scotland) Act 1995 and what panel members strive to implement, namely a balance between children's welfare and rights that involves a transparent and open process, takes on another meaning for the children and families concerned that is generally one of silence and circumspection. Such findings raise important questions about how the 'local' is to be perceived and located in relation to national and transnational processes that embrace law. For although the actors may be said to be 'local' in that they are located within the bounded space of a city, they nonetheless find themselves situated within very different types of networks that separate them from one another.

Thus children and families, while coming from different neighbourhoods all over Glasgow, share the common characteristics of living in areas that have high rates of poverty, deprivation, unemployment, lack of education, drug, alcohol and domestic abuse that set them apart from the panel members who deal with them. Although some panel members have knowledge of these neighbourhoods, they themselves, through their personal attainment and/or upwardly mobile life histories, find themselves living in a very different world from those of the children and families who come before hearings. These different worlds reflect differing priorities and values that have an impact on how law is perceived. In many cases what is important for children and families is the local, 'informal' law of family and neighbourhood that takes precedence over the national law that panel members seek to apply. Even though panel members themselves seek to 'localize' this national law to make it fit the circumstances in which they have to apply it (Griffiths and Kandel 2009a) they still encounter problems.

Despite panel members' valiant attempts to promote an open dialogue, power, inequality of status and class operate to create a division between the parties at a hearing that is hard to surmount. Understanding the factors that come into play and that give rise to differences is an important step in comprehending how abstract, theoretical propositions of law, embodied in transnational documents such as the Children's Convention or the European Right's Convention, take on significance in practice and acquire a reality that may subvert their original purpose. Being aware of what this entails is essential if policy makers and jurists are to engage in meaningful and effective law reform of the type that is currently under discussion by the Scottish Executive and the Scottish Parliament.

References

Benda-Beckmann, F. and K. and Griffiths, A. (eds) 2005. Introduction, in *Mobile People, Mobile Law: Expanding Legal Relations in a Contracting World.* Aldershot/UK and Burlington/USA: Ashgate Publishing Company, 1–35.

Foucault, M. 1980. Two lectures, in *Power/Knowledge Selected Interviews and Other Writings 1972–1977*, edited by C. Gordon. New York: Pantheon House, 78–108.

Giddens, A. 1984. *The Constitution of Society*. Cambridge: Polity Press.

Griffiths, A. 2001. Working towards consensus: Children's hearings in Scotland, in *Children in Society: Contemporary Theory, Policy and Practice*, edited by P. Foley, J. Roche and S. Tucker. New York/Basingstoke: Palgrave in association with the Open University, 121–132.

—— 2002. Legal pluralism, in *An Introduction to Law and Social Theory*, edited by R. Banakar and M. Travers. Oxford and Portland Oregon: Hart Publishing, 289–310.

—— 2004. Empowering children? Legal understandings and experiences of rights in the Scottish children's hearings system, in *Human Rights Brought Home: Socio-Legal Perspectives on Human Rights in the National Context,* edited by S. Halliday and P. Schmidt. Oxford and Portland Oregon: Hart Publishing, 231–255.

—— 2006. Children's confidentiality at the crossroads: Challenges for the Scottish children's hearings system. *Journal of Social Welfare and Family Law* 28, 2:135–150.

Griffths, A. and Kandel, R.F. 2000. Hearing children in children's hearings. *Child and Family Law Quarterly* 3:283–299.

—— 2005. Localizing the global: Rights of participation in the Scottish children's hearings system, in *Mobile People, Mobile Law: Expanding Legal Relations in a Contracting World*, edited by F. and K. von Benda-Beckmann and A. Griffiths. Aldershot, UK and Burlington, USA: Ashgate Publishing Company, 482–514.

—— 2009a. Half told truths and partial silence: Managing communication in Scottish children's hearings, in *The Power of Law: Anthropological Enquiries*, edited by F. and K. von Benda-Beckmann and A. Griffiths. Oxford: Berghahn Press, 176–195.

—— 2009b. The governance of children: From welfare justice to proactive regulation in the Scottish children's hearings system, in *Rules of Law and Laws of Ruling: On the Governance of Law*, edited by F. and K. von Benda-Beckmann and J. Eckert. Aldershot, UK and Burlington, USA: Ashgate Publishing Company, 171–189.

—— 2009c. The myth of the transparent table: Reconstructing space and legal interventions in Scottish children's hearings, in *Spatializing Law: An Anthropological Geography of Law in Society*, edited by F. and K. von Benda-Beckmann and A. Griffiths. Aldershot, UK and Burlington, USA: Ashgate Publishing Company, 157–175.

Hallett, C. and Murray, C. with Jamies, J. and Veitch, B. 1998. The Evaluation of Children's Hearings in Scotland, vol. 1: Deciding in Children's Interests. Edinburgh: The Scottish Office Central Research Unit.

Kilbrandon, L. 1964. *Report on Children and Young Persons, Scotland,* Camnd. 2306. Edinburgh: Scottish Home and Health department.

Marshall, K. 1997. *Children's Rights in the Balance: The Participation Protection Debate.* London: The Stationery Office.

Waterhouse, L. and McGhee, J. 2002. Children's hearings in Scotland: compulsion and disadvantage. *Journal of Social Welfare and Family Law* 24(3): 279–296.

Waterhouse, L., McGhee, J., Whyte, W.N., Loucks, N., Kay, H. and Stewart, R. 2000. Children in focus. *Evaluation of Children's Hearings System Vol 3*. Edinburgh: Scottish Office Central Research Unit, The Scottish Office.

Chapter 9
Business Lawyers in the Age of Globalization – A Comparison of the Situation in Norway and Germany

Knut Papendorf

Abstract

This chapter discusses the changes in the role of business lawyers in a time of increasing globalization. A comparative study of firms in Norway and Germany reveals strong growth in the number of law firms. This is due to changes in the needs of the large corporations that constitute the law firm's most important clients. These corporations hire law firms to handle their big and complex problems. In addition, they include business lawyers in their business activities, for example as members of the board. Thus lawyers who participate as strategic planners in the large corporations gain considerable power through their influence on the strategic choices of the corporations. At the same time that these developments are taking place we see increasing competition between law firms for the business opportunities that these corporations represent.

Introduction

This chapter examines the role business lawyers play in the process of globalization. Using Norwegian and German business lawyers as case studies, I investigate what power lawyers have in large corporations. I produced the Norwegian Power and Democracy (Committee) Report (1998–2003) (Papendorf 2002) which dealt with the dissemination of power in Norwegian society and included the role of business lawyers. As a result I became interested in the question of what power lawyers wield in today's global environment and, in pursuing this theme, expanded my study to include some German business lawyers for comparative purposes.

In addressing the business lawyer's role I first draw on some of the literature in the field of 'justice and the role of the business lawyer in a globalized world'. After an account of the method I used in this study, I turn to Norway and Germany as examples of the specialization and growth in the globalized lawyer market. One issue that arose in the development of this market is the importance of understanding how businesses adapt to the needs of trade and industry and what this entails for lawyers. This has had an impact on the globalized lawyers' market by creating competition among law firms, leading to their adopting certain strategies and internal restructuring to give them the edge in a competitive market. These processes give rise to something we may call 'transnational law' which I explore towards the end of the chapter, along with the question of the power lawyers wield within corporations.

A First Sketch

On summarizing a selection of the literature in this field, the following picture emerges. The state's legal monopoly – and its legislative monopoly in particular – is threatened by transnational powers. The state's role is taken over by very different organizations and cooperations. The globalized legal situation is characterized by a number of governance regimes (for example, the World Trade Organization), rather than by a single regime. In this context an abstract norm working as a mechanism of regulation is not relevant; what is required is a civil law that creates flexible, individual solutions to the problems at hand. In the development and practice of this new 'law', lawyers, rather than judges, are needed. With their legal way of thinking, the lawyers rule the mechanisms of globalization. Lawyers and legal experts establish influential networks that are organized transnationally. They develop strategies for globally-oriented corporations and generate rules for the world trade they will practice and interpret. We identify a culture of 'global lawyering', that may pose a threat to state sovereignty because it does not restrict itself to the application of law; moreover, it has control over legal production and legislation (Dezelay/Garth 1996, Teubner 1997 a and b, Vismann 2000).

Methodical Approach and First Answer

This research project started in June 2000 and the main work comprised an interview study that was carried out in the first six months of 2001. This involved interviewing nineteen Norwegian business lawyers, primarily from large and medium-sized law firms. Six German lawyers made up the comparative group. In addition I interviewed the director of a medium-sized firm in Oslo. The German lawyers also came mainly from large and medium-sized firms with their head offices in Hamburg and Cologne. I also carried out field work in lawyers' meeting places, for example, at a working exhibition for young lawyers in Berlin and at a refresher course arranged by the Norwegian Association of Lawyers in Oslo. This empirical work was prepared and supplemented by examining the discussion in sociology of law under the theme of lawyers in the process of globalization. Furthermore, I studied the presentations the firms had given of themselves on the Internet and their publicity strategies in the press. The first results from my study of the lawyers and their firms showed that one of the consequences of globalization is increasing specialization resulting in a swift process of restructuring firms into larger companies.

Specialization and Growth

In the course of the 1980s and 1990s the lawyer's role changed dramatically. The legal profession went from being a withdrawn professional group with a passive attitude, to becoming an integrated part of service companies and an active competitor among other participants in the market.

In parallel, one saw a steady growth which has intensified in the twenty-first century. My interviewees highlighted changes in clients' demands as the reason for this development. The demands primarily appear as what we could call an extended time of reaction. This has to do with technological development in communications as well as the increased frequency of transactions in the business world. However, what seems to be the most pressing issue is offering clients considerable legal competence. The clients' legal problems are clearly more complex than before, largely due to the globalization of international trade connections. The main route to solving the dramatically changed structural conditions of lawyers' trade internationally has been to create larger organization units. Size provides unconditional benefits for dealing with competition and a certain size is crucial, as all my interviewees agreed, in order to manage clients' demands for further specialization. Interviewees mentioned both restructuring the firms into businesses of knowledge and establishing new structures in the organizations geared towards different branches of trade and industry that form part of their clients' interests.

The Growth in the Norwegian Firms up to 2002

In discussing the importance of the dramatic growth in Norway's international lawyers' market, I focus on the five top firms in Oslo.[1] At the end of the 1989/90 period the firms *Thommessen & Krefting* in Oslo and *Greve, Greve, Greve & Lorentzen* in Bergen established an official cooperation. The latter firm merged with the former. The amalgamated firm acquired the name *Thommessen, Krefting & Greve* and became Norway's largest law firm with 61 lawyers, including 30 partners. A further step in expansion to provide the firm with an international profile and enhanced competitive edge led to it entering into close cooperation with a Swedish law firm, *Vinge KB*, and a Danish law firm, *Kromann og Münter*, with the aim of establishing a common office in London. In 1993 yet another firm, *Lund & Co* joined and the name of the firm changed yet again to *Thommessen, Krefting, Greve & Lund* (TKGL). In January 2002, as I collected my data, a total of 124 lawyers worked at *Thommessen, Krefting, Greve & Lund.*

In 1990 another three law firms merged: *Wiersholm, Bachke & Helliesen*; *Mellbye, Schjoldager, Seiersted & Tenden* and *Bech, Hirsch & Co* became *Wiersholm, Mellbye og Bech* (WMB). At the time *Wiersholm, Mellbye og Bech*

1 The number five seems to have an almost magic meaning in this context, particularly if one reads articles from journalists who focus on the lawyer market. In the case of London, they talk about a 'magic five' circle. The same is found in New York, but not in Germany.

comprised 50 lawyers but this had grown to 106 lawyers by 2002. Another important firm in Norway is *Schjødt* and this, too, was originally three firms, namely *Schjødt* in Oslo, *Martens* in Bergen and *Vaagland* in Trondheim. The merger took place at the end of 1993, a little later than the other two mergers mentioned. By 2002, *Schjødt* had 141 lawyers, working in five different places in Norway. Only 30 years ago, *Schjødt* was considered one of the largest law firms in Oslo with fewer than ten employees at that time.

While these three firms chose the model of the merger, the last two top firms I studied followed a more organic model of growth. *Wikborg, Rein & Co* (WR) grew approximately 30 per cent a year from 1999 onwards and expanded from 81 to 142 lawyers. *Bugge, Arentz-Hansen & Rasmussen* (BA-HR) estimated they had around 110 lawyers.

It seems inevitable that this rapid growth over such a short period of time would induce a number of problems, burdens and frustrations. Both the German and the Norwegian lawyers mentioned the division of profit between the partners as one of the main sources of conflict. The different business cultures were also ranked high on the list of potential conflict areas. Many described the loss of the feeling of intimacy that comes with working in a small firm as a big problem for them, especially since the possibility of withdrawing from time to time had lessened considerably. Many of the lawyers I spoke to felt reduced to an anonymous machine whose main task was to produce as many billing hours as possible. In the law firm *Haarmann, Hemmelrath and Partner,* one sees just such a conflict. The law firm wished to follow the trend and shift over to the shorter name *Haarmann and Hemmelrath* but this was not accepted by the Partner Assembly that demanded a 90 per cent majority vote (*Juve Rechtsmarkt* 2005:6). Last but not least, the most recent employees apparently had their career development potential reduced because of changes in the distribution of tasks and money relating to those who were partners and those who were merely employees. For, as the firms grow, the partners gain power at the expense of the employees.

General Considerations of the Concept of the 'Large' Law Firm

The lawyers generally view size as a criterion of success. It is important to note that we are not talking about size as something static, but about the development in law firms that takes place over a period of time. When comparing the growth of North American law firms with our own we recognize a dramatic development in the concept of size within the legal profession. In 1903 there were no law firms outside New York with more than nine employees. The concept of the 'law factory' originated as early as 1906 but, nevertheless, not one of the largest law firms at the time had more that 20 lawyers (Sander and Williams 1992:391). At the beginning of the 1960s hardly any North American law firms had more than 50 lawyers (Galanter and Palay 1991:15). At the beginning of the 1990s, the concept of the 'law factory' had gone through a complete change of character. The largest law firms now employ more than 1,000 lawyers (Sander and Williams 1992:392).

A firm with worldwide assignments like *Clifford Chance* with 30 offices in 21 countries was employing 3,700 legal advisors in 2009.

The fact that there is ongoing discussion about the ideal size for a law firm was confirmed by my interviewees. One ongoing strategy is to be represented in the important financial and economic centres of the world by establishing small offices in these areas or by associations with smaller firms there (worldwide model). *White & Case, Feddersen* employs this strategy. The law firm *Hengeler* on the other hand is following a strategic model where growth has taken place exclusively inside German borders. One of the fastest growing firms in Germany at the time of my research, *Haarmann & Hemmelrath*, established in 1987, chose a strategy of growth based on a concentration on several areas but an emphasis on expertise within business investigations and tax advice.

The size necessary to survive on the European and global lawyers' market remains an open question. One of my interviewees in Germany gave the following answer:

> This is the most difficult question today since we do not know what the development is going to be like. We suppose that we will need a certain number of lawyers to be able to cope with the really big assignments. We do not know what the necessary size is. When will size itself become a disadvantage? This we do not know.

My study was conducted at a time when there was a boom in mergers both in Norway and internationally. Given the signs of a weakening economy and the decline in confidence in the information technology and Internet business, even law firms now seem to favour slowing down their growth and want to consolidate their situation. The development in the Norwegian lawyers' market may at least be analyzed in this way. Three of the firms[2] I mentioned earlier – *Bugge, Arentz-Hansen & Rasmussen* (-19.1 per cent), *Schjødt* (-5.8 per cent) and *Thommessen* (-24.6 per cent) – considerably reduced the number of lawyers they employ over the 2002–2005 period. However, the picture is not clear nor is it unambiguous. During the same period *Wikborg Rein* increased their number of lawyers by 0.8 per cent and *Wiersholm* has had a 13.7 per cent increase in new employees. When this chapter was being written (mid-2009), after a new short period of growth in connection with a growing merger market, the business law firms had to react to a new crisis – the United States of America's mortgage disaster which reached Europe and Norway in the summer of 2007. The actual figures for the law firms in Norway mentioned before are as follows: *Bugge, Arentz-Hansen & Rasmussen*: approimately 100 lawyers; *Schjødt*: 125 lawyers; *Wiersholm*: 128 lawyers; *Thommessen*: 175 lawyers and *Wikborn Rein*: 185 lawyers. So the picture is still contradictory compared to the situation in 2002. Some firms, such as *Bugge, Arentz-Hansen & Rasmussen* and *Schjødt* are still reducing their number of lawyers, whereas others, like *Wiersholm, Thommessen* and *Wikborn Rein* continue to grow rapidly (*Thommessen* 41 per cent and *Wikborn Rein* 30 per cent).

2 I will from now use the actual names of the law firms.

The German Situation: Mergeritis – Fever of Change – Pedigrees

The large German firms, organized across the German regions, discussed their establishment abroad, for example in Brussels and in Asia, from around 1980. The same firms were also interested in contacts in the Anglo-American market.[3] The large, economically powerful, North American and English firms, on the other hand, were interested in gaining access to the European financial and economic centres. Germany was regarded as the most important market for growth and North American law firms were trying to establish themselves in Germany following an earlier, disastrous attempt to do so at the beginning of the 1990s. They no longer limited their interests to starting new establishments but also bought German firms. From 2000 onwards, the companies' strategies were first and foremost to supervise their clients in their financial projects. Another important dimension is the role that Germany plays in European industry. The European economy orients itself towards the capital market and becomes increasingly international (*JUVE Rechtsmarkt* 2001:6) as a result. The table opposite shows the development of some of the law firms.

First, it shows the great Anglo-American engagement in the German market. Second, it shows that some of the large firms have not yet taken part in any mergers, and appear as purely German firms (for example numbers 2, 7, 8, 9, 11, 13 and 19 in the table).

Contrary to the Norwegian law firms, the German law firms seem to have focused on commodity trading in the Anglo-American market. The *JUVE-Handbuch*[4] 1999/2000 (3) says: 'The Anglo-Saxon financial press treats the German market as the main scene for the strategic "final game" to gain power over the international lawyers' market'. The Norwegian law firms are definitely not subject to the same interest. This is for two reasons. The first concerns whether or not the Norwegian market holds an economically interesting potential for the kind of business that we are talking about. The second revolves around some structural peculiarities in Norway that seem to complicate the establishment of foreign law firms in the country. My interviewees referred to the difficulty of the Norwegian language and to the then established professional networks that would relegate the newly-established firms at the most to a place on the outskirts. The fact that Norway is presented as a 'country apart' in certain political ways also seems to lead to particular problems for foreign business lawyers in competition with Norwegian ones.

The German market for business lawyers, on the other hand, is a market in constant motion. The interviews I conducted with German business lawyers

3 The great enthusiasm in some of the big German law firms in this context may in part be attributed to younger partners' desire to hasten the necessary changes in generation and in structure in an ongoing merger process with a foreign firm (*JUVE-Handbuch* 2000/2001:3).

4 Publisher working with the ranking of law firms, see also section 4 in this chapter.

Table 9.1 Large national and transnational business law firms located in Germany (figures as of 1 July 2008)(a)

Ranking name		Number of lawyers in		Number of establishments in	
		Germany	Abroad	Germany	Abroad
1.	Freshfields Bruckhaus Deringer	594	1,966	6	21
2.	CMS Hasche Sigle	494	42	9	4
3.	Clifford Chance	427	3,707*	3	25
4.	Lovells	352	1,325	4	22
5.	Linklaters	288	2,560	4	26
6.	Taylor Wessing	285	423	5	8
7.	Luther	272	48	13	5
8.	Beiten Burkhardt	261	134	5	8
9.	Nörr Stiefenhofer Lutz	256	106	5	8
10.	White & Case	252	1,962	6	31
11.	Hengeler Mueller	228	15	4	2
13.	Gaedertz	195	9	9	1
14.	Baker & McKenzie	180	3,465	4	66
16.	Allen & Overy	151	2,539	4	25
17.	Latham & Watkins	136	2,012	3	23
19.	Graf von Westphalen	121	5	7	4
22.	Mayer Brown	118	1,963	3	19
24.	DLA Piper	113	3,623	4	60
40.	Heisse Kursawe Eversheds	73	2,720	1	39

Notes: The table is a condensed edition of the table in the *JUVE Handbuch* 2008/2009, Wirtschaftskanzleien, Köln, 11. edition 2008/2009:606.
*Legal advisors.

took place from December 2000 to January 2001. They point to a very different development in the German business market characterized by a rapidly changing global economic situation. According to the *Juve-Handbuch* of 2005/2006, German law firms had experienced a 'stony way' in the three years preceding. This involved processes of restructuring, reviewing business focus, retrenchments and closing branches. This phase seemed to end in 2005. Once again there appears to be a blossoming market providing clients like private equity houses and other investors such as *hedgefonds* (JUVE-Handbuch 2005/2006:23). However, this describes only a short time period. Already by the summer of 2007 the American mortgage disaster had reached Europe. As a result the business law firm market received another blow. The year 2008 was characterized by decreasing mandates, especially for firms specializing in mergers and acquisitions. This was an interesting development in the direction of greater segmentation of the market for law firms. The biggest firms and those who already had the highest turnover tried to concentrate on the most lucrative market segment which is mergers and acquisitions (*JUVE-Handbuch* 2008/2009:30). The law firms I interviewed may be seen as good examples of these rapid changes.

The law firm *Graf von Westphalen Fritze & Modeste*[5] planned a merger with their British working partner *Osborne Clark* at the beginning of 2001. In April 2001, *Osborne Clark* established their own office in Frankfurt but there was no progress in the process they had started with the German firm. The senior partner of the German firm, Dr Graf von Westphalen, was set against the merger. He wanted to continue to work in an independent office and had no wish to 'report to either London or Bristol' (*JUVE Rechtsmarkt* 4/2001:26). Halfway through 2001, nine partners and ten other lawyers left the branch office of the German firm in Cologne and established a new branch office for *Osborne Clark* in the same city. In 2002 *Graf von Westphalen Fritze & Modeste* merged with *Bappert Witz & Selbherr* to become *Graf von Westphalen Bappert & Modeste*. Since 2006 it has become known as *Graf von Westphalen* after a break up in the partnership that took place in 2003. At the time I did the interviews, the law firm *Gaedertz* was conducting intensive merger negotiations with the British firm *Norton Rose*. Some time after this, the Hamburg branch of *Gaedertz* merged with the American firm *Latham & Watkins* under the new name of *Latham & Watkins & Schön Nolte*. The original negotiations collapsed and the firm was divided into its regional parts (*JUVE-Rechtsmarkt* 2/2001:20). In May 2001 the *Gaedertz* branch in Leipzig was closed. Most of these lawyers joined *Haarmann, Hemmelrath & Partner*. In the meantime, the former branches in Cologne and Munich had merged with *Norton Rose* and became *Norten Rose Vieregge*. This spin-off process has continued until today. During that time, the third law firm that I contacted – *White & Case, Feddersen* – expanded its branch in Stockholm. From 2005 the name of this law firm in Germany was also shortened to *White & Case*. In 2007 and 2008, there were two new spin-offs. The fourth office – *Lovells Boesebeck Droste* – announced a merger with the French firm *Siméon & Associés* (Paris) as of 1 January 2001. *Lovells Boesebeck Droste* bought the Dutch firm *Ekelmans Den Hollander* in May 2001. In 2002 the name of that law firm in Germany was shortened to *Lovells*. In 2007 there were two spin-offs. The fifth firm that I had contact with – *Wessing* – gained access to the firm *Meibom*, specialists in competition law, at the beginning of 2001 and was thus able to expand their competition law specialization. In 2002, *Wessing* merged with *Taylor* becoming *Taylor Wessing*. In 2007, this had two spin-offs. The sixth firm – *Haarmann, Hemmelrath & Partner* – collapsed totally in 2006 because of conflicts about firm strategies among the leading partners.

This short examination of the processes of change in six law firms, chosen arbitrarily, clearly shows the speed with which restructuring processes take place. The restructuring is enforced by the processes of internationalization which materialize as mergers, buy-outs and new business establishments, in the

5 I will give a very short overview of their situation up to the middle of 2009 to describe later development.

form of branches at home and abroad. At the same time, Anglo-American firms establish branches in Germany. The process is marked by the ongoing exchange of highly specialized lawyers or whole teams of lawyers between the firms and by continuous peeling off and making new establishments. This rapid development opens up new possibilities in the market, even for the journalists that supervise the market, such as those connected with the *JUVE-Handbuch* that views itself as such a market observer. The *JUVE-Handbuch* offers columns and news about the most recent 'deals', the opening of new offices, latest trends, and so on. In the *JUVE-Handbuch's* annual edition, the law firms appear with their own 'pedigree', which simplifies the work for the supervisor of the market who wants to keep track of these developments.

Parallels of Economy: Understanding the Trade

The business lawyer today is confronted with assignments that reflect a totally different profile from before. Large corporations are only interested in the really big assignments and in a limited segment of the market. The mandate is usually complex in character since it is mostly a matter of particular cases within different legal specializations. Below is an example of a commentary on a buy-out and a merger and acquisition by a Norwegian lawyer who specializes in this field:

> In a buy-out situation your first concern is the structure of transaction that you aim for. If you are going to buy a business, you may generally either buy property and take over debts, or you may buy shares in a company. This could be a rather complicated matter. Taxes are almost always important, concession from the authorities is important and the consequences for deals with a third party may be important. We typically have to carry through a form of 'due diligence', going through the target company from a legal, economic and commercial angle. This means collecting and systematizing all legal material about the company. Whether you represent the seller or the buyer, you are involved. As a seller you prepare or organize, and as a buyer you conduct and document the research. Then you have the negotiation of the contract with a different situation every time, even though patterns can be found and practice for ordinary and non-ordinary deals develops over time. These are the three main components. When we are talking about a merger or a buy-out, we often run into extensive problems relating to competition law. The one that buys is normally in the same line of business as the one that is bought out and the goal of the buy-out is synergy, in other words, two and two should become more than four. Every time this happens the result is an increasing concentration in the market which involves competition law and the Office of Fair Trade in Norway and the commission in Brussels. A lot of labour legislation is involved too. First, the employees have a right to be involved and with a merger employees will often become redundant. Large retrenchment processes consume resources at the legal level. As corporate

> workers, we rely on specialists, typically experts on tax law, labour legislation and competition law. In some buy-out cases it may be very important to draw on experts on laws of immateriality. What often happens is that the lawyer of transactions becomes sort of a project coordinator. You need to be able to identify the problems that you need specialists for, and you need to have a fairly good understanding of the business aspects of the situation. This is essential if you are going to be able to assess the competition law aspects of the matter and to function as a go-between for business leaders and legal experts.

The problems of transaction described here and the legal problems that follow make up only a small part of the complicated everyday job of the business lawyer. Similar problems are linked to assignments of emissions.

The solution to this complex array of skills is first and foremost specialization. This means that the large and intricate assignments can only be carried through if you have a team of highly specialized and well-qualified lawyers who cooperate with other occupational groups, like banking investors. In order to meet the demand for profit, all the large and middle-sized Norwegian business law firms have made fundamental changes in their organizational structure. By and large, the traditional legal disciplines no longer form the basis of the internal organization. It seems more important to build an organization that is geared towards the client or the 'customer'. This allows for an understanding of the trade. One of my interviewees expressed this dramatic change in the image of the lawyer as follows:

> Earlier my firm was organized by the legal fields. A trade, on the other hand, deals with a larger spectrum of problems. If we want to give good legal advice to some lines of business, we do not just need legal experts. They also need to know the problems that are specific to this particular business.

If you study the largest Norwegian law firms' presentations of themselves on the Internet you see clearly how they have adapted to this new situation. The web page of the law firm *Wiersholm* shows the following organizational structure in business and activity areas:

> Shipping/transportation, taxes/duties, stock exchange/transactions, the European Union/legislation for competition, process law, industry/trade/public depreciation allowances, banking/finance, energy/construction activities/real property, information technology/communication/media.

With small variations, these areas of business are also undertaken by other large and middle sized Norwegian law firms.

In other words, Norwegian and German lawyers see themselves as providers of services; the client becomes a customer one is eager to please. The firms publish reviews of the legal development in different fields and arrange seminars on long-term strategies in order to keep former customers and attract new ones. When new colleagues are appointed this is duly announced in the (financial) papers, obviously for marketing purposes. The large firms regularly discuss advantages and disadvantages of management structures similar to the structures in the financial world. One of my German interviewees summed up this development:

> In the 1980s you had to work with many different things. Since the 1990s we have had to focus on core subjects. We have been through the same discussions as the financial world: Are we going to establish a firm with a total kind of service, or should we concentrate on the tasks that we are competent in doing?

The result of this reorientation and restructuring of the business law activity is not limited to the organization. One consequence is the expansion of traditional legal counselling. It now includes economic and strategic counselling. A review of the representation of lawyers on the boards of approximately 1,000 Norwegian limited companies shows this clearly. In May 2003, the five largest Norwegian business lawyer firms had 180 partners altogether and 137 of these lawyers were on the boards of 956 limited companies. On average each one of them had seven board posts (*Verdens Gang* 25.5.2003, s. 11). That interconnectedness with big Norwegian financial actors – understood as a role mixing legal advisor on one side and financial actor on the other – has led to major problems which, given this backdrop, is hardly surprising. Some of the law firms have reacted by reducing their involvement as members of boards or corporations.

The expansion towards more economic and strategic counselling has another interesting aspect to it which may be seen as parallel to the development in social and criminal policy. In the sense that it is a proactive interventionist model that aims to tackle problems at their roots within corporations. The business lawyer has gone from being someone who handles and solves conflicts to someone who prevents conflicts. The enormous economic consequences of a possible legal conflict have made this change in the field of counselling a major task for business lawyers. A parallel development which aggravates this for law firms is a new dispute culture in the economic sphere. This means for law firms that each merger listed on the stock exchange has to be made watertight against any possible legal actions. This requires high competence in litigation (*Juve Handbuch* 2007/2008:23).

Sharpened Competition includes Law Firm Ranking

There is no doubt that there is keen competition for assignments in the lawyers' market. This sort of competition requires a form of marketing that was unheard of in the Norwegian market just a couple of years ago. On the other hand the competition also reflects the existing hierarchy among the law firms which I return to later. My Norwegian interviewees described the competition among law firms as 'extremely keen', 'brutal' and 'huge'. The five largest Norwegian law firms view each other as rivals when it comes to large, lucrative cases, but still respect one another and even cooperate, for instance when it comes to postgraduate courses for young lawyers. However, the respect, especially for the clients in the competition, has its limits, as illustrated by this quote from one of my interviewees:

> A very offensive competition has developed between the law firms. You actually find lawyers calling up the clients of their rivals asking them permission to present themselves and the firm. They show up with video shows, PowerPoint presentations and God knows what.

Even clients promote this tight competition. This is because the structure of the assignments makes it impossible to stipulate the price in advance.

In this situation it is all the more important to be considered the best law firm in this particular class or else the best with regard to price. Another aspect of the increased competition is evident when it comes to complaints about lawyers. Clients are much less loyal than before and big clients frequently change their mandates so law firms rarely have exclusive rights to an assignment. In routine matters companies often make use of 'cheap' lawyers or their own law departments whereas they buy expert services from the large law firms when it comes to big and complex assignments.

Even in Norway there is ever-increasing supervision of business lawyers. Several companies work on the ranking of the firms.[6] This ranking indicates to firms where they stand in competition with other law firms, as well as where they stand when it comes to giving legal advice in different fields. It seems that the Norwegian media and the law firms themselves consider these ranking lists well-founded and objective, as if they were the result of independent research.

Yet another significant feature of the (global) competition in this field is that the firms seem to standardize the way they present themselves.[7] It is important to find office premises close to the large financial operators. We see this clearly both in Hamburg and in Oslo. It is equally important to be close to the large customers. Placing your office alongside the really important operators in the economy and finance business also holds symbolic value. In Oslo, *Aker Brygge*[8] *and Vika* are considered the economic and financial centre of Norway. Some of the power that radiates from the centre also rubs off on the law firms with offices within its orbit. The five firms mentioned earlier – *Bahr*, *Wiersholm*, *Wikborn Rein*, *Thommessen* and *Schjødt* – all have their headquarters within this centre. Since these law firms have expanded so much in the last years, some of them are short of space but moving to other areas in Oslo with more office space was never considered an

6 In the case of Norway we can, for example, mention the International Centre for Commercial Laws and Chambers and Partners and for Germany the already mentioned *JUVE-Handbuch* and *JUVE Rechtsmarkt*.

7 Lindemann's commentary titled 'Body politics – Lawyers in suits' may be taken as a little ironic sharpening of this issue (Lindemann 2009:84).

8 The Norwegian equivalent to the British Docklands in London.

option. Instead these firms have leased offices close by (satellite solution) or restructured their own buildings in order to house more lawyers in the same area. This has inevitably meant smaller offices for the lawyers. It is probably not the view of the beautiful Oslo fjord which keeps the firms located where they are but their interest in retaining business. However, a location near a fjord should not be underestimated. My interviews with partners in Hamburg, which included lawyers at some of the leading business law firms there, took place near a famous river and lake, Binnenalster, one of the most expensive regions in Hamburg. The atmosphere of economic power which accompanies top-rated districts like Aker Brygge cannot be downplayed. Albrechtsen (1974:54) reported the large concentration of law firms with an address in Oslo, the capital city, in the 1970s and, in 1971, 40 per cent of Norwegian Bar Association members had offices within a kilometre of the centre of Oslo. The unequal distribution of lawyers in a centre-periphery perspective and the associated preference lawyers have for business law has previously been discussed as a problem for legal security in Norway (Mathiesen 2005:93). In Marianne Bahus' research on lawyers in 2001, 95 per cent of those interviewed engaged in business law. Over 60 per cent of those interviewed were mainly engaged in business law. On the other hand, lawyers have little interest in or inadequate knowledge about law fields which have no economic benefits, such as social or penal law, in other words law fields relevant for poor people (Mathiesen 2005).

The Question of Transnational Law and the Role of Lawyers

As already suggested, the legal monopoly of the national state is threatened by transnational powers which we can generalize under 'governance regimes'. In this context we identify the origin of something we can call 'transnational law'. This new type of 'law' has the following characteristics:

- It is mainly created and carried out by private actors.
- It is based on general law principles, which are used in special fields of practice.
- It is mainly codified in standard contracts, moral codes and law standards (Quack 2008:1).

What is important in this context is the focus on private law and especially on venture company and commercial law.

The almost-autonomous actors in transnationalizing the law are, for example, the World Trade Organization, the International Monetary Fund or the World Bank (Günther/Randeria 2001). The World Trade Organization is an international organization dealing with international law and has its own competences designed to supervise and liberalize international trade. Anti-dumping rules and reducing limitations in trade are central here. In cases of violation of trade rules, World Trade

Organization members have agreed to use the organization's dispute settlement system instead of taking action unilaterally. In cases of disagreement on issues of law and legal interpretations, the decision of the Dispute Settlement Body, located in Geneva, can appeal to the Appelate Body, a permanent seven-member organ of mainly legal experts in international law. The judgments from this multi-step dispute settlement process are binding for member states, which is important in the context of transnational law. This dispute settlement process is constructed mainly as an arbitration type method but the World Trade Organization gets with it a mostly judicative power. Moreover, in the context of transnational law, their multi-step dispute settlement judgments will influence global law development in general, giving the organization almost a law-giver role.[9]

Lex mercatoria is another example of the development of transnational law. It is not a new phenomenon, with long traditions back to the Middle Ages as the universal 'law' for international commerce at that time. Today's *lex mercatoria* might be seen as a supplement to national law, which is understood as inadequate for the needs of international trade. The solution to this problem was seen as standard and sample contracts, which were interpreted locally according to the arbitration tribunals. According to Teubner (1997:769), *lex mercatoria* is:

> … the most successful case of law without a state (…), a transnational legal order of global markets that has developed outside national law and international law. Multinational enterprises now arrive at contracts which they submit neither to national jurisdiction nor to national substantive law. They agree on international arbitration and on the application of a transnational commercial law that is independent of any national law.

The interpretation of *lex mercatoria* as a kind of frontrunner of an autonomous transnational law is quite controversial. Sassen, for example, asks if *lex mercatoria* is actually pluralistic or in reality just an expansion of American commercial law, dominated by big American law firms. Sassen speaks in this context of an 'Americanization of law' (Sassen 1996:16).

Are Business Lawyers Powerful?

There is no doubt that lawyers and law firms have power but the question is, how much and in what context?[10] This question was the focus of the Norwegian Power and Democracy (Committee) Report that was the starting point for this research.

9 For more details see Papendorf (2002:122).

10 For a more thorough discussion concerning this question see Papendorf (2002: 136–183). I take as my starting point Max Weber's classic definition of power: '*Macht bedeutet jede Chance, innerhalb einer sozialen Beziehung den eigenen Willen auch gegen Widerstreben durchzusetzen, gleichviel worauf diese Chance beruht*' (Weber 2005:38).

I now address the potential of law and its application from a power perspective. Albrechtsen (1974b: 87) gives the law a function as a 'language' that turns technology, business management and other issues into relations between people and notions of rights, duties and competence. As a consequence, lawyers are especially qualified to attend to tasks linked to cooperation, representation and management, typically found in businesses (Albrechtsen 1974b).

Each business lawyer has power in relation to the client. My analysis shows that business lawyers have power when they give legal advice because they have the knowledge that the client does not have. So their power, if any, is *based on knowledge*. The lawyer may influence the result by using legal 'working tools' in order to rationalize, ensure, conserve and legitimize the client's activity. This can be called *instrumental* power. The advice the lawyer offers is supposed to serve a certain business idea and increase its potential for realization. The question of how comprehensive this power is, is empirical and dependent on each case. Accordingly, the lawyer's power has three different sources: from the extent of their companies' capital, from the reputation of the law firm and thirdly from the reputation of the client. The lawyers' assignment at this level may be large, legally interesting and difficult, and hold great potential for profit. Nevertheless, at this stage lawyers cannot escape the function and role of legal 'plumber'[11] no matter how well they are paid. If they succeed in using a sort of argumentative counter-power against the traditional monopolies of knowledge found among the administrative élite in the ministries, they can build a significant potential for power in their field of work and towards their legal adversaries.

As strategic legal advisors, lawyers are able to get very close to the financial centres of power. Through their legal arguments they not only have the potential to influence the result of the case but to influence strategic decisions during the process as well. Their power may be extended if they participate in and influence board decisions. This is when the lawyer leaves the role of legal plumber for the role of (business) architect or (business) door opener. The well-known Norwegian business lawyer, Krefting, had this function in the Swedish-Finnish bank, MeritaNordbanken, when it tried to buy the Norwegian bank, Kreditkassen. The positive result for the Swedish-Finnish bank was not least due to Krefting's work, although there was political resistance as well (see Papendorf 2002:152).

In order to achieve such a role, lawyers are dependent on good networks, both within in the financial world and in the politico-administrative system. This applies also to the role of legal advisor. However, for the role of strategic legal advisor, it seems especially important to have a brilliant political-administrative and economic network. The client makes use of the good name and reputation of the lawyer by 'pushing him upfront' in certain situations. The lawyer's 'credit worthiness' may only be put into action if the lawyer possesses adequate *social capital.* This social capital is based on how conscientiously the lawyer takes care of and renews her contacts. Thus, it makes sense to set up office in the same geographical area as the clients.

11 It was interesting that some of both the Norwegian and the German business lawyers in my research characterized themselves in such a way.

The lawyer who takes on the role of pseudo-lawmaker or legal planner is the one that, in historical perspective, comes closest to the formal power of the jurist. This was the kind of power Aubert (1960) attributed to the jurist in establishing Norway as an independent state in the 1880s. According to Albrechtsen (1974b:15), the lawyer's actions may gain current law status in two ways: either later through the lawmakers or immediately through legal practice as prevailing law.[12]

When corporations operating on the international capital market are looking for swift solutions to moving capital across national borders, we detect the rapidly growing power held by law firms working globally. Günther (2000:246) provided the following example: It became necessary to solve the problem of legal acceptance of clearing deals in derivative trading in situations where there was a danger of one contract partner being insolvent. By the prevailing law of the time the estate trustee could pick the best contracts ('cherry picking') and leave other claimants with the estate in bankruptcy. Transnationally organized business lawyers tried to intervene in order to minimize what they considered a danger to derivative trading. In order to secure that the clearing deals (made online and privately) would be accepted by the national bankruptcy proceedings, the law firms even put pressure on German lawmakers for a swift solution. One essential argument was the competition in the international financial market. Surprisingly, they were successful in changing the law. Within a few weeks a rule that acknowledged clearing deals was taken out of the long-term law-making process and moved into another process that was close to completion. The German *Bundestag* (parliament) adopted the proposition without further discussion. As we can see, the German lawmakers decided in the last resort but one still wonders if the lawmakers did not just bless the international capital market's demand for security of action. This example shows clearly how business lawyers operating globally make demands for economic functionality that become transnational law. Lawyers operating internationally or with an international network of lawyers undoubtedly have huge potential for power. These lawyers and the global networks of New York, London, Tokyo, Hong Kong and Frankfurt compete with the national lawmakers for the power to formulate and shape the regulation of international trade. Stichweh (1999:293) describes these lawyer networks as the 'motor of globalization'. When it comes to the global-lawyering level, the thesis of the 'century of the lawyer' seems totally justified.

However, in the end even this power is dependent on the clients' interests, their strategic choices and consequently on capitalist interests.

In conclusion, I look into the collective power of the law firms and large law corporations, in other words the development in the lawyer business where a group of (business) lawyers clearly holds a privileged position based on internal specialization and differentiation. Rogowski (1995:114) uses Weber and Luhmann to analyze the development in the business lawyer market as a process of social closure in a self-

12 In this article Albrechtsen has a more ambitious perspective. He identifies especially some non-democratic elements in the process of legal innovations, because capital interests can force a direct change in relation to the law.

regulating system. The so-called privileged position of these lawyers may be described empirically through the system of recruitment and selection for these business lawyers. It focuses on grades, internal postgraduate courses and forums for discussions as well as on keeping offices close to the important clients and concentrating on the large and lucrative assignments. These firms or, rather, large corporations themselves appear to be a considerable economic, corporative and political factor of power.[13]

Weber's final thesis is based on the economic compulsion found in every business, which is the attempt to gain a monopoly by distinguishing oneself from the competitors (2005:260). Rogowski connects Weber's theory to Luhmann's system theory. Luhmann believes the process of closure, described by Weber, is explained by the fact that all systems, including the subsystem of business lawyers, are guided by a need to reproduce themselves. The legal system can be seen as a closed system constantly working on its own autonomy and reproducing its process of self regulation:

> It is characterized by the fact that it produces and restrains the operating unity of elements (in our case the legally relevant events and decisions) through the way the elements are treated, and it is just this self-regulating process that gives the system its own unity (Luhmann 1987:355).

We seem to face a paradoxical situation. On one hand we observe the closure of social positions in the form of growing specialization in the legal business, on the other, profound restructuring processes characterized by a clear understanding of trade. My research shows that the business lawyer not only has to be open to the pronounced forms of specialization, but also to the surroundings and to economic and technological developments. Luhmann (1987:357) argues that a system – in our case the business lawyers – is capable of combining openness and isolation in such a way that one is both normatively closed as well as operating as a cognitively open system: 'Consequently, it may, to a great extent, bring out a willingness to learn whilst being ever dependent on the normatively closed reproduction of itself'. Rogowski (1995:131) poses a relevant question which is the final one in this chapter: Have the business lawyers from the globalized corporations not gone a bit too far when it comes to adapting the legal core sphere of activity to the economic framework?[14]

13 This can, for example, be illustrated by the turnover figures for American and British business law firms operating globally. Taking the figures from 2008, there are six law firms with a turnover of over a milliard euros. Nineteen have a turnover of between 957 and 611 million euros. But the United Kingdom also had four law firms with a turnover of over a milliard euros. Twenty-one law firms had a turnover of between 672 and 176 million euros. The highest turnover was Clifford Chance with 1.863 million euros followed closely by Linklaters with 1.813 million euros and Freshfield Bruckhaus Deringer with 1.651 million euros (Griffiths 2008:33ff).

14 The numbers I mentioned earlier when presenting Norwegian business lawyers in boards may illustrate this aspect.

References

Albrechtsen, E. 1974a. Kritikk av den rene jus I: Jus og politikk. *Tidsskrift for Samfunnsforskning:* 1.

—— 1974b. Kritikk av den rene jus II: Jurister og kapitalinteresser. *Tidsskrift for Samfunnsforskning:* 87.

Aubert, V. *et al.* 1960. Akademikere i norsk samfunnsstruktur. *Tidsskrift for Samfunnsforskning*: 185.

Bahus, M. 2001. Kvinner i advokatyrket – proletarier i advokatfullmektigham. *Lov og rett* 7:413.

Dezelay, Y. and Garth, B. 1996. *Dealing in Virtue. International Commercial Arbitration and The Construction of a Transnational Legal Order*. Chicago: University of Chicago Press.

Galanter, M. and Palay, T. 1991. *Tournament of Lawyers. The Transformation of the Big Law Firm*. Chicago: University of Chicago Press.

Griffiths, C. 2004. Der Preis globaler Präsenz. *Juve Rechtsmarkt* 10:32.

Griffiths, A. 2008. Magere Zeiten in Aussicht, *Juve Rechtsmarkt* 10:32.

Günther, K. 2000. Alles richtig! Otfried Höffes Entwurf einer subsidiären und föderalen Weltrepublik auf der Basis des Allgemeinmenschlichen. *Rechtshistorisches Journal* 19:232.

Günther, K. and Randeria, S. 2001. Recht, Kultur und Gesellschaft im Prozess der Globalisierung. Schriftenreihe Suchprozesse für innovative Fragestellungen in der Wissenschaft, Heft Nr. 4, herausgegeben vom Programmbeirat der Werner Reimers Konferenzen, Bad Homburg.

Juve Verlag 1999/2000. *Juve Handbuch* 1999/2000. Third edition, Köln: Wirtschaftskanzleien.

—— 2005/2006. *Juve Handbuch* 2005/2006. Eighth edition, Köln: Wirtschaftskanzleien.

—— 2006/2007. *Juve Handbuch* 2006/2007. Ninth edition, Köln: Wirtschaftskanzleien.

—— 2007/2008. *Juve Handbuch* 2007/2008. Tenth edition, Köln: Wirtschaftskanzleien.

—— 2008/2009. *Juve Handbuch* 2008/2009. Eleventh edition, Köln: Wirtschaftskanzleien.

Lindemann, O. 2009. Body Politics – Anwälte in Anzügen. Kritische Justiz – *Heft* 1:84.

Luhmann, N. 1987. *Rechtssoziologie*. Third edition. Opladen: Westdeutscher Verlag.

Mathiesen, T. 2005. *Retten i samfunnet. En Innføring i rettssosiologi*. Fifth edition, Oslo: Pax.

Papendorf, K. 2002. Advokatens århundre? Globalisering og dens følger for Advokatmarkedet. *Makt- og demokratiutredningen* 1998–2003, rapportserie nr. 47.

Quack, S. 2008. Governance durch Praktiker: Vom privatrechtlichen Vertrag zur transnationalen Rechtsnorm. Vortrag auf dem Kongress 'Wie wirkt Recht' der deutschsprachigen Rechtssoziologie-Vereinigung, Universität Luzern 4–6 September 2008 (unpublished manuscript).

Rogowski, R. 1995. German corporate lawyers. Social closure in autopoietic perspective, in *Professional Competition and Professional Power. Lawyers, Accountants and the Social Construction of Markets*, edited by Y. Dezalay and D. Sugarman. London/New York: Routledge, 114.

Sander, R. and Williams, E. 1992. A little theorizing about the big law firm: Galanter, Palay, and the Economics of Growth. *Law and Social Inquiry* 17, 3:391–414.

Sassen, S. 1996. *Losing Control?* New York: Columbia University Press.

Stichweh, R. 1999. Zur Genese der Weltgesellschaft – Innovationen und Mechnismen, *Wege – Bilder – Spiele. Festschrift zum 60, Geburtstag von Jürgen Frese*, edited by Baumschulte, Krech, Landweer. Bielefeld: Aisthesis.

Teubner, G. 1997a. *Global Law Without a State*. Aldershot: Ashgate.

Teubner, G. 1997b. The king´s many bodies: The self-deconstruction of law's hierarchy. *Law and Society Review* 31, 4:763.

Vismann, C. 2000. Das Jahrhundert der Rechtsanwälte. Verträge statt Gesetze: Der Staat muβ sein Monopol mehr und mehr aufgeben. *Frankfurter Rundschau* 14, 3:22.

Weber, M. 2005. *Wirtschaft und Gesellschaft*. Frankfurt/Main: Zweitausendundeins.

Chapter 10
Regulating Cyberspace: Modes of Production, Modes of Regulation and Modes of Resistance

Abdul Paliwala

> The Pirate Party wants to fundamentally reform copyright law, get rid of the patent system, and ensure that citizens' rights to privacy are respected. With this agenda, and only this, we are making a bid for representation in the European and Swedish parliaments.
>
> The Pirate Party http://www.piratpartiet.se/international/english. Accessed: 24 July 2009

Introduction

The interest in the rising popularity of the Swedish Pirate Party, which captured a seat in the 2009 European Parliamentary elections, its popularity among younger voters and especially the international spread of its appeal, raises interesting questions about the transculture of the net and fundamental socio-economic relationships, including property rights, modes of regulation and modes of resistance.

This chapter explores the way cyberspace's construction of new Internet cultures also transforms economic and regulatory cultures – that is modes of production and regulation. However, there is a marked difference between emancipatory visions such as Benkler's (2003, 2006) which promotes a new network culture of collaborative non-capitalist development and the less redemptive visions of Klein (2005), Baxi (2006) and Rajan (2006) which suggest that capital power persists but is transformed through new modes of production. These modes of production have been characterized variously as the 'network information economy' (Benkler 2003, 2006), the 'network informational society' (Castells 2000) or the 'techno-scientific mode of production' (Klein 2005, Baxi 2006).

This results in transformation of modes of regulation from hierarchical to complex network modes which involve shifts from Westphalian hierarchies to nodal networks involving global, national, state, business and non-governmental organizations (Burris *et al.* 2005, Drahos 2004). Technology itself provides new regulatory forms, for example in the development of new forms of surveillance and, more significantly, Lessig's *Code* (Lessig 1999, 2006), to supplement other regulatory forms such as market competition and community norms.

The question is – how does this affect the complex relationships juxtaposing an invasion of the global commons by state and property interests and an emancipatory expansion of collaborative non-capitalist non-state creativity which enhances new trans- and hyper-cultural identities?

Using examples from intellectual property and Internet governance, I suggest that while alliances between capital, state and law promote one type of information society, these are resisted by new forms of cyber-capitalism, the commons movement, the right to development movement and piracy. Therefore struggles for social justice for new cyber-identities and the excluded have to take into account the complex realities of the new modes of regulation.

The Global Commons as a Transnational/Transcultural Information Space

Commons as Tragedy

Hardin's 'tragedy of the commons' suggests that freedom in the commons – whether it is freedom to breed, to farm or pollute – will inevitably result in forms of overuse and destruction of the commons. Such freedom can be constrained, not by technical solutions but by social solutions such as property rights and moral values. Thus, eighteenth-century enclosure of the English commons was justified by Locke as private property prevents destructive anarchy (Radkau 2008). Radkau suggests, however, that commons were not anarchic spaces but regulated by those involved in their use. In well-regulated commons, humans were in symbiosis with nature, a symbiosis sundered by the primitive accumulation of the enclosure movement. The idea of the commons takes very different dimensions in their application to knowledge commons:

> In the tragedy of the commons, activities include overgrazing, dirtying the water and air, and breeding. These activities lead to the overuse of the commons. For intellectual property, the activities at issue are creating and innovating, processes that in effect lead to the expansion of existing commons rather than their overuse. Hardin's tragedy is about the commons looking in; intellectual property is about looking out from existing commons to more expansive horizons (Ghosh 2007:858, see also Rose 1986, Ostrom 1999).

Digitalized knowledge is a non-rivalled non-excludable *public good*, as consumption by one individual does not reduce or prevent consumption by others, who can only be excluded by legal or technological devices. Moreover, the expansion of digital information in cyberspace has resulted in the growth of knowledge networks which provide space for new forms of collaborative and creative work and for transnational and transcultural interaction which can be restricted by excessive intellectual property rights (Uhlir and Schröder 2007, Murray and Stern 2007).

A Collaborative Commons?

Thus, cyberspace is a diverse and plural space with all its advantages and dangers. Its fundamental feature is communicative collaboration which has transformed text and textuality. This is so even in the form of its most individualist mode, the individual blog, there for others to read and interact with. The classic examples are GNU/LINUX software and Wikipedia, a cyber-encyclopaedia. Wikipedia's success relies on people making use of the ease of Internet communication, so that anyone can:

- be an author;
- improve an article – there is no concept of original ownership;
- be involved in editorial oversight of articles to prevent abuses; and
- read freely.

This apparent participatory democracy seems to work!

Collaborative forms include the blogsite with comments by users – a contemporary form of the medieval Glossa (Maharg 2008:125–35). Collaborative endeavours such as Wikipedia and GNU/LINUX, in which each individual assists democratically in the development of the whole, are new forms of evolving storytelling and folksongs. The distinction between creation and communication of knowledge becomes blurred and the communicator has a crucial role in the construction and maintenance of communities linked by knowledge. In new authoring cultures, individual hard copy authoring is replaced by collaborative multimedia e-authoring (Coombe 1998).

A Transcultural and Netizen Culture?

Cyberspace transcends territorial space not merely by enabling inter-territorial interaction but by making territoriality irrelevant in interactions. This has complex effects on identities. Cyberspace promotes interaction based on national, cultural, religious and sexual identities. Within territorial boundaries it can enable communication and solidarity space for minorities and social movements, whether progressive or reactionary. However, cyberspace also supports trans-border identities, for example, linking diasporic communities and the homeland. Students, migrants and refugees living in global diasporas can use the Internet to connect with others who share their identity.

More significantly, the expansion of digital information in cyberspace has resulted in the growth of knowledge networks which provide space for transnational and transcultural interaction and identities (Lury 1993, O'Neil 2009). The Internet enhances the variety of identities linked to *Global Islam*. And yet, it permits users to create their own virtual multiple identities such as *Second Life* avatars.

Transcultural development may involve the globalization of an existing local culture (Santos 2002), for example, the global spread of Hollywood culture. Alternatively, communities that work together globally through the medium of cyberspace, such as software developers in Bangalore, Silicone Valley and Montpellier, by working together may develop a transculture which is independent of their physical localities and identities. Of course, the singular Silicone Valley culture may be the dominant influence. Shared respect, as is the case with World Music, may produce more egalitarian transcultural identities. The World Social Forum – which, with all its limitations, represents a globalized subaltern counter-hegemonic identity – would not be possible without the Internet (Santos and Rodriguez-Garavito 2005).

By the same token cyberspace promotes the hyperidentity of the 'netizen'. Hauben (1996) begins:

> Welcome to the twenty-first century. You are a Netizen (a Net Citizen), and you exist as a citizen of the world thanks to the global connectivity that the Net makes possible. You consider everyone as your compatriot. You physically live in one country but you are in contact with much of the world via the global computer network. Virtually you live next door to every other single Netizen in the world. Geographical separation is replaced by existence in the same virtual space.

This seems to include every user of the Internet as a net citizen. However, Hauben also suggests that a second usage of a responsible netizen is closer to his understanding:

> People who care about Usenet and the bigger Net and work towards building the cooperative and collective nature which benefits the larger world.

This *cyberspace cosmopolitan* actively engages in the creation and governance of cyberspace. This may constitute an identity which transcends both territorial culture and transculture and be an identity linked specifically to cyberculture. O'Neil (2009:2) suggests that it is these super-cybercitizens who enable effective self-organization and self-expression:

> The authority of experts is traditionally subordinated to the authority of leaders. However, when the internet developed, learned authority to a great extent determined administrative authority for the simple reason that only computer hackers knew how to run the systems ... expertise on the internet became dependent not on credentials issued by an institution to an individual, in the shape of a diploma or professional certificate, but on an individual's unique skill, developed over time, and publicly demonstrated.

The Net-excluded Non-netizens

Yet, netizen or cybercitizen cosmopolitanism is dominated by values which are perhaps distinctive to Silicone Valley. In North-South terms it is Northern values that predominate. Even more significantly, there is a huge swathe of the global population which either does not participate at all or participates only marginally in cyberculture – leading to exclusion or marginalization (Paliwala 2004, Norris 2001, Warschauer 2002):

> In the information age, the critical organizational form is networking. The most critical distinction in this organizational logic is to be or not to be – in the network. Be in the network and you can share and, over time, increase your chances. Be out of the network or become switched off, and your chances vanish since everything that counts is organized around a worldwide web of interacting networks (Castells 1998).

They may be linked to the information society through occasional use of a cellphone (as in Africa) or through village telecentres but they do not really have the full participatory benefits of cybercitizenship:

> The most important digital divide is not access to a box. It's the ability to be empowered with the language that the box works in. Otherwise only a very few people can write with this language, and all the rest of us are reduced to being read-only (Daley cited in Lessig 2004:37).

While there is general recognition of the need to deal with digital divides, for example in the World Summit on the Information Society principles, it is not always appreciated that the digitally marginalized may have their own subjectivities in engaging with cyberculture (Paliwala 2007, Endeshaw 2008).

Cyberculture and Modes of Production

The collaborative and transcultural aspects of cyberspace have resulted in suggestions that cyberculture is a new culture but not an uncontested emancipatory phenomenon:

> There are many internet cultures, made up by many different kinds of storytellers, all trying to maintain their own voice and identity. In the current and more subdued mood, internet communities are fighting to keep their cultures alive among fears they are bound to be swamped – by bad code, bad businesses, bad practices, bad people, bad organizations, bad laws, bad courts and bad governments. Evil doers and dangerous idiots can be found at all levels and in all places and directions, depending upon whom you ask (Bowery 2005:15).

The underlying emancipatory aspect of cyberculture is reflected in Benkler's notion of a *network information economy* as a distinct mode of production (Benkler 2003, 2006). Benkler distinguishes between the network and industrial information economies. The *industrial information economy* was centred on information (financial services, accounting, software, science) and cultural production (films, music), the manipulation of symbols (brands, for example, Nike) and mega-corporations, such as Nike, Microsoft, News International and Monsanto. With the assistance of control systems, media advertising and intellectual property laws, it created passive workers who had no control over what they produced or consumed. The *network information economy* involves paradigmatic change involving communicative networked information in which collaborative non-market production plays a key role typified by GNU or Linux software, Wikipedia and community-based public domain biotechnologies.

For Benkler (2003, 2006) the new networked information society goes to the core of metropolitan production relations. Those who have developed Linux and other successful applications have been leading-edge developers giving their time to something they believe in. They do not start from a position of financial poverty but have surplus resources of time, money, equipment and skills. However, they contest the legal economic frameworks, particularly in relation to intellectual property, which restrict their capacity for innovative development. It is because they can work collaboratively in the non-market environment, avoiding the drudgery of neo-Taylorist production processes, that the systems they create are successful. This new mode of non-market production has echoes in family and gift-exchange modes of production created by Hauben's cosmopolitan cybercitizens.

In 'Empire' (2001) Hardt and Negri argue that in the era of globalization, sovereignty has taken a new form, composed of a series of national and supranational organisms united under a single logic of rule – of empire. While many may fear the new globalism for the domination of multinational corporations armed with new forms of property in knowledge – whether information or biotechnological – there is potential for fundamental leftist democratic development in empire through *immaterial labour* and the *multitude* is a key political constituent of such labour. The rise of Free/Libre and Open Software and content (FLOSS-C) provided Hardt and Negri in 'Multitude: War and Democracy in the Age of Empire' with a concrete example of immaterial labour:

> The information and knowledge is produced by human labour, experience and ingenuity, but in neither case can that labour be isolated to an individual. Such knowledge is always produced in collaboration and communication, by working in common in expansive and indefinite social networks (Hardt and Negri 2004:187).

In this collaborative communicative form of work, the workers of the multitude find the potential to free themselves from the shackles of corporate control and enclosure of the global commons in intellectual property. Thus, similarly to Benkler, they suggest that the new ideas in intellectual property, such as the creative commons and free and open source movements, signify the rising power of the *multitude*.

Benkler is unclear on the exact relationship between the two modes of production. His larger claim is that the new network information mode of production is in a state of struggle with the old/new industrial information in which none of the industrial giants of yore are going to take this redistribution lying down (Benkler 2003:1249). That is, the promise of the Benkler analysis is very fragile; it is subject to dominant powerful forces. His more circumspect claim, reinforced in Benkler (2006), is that there will not necessarily be a complete substitution of market by non-market:

> None of this is to say that non-market and decentralized production will completely displace firms and markets. That is not the point. The point is that the networked information economy makes it possible for non-market and decentralized models of production to increase their presence alongside the more traditional models, causing some displacement, but increasing the diversity of ways of organizing production rather than replacing one with the other (Benkler 2003:1249).

It is not clear from his reasoning whether we are in a transitional phase of co-existence, to be replaced by a new phase or in a state of perpetual transition (cf Benkler 2006:123).

There is a distinct difference between Benkler's emancipatory vision and techno-scientific mode of production (Klein 2005, Baxi 2006). Baxi, in *The Future of Human Rights* (2006:264), puts the debates about the redemptive potential of new technologies within the context of 'the techno-scientific mode of production and the accompanying organic ideology (in the Gramscian sense) that presents itself as redemptive of human suffering'. The concept of techno-science integrates a range of technologies including digital, nuclear, bio and nano technologies. His suggestion is that we should be suspicious of millennial ideologies which accompany new modes of production, because they are likely to disguise new modes of domination. Such modes are represented in human rights language by what he terms 'market-friendly human rights'. Rajan's (2006) concept of 'bio-capital' is based on a narrower framework of biotechnologies but involves a similar exploration of the relationship between capitalism and biotechnologies. He suggests (following Althusser) that while there is no necessary causal relationship between capitalism and life sciences, the latter are *overdetermined* by the capitalist political economic structures which *disproportionately* set the stage within which the life sciences emerge (Rajan 2006:6).

Benkler, Baxi and Rajan would all agree that there is a paradigmatic change in modes of production, whether brought about by network information, techno-science or bio-capital. Whereas Benkler and Hardt and Negri see a source of redemption in the transformative potential of non-capitalist production systems,

Baxi and Rajan appear to be more aligned with Castells (2000) for whom the *network informational society* may be as empowering of global business as it is of alternative social and other groups. It is probable that neither the muted determinism of Benkler nor Althusserian *over-determination* can provide the answer as to the economic and power relationships likely to ensue within the new modes of production. Berry (2008) suggests that ultimately the answer may lie in the politics of culture change.

From Modes of Production to Modes of Regulation

In this condition of uncertainty, the nature, processes and political economy of regulation become very significant. Regulation theory[1] suggests that modes of regulation shift with shifts in modes of production. The Fordist/Keynesian mode of production was typical of industrial production in the twentieth century and was a key aspect of the industrial information society or economy for Benkler (2003) and Castells (2000). The current shift to a networked or, for Baxi (2006) and Rajan (2006), the techno-scientific or bio-capital mode, should involve equivalent shifts in regulatory modes.

There is considerable evidence of changes in modes of regulation which have accompanied late twentieth-century developments. For example, Tshuma (2000) suggested that the Fordist/Keynsian hierarchical mode of regulation was being replaced by a more flexible mode of regulation. Indeed, the increasing use of the terms 'regulation' or 'governance' in contrast to 'law' and 'government' signifies the growth of a new regulatory paradigm. Much is attributed to globalization. Braithwaite and Drahos (2000) outline how global businesses and groups of national and international regulators are creating new regulatory environments in areas such as telecommunications and trade. The changing culture also provides potential for consumer and other groups to resist these modes. The significant feature of their analysis is not just the global development of regulation but that new regulatory modes shift from Westphalian hierarchies to nodal networks in which there are increasingly complex interactions between global and national state and non-governmental organizations as well as global businesses (Braithwaite and Drahos 2000, Drahos 2004, Burris *et al.* 2005). Technology itself provides new regulatory forms, for example in new forms of surveillance. More significantly, Lessig in his 'Code and other Laws of Cyberspace' (1999) suggests that the technical architecture of cyberspace becomes a regulatory form which technically shapes behaviour to suit the needs of those controlling the technology.

1 Boyer and Saillard (2002). See the journal *Issues in Regulation Theory*, for the literature on the subject. Available at: http://web.upmf-grenoble.fr/lepii/regulation/Issue_Regulation_theory/ (accessed on 24 July 2009). See also the Recherche and Régulation website http://www.theorie-regulation.org (accessed on 24 July 2009).

> In real space we recognize how laws regulate – through constitutions, statutes and other legal codes. In cyberspace we must understand how Code regulates – how the software and hardware that make cyberspace what it is *regulate* cyberspace as it is. As William Mitchell puts it, this Code is cyberspace's 'law'. Code *is law* (Lessig 1999:6, Lessig 2006).

Such a code includes ubiquitous password control systems as well as the finer arts of encryption and digital rights mechanisms. For Lessig, law in the form of positive law becomes only one mode of regulation. The market becomes an increasing regulatory force through the use of mechanisms such as licensing. The third form is individually and collectively enforced behavioural norms. Finally, there is Code:

> This code presents the greatest threat to liberal or libertarian ideals, as well as their greatest promise. We can build or architect, or code cyberspace to protect values that we believe are fundamental, or we can build, or architect, or code cyberspace to allow those values to disappear (Lessig 1999:6).

Lessig locates himself in the United States' liberal discourse as 'fanatically pro-market' and pro-property. However, as a libertarian, he sees control culture as restrictive of ideas and innovation which depend to a great degree on nurturing the global commons in ideas (Lessig 2001:6).

Murray (2007) frees us from Lessig's United States-centrism by suggesting that regulatory frameworks emerge as reflexive and complex phenomena from autopoietic communities within which they are located. Bowery (2005) presents Internet culture both within a more global framework and a Foucaultian/Deleuzian discourse with wider consideration of cultures of control as well as resistance. I suggest that this global frame has to include the digitally-excluded 'non-netizen'.

Regulation in the Global Knowledge Commons

Thus various modes of regulation affect the developing conflicts between cultures of control in the interest of property rights and state security, and the collaborative transculture of the Internet. Old forms of intellectual property law are being applied and extended to new cultural forms of cyberspace in an attempt to prevent the development of a collaborative cyberculture and to put up barriers against the digitally excluded. These applications arise at various levels but represent a globalization of United States' approaches.

Battles in United States Courts

The *Napste*r and *Grokster* cases have become iconic representations of these developments against the collaborative file-sharing culture of the Internet. They involve decisions about the attempted copyright breach actions by the music industry against the providers of systems of Person to Person (P2P) file sharing. Old property forms are extended to provide protection for business in a way that fails to recognize the changed universe of information. Only occasionally is there a realization of the networked mode and this may prove to be very fragile, as happened in the *Grokster* case.

Briefly, in the *Napster* case it was decided that such file sharing, which involved uploading and downloading files from the defendant's file server, was in breach of copyright. In the *Grokster* case, the defendants, StreamCast, merely distributed P2P file-sharing software and did not maintain a fileserver from which files could be uploaded or downloaded. In the district court, it was decided that there was no breach as there was no single file serving facility. The United States Supreme Court decided in the *Grokster* case, following the *Sony Betamax* case, that the distribution of software by itself does not constitute an infringement if there were also non-infringing uses. However, there may nevertheless be a breach if an intent to foster infringement could be found.

Thus there is a clear technical difference between the district court decisions in the *Napster* and *Grokster* cases. Nevertheless, the explanation for the decisions also resides in two different conceptions of the information society. In the *Napster* case, Justice Patel was keen to acknowledge the need to protect the investment of the traditional property owner, the record company, while ignoring the extent of the investment made by Napster. For Bowery the decision highlights law's ties with the established power of business interests but also an inability to contest change (Bowery 2005:152).

On the other hand, in the *Grokster* case, Justice Thomas was willing to seize on the new networked mode of operation of information technology and used language such as: 'It is the users of the software who, by connecting to each other over the internet, create the network and provide the access'. He also emphasized the network dimension: '(t)he technology has numerous other uses, significantly reducing the distribution costs of public domain and permissively shared art and speech, as well as reducing the centralized control of that distribution' (*Grokster* District Court 1740–41) (Bowery 2005:154).

In the *Grokster* district court case, law is showing its non-conservative face, its historic tendency to adapt ultimately to changed social circumstances; an adaptability which Fitzpatrick (2001) considers to be the creative force for law's own survival. The conservatism of Patel in the *Napster* case and the adaptability of Thomas in the *Grokster* case are both part of the creative tension of the law: tensions which make advances fragile in proportion to the strength of the continuing alliance between legal institutions and business interests. The conservative approach of the Supreme Court's *inducement doctrine* in its hearing of *Grokster* on appeal provides a graphic indication of this fragility:

> … [o]ne who distributes a device with the object of promoting its use to infringe copyright, as shown by the clear expression or other affirmative steps taken to foster infringement, is liable for the resulting acts of infringement by third parties.

There was no actual finding of inducement and there was a difference between the different concurring judgments with Justice Ginsberg using Napster type language and Justice Breyer using language similar to Thomas in Grokster. While this leaves the law in a state of uncertainty, the practical result was that the Grokster site stopped operating in November 2005.

If *Napster* and *Grokster* were isolated examples, it might be possible to see a strong potential for the new to ultimately replace the old, as the new logic of Internet culture takes hold among a new generation of lawyers and judges. The *Grokster* issue remains unresolved but attention has shifted to alternative strategies of enforcement and globalization.

BitTorrent sites have provided the next technical phase of file sharing in which those being sued merely provide cataloguing facilities without any actual copies of copyright or other material. Rather than rely on or wait for a superior court decision, the film and music industry have targeted Torrent cataloguers, Internet service providers and individual users in attempts to disrupt traffic or shut down Torrent sites. This strategy has had mixed success in the United States, on the other hand, as the recent *Pirate Bay* decision in Sweden indicates, courts worldwide are likely to assert that there is copyright infringement.[2]

The second strategy is to pursue litigation until compromises are reached which make sharing sites compliant. This is the case with two pieces of litigation against Google for alleged violations in relation to *Google Books* and *YouTube*. Google's innovative Library Project is an attempt to create digitized copies of entire catalogues of its library and publisher partners (books.google.com/googlebooks/library.html). Books out of copyright are available in full, books in copyright are only available with permission either as full copies, previews or card catalogue entries. This service attracted litigation because in most cases the whole book was scanned but Google permitted the searcher to browse limited sections of any particular work in an attempt to stay within *fair use* exceptions to copyright. However, it was questionable whether Google as a commercial organization would have been entitled to fair use. In the end Google compromised with an agreement to make substantial payments to rights holders. In the YouTube litigation, Google has relented by taking music videos off its site. Remarkably, the Google litigation is against a new cyber-capital giant by old content capital indicating that Google has more legal muscle than non-capitalist organizations.

Code's Law

Code- or design-based control has had a significant regulatory influence, especially on ways of technically locking in digital rights to prevent sharing

2 These have not always succeeded, however as the action against Comcast before the Federal Communications Commission indicates (Lohmann 2008). In the Danish SONOFON case the action succeeded against the Internet service provider for allowing access to Pirate Bay.

activity. The communicative freedom of cyberspace which supports collaborative behaviours, such as file sharing, arises because of the architecture of the Internet itself. The development of access control technologies attempt to ensure that activities considered undesirable will not be permitted. Digital rights management systems (DRM) are an example. The technical freedom of the Internet and its communicative efficacy result in the failure of most attempts to prevent copying or enable censorship. Clever netizens have circumvented them or consumers have shunned them. Successful controls, such as with the *iPod,* have done so not because of their technical achievement but because of consumer inertia – in spite of significant circumvention. Zittrain, however, suggests that we may be moving into a new generation of perfect enforcement of *tethered* appliances:

> Those who control the tethered appliance can control the behaviour undertaken with the device in a number of ways: pre-emption, specific injunction and surveillance (Zittrain 2008:107).

Such appliances include DVD appliances with Macrovision copy protection. Television set top recording appliances and GPS in-car computers allow remote controlled modification and surveillance (Zittrain 2008:109). The very tethering makes the appliance secure and easy to use thus increasing its appeal to the user.

Old Capital in Alliance with Legislators

Perhaps an even more significant alliance has been between legislators and industry. This alliance has had the effect in the late twentieth century of changing the balance between the interests of creators and those of the community in the Progress Clause Article I.8.8 of the United States Constitution. The rationale of intellectual property law has been to provide authors and inventors with exclusive rights as an incentive for creativity but to enable ultimate public access and innovation for limited times (Lessig 2004:130). However, Congress has willingly provided extensions to copyright through the *Copyright Term Extension Act* (the Sonny Bono Act) by extending the copyright term by 20 years to 70 years. Subsequently the Supreme Court in *Eldred v Ashcroft* abdicated its constitutional responsibility by suggesting that it was for 'Congress not the courts how best to pursue the copyright clauses objectives'. The Digital Millennium Copyright Act 1998 enables enforcement of code-based digital rights management technologies by prohibiting any removal or alteration of systems or their distribution. However, the Act is a little more circumspect in not imposing a duty on Internet service providers or intermediaries to pre-emptively remove material considered to be in breach of copyright. Instead, it is up to the right-holder to seek such enforcement. These tendencies are being followed worldwide. The French legislature has enacted even more drastic provisions making P2P sharing of copyrighted works and circumvention of digital rights management systems into criminal offences.[3]

Global Fencing

Thus, an impressive recent phenomenon has been the globalization of United States' ideas and concepts related to information technology, what Santos (2002) terms 'localized globalism'. With this globalization, information became a key commodity. Information technology, especially software, as the gateway to the control of information, became the crucial arena for advancement of corporate power over the global commons. The underlying thrust behind globalization has been a combination of scientific, cultural, intellectual and political leadership of United States persons and institutions. United States leadership has affected both the property fencing of the global digital knowledge commons and the radical opposition to it. The United States (with European Union support) was the primary influence in the achievement of the WTO TRIPS Agreement which requires countries to adopt minimum standards of intellectual property protection. United States' economic interests shaped the negotiations and text with the assistance of the United States Trade Representative (Braithwaite and Drahos 2002). The Trade Representative used inducements and threats, including the use of trade sanctions under Section 301 of the United States Trade Act, to secure compliance (Drahos 2001). However, TRIPS merely set the minimum standards and the growing opposition to the Agreement has led the United States (again with European Union support) to ratchet up property standards in further multilateral negotiations and Bilateral Investment (BITS) and Intellectual Property Agreements (BIPS) (Drahos 2001, Dwyer 2007).

However, a variety of other influences has been brought to bear on the spread of these ideas. This message of *common sense* had nearly unrivalled acceptance until recently because it was the dominant discourse of United States and European literature and law schools and was spread further by specialist World Intellectual Property Organization (WIPO) courses to developing countries through what Braithwaite and Drahos (2000) have termed 'model missionaries and mercenaries'.

On the whole, therefore, legislatures, courts and legal authorities have tended to follow the established model in ways which are resulting in global harmonization of laws and practices. Thus the European Electronic Commerce and Digital Copyright Directives follow similar principles to those established in the United States. In some ways the United Kingdom law provides greater protection to rights holders because fair dealing provisions are weaker than the United States' fair use (Stokes 2005:129). BitTorrent sites have been closed down all over the world and file sharers sued or prosecuted (Wang 2009).

3 Loi sur le Droit d'Auteur et les Droits Voisins dans la Société de l'Information (DADVSI) 2006.

The Normative Message

Lessig (1999 and 2005) suggests that the impact of digital copyright extension is to distance social norms from law, market and code. However, society refuses to accept the prevention of a flourishing digital culture by copyright extension. The continued persistence of this phenomenon has been in spite of attempts by the alliance between government and the content industry to promote the 'copyright violation is piracy' message on television, CDs, DVDs and in cinemas. It is supplemented by government propaganda and highly publicized trials of copyright infringers and reinforced by laws such as the Digital Millennium Copyright Act (Lessig 2005:122).

This inability of regulators to come to terms with and to obstruct the flourishing Internet culture can be contrasted with the relative success of new forms of legal pluralism, of self-governing communities of netizens (Rose 1986:742, O'Neil 2009). It is these self-governing communities that have sustained and developed the Internet through groups such as the Internet Society (ISOC), World Wide Web Consortium (W3C), Internet Engineering Task Force (IETF) and the Internet Research Task Force (IRTF) (O'Neil 2009, Murray 2007). The remarkable feature of the work practices of all these organizations is their openness. Groups are not appointed, only chairs are appointed. Membership is open to all interested parties. This radical non-bureaucratic system of self-governance is what has given the Internet community its peculiar strength and politics of a cultural revolution. The culture of self-governance has seeped into the software and content fields through the development of the *Free/Libre and Open Source Software and Content* movements (FLOSS-C) and thus strengthens the argument for a new mode of regulation of cyberspace.

It is therefore hardly surprising that the organization which fits least within this mode, the *Internet Corporation for Assigned Names and Numbers (ICANN)* and which is based on a corporatist stakeholder model has been the most contentious (Palfrey 2006).

On Modes of Resistance

The attempted fencing through legal, commercial market power and code therefore comes up against forms of resistance. These resistances are far from uniform and arise from different positions of power, positions that are linked to debates about modes of production and their connection with capital.

New Network Capitalism

Thus, the file sharing service providers involved in Napster, Grokster and so on, involved new business models for capital in a new culture of the Internet. Perhaps the most significant example of contestation between different modes of capital is Google. Google commenced operation through the ethic of the Internet as a collaborative free resource. The freeness of the resource, combined with its innovative operation led it to capture a global market – and this leads to the development of an innovative business model for advertising revenue. Unsurprisingly it has come up against old content providers in a number of disputes, especially those relating to YouTube and the Google Library. Unlike Napster and Grokster, Google's market power and utility gives it muscle for resistance. The above mentioned compromises in removing music videos from YouTube do not affect YouTube's effectiveness and Google can afford the money for the library. In the meantime, Google and other new powerful players can wait for techno-capital power to shift in ways envisaged by Justice Thomas in the *Grokster* case.

Commons Movement

A different form of resistance is the commons movement. We noted above that Hardt and Negri (2004) see in this movement the potential challenge by the 'multitude' to the new 'Empire'. Benkler (2003, 2006) sees similar emancipatory potential. Yet the intellectual argument for the commons is not uniform (Rose 1986, Boyle 2004, Lessig 2001, Berry 2008).

A principle reason for its creative survival is that organizations such as ISOC, W3C, IETF and IRTF (described above) support the Internet's open architecture. Their power resides in the serendipity between their participatory, democratic, pluralist, informal mode of operation, their approach to regulation and their shaping of *Code* or Internet architecture. This regulatory power is further sustained by a range of participatory democratic community activitist groups loosely coordinated by the Global Internet Liberty Campaign (GILC) (http://gilc.org/about/members.html). Much of the dynamism of these groups emerges from the United States with the Electronic Frontiers Foundation (EFF) leading a position that is classically based in the United States Civil Libertarian perspective symbolized by the American Civil Liberties Union (ACLU). On the other hand, SARAI and the Alternative Law Forum in India with the *commons-law* list (commons-law@sarai.net) take a much broader subaltern perspective within a free discursive framework (www.sarai.net).

Community-based regulatory power has created cultural space for the Free/Libre and Open Source Systems (FLOSS) and Content movements (FLOSS-C).[4] Nevertheless, the FLOSS-C repositories of software and content avoid the barrier created by intellectual property rights without challenging these rights. For example, the Creative Commons movement (www.creativecommons.org)

4 Free software is not necessarily free but gives unrestricted use to the user (www.fsf.org); Open Source gives users access to source code to enable creativity (www.opensource.org). Free content gives users free access to materials. Berry (2008) identifies the differences between the movements in terms of communal rights as opposed to technical efficiency and neo-liberalism.

promotes the development of an alternative open form of intellectual property rights according to Lessig's libertarian principles. The GNU/Linux operating system (www.gnu.org), copyleft (www.gnu.org/copyleft) or creative commons licence forms enable authors to license their copyright on a basis which permits openness in adaptation and/or free pricing, with protection against abuse. The World Legal Information Institute (www.worldlii.org) has created global free legal databases of public legal information through careful negotiation around existing intellectual property rights.

The critical advantage of FLOSS software is that it enables easy and free adaptation to the needs of particular countries and peoples. Some of the biggest users of FLOSS are government agencies, often in developed countries such as Germany. Lawyers worldwide have benefited from the provision of free law. For the global South, FLOSS-C provides scope for agency and autonomous development of new content or modification.

There are a number of obstacles to the effect of the FLOSS-C movement in countries of the South. Implementing Linux, for example, is not merely about the software itself, but the paraphernalia of systems knowledge, engineering, attitudes, consultancies and aid finance which form obstacles to overcoming pro-Microsoft tendencies.

Thus for developing countries, the relationship between FLOSS-C and TRIPS and WIPO sanctioned intellectual property rights becomes significant and may mean that FLOSS-C's location within acceptance of property rights framework means its subordination to interests of capital.

The Right to Development

One way of undermining this subordination would have been through global effort to promote a greater role for FLOSS-C. However, as argued elsewhere (Paliwala 2007) DOT (Digital Opportunity Task Force 2001), led by the Organization for Economic Cooperation and Development, and the World Summit on the Information Society (WSIS, 2003, 2004, 2005a, 2005b) have failed in this task, with fairly anodyne support for the promotion of all software models. The inability to question the current state of intellectual rights questions the costs and benefits and suggests a better balance between intellectual property and developing country interests (WIPO 2004, Paliwala 2007, Endeshaw 2008). The underlying problem is that international human rights norms are located in what Baxi (2006) terms 'trade-related, market-friendly human rights'. Modification of such norms can only take place through broad-based social struggles which transcend current conceptions of property. Harvey (2000:251) suggests a scope for such social struggles around the right to collective control of common property resources. The Pirate Party provides a different political forum.

Piracy as Enforcer of Right to Knowledge Commons

The strong attempts by the Content industry to brand infringers of their copyright claims as pirates, to pursue and shut down file sharing organizations, to pursue individuals through civil and criminal process, to make judiciaries and legislatures (national and global) their allies in these pursuits, to attempt (though somewhat unsuccessfully) to massage public opinion, has an analogy with the eighteenth-century Black Act. Under this Act, blackening your face at night, with or without proof of attempt to poach on what formerly was common land, could secure capital punishment (Thompson 1985). Piracy is the unwelcome 'other' of the new righteous invasion of the commons.

From the perspective of the global South, the challenge is to the general principle under which property rights are claimed and established over the commons. Just as the eighteenth-century enclosures drove the peasantry off the land and into towns in Britain, the new enclosure digitally divides the world through its property fences, of law and *Code.* Barbed wire fences were also a means of enclosure in the United States' Wild West (Razac 2000). Yet, property rights and dynamic capitalism in the United States were not built on the basis of traditional legitimacy but through legitimation under pressure of rights of squatters and others (De Soto 2001) and expropriation of Native Americans' property. Yesterday's pirates become today's lauded entrepreneurs.

The piracy label also confuses those who are acting to secure use of information software or content for personal purposes and those who enable this commercially. However, from the perspective of the excluded, especially of the developing countries, it is difficult to see any conduct, including commercial activity to spread the information, as piracy.

Lessig (2004) attempts to distinguish good pirates from bad pirates. The good pirates are those like student music file sharers who are part of a new culture of creativity. Their intention is not to cheat the record or software companies and they may be good buyers through official sources. They are creative participants in the Internet as it should be used, as a sharing caring medium of the Network Information Society/Economy (Benkler 2003). For Lessig (2004) the bad pirates are those who produce and sell for personal profit, whether or not linked to organized crime. The underlying issue is protection and promotion of innovation. Mafia-type piracy does not do this, whereas P2P Internet culture resists invasion of the global commons.

The fine distinctions between file sharing which is dependent on networks, and file sharing which is dependent on some form of commercial production of tapes or CDs might be contestable in developed countries. However, it is completely problematic in societies where there are no broadband networks that allow music sharing (Liang 2004a, 2004b) and do not take account of either local cultural traditions or political economy (Yu 2001). The deconstruction of claims to intellectual property rights results in new uncertainties about the nature of legality – on the one hand of property rights claims and on the other of piratical conduct. Liang (2004a) uses porous legality to index the whole complex of creative networks which are producing a vital information society in developing countries such as India. Far from Lessig's legal, semi-legal and illegal occupying separate spheres, they may be involved in complex relationships with one another (cf Murray 2007). For example, legal record companies may do deals with 'illegals' because it suits their interests (Liang 2004a). These complex relationships are part of the subversive but vital soup of network or techno-capitalist economies. The porous legal vitality in the development of the global South information society requires recognition of new forms of power, a counterpoint to the attempted capture of global commons. It may promote innovation and global social justice for the digitally excluded. Yet, porous legalities do not fit easily into the language of market-friendly human rights nor with rights-based subaltern approaches in the global South. Subaltern social movements do not necessarily have to operate within the law; they arise from the tradition of civil disobedience (Santos 2002, Santos and Rodriguez-Garavito 2005, Rajagopal 2003). Nevertheless, they do not countenance the complexities of software piracy under which yesterday's pirate can become today's legal entrepreneur.

Therefore struggles for social justice in cyberspace: for the sustenance of the new collaborative network culture, of new trans and hyper cultural identities, and for the digitally marginalized and excluded, need to take account of the complex realities of porous legalities which are embedded in new modes of regulation.

References

Baxi, U. 2006. *The Future of Human Rights*. New Delhi: Oxford University Press.

Benkler, Y. 2003. Freedom in the commons: Towards a political economy of information. *Duke Law Journal* 52:1245–1276.

Benkler, Y. 2006. *The Wealth of Networks: How Social Production Transforms Markets and Freedom*. Yale: Yale University Press. Available at: http://www.benkler.org/Benkler_Wealth_Of_Networks.pdf (accessed on 24 July 2009).

Bowery, K. 2005. *Law and Internet Cultures*. Cambridge: Cambridge University Press.

Boyer, R. and Saillard, Y. (eds) 2002. *Régulation Theory: The State of the Art*. London: Routledge.

Boyle, J. 2004. A manifesto on WIPO and the future of intellectual property. *Duke Law and Technology Review* 9:1–11.

Braithwaite, J. and Drahos, P. 2000. *Global Business Regulation*. Cambridge: Cambridge University Press.

Burris, S.C., Drahos, P. and Shearing, C. 2005. Nodal governance. *Australian Journal of Legal Philosophy Vol. 30*. Available at SSRN: http://ssrn.com/abstract=760928 (accessed 25 July 2009).

Castells, M. 1996. *The Information Age: Economy, Society, Culture. Volume 1: The Rise of the Network Society*. Oxford: Blackwell.

—— 1998. Information technology, globalization and social development, in Conference on Information Technology and Development Geneva, United Nations Research Institute for Social Devlopment. Available at: http://www.unrisd.org/infotech/conferen/castelp1.htm. Accessed on 25 July 2009.

Commons-Law. Available at: CommonsLaw@sarai.net http://mail.sarai.net/mailman/listinfo/commonslaw. Accessed on 25 July 2009.

Coombe, R. 1998. *The Cultural Life of Intellectual Properties: Authorship, Appropriation and the Law.* Durham and London: Duke University Press.

Davoudi, S. and Bradshaw, T. 2009. Pirates on parade. File sharing: film, television and music companies are all losing the fight against the illicit use of their products as consumers tap into new means of access. *Financial Times* 22 July 2009:11.

De Soto, H. 2001. *The Mystery of Capital London*: Black Swan.

DOT Report 2001. Digital Opportunities for All: Meeting the Challenge, Report of the Digital Opportunity Task Force DOT Force including a proposal for a Genoa Plan of Action 11 May 2001. Available at: http://www.dotforce.org/reports/. Accessed on 24 July 2009.

Drahos, P. 2001. *Bilateralism in Intellectual Property*. Oxford: Oxfam.

Drahos, P. 2004. Intellectual property and pharmaceutical markets: A nodal governance approach. *Temple Law Review* 77:401.

Drahos, P. and Braithwaite, J. 2003. *Information Feudalism*. New York: W.W. Norton.

Dwyer, L. 2007. Patent protection and access to medicine: The Colombian and Peruvian trade promotion agreements. *Law and Business Review of the Americas* 13:825.

Endeshaw, A. 2008. Intellectual property and the digital divide. *The Journal of Information, Law and Technology (JILT)* 2008 (1). Available at: http://www2.warwick.ac.uk/fac/soc/law/elj/jilt/2008_1/endeshaw. Accessed on 25 July 2009.

Fitzpatrick, P. 2001. *Modernism and the Grounds of Law*. Cambridge: Cambridge University Press.

Ghosh, S. 2007. The fable of the commons: Exclusivity and the construction of intellectual property markets. *UC Davis Law Review* 40:855.

Hardin, G. 1968. The tragedy of the commons, *Science* 162: (3859) 13 December: 1243–1248.

—— 1998. Extensions of the tragedy of the commons. *Science* (280 5364): 682–683. Available at: DOI: 10.1126/science.280.5364.682. Accessed on 25 July 2009.

Hardt, M. and Negri, A. 2001. *Empire*. Cambridge and London: Harvard University Press.

—— 2004. *Multitude: War and Democracy in the Age of Empire*. London: Penguin.

Hauben, M. 1996. *Netizens: An Anthology*. Columbia: Columbia University. Available at: http://www.columbia.edu/~rh120/. Accessed on 25 July 2009.

Klein, U. 2005. Introduction: Techno-scientific productivity, *Perspectives on Science* 13 (2) 139–141.

Lessig, L. 1999. *Code and Other Laws of Cyberspace*. New York: Basic Books.

—— 2001. *The Future of Ideas: The Fate of the Commons in a Connected World*. New York: Vintage Books.

—— 2004. *Free Culture: How Big Media uses Technology and the Law to Lock Down Culture and Control Creativity*. London and New York: Penguin Press.

—— 2006. *Code Version 2.0*. New York: Basic Books.

Li, M. 2009. The Pirate Party and the Pirate Bay: How the Pirate Bay influences Sweden and international copyright relations. *Pace International Law Review*. Available at: http://digitalcommons.pace.edu/intlaw/290. Accessed on 25 July 2009.

Liang, L. 2004a. Porous legality: An argument for media piracy. Seminar paper. Warwick: University of Warwick. May.

—— 2004b. *A Guide to Open Content Licensing*. Amsterdam: Piet Zwart Institute.

Lury, C. 1993. *Cultural Rights. Technology, Legality and Personality*. London: Routledge.

Moffitt, R. 2008. Resistance is futile. *The Journal of World Intellectual Property* 12 (1): 75–87.

Murray, A. 2007. *The Regulation of Cyberspace*. London: Routledge-Cavendish.

Murray, F. and Stern, S. 2007. Do formal intellectual property rights hinder the free flow of scientific knowledge? An empirical test of the anti-commons hypothesis. *Journal of Economic Behavior and Organization* 63:648–687.

Norris, P. 2001. *Digital Divide: Civic Engagement, Information Poverty, and the Internet Worldwide*. Cambridge: Cambridge University Press.

O'Neil, M. 2009. *Cyberchiefs: Autonomy and Authority in Online Tribes*. London: Pluto.

Ostrom, E. *et al.* 1999. Revisiting the commons: Local lessons, global challenges. *Science* 284 (9 April): 278–282.

Palfrey, J. 2006. The end of the experiment: The failure of democracy in ICANN, in *Reformatting Politics*, edited by J. Anderson, J. Dean and G. Lovink. London: Routledge, 161–180.

Paliwala, A. 2004. Legal regulation and uneven global digital diffusion. *UTS Law Review* 6:26.

Radkau, J. 2008. *Nature and Power: A Global History of the Environment*. Cambridge: Cambridge University Press.

Rajan, K.S. 2006. *Biocapital: The Constitution of Postgenomic Life*. Durham: Duke University Press.

Rose, C. 1986. The comedy of the commons: Custom, commerce, and inherently public property. *University of Chicago Law Review* 53:711.

Santos, B. 2002. *Towards a New Legal Common Sense: Law, Globalization and Emancipation*. London: Butterworths.

Santos, B. and Rodriguez-Garavito, A. (eds) 2005. *Law and Globalization from Below.* Cambridge: Cambridge University Press.

Stokes, S. 2005. *Digital Copyright: Law and Practice*. Oxford: Hart Publishing.

Thompson E.P. 1985. *Whigs and Hunters: Origin of the Black Act*. London: Harmondsworth.

Tickell, A. and Peck, J. 1999. Social regulation after Fordism: Regulation theory, neo-liberalism and the global–local nexus. *Economy and Society* 24 (3): 357–386.

Tshuma, L. 2000. Hierarchies and government versus networks and governance: Competing regulatory paradigms in global economic regulation. *Law, Social Justice and Global Development (LGD)* (1). Available at: http://www2.warwick.ac.uk/fac/soc/law/elj/lgd/2000_1/tshuma/. Accessed on 25 July 2009.

Uhlir, P. and Schröder, P. 2007. Open data for global science. *Data Science Journal* 6 (Open Data Issue) 17 June 2007.

Von Lohmann, F. 2008. FCC Rules Against Comcast for BitTorrent Blocking. Electronic Frontier Foundation. Available at: http://www.eff.org/deeplinks/2008/08/fcc-rules-against-comcast-bit-torrent-blocking. Accessed on 25 July 2009.

Wang, Y. 2009. Fair Use and File Sharing in Research and Education. PhD Thesis. Southampton: School of Law University of Southampton. Available at http://eprints.soton.ac.uk/67657/ after 1 September 2010.

Warschauer, M. 2002. *Technology and Social Inclusion: Rethinking the Digital Divide*. Cambridge: MIT Press.

World Intellectual Property Organization (WIPO) 2004. *Proposal by Argentina and Brazil for the Establishment of a Development Agenda for WIPO*. Geneva: WIPO.

World Summit on the Information Society (WSIS) 2003. World Summit on the Information Society: Declaration of Principles, Building the Information Society: a Global Challenge in the New Millennium, WSIS-03/GENEVA/DOC/4-E 12.12.2003.

—— 2004. Report of the Geneva Phase of the World Summit on the Information Society. WSIS-03/GENEVA/9(Rev.1)-E 18.2.2004.

—— 2005a. Tunis Agenda for the Information Society. WSIS-05/TUNIS/DOC/6 (Rev. 1)-E 18.11.2005.

—— 2005b. Tunis Commitment. WSIS-05/TUNIS/DOC/7-E 18.11.2005.

Yu, P.K. 2001. Piracy, Prejudice, and Perspectives: An Attempt to Use Shakespeare to Reconfigure the US–China Intellectual Property Debate. Working Paper Series No. 38. Cardozo Law School. Available at: http://papers.ssrn.com/paper.taf?abstract_id=262530. Accessed on 25 July 2009.

Zittrain, J. 2008. *The Future of the Internet and How to Stop It.* New Haven: Yale University Press.

List of Cases

Eldred v Ashcroft (2003) 123 S. Ct. 769, p 785 (US).

Grokster (2003) and (2005) *MGM Studios Inc et al. v Grokster Ltd et al.* 259 F. Supp. 2d 1029 (C.D. Cal., April 2003) pp 11740–41 (2003).

MGM Studios Inc et al. v Grokster Ltd et al. Supreme Court (04-0480), 545 U.S., 125 S. Ct. 2764 (2005) (US). For full information see Electronic Frontier Foundation MGM v Grokster http://w2.eff.org/IP/P2P/MGM_v_Grokster/.

Napster (2000) *A & M Records Inc & Ors v Napster Inc* 114 F Supp 2d 896 (ND Cal 2000) (US); See generally Electronic Frontier Foundation, *Napster* Cases http://w2.eff.org/IP/P2P/Napster/ (Accessed 25 July 2009).

Pirate Bay (2009) *Public Prosecutor v Neij Unreported* 17 April 2009 (TR (Stockholm, Sweden) (Davoudi and Bradshaw 2009).

SONOFON (2008) *SONOFON A/S (formerly DMT2 A/S) v IFPI Danmark,Ostre Landsret (Denmark)* 26 November 2008 [2009] E.C.D.R. 10 (Denmark).

Sony Betamax (1984) *Sony Corporation of America v Universal City Studios Inc* 464 US 417 (1984) (US).

Chapter 11

Post September 11 Legal Regulations of the *Hawala* System: The Predicament of Somalis in Norway

Sarvendra Tharmalingam and Mohamed Husein Gaas
with Thomas Hylland Eriksen

Introduction

Unprecedented transnational human mobility and flows of capital and ideas are characteristics of a world that is, arguably, more globalized than ever. De-localization, acceleration, standardization, interconnectedness, movement, mixing, vulnerability and various counter-reactions that could be labelled 're-embedding', are elements of globalization that are all interlinked and influence one another (Eriksen 2007). This dynamic process has had the effect of creating transnational diaspora communities and has also contributed to the growth of transnational practices engaged in by such communities.[1] Remittances are one of the key transnational practices engaged in by diaspora communities all over the globe. The remittances from the United States of America were, by the early twenty-first century, several times larger than the total value of official American development aid. Estimates in 2009 suggest that the total amount of remittances sent overseas by migrants is somewhere between $250 billion and $400 billion, in any case far exceeding the amount given in development assistance from rich countries to poor ones.

Following the September 11 terror attacks on the United States of America, remittance as a transnational practice has attracted considerable attention from scholars, policy makers and security establishments. Resulting from this, the

---

1 The transnationalism of migrants (diaspora) communities can be seen as the 'process by which immigrants forge and sustain multi-stranded social relations that link together their societies of origin and settlement' (Basch *et al.* 1994). Within transnational migration scholarship, the diaspora, transnational communities, immigrants and refugees are different key concepts with varying conceptualization by scholars. Here we use the term 'diaspora communities' to denote the category of people who have migrated from their country of origin and live in another country, without going into the details of these conceptual differences.

concept of 'the enemy within' has emerged as a new migration–security nexus paradigm. While the old migration–development nexus paradigm sees international migration as a positive in the sense that diaspora communities develop and sustain their homeland through remittances and other kinds of resource transfer, the migration–security nexus treats international migration as a threat to internal and global security: migrant's radicalization and the possibility of transmitting funds to 'terrorist and criminal networks' channelled through informal transfer systems including the Somali *hawala* institution. Such tensions between the two approaches reflect how transnational remittance transfers intended for the communities in the south, including Somalis, are increasingly at conflict with national laws.

As a consequence of this, one of the leading Somali *hawala* organizations, Al-Barakaat, was closed, and its funds were frozen in November 2001 by the United States authorities which led to a total collapse of Al Barakaat's operations globally.[2] Al-Barakaat was accused of having connections with Al-Qaeda and carrying out illegal money transfers. But no evidence substantiating these allegations has been put forward (Lindley 2005, Host and Van Hear 2005). However, addressing the dangers of *hawala* or informal money transfer systems in the context of financing terrorism was given political priority. The closure of Al-Barakaat created hardships for many immediately after the closure and caused panic among the Somalis as well as the *hawala* companies. It was feared that if the flow of remittances through Somali remittance companies was affected due to new regulations, it would create tremendous adverse consequences to Somali people who have been suffering a lot due to ongoing war and conflict since 1991. In this context, the need to match the expectations of the Financial Action Task Force (FATF) and the money transfer procedures of Somali *hawala* companies was realized and the United Nations Development Programme (UNDP) in Somalia intervened and became involved in the formalization process. UNDP's task was to help the Somali remittance companies transform themselves to conform to the minimum legal structure acceptable in order to address the fears of international governments with regard to informal remittance systems and to be able to fulfil the legitimate remittance needs of the Somali people.

While many countries understood the relevance of *hawala* and adopted moderate regulations, a few countries, including Norway, adopted difficult measures for the *hawala* companies to comply with. Consequently, Somalis in Norway face the dilemma of not sending money to their relatives, which is not an option, yet legally sending money from Norway is impossible.

---

2 Al-Barakaat was the leading remittance transfer company among Somalis and the largest infrastructure (telecommunication) and employment provider in Somalia at the time of its closure. It was reported that Al-Barakaat operated in 40 countries and handled about 140 million United States dollars annually from the Somali diaspora. It was claimed at the time of its closure that United States authorities had proof that Al-Barakaat was providing 25 million United States dollars in aid a year to Osama Bin Laden (West 2006:15 in Maimbo 2006).

This chapter deals with a number of overlapping, supplementary and conflicting formal and informal, local, international and transnational norms that inform the transfer of money from immigrants to family, local communities or local businesses in the south. The Somalis in Norway provide the focus for this study which aims to explore and understand transnational relations and their impact on transnational law formation.

We use data collected from both primary and secondary sources, including individual and key informant interviews with a dozen Somalis living in Norway, and participatory observation. This chapter focuses on how, in the aftermath of September 11, the broadening and elusive notion of security in international and national laws and policies impacted on Somali remittance companies and Somali diaspora communities trying to fulfill their financial and family obligations in terms of economic support to relatives at home. Thus, we discuss the regulatory process of *hawala*-based remittance transfers that was initiated after September 11 and the experiences of the Somali *hawala* companies in the formalizing process. As the Norwegian context is central, the implication of Norwegian measures to formalize the informal remittance transfer system is given special attention.

Somalia and the *Hawala* in Context

Factors such as the unfortunate legacies of colonialism, Siyaad Barre's dictatorship regime and the prevalence of clan loyalties rather than state legitimacy eventually led to the de facto collapse of the Somali government in the 1990s (Waldorn and Hasci 1995, Hyndman 2000, Gaas 2007). The rebel movements that ousted Siyaad´s regime eventually turned against each other and full-scale clan warfare broke out in 1991. Since then, a million civilians have died and Somalia has descended into chaos with massive displacement, destruction of livelihood sources and basic infrastructures, and wide looting of public property (Gaas 2007). In an attempt to quell the chaos and help relief agencies deliver aid, the United States of America intervened in Somalia, followed by UNISOM 1 and 2, but these initiatives failed to restore peace in Somalia and ended disastrously in 1995. The country has been divided and ruled by warlords and clan-militias ever since. Puntland and Somaliland in the north remained exceptions to this general development. Somaliland declared its independence from the rest of Somalia in 1991 but this is still unrecognized, while Puntland declared its autonomy rather than independence in 1998 and remains a regional state within Somalia (Gaas 2007). Over these years various endeavours have been made towards reconciliation and reconstruction in Somalia but none produced any results with the exception of the fourteenth attempt which created the Transitional Somali Government in 2004 (Gaas 2009). Despite this, warfare between Alshebaab and Hisbil-islmam on one side and the Transitional Somali Government and AMISOM troops on the other continue in the country (ibid.).

Xawaalad or *xawilaad* is an informal money transfer system used and operated mainly by Somalis.[3] However, Kenyans, Ethiopians and Sudanese refugees and immigrants also use the Somali's *hawala* to send remittances to their relatives and families. The system operates wherever a sizeable population of Somalis is found (Cf, Horst 2002, Horst and Van Hear 2002). *Hawala* is not new; it is old and indigenous and has been practised by Somali pastoral nomads for centuries, previously known as an *abbaan* (Yusuf 2006). *Abbaan* is a security arrangement that guarantees the protected route of goods carried by camel or donkey convoys within and between the different clans and their territories, regardless of whether those respective clans are hostile to and among each other (ibid.). However, due to civil war, loss of banking institutions in Somalia and forced migration since 1991, the *abbaan* has evolved and renamed itself *xawaalad* (*hawala*). It has become increasingly popular as a means of Somalis sending and receiving money as they are dispersed across all continents.[4] Like the *abbaan*, *hawala* is a trust-based system characterized by simplicity and time and cost efficiency (Horst 2002, Horst and Van Hear 2002, Yusuf 2006, Lindley 2005). Further, unlike the other formal financial institutions, such as banks, there is almost no bureaucracy involved in sending or receiving money through *hawala*. For instance, if you have to send money to relatives anywhere in the world, all you have to do is hand over the amount of money you want to remit to one of the *hawala* agents and provide him with the contact and personal details of the recipient. How fast the money is received usually depends on how urgently the sender wants the money delivered to its final destination. All in all, the time between the remittance being sent and it being received ranges from a few minutes to a few hours and up to, at most, two or three days (C.f., Horst 2002, Horst and Van Hear 2002, Lindley 2005).

In the absence of formal financial institutions, remittance transfers to Somalia from other countries, including Norway, have increasingly taken alternative forms of transaction such as hand delivery, trade-based transactions and transactions through *hawala*-based remittance companies (Lindly 2005). *Hawala*-based transactions are described as an integral part of informal money or value transfer systems (IMTS or IVTS).[5] However, this system cannot be fully characterized as

3 Though we have used the term *xawaalad* or *xawilaad* here, it is also important to note the present mode of operation of Somali remittance companies cannot wholly be characterized as *hawala* in the traditional sense. The operation of Somali remittance companies are increasingly centralized and coordinated in contrast to traditional *hawala*.

4 Here, it should be noted that this claim is contestable and further study is needed to explore the connections between *abbaan* and *hawala*.

5 'Informal money transfer system' (IMTS) (Buencamino and Gorbunov 2002), 'informal value transfer system' (IVTS) (Passas 1999, 2003, 2005, 2006), 'alternative remittance system' (FATF 2002, 2003) and 'underground banking' are some of the terms that are being used for the same kind of activity. Passas argues that IVTS is a more suitable term and tries to make a distinction between an informal fund transfer system (IFTS) and an informal value transfer method (IVTM). According to Passas, an informal fund transfer system and an informal value transfer method are 'within the wider category of the informal

illegal all over the world (Carling 2005). Some scholars are reluctant to use the term 'informal money or value transfer system' due to the long tradition of the system and the sophistication adopted by the actors in the system. In this sense Somali remittance companies are also described as an 'alternative banking system' rather than an informal one (Lindly 2005). Not only among Somalis but also among other transnational communities, the *hawala* system[6] has become popular due to its trustworthiness, fast service, lower cost of transfer, fewer formalities, familiarity with local cultural values and flexibility.

The Significance of *Hawala* and Remittances to Somalia and Somalis

Besides the low cost, time efficiency and simplicity in receiving and sending money through *hawala*, one may still question why Somalis, including those in Norway, still use *hawala* since it is not legal. There are several reasons for this.

Firstly, *hawala* is crucial, not only for Somalis in Somalia or in the countries of the Horn where large numbers have been displaced to but also for the Somali economy at large. *Hawala* played and continues to play a lifeline role in the survival of the country and its population, ravaged by a never-ending civil war since 1991. As a consequence of this, the country's basic economic infrastructure has been either destroyed or looted (Gaas 2007, 2009). Despite these formidable constraints, the Somali economy strives to and continues to grow. This is mainly due to the *hawala* which fills the vacuum created by the loss of a formal Somali banking system and thus plays a facilitating role for entrepreneurs and business people who can conduct their activities easily in Somalia and beyond.

Further, because remittances through the *hawala* system provide hard currency, they increase the purchasing power at local markets in Somalia, as evidenced by the continued economic growth in Somalia's export, import, telecommunications and small-scale manufacturing sectors. Thus, it has been suggested that the per capita income of the Somali population (USD283) exceeds that for the population in neighbouring, stable Ethiopia (USD164) as the United Nations reported in 2006 (Gaas 2009):

> … despite the civil war, Somalia is by no means economically isolated by its lack of government. In the 1990s, transit trade emerged as a key sector of the

---

value transfer system, but the latter almost always involves crimes and other misconduct, whereas the former are primarily serving legitimate customers' (2003b).

6 *Hawala* is one of the well-known forms of informal money or value transfer systems. The *hawala* system is called different names in different places such as *hawala* in India and the Middle-East, *hundi* in Pakistan and Bangladesh, *fei ch'ien* in China, *padala* in the Philippines, *hui kuan* in Hong Kong, *phoe kuan* in Thailand, *casa de cambio* in Latin America (Passas 2003), *xawaalad or xawilaad* in Somalia and *undiyal* among Tamils from Sri Lanka. For an anthological analysis of the *hawala* system, see Ballard 2003.

> economy. The Somali ports of Mogadishu, Marka and Kismaayo all serve as an entry point for goods bound for destinations throughout East Africa, while Berbera and Boosaaso provide a similar function for the northern Horn. Much of this trade is illicit. Six privately-owned air companies also operate between Somalia and neighbouring countries. Telecommunications have also emerged as a primary sector of economic growth, with twelve different companies in Somalia providing the cheapest and most reliable telephone services in the region (Gaas 2009:27).

In 1998, it was estimated that *hawala*-based remittance companies fulfilled around two-thirds of total remittance transfers (Menkhaus 2001).

Secondly, remittances are considered more vital for the Somali people's survival than trade and aid put together (Gundel 2002). It is estimated that remittances worth from approximately 120 million (Montclos and Kawanija, 2000)[7] up to the UNDP figure of between 750 million and 1 billion (Omer 2002) United States dollars are transferred annually by the Somali diaspora, including those in Norway, to Somalia and into the Horn of Africa through the *hawala* system. As the Somali diaspora are believed to number at least one million, other estimates suggest that no less than 1 billion United States dollars' worth of remittances are remitted by the Somali diaspora (Maimbo 2006). UNDP has also estimated that a considerable sum of approximately 360 million dollars is transferred for livelihood purposes alone for nearly two million Somalis (Omer 2002).[8]

Thirdly, at household and individual level, Somali diaspora remittances play an indispensable role concerning any welfare issues of Somali individuals and households (Horst and Gaas 2008). Besides covering monthly family and individual bills, even fleeing into safer places in or outside the country on the eve of increased conflicts is facilitated by remittances. Furthermore, services such as schooling, health facilities and universities are created and maintained by the remittances flow.

Finally, *hawala* companies are present anywhere where considerable populations of Somali people are found. Sending money through *hawala* takes less time and costs less than through banks or 'money grams'. Also, the *hawala* system is less bureaucratic than its alternatives and is therefore suitable for the locally decentralized and globally dispersed nature of Somalis since *hawala* agents can deliver money remitted to remote places.

---

7 As referred to in Sørensen (2004).

8 It would be appropriate to add a note of caution about the figures on the volume of remittances transferred. It is important to note that the figures are all estimates and transparency on the sources and methods of estimation is lacking.

Somalis in Norway: How They are Seen and Portrayed in the Media

Migration of Somalis into Norway and other *Western* countries has taken place in three distinct phases. In the 1970s, the first Somalis came to Norway as migrant workers in the Norwegian shipping industry. This was followed in 1980 by the second wave, who were refugees fleeing the fighting between the insurgents and the last Somali regime. However, the third wave of Somalis coming into Norway started in the 1990s and still continues. As the civil war broke out and the conflict intensified in Somalia, the population has increasingly been fleeing into the neighbouring countries in the region and further afield to *Western* countries (Gaas 2007). According to the Norwegian Statistics Bureau, by January 2009 the Somali population in Norway totalled almost 23,500 (Norwegian Statistics Bureau 2009), with just half living in Oslo and the rest being scattered around other parts of Norway (ibid.). There are several characteristics that differentiate Somalis from the other migrants in Norway. The group constitutes the latest arrivals when compared with other migrant groups and most of the Somali population is relatively young (Gaas 2007). Somalis are among the largest refugee groups in Norway and make up the largest African population in Norway (ibid., Horst and Gaas 2008). Furthermore, compared to other groups, Somalis have arrived the most recently, stayed the shortest time in Norway and have the highest unemployment (Horst and Gaas 2008). They are the only migrants in Norway who have come from a country whose state is not functional and where traditional laws (*Xeer*), as non-state regulations, and informal institutions, including *hawala*, play significant roles in every aspect of the country – the life and welfare of Somali individuals, families and society at large (Gundel 2006). However, it is amply documented that Somalis face challenges in integration and have an uneasy relationship with welfare institutions (Fangen 2006, Engebrigtsen and Fuglerud 2006). There are perceptibly negative stereotypes of Somalis in the Norwegian media and press (Gaas 2007). In this respect, it has been argued that 'being Somali is seen by the Norwegian public as being synonymous with crime, drugs, smuggling, unlawfulness, exploitation of the welfare system and having more than two spouses' (Fangen 2006). In a sense, it may be said that the Somalis in Norway are doubly disadvantaged, being simultaneously black and Muslim. They have become, in the popular imagination, a paradigm case of the 'poorly integrated immigrant', a fact that generates a number of vicious circles: exclusion from the labour market, poor housing, problems at school and over-representation in adolescent drug use and petty crime.

Despite their stigma and the fact that Somalis are among the poorest in Norway, it has been suggested that they manage to transmit 60 million Norwegian kroner (about 7 million euros) annually through *hawala* (*Verdens Gang* 2001). However, unlike many other *Western* countries, including the United States of America, *hawala* companies in Norway operate informally. Although *hawala* operates openly, it is considered illegal. Yet, Somalis in Norway use this as the only viable channel to transmit money to people in Somalia to whom they have obligations (Carling *et al.* 2007).

Dynamics and Motivations for Remitting

The remittance activities of Somalis in Norway are not well documented so we do not have access to all the details of the population that sends money, the amount of money involved or the frequency of their remittances. Consequently, people may assume that all Somalis in Norway send money back home but, in reality, there are various reasons why this is not so. For instance, a study carried out on this in the United Kingdom suggested that not all Somalis there send money as some individuals do not have a family member 'in need' or they may just decide not to remit any money at all (Lindley 2007). In Norway, recent statistics from the Statistics Bureau suggest that 74 per cent of Somalis in Norway remit money and 38 per cent of these send money on a monthly basis to their relatives and immediate families left back in Somalia or elsewhere in other countries (SSB 2008).[9]

Motivation for sending money among Somalis is diversified: philanthropic, political and kinship or family obligations but purposes are mainly for livelihood and sustenance of family and relatives, education of children, development and humanitarian relief in the homeland. Somalis sending money falls within and should be seen as a culture of collectivism rather than individualism. When asked why Somalis send money, our informants argued that: 'Among Somalis there is a culture where a (needy) person should be fed and given shelter, and this money sending is an extension of that, where the powerful person or the able one helps those who are weak or are not able to survive on their own'. Transfers from Somalis in Norway are essential for the survival of relatives in Somalia. As one Somali informant interviewed put it:

> … nobody wants to eat food when his or her mother is hungry! When a relative calls you from Somalia and tells you that she did not have lunch today or that there is a sick person in the family, you have to send …

And remittances are crucial for those sending money as well, a number of people we talked to stressed that in order for them to function well in Norway, they needed to know that their relatives were fine. A woman informant when asked why she remits money said that one cannot just live for and by oneself; you have to take care of people who are hungry or sick. She stressed that:

> … the purpose that [I] send money is so that [my] mother does not face hunger and other problems that come with not having money to survive. My mother raised me and if I cannot send money for her to survive, for my mum, when there

9 In a workshop organized by PRIO in Oslo on 30 October 2007 on Somali remittances, it was revealed by members of the Somali diaspora in Norway that most of the Somali diaspora remit money to their kith and kin in Somalia and surrounding areas. A small section of non-remitters also exist. They are mostly from second generation Somalis and those who have little contact with Somalia.

> is no other way that she can sustain her life in the midst of chaos, displacement and conflicts that Somalia endures, then why did she raise me?

Besides for developmental and relief purposes, remittances are also sent for political purposes, for peace building and reconciliation as well as, in some cases, supporting conflicts between clans in Somalia (see Horst and Gaas 2008). Contrary to the common perception that remittances are a one-way flow of money – that the money is always sent out of Norway – there are some Somalis who receive money through *hawala* in Norway. This happens in cases where a person in Norway is in financial difficulty and has family, relatives or friends who can help in other Western countries. For instance, several people we interviewed said that they have received money from family members, relatives and friends when they were in a difficult economic position – when they did not have work and had huge bills to pay or needed to travel but could not cover the expenses of the journey.

Post September 11 Legal Regulations and Somali Remittance Sector

Widespread misconceptions prevailed among policy makers, the media and vast sections of the general public that finance for Al Qaeda was largely channelled through the informal systems as such suspicion and hostility towards these systems dominated political discourse in the United States and other Western countries (Geode 2003). To this end the *hawala* system was described as 'the terrorist's informal financial mechanism' (Looney 2003). An article that appeared in *Time* magazine reflected that misconception, as it described the *hawala* system as an 'international underground banking system that allows money to show up in the bank accounts or pockets of men like hijacker Mohammed Atta, without leaving a paper trail' (Ganguly 2001).[10] While discussing the prevailing discourse critically, Geode observes that an 'us and them' divide of banking practices lies behind such discourse (Geode 2003). The suspicions or allegations about *hawala* as the only or main channel for transferring finance for the September 11 terror attacks was contrary to the evidence that emerged later. It was documented that funds for the Al Qaeda network terror attacks were largely channelled through formal institutions. Willman (2001) describes how Al Qaeda was able to use formal financial institutions for their funds transfers:

> Al-Qaeda has been able to move money around the world through al-Shamal's correspondent network of banks that cooperate with the Sudanese bank in cross-border transactions. Al-Shamal's correspondents have included France's Credit Lyonnais, Germany's Commerzbank, Standard Bank of South Africa and Saudi Hollandi bank in Jeddah in which ABN Amro of the Netherlands has a 40 per cent stake.[11]

10 http://www.time.com/time/world/article/0,8599,178227,00.html.

11 http://specials.ft.com/attackonterrorism/FT3RNR3XMUC.html.

It was also revealed that the *hawala* system was 'by no means the only or main vehicle of illegal fund transfers or financing of terrible acts' (Passas 2003a). Despite this, officials' hostility towards *hawala* continues as in 2004 two United States officials in a BBC interview stated:

> Certainly, in terms of *hawala*, we are concerned that any time you have a lack of transparency, a lack of accountability with respect to the movement of money, there is potential that that medium can be used by terrorists and criminals (Treasury Deputy Assistant Secretary Juan Zerati, BBC, 6 February 2004).

In the same news report, Danny Glazer, Director of the United States Treasury's Executive Office of Terrorist Financing said:

> *Hawala* is one of the important things that everybody needs to be focusing on. We have to make sure that all methods for transferring money – particularly for transferring funds across borders – are covered by effective anti-money laundering and counter-terrorist financing regimes.

Guidelines for the Financial Action Task Force (FATF)

The responsibility of regulating informal systems was given to the Financial Action Task Force (FATF), an inter-governmental body that consists of 33 countries and two international organizations as members and one country as observer at present.[12] The Task Force issued certain guidelines and recommendations for the member states in relation to money transfers to combat money laundering and illegal money transfer practices. In addition to the 40 recommendations given for the fight against money laundering and illegal money transfer practices before September 2001, the Task Force issued nine special recommendations on terrorist financing on 31 October 2001.[13] Among these, the recommendation for alternative remittances notes as follows:

---

12 The FATF member countries are: Argentina, Australia, Austria, Belgium, Brazil, Canada, China Denmark, Finland, France, Germany, Greece, Hong Kong – China, Iceland, Ireland, Italy, Japan, Luxembourg, Mexico, the Netherlands, New Zealand, Norway, Portugal, Republic of Korea, Russian Federation, Singapore, South Africa, Spain, Sweden, Switzerland, Turkey, the United Kingdom and the United States. The two international organizations are the European Commission and the Gulf Cooperation Council. India is the country with observer status. For further details of associate members, observer bodies and FATF organizations, see: http://www.fatf-gafi.org/pages/0,2966,en_32250379_32236869_1_1_1_1_1,00.html, last accessed 7 December 2009.

13 Until 22 October 2004, there were eight recommendations and the ninth recommendation on cross-border cash movement was adopted by FATF in meeting held in France. For the details of these nine recommendations, see:http://www.fatfgafi.org/

> Each country should take measures to ensure that persons or legal entities, including agents, that provide a service for the transmission of money or value, including transmission through an informal money or value transfer system or network, should be licensed or registered and subject to all the FATF recommendations that apply to banks and non-bank financial institutions. Each country should ensure that persons or legal entities that carry out this service illegally are subject to administrative, civil or criminal sanctions (FATF 2001, 6th recommendation on terrorist financing).

In June 2003, the Financial Action Task Force released a document to recommend international best practices in combating the abuse of alternative remittance systems. These focus on five areas, namely: licensing and registration; identification and raising awareness; anti-money laundering regulations; compliance monitoring; and sanctions.[14]

The Task Force's detailed guidance can be seen as an international legal framework for informal remittance systems and this framework has transnational implications. Here it is useful to note a conceptual difference between 'international' and 'transnational': 'international' denotes a scenario where relationships are sustained between nations and states whereas 'transnational' suggests that relationships are sustained beyond nations and states (Kjeldstadli 2008:59). When transnational practices such as sending remittances through informal or alternative transfer mechanisms are seen from the perspective of the migration–security nexus and considered a security threat to states, states join hands to restrict or regulate the transnational practices taking place beyond the states' jurisdiction which has a huge impact on the transnational practices of diaspora communities. In this context, it is important to note that in the case of Somalia, states do not have an effective counterpart within Somalia due to the lack of an effective state mechanism.[15]

Based on the recommendations of the Task Force, many member countries introduced laws and regulations to register, licence and monitor informal money transfer companies. In the United States registration and licensing are managed by state, not federal, authorities. European countries implement different national laws and regulations rather than use common European Union regulations. Some European Union countries, such as France and the Netherlands, adopted tough

document/9/0,3343,en_32250379_32236920_34032073_1_1_1_1,00.html#VIAR, last accessed 7 December 2009.

14 For details of the international best practices for combating the abuse of alternative remittance systems recommended by FATF, see http://www.fatf-gafi.org/dataoecd/32/15/34255005.pdf, last accessed 9 December 2009.

15 Though Somalia has had a transitional government for the last few years, its control over the territory of Somalia is minimal. The self-declared state of Somaliland in the northern part of Somalia is not officially recognized as a state by the international community.

regulatory processes while others like the United Kingdom took a moderate approach. Norway's approach to the regulatory process is also considered tough.

However, the outcome of these measures adopted has now become a subject of controversy (McCulloch and Pickering 2005, Passas 2006). Passas (2006), in his article, 'Fighting terror with error: the counter-productive regulation of informal value transfers', questions the wisdom in regulatory processes as follows:

> The findings suggest that some practices may constitute an overly aggressive and costly approach, insensitive to cultural and socio-economic factors in both the labour importing and labour exporting countries. Such approaches appear to produce the opposite from desired effects, including higher remittance costs, fewer options for remitters, unnecessary criminalization of economic sectors and ethnic groups, lower transparency and traceability of transactions, alienation and mistrust between ethnic communities and authorities.

The Case of the Somali Remittance Sector

The closure of Al Barakaat and its network by the United States authorities on 7 November 2001[16] had a negative impact on the Somali economy and trade. In a CERI-CNRS working paper entitled 'Outcomes of the United States decision on Al-Barakaat', Roland Marcel points out the negative effects of its closure, as follows:

> Many small and middle rank traders have therefore lost most of their capital and are now excluded from the market. Many who put their money in the company are facing problems. Many traders were using Al Barakaat to send their money to Dubai, Djibouti and Yemen: that money is also lost (referred to in Omer 2002).

It was also claimed that the amount lost by the closure of Al Barakaat was nearly 9 million USD.[17] Though it was feared that the closure of Al Barakaat would lead to an escalation in the crisis of many Somali livelihoods by blocking any remittance flows, the actual impact was less damaging than feared in terms of transfer of remittances. Other remittance companies filled

16 It is important to note that though Al-Barakaat and its network all over the world were closed on allegations of financing terrorism and links with Al-Qaeda, until now there was no such evidence documented in any of the courts in the United States or any other countries. The owner of Al-Barakaat was found guilty in a United States court for running a remittance company without having a licence and sentenced to one and a half years in prison, but not for any connections with Al-Qaeda or for financing terrorism (Medani 2002).

17 This claim was made by the manager of the Al-Barakaat company in Somalia to the Somali country representative of UNDP (Omer 2002).

the vacuum created by the closure of Al Barakaat and the flow of remittances continued (Omer 2002). But the international community's new regulatory measures have had impacts on other remittance companies as well. These new regulations and the surveillance of remittance transfers affected the operation of the Somali remittance companies and contributed to new challenges for the Somali remittance sector (Omer 2002). Though there is a high risk of terror and criminal networks using the *hawala* system, scholars who understand the formal and informal financial transfer systems argue that such risks are also high for formal financial transfer channels (Geode 2003, Passas 2003a, 2003b, 2006, Maimbo 2004).

In this context, Somali remittance companies faced two major challenges. The first related to legalizing their operations in the countries where they were operating and the second was facing and fighting the negative discourse about the informal remittance transfer system (Omer 2002). The two tasks were interrelated and had to be dealt with using a common strategic plan. In a situation where a secure remittance transfer system is necessary for the wellbeing of the Somali people, formalizing the operating mode of Somali remittance companies was essential. Fortunately, many international governments also had a reasonable understanding of the need for the services of the Somali remittance companies due to the non-existence of a formal money transfer system in Somalia.[18] The United Nations Development Programme (UNDP) in Somalia realized the importance of the effective functioning of the Somali remittance companies and became involved in the process of formalizing them within an acceptable legal framework. It is important to note here that the 'acceptable legal framework' has varied from country to country based on respective national laws and policy positions.

To address the challenges faced by the Somali remittance companies UNDP identified the needs of the Somali remittance companies and recommended short-, medium- and long-term tasks for them (for further details, see Omer 2002). In addition to this, as a medium term plan, an association of Somali remittance companies was formed to represent their interests with Western governments and the other stakeholders. The long-term plan is to establish a formal commercial banking sector in Somalia. The Somali Financial Services Association (SFSA) was formed in December 2003. It was launched in London at a conference held to promote understanding of the remittance sector and the regulations that

18 Even the United States government, while on the one hand being concerned about the possible misuse of the *hawala* system in financing terrorism, on the other hand recognizes the necessity for the services of informal remittance companies to the places where formal money transfer systems have limited access. Based also on this recognition, it was decided not to ban the informal remittance companies but to regulate and formalize them within an acceptable legal framework.

govern it.[19] Participants included: remittance regulators representing some European governments, such as Norway, United Kingdom, Sweden, the Netherlands and Germany; representatives of the Somali remittance companies; and some international experts and observers who participated with the facilitation of UNDP–Somalia. European remittance regulators explained the regulations regarding the flow of remittances from their countries and the Somali remittance companies presented their needs and problems. In 2006, another organization called the Somali Money Remitters Association (SOMTA) was formed, also with the help of UNDP–Somalia. Most of the Somali remittance companies have become members of either the Somali Financial Services Association or the Somali Money Remitters Association.

Based on their commitment to following international standards, Somali remittance companies have started adopting the best practices recommended by the Task Force and follow-up studies show they have made reasonable progress in this. A study, 'Feasibility of study on financial services in Somalia' (2004), was jointly funded by UNDP and the European Commission Somalia unit and carried out by KPMG East Africa Limited. Interviews were held with Somali remittance companies like Amal, Barwaqo, Dahabsshiil, Dalsan, Global and Towfiq to discuss progress made in the formalization processes that were initiated after September 11. In these interviews, companies revealed the actions they had taken since September 11 to formalize their businesses. Almost all the companies have begun to strictly impose the customer identification practice known as 'know your customer'. The common strategy among Somali remittance companies in this regard is to carry out transactions with known Somalis. The companies have also ensured that accounts are produced in accordance with international accounting standards and have organized an internal and external audit system. The companies have also made progress in becoming registered and obtaining licences for their operations. For example, it is mentioned in the study that the Somali remittance company, Dahabshiil, has registered their business in the United States, like many other big remittance companies. Progress has also been made in formalizing ownership, capital and management structures. For example, the remittance company, Amal, has separated the shareholders from the executive management structure. Amal has also organized a decentralized structure with agents, branches, regional centres and a head office in order to manage the widespread remittance transfer activities. At the same time, companies have developed new software to keep records and monitor any suspicious transactions.

19 The conference was organized by UNDP Somalia who appointed KPMG East Africa Limited to coordinate the conference with the support of the Department for International Development (DFID) UK. The conference was titled: 'Conference on the Somali remittance sector: Understanding the Somali remittance sector and the regulations that govern it' that was held in London on 3 and 4 December 2003.

Establishing a Formal Banking Sector

One of the regulators' strategies to overcome the risks in the *hawala* money transfer system is to establish or broaden the formal financial service networks. This kind of commercial banking service is also considered important and beneficial for Somali trade and the Somali economy.

The lack of government-sponsored banking institutions in Somalia has contributed to the crucial role of remittance companies in transferring money to and from Somalia. There were some government-controlled banking institutions operating in Somalia prior to the civil war, such as the Central Bank of Somalia, the Somali Savings and Commercial Bank, the Commercial Bank of Somalia, the Somali Development Bank and the Somali Insurance Company (Omer 2002). These banking institutions went bankrupt during the civil war. Now Somalis have less confidence in the government-sponsored financial sector because of their bad experiences in the pre-civil war period. This opinion is reflected in the study commissioned by UNDP:

> As one businessman reflected, 'it is hard to persuade a Somali to use a commercial bank controlled and owned by a Somali government.' This sentiment is reflected in the people's use of remittance companies to conduct their business and utilization of them as banks for deposits (Omer 2002).

In the KPMG study (2004) of the financial sector in Somalia, the feasibility of developing a commercial banking sector was explored as well as a strategy for developing a banking sector in Somalia. The KPMG study included a survey to assess demands for various banking services.[20] As one of the key findings, it was revealed that while the business sector has been using the remittance transfer companies for money transfers and foreign exchange transactions, they have less confidence in the remittance companies' ability to become banks in the future.[21] This scepticism within the Somali business sector emerged from the KPMG study with business people citing some potential problems, for example, lack of security, lack of the necessary and sufficient finances, lack of experience and ethics, lack of ties with the international financial institutions and the fear of potential corruption if such banks were set up (KPMG 2004:70).

Due to the ongoing conflict and war in Somalia, establishing internationally regulated commercial banks and a central bank is not highly feasible until a stable central government is installed and rule and order restored. However, Somaliland has managed to establish a central bank, the Bank of Somaliland, due to the relative peace and harmony in the territory. In 2004 the Bank of Somaliland had

20 Questionnaires were sent to 100 businesses throughout Somalia of which 67 responded.

21 At the same time, it is important to note that some remittance companies do take deposits from businesses and effectively perform some banking functions.

eleven branches spread over the six regions of Somaliland and operated with the dual functions of central bank and commercial bank. The KPMG study (2004) also revealed that due to the history of civic unrest, the general public lacked confidence in the Bank of Somaliland. The bank was aware of this problem and considered separating the central and commercial bank functions as a way of increasing public confidence in the banking sector. Puntland also has a bank, the State Bank of Puntland, which has limited modern central bank functions.

The willingness of the Somali remittance companies to adopt the Task Force recommendations has facilitated the sector's effective functioning. At the same time, due to the Somali political and security situation, forming a formal banking sector would not be practical in the near future. Though the flow of remittances has not been affected in many countries due to the Somali remittance companies being able to function within a legal framework, in a few countries the remittance transfers to Somalia are still trapped in a status of illegality. Norway is one such country where *hawala*-based remittance transactions are considered illegal. The formalizing process of Somali remittance companies has not taken place in Norway because of the tough regulations involved. The experience of the Somali remittance sector in Norway since September 11 is dealt with in the next section.

Norwegian Response to the Post September 11 Era

Following the closure of Al-Barakaat offices in the United States, some countries, including Ethiopia, closed all Somali *hawala* company offices (Lindley 2005). However, European countries were divided on their measures against legalizing *hawala* companies. These measures ranged from reasonable and more liberal to stricter and difficult to comply with (ibid.) formalization processes. In countries such as Sweden and the United Kingdom, the legalization process for *hawala* companies was reasonable and all remittance companies were legalized and registered with the concerned authorities in these countries. Norway, Germany and France, however, imposed difficult regulatory processes for *hawala* companies to operate legally (ibid.).

Norway, as a member of the Financial Action Task Force, has intensified control on informal money transfer systems in the post September 11 era. The Norwegian response started with the arrest of seven Norwegian Somalis, Al Barakaat and Dahabshiil operatives, in Oslo in October 2001. Making illegal transfers of nearly 60 million kroner every year out of Norway that may have had links with terrorism constituted the allegations made against them (Carling 2005, *Verdens Gang* 2001). Investigation was undertaken by Økokrim, a Norwegian police division responsible for economic crimes. The investigation aimed to find out:

1. Whether the money sent by the *hawala* system had any connection with criminal actions within or outside Norway.

2. How it was possible for individuals with no permanent job to send millions of kroner out of Norway.
3. Whether these transactions were made in accordance with Norwegian law.

Following the investigation, the initial allegations were not substantiated so no 'smoking gun' was found. However, the police charged a number of Somalis with money laundering and violation of the Tax Act, Accounting Act and Currency Act (Carling 2005, Stortinget, 2007).[22] Out of the seven Somalis arrested, two were given 14 and 18 months imprisonment and the other five received sentences of 30 to 45 days. These sentences were appealed and while the Appeal Court upheld the charges, it reduced the punishment. The Appeal Court also mentioned in its verdict that the reasons for reducing the punishments were related to the humanitarian motives for the money transfers, according to the thorough investigation by Økokrim. It also reported that one of the convicted people, the manager of Dahabshiil, was trying to establish regulated remittance services from Norway to Somalia but his request was rejected by the Norwegian authorities (Carling 2005).

We are able to observe two important but conflicting perspectives on the police action. Firstly, the attitude of the authority was over-anxious, restrictive and largely based on the assumption that *hawala* could be used by 'terrorists'. The argument used was that since there were around 12,000 Somalis in Norway at that time and many of them were unemployed[23] how could they send out 60 million Norwegian kroner annually? As noted in the introduction, this perspective was rooted in the migration–security nexus paradigm.

The second perspective, based on the migration–development nexus paradigm, argues that there was no law in Norway to guide the *hawala* financial transfers and Somalis have no other option for sending money back home to people in need. It was further argued that more than 10,000 people, also from Sweden, Denmark and Finland, were customers of the *hawala* system.[24] If they sent 60 million kroner annually, the average amount was 6,000 kroner each per year – not a huge sum, as the police admitted. This perspective further emphasized the need for remittances to provide livelihoods for Somalis and help the country as whole to survive.

Although Norway is seen as a country that values the development and humanitarian concerns of developing nations, in the post September 11 era, in the case of informal money transfer mechanisms, it adopted a hard-line approach based on the remittance–security paradigm. Økokrim began investigating informal money transfer systems and the rationales behind this were: partly to fulfil Norway's international obligations to follow the recommendations of the Financial Action Task Force; to answer national concerns about monitoring illegal money transfers

22 Source: http://epos.stortinget.no/SpmDetalj.aspx?id=36541.

23 This information was revealed by the Norwegian official who participated in the conference organized by UNDP Somalia in London in December 2003.

24 The figure was from the *hawala* operatives in Norway.

to criminal and terror networks; and to maintain law and order in the country. During these investigations, Økokrim was able to monitor and investigate nine informal money transfer systems or *hawala* networks. Out of these nine, two were Somali, as mentioned above, and the other seven were run by Iraqi Kurds. The operations of the networks were traced back to 1999 and revealed that around 600 million Norwegian kroner had been transferred out of the country (Økokrim 2007). The largest network channelled around 45 million Norwegian kroner annually on average and the smallest around 2 million Norwegian kroner (Økokrim 2007). The longest duration of the network was around four years and the shortest around five months. There were seven cases filed at court. Out of these, in five cases the accused were convicted, one case was rejected and the other was about to go to ruling at the time of Økokrim's report. Altogether nineteen people were punished, seven were given prison sentences and others were given fines of between 10,000 and 30,000 Norwegian kroner (Økokrim 2007).

While these investigations and actions were in motion, affected communities, especially the Somali community in Norway, started to respond and pointed out the significance of remittances for the people left back in the homeland. People who advocate the remittance–development nexus paradigm within academia, policy-makers and journalists have also expressed concerns about the danger of a humanitarian catastrophe emerging if the remittance lifeline was closed.

However, the imperative but difficult issue is how to reconcile these two legitimate necessities and concerns of the migration–development nexus and the migration–security nexus. That is, how can Somali remittance companies continue to function in Norway to facilitate remittance transfers in accordance with the Norwegian law?

Norway introduced a new law in early 2004. According to the new law, the Currency Act and the Norwegian central bank's (Norges Bank) foreign exchange regulations were to be abolished and regulation of foreign exchange activity was to be transferred to a new Financial Institutions Act. According to the Financial Institution Act, Somali remittance companies can register themselves as finance companies and function in Norway. But according to this law, any financial institution that intends to get licensed should have a start-up capital of 5 million euros and, if the institution is to engage with only money transfer services, the start-up capital can be reduced to 1 million euros (Økokrim 2007, Kredittilsynet 2008). The law also demands a lot of different procedures and paperwork in the company registration and licensing process. In the UNDP conference report (2003) a Norwegian official stated the following:

> A Somali remittance company will be able to conduct its business if it is licensed as a financial company. To obtain such a licence, firstly, the company must be established under the Norwegian laws with minimum share capital of Norwegian kroner equivalent to 5 million euros, although the King of Norway may lower this minimum amount to 1 million euros in special cases. The following must then be submitted with an application to Kredittilsynet: 1) The company's corporate

> structure; 2) An overview of the operating set-up and policies/procedures of the business and services that the company intends to offer; 3) Information about the company's capital composition; 4) Budgets for establishment and administrative costs; 5) Budgets including the profit and loss account, balance sheet and funds flow statement for the first three years; and 6) forecast of the financial position for each of the first three years. As such, subject to Kredittilsynet being satisfied with the above requirements and the requirement of 'fit and proper' management under the Financial Services Act, a licence may be granted.

The above Norwegian regulations are tough compared to some other European countries. For example, in Sweden *hawala*-based remittance companies can start their business if they register with the Swedish Financial Supervisory Authority (Finansinspektionen – FI) and have approval from them. The Swedish Financial Supervisory Authority charges 3,000 Swedish kronor for private individuals and 10,000 Swedish kronor for judicial persons as an annual fee for their regulation formalities. In the United Kingdom, *hawala*-based remittance transfer companies can start their business by registering themselves and paying 60 pounds as a registration fee (Økokrim 2007). While the United Kingdom has adopted a much lower cost requirement for the establishment of money transfer companies, they have adopted more sophisticated monitoring mechanisms to prevent or reduce the level of misuse.

At the UNDP conference held in the United Kingdom in 2003, it was pointed out that Norway's regulations were too tough for any Somali remittance companies to conform to and, in a practical sense, Norway has prohibited the operations of these companies. Despite the new Financial Institution Act being introduced, to our knowledge there is not a single formalized *hawala* company in Norway.

Nevertheless, all of them, except Al-Barakaat, are transferring remittances to Somalia and elsewhere. However, the Act has given little consideration to the legitimate needs of the Somalis and has imposed virtually impossible conditions on *hawala* companies. Consequently, while the new Act has failed to formalize the Somalis remittance companies, it has succeeded in creating fear and insecurity among Somalis, whether they are sending or receiving money. Further, it may result in people developing an 'underground' or alternative system for transferring money and the transparency and accountability of such systems would be difficult to ascertain.

The current situation with regard to Somali remittances is that the policy makers need to find a balance between their different approaches but they realize this and have resolved to work on it. This was also reflected in the approach taken by the Norwegian national security service (PST) during the arrest of three Somalis amidst allegations of terror funding in 2008. Apparently the security service was keen to identify whom the funds were channelled to but not how they were channelled to them.

Although Norway has not yet softened its regulations for remittance companies, there has been considerable progress in making it easier to register and licence financial transfer operations. Økokrim, who carried out the investigation on *hawala* networks, recognized concerns based on both the migration–development nexus paradigm and the migration–security nexus paradigm. It suggested a two-prong strategy to the Norwegian Government (Ministry of Justice) which would address both legitimate concerns through more police control to prevent or reduce the misuse of financial transfer activities and less formal demands in establishing money transfer companies. The Ministry of Justice forwarded Økokrim's suggestion to the Ministry of Finance for consideration and the Ministry advised Kredittilsynet to submit a report on the issue. Their report, completed in September 2008, recommended less restrictive regulations for establishing money transfer companies. In the meantime, the Norwegian Government had decided to implement Directive 2007/64/EC of the European Parliament and of the Council on payment services in the internal market. The Norwegian Ministry of Finance had sent its proposal for public hearing and the responses were to be registered by15 September 2009.

If the suggestions become law, remittance companies can start their businesses and get licensed with a start-up capital of20,000 euros (stated as 160,000 Norwegian kroner in the Norwegian proposal) if the company is to engage with only direct money transfer activities. If the company plans to engage in the 'execution of payment where the consent of the payer to execute a payment is given by means of any telecommunication, digital or IT device and the payment is made to the telecommunication, IT system or network operator (as stated in the EU directive), then the start-up capital would be 50,000 euros (400,000 Norwegian kroner). For the other services, defined as payment services in the European Union directive that include account-based remittance services, a higher start-up capital of 125,000 euros (1 million Norwegian kroner) is expected.

Conclusion

Globally, migrant remittances amount to more than double the official development aid. The money that is sent by migrants through informal transfer systems, including *hawala*, for example, from Norway, thus contributes to the survival of millions of individuals and development processes in many countries in the South. Somalia is amongst the most remittance-dependent countries in the world, with most recent estimates suggesting an annual remittance inflow of up to one billion. For immigrants of Somali origin in Norway, transfers back home are not available within the legal sector. Neither banks nor transfer companies, such as Western Union or Forex/Money gram, provide services to Somalia, and transfers through *hawala* operators are currently illegal.[25]

25 Though there is a Western Union facility in Somaliland, people are unlikely to use the service due to higher transfer charges.

Nevertheless, transfers from migrants are essential for the survival of relatives in Somalia, a country that has been without a functioning state for over fifteen years. And sending remittances is crucial for the senders as well, as in order to function in Norway, they need to know that their relatives and friends are not starving or trapped in conflict zones of the country when they needed to flee. For Somalis in Norway, the *hawala* system is the only transfer mechanism available for remitting money to Somalia.

Meanwhile several *hawala* operators who operate legally from Sweden, the United States and the United Kingdom, have put their own safeguards in place in order to combat money laundering and financing of terrorism, in accordance with the Financial Action Task Force recommendations. Norwegian authorities have cited these recommendations in defence of Norway's restrictive regulatory environment. The significant challenge here lies not only in the legal and technical issues of regularizing *hawala* but, at a more fundamental level, this issue relates to how these businesses are being received when they seek regularization.

The disadvantage of the situation at the end of 2009 is that the consumer interests of those wishing to make international transfers, including migrants in Norway, are not being protected. The Financial Action Task Force has stressed the need for remittance regulations to be flexible and proportional to the risks they pose. The World Bank and the International Monetary Fund point out that consumer protection in the financial system involves the availability of accessible and affordable remittance services. In order to work towards the inclusion and equality of migrants in Norway, these issues need to be addressed. A recent report from the Norwegian Statistics Bureau about the living conditions of immigrants in Norway indicates that Somalis feel a high affiliation with Norway, despite the relatively short time they have been living there and the many social and economic challenges they face. Are they being met with equality and respect, as part of the policy of inclusion in a multicultural Norway?

The Norwegian government policy related to migrant remittances must respect the right of immigrants to prioritize the spending of their money, within a legal context. The fact that millions of displaced civilians depend on the *hawala* for their livelihoods and survival should not be forgotten when practical and administrative procedures are considered.

References

Ballard, R. 2003. A background report on the operation of informal value transfer systems (*hawala*). Manchester: University of Manchester Centre for Applied South Asian Studies. Red Croft, UK.

Carling, J. 2005. Migrant Remittances and Development Cooperation. PRIO Report. Oslo: International Peace Research Institute (PRIO).

Carling, J., Erdal, M.B., Horst, C. and Wallacher, H. *et al.* 2007. Legal, Rapid and Reasonably Priced? A Survey of Remittance Services in Norway, PRIO Report. Oslo: International Peace Research Institute (PRIO).

Congressional Budget Office (CBO) 2005. *Remittances: International Payments by Migrants*. Washington DC: Congress of the United States.

Eriksen, T.H. 2007. *Globalization: The Key Concepts*. Oxford: Berg.

Fangen, K. 2006. Humiliation as experienced by Somalis in Norway, *Journal of Refugee Studies* 19:69–93.

Financial Action Task Force (FATF) 2003. Combating the Abuse of Alternative Remittance Systems: International Best Practices. Paris: FATF.

Fuglerud, Ø. and Engebrigtsen, A. 2006. Culture, networks and social capital: Tamil and Somali immigrants in Norway. *Ethnic and Racial Studies*, 29: 1118–1134.

Gaas, M.H. 2007. Flight, resettlement and employment constraints of Somali refugees in Oslo, Norway. MSc Thesis. Aas, Norway: Department of International Environment and Development Studies, Norwegian University for Life Science (UMB).

—— 2009. A new hope? Former rebel takes over as Somali president. *Jane's Intelligence Review*: March: 24–29.

Geode, de M. 2003. *Hawala* discourses and the war on terrorist finance. *Environment and Planning D. Society and Space* 21:513–532.

Gundel, J. 2002. The migration–development nexus: Somalia case study. *International Migration* 4:5.

—— 2006. The Predicament of the 'Oday': The role of traditional structures in security, rights, law and development in Somalia, Copenhagen: Danish Refugee Council and Novib-Oxfam.

Horst, C. and Gaas, M.H. 2008. Remittances for peace? The transnational political engagements of Somalis in Norway. PRIO Papers. Oslo: PRIO.

Horst, C. and Van Hear, N. 2002. Counting the cost: refugees, remittances and the 'war against terrorism'. *Forced Migration Review* 14.

Hyndman, J. 2000. Managing displacement: Refugees and the politics of humanitarianism. *Borderlines* 16. Minneapolis and London: University of Minnesota Press.

KPMG 2004. Feasibility Study on Financial Services in Somalia. Updated Final Report, Nairobi: UNDP.

Kredittilsynet 2008. Reguleringen av pengeoverføringer fra Norge – en vurdering av muligheten for å gjøre pengeoverføring enklere, rimeligere, og lovlig. Accessed on 7 December 2009 at: http://www.kredittilsynet.no/archive/f-avd_pdf/01/04/20080035.pdf.

Lindley, A. 2005. Somalia country study: A part of the report on informal remittance systems in Africa, Caribbean and Pacific (ACP) countries (Ref: RO2CS008). DFID UK, EC-PREP and Deloitte and Touche. Oxford: University of Oxford Centre on Migration, Policy and Society (COMPAS).

Looney, P. 2003. *Hawala*: the terrorist's informal financial mechanism. *Middle East Policy* X:1 Spring.

Maimbo, S.M. 2004. The regulation and supervision of informal remittance systems: Emerging oversight strategies. Paper submitted for the Seminar on Current Developments In Monetary and Financial Law. Washington DC. Accessed at: http://www.imf.org/external/np/leg/sem/2004/cdmfl/eng/maimbo.pdf.

—— (ed.) 2006. Remittances and Economic Development in Somalia. Social Development Papers, Conflict Prevention and Reconstruction, Paper No. 38 November. Washington DC: World Bank.

McCulloch, J. and Pickering, S. 2005. Suppressing the financing of terrorism: Proliferating state crime, eroding censure and extending neo-colonialism. *British Journal of Criminology* 45: 470–486.

Medani, K.M. 2002. Financing terrorism or survival? Informal finance and state collapse in Somalia and the United States War on Terrorism. *Middle East Report* No. 223:2–9 Summer.

Norwegian Statistics Bureau (SSB) 2005. Information available at: http://www.ssb.no/vis/emner/02/01/10/innvbef/art-2006-05-11-01.html.

Økokrim 2007. Uformelle verdioverføringssytemer i Norge: En strategisk analyse. Accesed at: http://www.okokrim.no/www/okokrim/home.nsf/Attachments/784F4CBC7A4B6F79C12575A700167E8A/$FILE/UVSrapport.pdf.

Omer, A. 2002. A report on supporting systems and procedures for the effective regulation and monitoring of Somali remittance companies (*hawala*). Somalia: UNDP.

Parker, K., Browdidge, J. and Chang, C.E. 2004. *Hawala* and Terrorist Financing. Accessed on 7 June 2007 at: http://faculty.concord.edu/chrisz/M-AIB-05/PDFs/11HawalaandTerroristFin.pdf.

Passas, N. 2003a. *Hawala* and other informal value transfer systems: How to regulate them? *Journal of Risk Management* 5(2), 49–59. Accessed on 7 June 2007 at: http://usinfo.state.gov/eap/Archive_Index/Hawala_and_Other_Informal_Value_Transfer_Systems_How_to_Regulate_Them.html.

—— 2003b. Informal value transfer systems, terrorism and money laundering: a report to the National Institute of Justice. Available at: www.ncjrs.gov/pdffiles1/nij/grants/208301.pdf.

—— 2006. Fighting terror with error: The counter-productive regulation of informal value transfers. *Crime, Law and Social Change* 45:315–336.

Sørensen, N.N. 2004. Opportunities and Pitfalls in the Migration–Development Nexus: Somaliland and Beyond, DIIS Working Paper 21. Oslo: Danish Institute for International Studies.

UNDP 2003. Conference on the Somali Remittance Sector: Understanding the Somali Remittance Sector and the regulation that govern it. 3–4 December Conference Report. London: UNDP.

Verdens Gang Nett 2001. Bin Laden kobles til norsk nettverk: 60 millioner sendt ut av Norge årlig, mener Økokrim. Accessed on 4 June 2007 at: http://www.vg.no/pub/vgart.hbs?artid=2611834.

Waldron, S. and Hasci, N.A. 1995. Somali refugees in the Horn of Africa: State of the art literature review. *Studies on Emergencies and Disaster Relief Report* 3. Uppsala: Nordiska Afrikainstitutet.

Yusuf, A.W. 2006. Somali enterprises: Making peace their business. Available at: http://www.international-alert.org/pdfs/lblp_Somalia.pdf.

PART IV
Transnational Media and Freedom of Expression: Human Rights Paradoxes

Chapter 12

Differing Standards of Free Expression: Clashes of Laws during the Cartoon Controversy?

Elisabeth Eide[1]

Abstract

This chapter studies how the crisis developing after the publication of the twelve Mohammed cartoons in Denmark's largest newspaper, demonstrated a variety of interpretations of freedom of expression as well as the international conventions and national constitutions and punitive laws treating this right. This is based on a larger study of media representation of the cartoon issue in several countries, but with a special focus on Pakistan. The study applies representation theories – the Orientalism critique and theories of its supposed adversary, Occidentalism – as well as critical discourse analysis. Among the cases mentioned is the sentencing of Holocaust-denier, David Irving, which was perceived in Pakistan as an example of European double standards and the debates preceding the Durban II conference in Geneva.

Introduction

In 2005 twelve cartoons of the Prophet Mohammed were published in Denmark's largest newspaper, *Jyllands-Posten.* The event initially caused critical reactions among Danish Muslims and some of the cartoons were published in a few other countries, for example in the Egyptian paper *Al Fagr.* In 2006, after more widespread publishing in Europe, the world witnessed a variety of protests around the world, some of them violent, particularly in the parts of the world where Islam plays an important role.[2]

---

1 Elisabeth Eide is Associate Professor (PhD) in Journalism Studies at Oslo University College.

2 From a Muslim perspective, the cartoon depicting the prophet Mohammed with a bomb in his turban and an inscription of the Islamic decree of faith in the turban as well, was the most provocative one. The event was triggered by *Jyllands-Posten* inviting cartoonists to draw the Prophet Mohammed, allegedly because there was a growing danger of self censorship *vis-à-vis* the Muslim population in Denmark.

The publication of the Mohammed cartoons happened in a tense, transnational discursive situation framed by the 'war on terror', and as the controversy developed in February and March 2006, the discourse of the 'clash of civilizations' (Lewis 1990, Huntington 1993, 1996) was revived. In many countries the cartoons were labelled as blasphemous and insulting to the world's 1.3 billion Muslims. Demands for punishment of the artists by referrals to blasphemy law were raised on several occasions, including in Europe.

It became increasingly clear that the perceptions of blasphemy as a punishable crime varied widely. While in most of Europe laws on blasphemy still exist, they are rarely applied; but in other countries outside the West, such laws are actively used against dissenters and proponents for freedom of expression.

The cartoon controversy also made its mark on the debate on defamation of religion leading up to the United Nations conference on racism in Durban in 2009[3] and the preceding debate concerning the mandate of the United Nations' special rapporteur on freedom of expression and human rights (this was most likely – at least partly – derived from the cartoon controversy).

This chapter gives an outline of the caricature crisis as a transnational media event. It raises questions about how different interpretations of freedom of speech and blasphemy law figured in the media representations; and how freedom of speech – recognized by most states as a universal human right – was interpreted differently in media representations during the cartoon controversy. How the 'clash of civilizations' discourse comes into play in the coverage of the cartoons, particularly concentrating on the coverage in one predominantly Muslim country, is illustrated through examples from Pakistan.[4] The Pakistani case study shows how some actors represented in the Pakistani press treated what they saw as 'European inconsistency' and the 'double standards of the West', using legal arguments. As part of the conclusion I address the pre-Geneva controversies.

Transnational Media Events

The concept of a 'media event' has traditionally been linked to the medium of television and implies an immediacy of reporting, often transgressing national borders. According to Dayan and Katz, they:

> [...] include epic contests of politics and sports, charismatic missions, and the rites of passage of the great – what we call Contests, Conquests and Coronations. In spite of the differences among them, events such as the Olympic Games,

3 Also called the Durban II or the Durban Review Conference; Geneva 22–24 April 2009.

4 This researcher lived and worked in Pakistan the first half year of 2006 and thus had easy access to the sentiments and the media representations of the controversy as it developed there.

> Anwar el-Sadat's journey to Jerusalem and the funeral of John F. Kennedy have given shape to a new narrative genre that employs the unique potential of the electronic media to command attention universally and simultaneously in order to tell a primordial story about current affairs (Dayan and Katz 1992:1).

Some of these events may be characterized by being prearranged, for example the funeral of the late Princess Diana was broadcast to many corners of the world (Ramonet 1999). One could also see how the terrorist attack of September 11, 2001 developed into one of the major transnational media events of our time. That event in turn contributed to a transnational discursive situation which may have had an impact on the various interpretations of the Mohammed cartoons and the way the media treated them in different national contexts. The 'nine-eleven' attack may also have affected how different understandings of freedom of speech and blasphemy mushroomed as laws were mobilized in a highly politicized transnational context.

The publication of the cartoons did not immediately stir the world media and so this did not qualify as a transnational media event in the strict sense. We may, however, need to look at informal networking – not least due to the increasing diaspora – and the way in which images inviting various interpretations travelled, and thus opt for a revised definition of the concept. Dayan and Katz's book was published in 1992 and since then a range of new media have become more prominent, allowing for a line-up of new communicative options. This rethinking may be important to allow both for including diasporic practices and (re)actions and new participatory media, for example web logs. Furthermore it is necessary to take into consideration how this new media situation, for example, makes it possible to transfer a drawing of the Prophet Mohammed, published in a mid-Norwegian town, in a split second through MMS communication to Muslim *madrasa* students in Taliban-controlled areas in Pakistan (Eide 2009).[5] Needless to say, the understanding of law and freedom of expression in mid-Norway and the tribal areas in Pakistan (FATA)[6] differs substantially.

5 Dayan has recently published a new contribution taking into consideration both the development and critique since 1992 (Dayan 2010).

6 FATA = Federally Administered Tribal Areas, an area between Pakistan and Afghanistan where the tribal leaders traditionally exercise control without much interference from Pakistani authorities but where Taliban have gained considerable influence during the last decade. *Madrasa* = religious school. In this particular case, a rather insulting cartoon was received by religious students while a Norwegian reporter was present and thereby threatened – he was almost beaten up before he was allowed to leave. The same reporter wrote a weblog about his experiences, mentioning that he also faced danger in Gaza in 2006 due to the Mohammed cartoon controversy, since he was from Norway.

A Clash of Representations?

The research project which inspired this chapter was initiated in February 2006 and called 'Freedom of speech as a news item. An international analysis of the press discourses on the Mohammed caricatures'. One of the most prominent research questions investigated how freedom of speech was defined in the context of a 'global' news event – by editors, reporters and other public actors who had access to the press. For the study, both news items and opinion articles were investigated in five or six publications in each country, from late January to early March 2006, the period in which the conflict was most highlighted.[7] We found that both publication practices and reactions to the cartoons varied to a great extent around the world, even between neighbouring countries thought to be culturally close. In demonstrations linked to protests against the cartoons, several people were killed by police or paramilitaries: five people in Afghanistan, eleven in Libya, 140 in Nigeria and five in Pakistan. Some journalists lost their jobs and a couple of reporters were imprisoned due to their involvement in publishing one or several cartoons. The mapping of various constitutions and their way of defining free expression was also an essential part of the project.

Since most countries, including Pakistan, are signatories to a wide variety of human rights conventions protecting freedom of speech, one might expect the political leaders as well as the press or media to interpret their constitutions in the light of these universal standards.

The variety of practices and interpretations, however, suggest three main attitudes to the controversy:

1. The printing of the cartoons was justified as an exercise of free expression in a context where this right is under threat – often from fundamentalist Muslims;
2. The right to print such cartoons is indisputable but one may question whether the act itself was wise and sensitive in the present diverse societies we all face;
3. The printing was insensitive and should be dealt with by law as an example of blasphemy.

Interestingly, some of the divisions occurred between countries perceived as culturally close, for example Denmark and Sweden (in the latter the cartoons were not printed); and France and the United Kingdom (in the latter the cartoons were almost only found on the website of the extreme right wing British Nationalist Party). In both Denmark and France groups of Muslims tried to bring

7 The project was funded by *Helsingin Sanomat Foundation*, later also by Culcom, at the University of Oslo. A working report (Kunelius, Eide *et al.* 2007) as well as a book (Eide, Kunelius and Phillips 2008) have been published.

the publishers to court; in Denmark the case was rejected, in France the court case happened but the Muslims lost.[8]

Orientalism, Occidentalism

Edward Said's Orientalism critique (1981, 1994, 1995, 2003), as well as theories of Occidentalism (Carrier 1995, Chen 2000, Buruma and Margalit 2004), often seen as an attempt at creating an adversary to Orientalism, offer a framework to understand this transnational media event. Are the traits of Orientalism still to be found in the media coverage of Islam and Muslims during the controversy, as Said observed in his study of how the Iranian revolution was represented in the Western media (1981)? Is Occidentalism – the study of the West from a non-Western point of view (Hanafi 2005) – an adequate theory for understanding the way in which 'Eastern' media covers such an event?[9] In the following the pronouns *we* and *they* are looked at as discursive categories which may be both inclusive and exclusive. Often these pronouns may take the shape of broad categories as 'the West', 'the East' or 'the Muslim world', for example, which are open to sweeping generalizations. Critical discursive analysis (Fairclough 1995, 2003) adds to the perspectives.

Categories are always a problem. As Said wrote:

> [...] how prevalent it has become for people to speak now in the name of large, and in my opinion, undesirably vague and manipulable, abstractions like the West or Japanese or Slavic culture, Islam or Confucianism, labels that collapse religions, races, and ethnicities into ideologies that are considerably more unpleasant and provocative [...] (2003).

The above citation is from an essay called 'The clash of definitions', the title revealing an inter-textual reference to the works of Huntington and Lewis. Said's aim in this late work seems to be a warning against simplifications by emphasizing diversity.

Still, the press, often perceived as a conservative institution in modern society, would frequently apply the broad concepts in an ideological way, without

8 Reported in a documentary directed by Daniel Leconte '*C'est dure d'etre aimé par des cons*' (2008).

9 Some knowledge of the Orientalism critique is presupposed here. Its younger adversary is less well known, and in addition to Hanafi's initial definition, Occidentalism may be seen as a process of liberation, a counter-discourse, through which academics and other representing intellectuals (including media workers) talk back to the 'West' from an upgraded status of observer. It may take the shape of seeing the Western Other as amoral, insensitive, extremely secular and so on (See also Eide 2008).

recognizing these flows and the new societies they contribute to shaping. One example is how the cartoons were perceived by a Canadian daily:

> The key issue at stake in the battle over the twelve Danish cartoons of the Muslim prophet Muhammad is this: Will the West stand up for its customs and mores, including freedom of speech, or will Muslims impose their way of life on the West? (*The Montreal Gazette*, Canada 7 February 2006).

This statement presupposes that 'Muslims' have one particular 'way of life', and underlying these sentences seems to be the fear of a Muslim invasion due to their rules and lifestyles. Implicit in the last sentence is an assumption that Muslims will curb Western freedoms by their stricter rules.

Several other papers in the so-called West would echo this kind of argument but other voices were also important. Not least in Denmark, where two other large dailies (*Berlingske Tidende* and *Politiken*) did not initially publish the twelve cartoons and *Politiken* was critical of the act.[10]

A main Russian newspaper would argue against publication of the cartoons referring to historical experience.

> Yes, Russia is often called a barbarian country. In fact we have a problem with culture. But no one will be as rude as some European newspapers have been. In Russia we have our common historical experience of coexistence of different peoples and nationalities (*Argumenty i Fakty, Russia*, 15 February 2006).

On the other hand, in Russia, some journalists were arrested after they published the cartoons and the country's general practice of freedom of the press may indicate that behind the rhetoric of not being rude and of taking coexistence into consideration, there may be other concerns. In China none of the cartoons were published and there was minimal coverage of the event, in spite of the fact that the country has 20 million Muslims. The overall state control of media combined with the 'harmony model' (Zhengrong and Liang 2007) were the main reasons for this.

East and West …

The debate which occurred in Norway after a Christian weekly, *Magazinet*, published the cartoons on 10 January 2006 was partly characterized by the government taking a stand, prioritising dialogue above confrontation. For this they harvested criticism from some of the press and from lay people and politicians:

10 Later, however, when the cartoonist who had delivered the most provocative cartoon (of the Prophet Mohammed with a bomb in his turban, with part of the Muslim declaration of faith inscribed) received death threats and had an attempt on his life, the other papers *did* print the cartoons, as a gesture of solidarity.

'There does not exist any nuances of grey when it comes to freedom of speech' wrote the leader of the Party of Progress, the main opposition party (Dagens Næringsliv 18 February 2006). On the other hand, several Muslim leaders favoured the government position. In the autumn of 2006, the editor of *Magazinet*, Vebjørn Selbekk, published a book called *Threatened by Islamists*,[11] highlighting his experiences (among them death threats) after the publication. In this context, the Secretary General of the Norwegian Press Council, Per Edgar Kokkvold, who had written a preface to the book, said the following in a press interview:

> We cannot step by step accept claims from Islamists which put our society back to medieval times, because somebody does not accept modernity and democracy – which enable Muslims to exercise their beliefs in our society, says Kokkvold (bt.no 3 October 2006, my translation).

This quote places the protestors against the publication of the Mohammed cartoons at another stage of history, a well-known Orientalist feature; thus linking protests to the negation of modernity and democracy. Furthermore it echoes the fear of censorship mentioned in the Canadian newspaper. Last, but not least, it illustrates how the national *we* is established as a category of ownership not including Muslims ('*their* belief in *our* society'). However, this use of pronouns is fairly widespread both within and outside the so-called West; the latter can be seen from the headlines of two Egyptian newspapers:

> The religious East and secular West can never meet (*Al-Wafid*, Egypt, 15 February 2006).

> The West dictates to us how to react to the cartoon controversy (*Akhbar Al-Alyoum*, Egypt, 11 February 2006).

> There is a Western conspiracy against the Muslims. Freedom does not guarantee the right of blasphemy (*Akhbar Al-Alyoum*, Egypt, 11 February 2006).

The headlines were rather harsh and established an *Us* ('Muslims'), counterpoised to a perceived *West* during the heat of the cartoon crisis. Conspiracy theories were amply present in several Pakistani media linked to the publication of the cartoons (Eide 2007). This way of representing the West as a unit, corresponds with what James Carrier writes about Occidentalism, as occurring 'in studies of the ways that people outside the West imagine themselves, for their self-image often develops in contrast to their stylized image of the West' (Carrier 1995). From the last headline an argument occurs that has to do with law. The interpretation is that freedom to express oneself is something apart from blasphemy. And if one transcends the blasphemy border, one has to face the law (as one is no longer exercising a given right).

11 *Truet av islamister.*

Discourse of Disgust

The conservative-leaning Urdu newspaper in Pakistan, *Nawa-e-Waqt*,[12] describes the caricatures as blasphemous, hurtful, shameless and undignified – thus introducing a *discourse of disgust*. The editorial sees the publication as part of a larger strategy:

> Freedom of expression does not imply freedom from morals, values and regulations but stands for the protection and respect of religious and social values. [...] Every enlightened Jew and Christian scholar and journalist is well aware of Muslims' sentiments and beliefs regarding Prophet Mohammad (PBUH).[13] In this context the publication of the cartoons and their defence on the pretext of freedom of expression appears to be a well thought-out strategy (*Nawa-e-Waqt* 8 February 2006: 'The clash of civilizations continues').

Freedom of expression is here seen as coherent with the respect for religious and social values. And in a country with strict blasphemy laws this argument may seem valid. Furthermore, the 'shameless' definition may be associated with the way in which Buruma and Margalit define Occidentalism, as a representation of the West as hyper-secular and promiscuous (2004). What this Urdu newspaper adds here is the already mentioned *discourse of conspiracy*. They suggest that the cartoons were well planned and meant to provoke, and the headline repeating Huntington's title underlines the *us/them*-theme of the text. Seen as provocations, the moral argument against the cartoons is reinforced.

Reactions to the cartoons in Indonesia were divided. A conservative religious newspaper, *Republika*, wrote that:

> The argument of freedom of expression that is repeatedly used is merely a way of concealing Western inferiority. Apart from all their material achievements, the West has this religious complex: they hate their religion. Ironically, this feeling of hatred is generalized towards all religions (11 February 2006).

This argument is very much in line with the Occidentalist notion of 'the West' being extremist secularists (and Occidentalism's advocates representing a 'revolt against rationalism'), as observed by Buruma and Margalit (2004:95). But while they argue that the Occidentalist representations often stem from a position of inferiority, we can observe that, at least rhetorically, the above newspaper seems to do the opposite, by using the expression 'Western inferiority'.

From the various excerpts it is evident that *freedom of speech* is a concept understood in a variety of ways and seen as relative to values and regulations,

12 A rather religious-conservative leaning newspaper.

13 PBUH means 'Peace be upon him', very often quoted when mentioning the Prophet Mohammed. Urdu quotes translated by Beenish Cheema.

and in many countries arguments were raised about freedom not implying the freedom to insult.

Accusations travelled both ways. An underlying discourse which seems to have been more important in countries where many felt offended by the cartoons was the reference to *law*, as a solution to the problem of insult, including demands for bringing the perpetrators (the cartoonists) to justice.

These conflicting views did not correspond with geographical boundaries. Within all societies, there were differing views. In Pakistan one of the monthly *Herald*'s columnists supported the printing of the cartoons; in Norway most editors refrained from printing them followed by arguments of sensitivity to religious feelings. The differences were more marked when it comes to the interpretation of law.

A Clash of Laws?

At a conference aimed at bridging gaps between media professionals around the world, the Global Inter Media Dialogue (I)[14] in Bali in August 2006, several delegates from the Muslim world suggested that it would be a good idea to have a global code of ethics, including some guidelines on how to deal with religion in a non-defamatory way.[15] This suggestion was met with resistance and scepticism from many Western delegates. It may perhaps seem paradoxical that proponents of universal rights to free expression reject suggestions of universal ethical guidelines. However, behind the scepticism there is no doubt a perception of the danger that universal ethical guidelines may develop into obstacles to this universal freedom. This is just one of several dilemmas exposed during the cartoon controversy.

Article 100 in the Norwegian constitution states:

> There shall be freedom of expression.
>
> No person may be held liable in law for having imparted or received information, ideas or messages unless this can be justified in relation to the grounds for freedom of expression, which are the seeking of truth, the promotion of democracy and the individual's freedom to form opinions. Such legal liability shall be prescribed by law.
>
> Everyone shall be free to speak his mind frankly on the administration of the State and on any other subject whatsoever. Clearly defined limitations to this

14 The conferences, altogether three (Bali I, Oslo, Bali II), were the result of an initiative from the Norwegian and Indonesian ministries of foreign affairs, obviously initiated after seeing the extensive reactions to the publications of the Mohammed cartoons, which were also a topic of discussion at the first one.

15 I was present at all these conferences and the reference is from my own memory.

> right may only be imposed when particularly weighty considerations so justify in relation to the grounds for freedom of expression.
>
> Prior censorship and other preventive measures may not be applied unless so required in order to protect children and young persons from the harmful influence of moving pictures. Censorship of letters may only be imposed in institutions.

This paragraph's only limitation has to do with the rights of children and youngsters to be protected from harmful influences and the article is a little more detailed than Article 19 in the United Nations Universal Declaration of Human Rights, stating that:

> Everyone has the right to freedom of opinion and expression; this right includes freedom to hold opinions without interference and to seek, receive and impart information and ideas through any media and regardless of frontiers.

In addition, till May 2009 there was an article against blasphemy in the Norwegian punitive law. The parliament abandoned this paragraph both since it has not been actively used since the 1930s and presumably also as a result of the debate in the aftermath of the cartoon crisis. The government initially opted for a new version banning blasphemy but was taken to task by the press and by freedom of expression organizations for this; and subsequently withdrew this proposal.[16] In the end, only the Norwegian Christian Democratic Party voted against this motion.

Writers and commentators engaged in the Norwegian debate in 2006 were aware of this paragraph in the Penal Code. The leader of the Freedom of Expression Commission in Norway, Francis Sejersted, said that 'punitive laws on blasphemy do not belong in our way of thinking'.[17] Other international sources were of a different opinion. The Norwegian News Agency (NTB) interviewed the United Nations Special Rapporteur on contemporary forms of racism, racial discrimination, xenophobia and related intolerance, Doudou Diene; and he was deeply worried after the publication of the cartoons:

> He claims that the Danish government broke with international law, under which it is its duty to protect civilian and political rights, since the government did not officially take a stand on the cartoons. This also shows that Islamophobia – fear of Islam – has been politically banalized, claims Diene (NTB 17 March 2006).

---

16 Article 142 in the Penal Code stated that it is punishable in words or deeds to publicly defame or in other hurtful ways demonstrate contempt for any belief whose practice is legal in this country, or any lawful religious community's religious learning or worship. Available at: http://www.regjeringen.no/nb/dep/jd/dok/regpubl/otprp/2008-2009/otprp-nr-22-2008-2009-/13/2.html?id=540706, accessed on 17 August 2009.

17 Quoted in *Dagbladet* 18 February 2006, in an article 'Det usmakelige' (the distatsteful) by author Roy Jacobsen.

By using the word 'claims', the journalist demonstrates that he or she is not endorsing Diene's view or worries on this issue. The same agency in another news story cites the Pakistani Minister of Religion, Ijaz ul-Haq, who wants the United Nations to adopt guidelines for journalists to avoid future cases of blasphemy (7 March 2006). It also refers to a conference of Arab and European parliamentarians where a representative from Egypt opted for a more authoritarian Human Rights Commission in the United Nations to prevent 'repetition of this unusual way of using freedom of expression' – and to the Organization of the Islamic Conference that had already suggested a ban on blasphemy to the United Nations. Simultaneously it refers to the European parliamentarians as rejecting all claims of censorship (ibid.).

The Norwegian Association of Editors in a letter to the Norwegian Ministry of Foreign Affairs urged the Minister, Jonas Gahr Støre, to take action concerning editors being imprisoned in Yemen and Jordan due to their publication of the cartoons (*Dagens Næringsliv* 17 March 2006). In the same letter the editors warn the government against encouraging the 'forces who want our courts to put into usage *the dormant article on blasphemy* or other increments against freedom of expression' (ibid. emphasis added).

Several newspapers also referred to Pakistan and the fact that blasphemers there risked being sentenced to death. The large regional newspaper, *Stavanger Aftenblad*, in an editorial column tried to answer questions linked to the ongoing crisis: 'What are the blasphemy laws in Islamic countries? We can take Pakistan as an example. There blasphemy is punishable by death. And there is no milder sentence for the one who is found guilty' (*Stavanger Aftenblad* 6 February 2006). The question is not raised whether the ones found guilty are actually executed or whether all cases are punishable by death. From a closer look at the Pakistani laws and practices this seems not to be the case.

Constitutional Dilemmas

Pakistan is a signatory to the international treaties on human rights and freedom of expression. However, in their national laws, freedom of expression is represented with distinct restrictions attached to it. The Constitution of Pakistan states in its Article 19 that:

> Every citizen shall have the right to freedom of speech and expression, and there shall be freedom of the press, subject to any reasonable restrictions imposed by law in the interest of the glory of Islam or the integrity, security or defence of Pakistan or any part thereof, friendly relations with foreign States, public order, decency or morality, or in relation to contempt of court, commission of or incitement to an offence.[18]

18 Available at: http://www.pakistani.org/pakistan/constitution/part2.ch1.html, accessed 12 November 2009.

The reference to Islam in the article illustrates part of Pakistan's dilemma with Islamic and secular law and law execution. In addition to this article, the country has a strict and detailed law on blasphemy (Articles 295 and 298 of the Pakistan Penal Code); due to which several death sentences have been passed, though not executed.[19] The articles ban damaging or defiling places of worship or sacred objects; defiling the *Qur'an* (life sentence) or defiling the Prophet Mohammed (Article 295C; death sentence). If someone is charged with the latter insult, a Muslim judge is required to preside over the Court of Session.

In other countries, for example, Afghanistan, the constitution guarantees freedom of expression with fewer constraints,[20] but Article 3 in Chapter 1 states, 'In Afghanistan, no law can be contrary to the beliefs and provisions of the sacred religion of Islam'. Thus the constitution leaves it to the judicial system (largely dominated by conservative Muslim scholars) to interpret what is contrary to Islam and what is not. A recent example is the death sentence (later modified to 20 years' imprisonment) for a young journalism student, Seyed Pervez Kambakhsh, for allegedly downloading an article from the Internet criticizing Islam's view on women's rights.[21] This latter example clearly demonstrates how access to modern transnational media, and thus to all kinds of critical debates, collides with national law or regional religious-inspired interpretations of law and of rights and insults.

David Irving as Seen from Pakistan

The cartoon debate and crisis received wide coverage in the national and local media in Pakistan (Eide 2007). The coverage can roughly be divided into three phases. The first phase, starting around 1 February, after a string of European newspapers had followed the Norwegian weekly and published the twelve cartoons, was characterized by a rather unanimous condemnation of the cartoons as blasphemous and insulting, aimed at provoking the Muslim world. Several columnists advocated *legal action* against the cartoonists and the editors of *Jyllands-Posten.* This changed in the second phase, in mid-February, due to violent demonstrations (particularly in Lahore and Peshawar) in which lives were lost

19 The present government in Pakistan headed by Asif Ali Zardari, has promised a revision of these laws. Available at: http://en.wikipedia.org/wiki/Blasphemy_law_in_Pakistan, accessed 20 July 2009.

20 Article 34: 'Freedom of expression is inviolable. Every Afghan has the right to express his thoughts through speech, writing or illustration or other means, by observing the provisions stated in this Constitution. Every Afghan has the right to print or publish topics without prior submission to the state authorities in accordance with the law. Directives related to printing houses, radio, television, press, and other mass media, will be regulated by the law' (http://www.afghan-web.com/politics/current_constitution.html#chaptertwo).

21 Available at: http://en.wikipedia.org/wiki/Sayed_Pervez_Kambaksh. In September 2009 Kambaksh was freed after strong national and international pressure.

and private and public property damaged or looted. The attention was then turned more inwards and was characterized by self-examination. Questions were raised as to which interests were served by the outbursts and what image of Pakistan this presented to the rest of the world.

A third phase might be said to have started after information about Holocaust-denier David Irving's sentence in Austria reached the subcontinent.[22] The law which led to this sentence originates from the Verbotsgesetz 1947 aimed at a de-nazification of the country:

> National Socialism Prohibition Law (1947, amendments of 1992)
>
> § 3g. He who operates in a manner characterized other than that in § § 3a – 3f will be punished (revitalizing of the NSDAP or identification with), with imprisonment from one to up to ten years, and in cases of particularly dangerous suspects or activity, be punished with up to twenty years imprisonment.
>
> § 3h. As an amendment to § 3g., whoever denies, grossly plays down, approves or tries to excuse the National Socialist genocide or other National Socialist crimes against humanity in a print publication, in broadcast or other media.[23]

Several editorials and columnists in Pakistani newspapers commented on this sentence and asked how Irving could be brought to justice in this manner, whilst no European leaders seemed willing to consider bringing the Danish cartoonists or editors to justice. In this phase of the coverage, several explicit references to the judiciary were made.

One of the regular opinion writers for the Urdu newspaper *Nawa-e-Waqt*, Qazi Mustafa Kamil, calls the Western defence of freedom of expression 'false' by referring to David Irving's lack of freedom to air his views or to insult Jews (28 February 2006).

The English language daily, *The Nation*, belonging to the same newspaper house, in its editorial on the issue, highlights what it considers to be European double standards and states that in spite of David Irving having expressed his regrets, he is still sentenced.

---

22 The European Union has not prohibited Holocaust denial outright, but 11 states have laws that do. David Irving, a famous Holocaust-denier, was sentenced to three years imprisonment in Austria for his views on the Holocaust, expressed during speeches he made in 1989. Suggestions of banning Holocaust denial have been raised within the European Union but due to concerns about free expression, expressed, among others, by the United Kingdom and the Nordic countries, no strict law has been voted. Available at: http://en.wikipedia.org/wiki/Holocaust_denial#European_Union. Accessed on 30 July 2009 and http://www.nationmaster.com/graph/gov_law_aga_hol_den_pen_for_vio_min-holocaust-denial-penalties-violation-minimum. Accessed on 5 March 2010.

23 Available at: http://en.wikipedia.org/wiki/Laws_against_Holocaust_denial#Austria. Accessed on 12 November 2009.

> Mr Irving's sentence comes at a time when the West is dishing out the popular theory of freedom of expression to the Muslim World in support of publishing blasphemous cartoons. This lays bare the hypocrisy lying at the very roots of Western ideology. '[...] It goes without saying that the intensity of the blasphemous cartoons is much more on religious grounds compared to the ethnic context of the Holocaust. Still the West makes it an issue of freedom of expression' (*The Nation*, editorial, 22 February 2006).

The way in which freedom of expression is represented as a 'popular theory' rather than a universal legal principle seems disturbing and may still also be interpreted as sarcasm linked to the way in which, in practice, Irving is denied this right. The weighting of context (insult of Muslims versus the 'ethnic' aspects of the Holocaust) demonstrates forcefully that the views on the gravity of the Holocaust vary across continents.

'Freedom Myths'

Already, before Irving was sentenced (1 March 2006), Shireen M. Mazari, a columnist (and an academic and defence analyst) for the Pakistani English language newspaper, *The News*, had expressed her views in an article under the headline 'Exposing freedom myths legally':

> So let us be clear about this so-called 'freedom of expression' and the claimed legal helplessness of the European governments to take action against the papers printing the offensive cartoons. All this is absolute rubbish and this is where Muslims can take on the guilty in a non-violent and legal manner (Mazari 2006).

The writer demonstrates that she does not trust the European leaders to help Muslims be rid of insulting cartoons. What makes the piece particularly interesting, is that the writer refers to the European Convention for the Protection of Human rights and Fundamental Freedoms (Article 10.2, which includes the 'protection or rights of others'),[24] as well as the constitutions of Norway and

24 The full text: 'The exercise of these freedoms, since it carries with it duties and responsibilities, may be subject to such formalities, conditions, restrictions or penalties as are prescribed by law and are necessary in a democratic society, in the interests of national security, territorial integrity or public safety, for the prevention of disorder or crime, for the protection of health or morals, for the protection of the reputation or rights of others, for preventing the disclosure of information received in confidence, or for maintaining the authority and impartiality of the judiciary.' Available at: http://conventions.coe.int/treaty/EN/Treaties/html/005.htm. Accessed 12 November 2009.

France.[25] The way she sees it, there is no reason why the 'French and Norwegian governments claim an inability to take legal action against those newspapers that have clearly violated their countries' constitutions' (Mazari 2006), and furthermore she advises the Muslims in Europe to use the legal route (and sue the newspapers) in addition to the street protests.

Mazari furthermore cites another article from the European convention, Article 18.2, where it is stated that the exercise of the freedoms carries with it:

> [...] duties and responsibilities; [that] may be subject to such formalities, conditions, restrictions or penalties as are prescribed by law and are necessary in a democratic society, in the interests of national security, territorial integrity or public safety, for the prevention of disorder or crime, for the protection of health or morals, for the protection or rights of others.

This article may be seen as an articulation of a legal discourse but simultaneously adheres to a larger 'responsibility discourse' which was frequently represented in the Pakistani press following the cartoon event. In a society where religious sensitivity is a major issue, one may be prone to interpret the above excerpt as a licence to punish those who, through their publications, insult, for example, the Prophet of Islam. This demonstrates the variety of 'communities of interpretation' that coexist in the present world as well as the linking of law and morale (sensitivity, responsibility). In 2009, this article seems to have been changed. According to the website of the Council of Europe, Article 18 now reads: 'The restrictions permitted under this Convention to the said rights and freedoms shall not be applied for any purpose other than those for which they have been prescribed'.[26]

Mazari was at the time Director General of the Institute of Strategic Studies in the capital, Islamabad,[27] a medium-to-large think-tank. She refers to the event of printing the cartoons as the 'almost conspiratorial approach of the primarily European press to keep Muslim passions inflamed by reprinting these' (Mazari 2006) and refers to the freedom of expression argument as a 'guise', before she discusses the legal aspects in detail.

25 The French constitution's Article 11 is cited: 'The free communication of ideas and opinions is one of the most precious of the rights of man. Every citizen may, accordingly, speak, write and print with freedom, but shall be responsible for such abuses of this freedom as shall be defined by law' (ibid.).

26 Available at: http://conventions.coe.int/treaty/EN/Treaties/html/005.htm#FN1. Accessed on 12 November 2009.

27 In 2008, she joined the Tehrik-e-Insaf party, headed by Imran Khan, who boycotted the last elections in Pakistan due to the precarious situation of the judiciary. Subsequently she was sacked from her position by the present government (Zardari).

Aggressive Defence …

Dawn, the largest English daily in Pakistan and somewhat less conservative than *The Nation*, refers to the European countries 'aggressively defending the right to freedom of speech' and concludes that the sentencing of David Irving is 'bound to open a debate on Western double standards'. The editorial reminds readers that the cartoons were defended by both editors and the European Union itself 'which attaches a great deal of importance to the freedom of expression but criminalizes any denial of the Holocaust'.[28]

> If Europe is sincere about defending its societies' right to freedom of speech, it must also concede the right to question the veracity of historical experiences, however uncomfortable it may make society feel in some cases. The Holocaust was a tragic event but any study or analysis of it cannot be hampered by laws that do not allow an honest exploration of the events surrounding it. […] If the Muslim world has to learn to respect ideals that go against its beliefs and convictions, the same must be true of Europeans. People must be allowed to hear all views and come to their own conclusions (*Dawn*, 23 February 2006).

The above text presupposes that David Irving may be viewed as an 'honest explorer' of the Holocaust, and that more exploration into this history is needed, even if 'uncomfortable'. The fact that the Holocaust itself is characterized as a 'tragic event' may further underline the differing views on this history.

On the other hand, the *Dawn* editorial may be interpreted as contradicting earlier editorials aimed at condemning the cartoons, being now more positively inclined towards an extended freedom of expression ('If the Muslim world has to …').

'Forget the Muslims' …

The newcomer publication, the liberal-leaning *Daily Times*, addresses the same issue two days later, and the editorial starts very distinctly by declaring that 'Free Europe is not so free after all'. It then gives an outline of David Irving's sentence and the law he was violating. The text also compares Irving to other academics who have been disgraced for plagiarism or for faking research, plus athletes caught using drugs. 'But none has ever gone to jail. The disgrace itself is enough'. The editor questions the fairness of jailing Irving for his views, 'even if he is wrong':

> Furthermore, his sentence could not have come at a more unpropitious time, just as Europe is raising the flag of 'free speech' to justify the publication of

28 As seen from the above, the European landscape is more diverse. Furthermore several freedom of expression organizations (International PEN, Index on Censorship and so on), protested against the Irving sentence.

> grossly offensive caricatures of Prophet Muhammad. [...] If free speech indeed means no holds barred, then Mr Irving should be a free man. That he is not makes it important to put the cartoon affair in the proper context. [...] Europe cannot afford to go back to its anti-Semitic past whose name still stands out in the existence of the word pogrom. All this is fine. But why can we not apply the same benchmark to other sensitivities involving over a billion people? If it is clear that some people – forget the Muslims – revere their prophet, should others be allowed to make fun of their beliefs, especially if it can be proved – and is clear – that such an action is based on racism and double standards? (*Daily Times*, 25 February 2006).

The editorial, by the excerpt 'forget the Muslims', recommends universalist approaches to insult, implying that this controversy is more about decency towards religious people in general. It is also, more explicitly than *Dawn*, in line with the 'European' view on the Holocaust, demonstrating knowledge about how the history of anti-Semitism paved the way for the Nazi regime. But the *double standards discourse* seems to be the most prominent: where to draw the line when it comes to insulting other peoples' feelings and beliefs? The question seems to be raised of whether the threshold for freedom of speech should be lower when it comes to insulting Muslims than when insulting Jews.

Judging from the arguments raised in these two editorials, among others, the legal arguments concerning the cartoons may take two directions: either support the punishment of David Irving but then also take legal action against those who insult Islam – *or* accuse the Austrian authorities of disregard for Irving's freedom of expression but then also admit that at least in Europe (and maybe elsewhere?) the tradition of free expression must also include the right to insult religion, including Islam.

Guantanamo and Abu Ghraib

In the Irving debate 'Europe' is again often represented as an entity, in the same way as European media often treat 'Muslims' or 'Islam' as an entity, thus depriving the diverse communities where Muslims live by their variety of ideas, traditions and practices.

The debate in Pakistan demonstrated a strong concern with a perceived Western inconsistency and double standards but, simultaneously, there were a few voices reminding the public of national inconsistency – of the discrimination of religious minorities in Pakistan (see Eide 2007).

A more overarching characteristic of the discursive situation in Pakistan post nine-eleven, into which the cartoon affair landed (and most likely in other countries with a Muslim majority), was the referral to double standards in the 'war on terror'. The press often reminded readers of the unlawful treatment of the Guantanamo prisoners, the torture of prisoners in Abu Ghraib, Baghdad, and civilian casualties due to American (and other) bombardments in Afghanistan. The election victory of Hamas in Palestine, not being recognized by most Western powers, was yet another concern.

These streams were amply demonstrated at street level during the cartoon crisis, by demonstrators burning effigies not only of the Danish Prime Minister, Anders Fogh Rasmussen, but also of President George W. Bush, in spite of his resolute condemnation of the cartoons.[29]

Afterthought and Reflections

Afterthoughts and reflections were occurring in many of the countries where the media debate had been heated. In Pakistan there were some publications even supporting the publication of the Mohammed cartoons, arguing much along the same lines as several European newspapers did (See Eide 2007, 2008). Concerns were raised as to what images were given of the protests on a global scale – and how that might hurt the image of Pakistan and of Muslims in general. One Egyptian newspaper headline read like this:

> We […] helped to frame ourselves as terrorist groups (*Al-ahaly*, Egypt 15 February 2006).

The Pakistani *Dawn*, taking into consideration the fundamentalists and their attempts to exploit the affair to their own benefit, would conclude as follows, after seeing the riots and the damage done in Pakistan:

> Governments in Muslim countries seeking to sponsor or participate in the anti-blasphemy demonstration should be careful: in their effort to take the sting out of the fundamentalists' frenzy or to prove themselves more Muslim than the latter, they might only be weakening their own position (*Dawn*, editorial, 16 February 2006).

The intertextual reference to 'more religious than the Pope', situates the liberal paper in a middle ground of sorts, observing how some of the reactions to the cartoons, when becoming unlawful, harmed Pakistan's reputation.

Aftermath: The Geneva Controversy

In the rhetoric in several Muslim countries, 'responsibility' frequently occurred with reference to how people – both globally and in nation states with growing

29 Some papers simultaneously lauded Bush for his opinion on this issue.

Muslim minorities – ought to act towards each other and, if they did not show a degree of sensitivity, should face punishment.

A particular discursive situation occurred in the early months of 2009. Blasphemy laws in some Western countries, having long been dormant, were now suggested being abandoned, as in Norway, and one may presume that the cartoon crisis played a role in this process. On the other hand, on the global scene, suggestions for universal rules against defamation of religion were introduced in resolution drafts prior to the Geneva conference. These events must be seen in the light of the firmly disputed suggested change in the guidelines for the United Nations Special Rapporteur for Human Rights; where reporting on 'insults against religion' was suggested as an addition to the mandate. Furthermore, a dispute occurred which led to several nations' boycott of the Durban Review (Durban II) conference in Geneva,[30] referring to the draft document which included 'defamation of religion' as part of the work against racism.

These suggestions were, as we shall see, largely rejected at the actual conference.

On the other hand, the fact that they were raised may to a certain extent be seen in the light of the experiences from the cartoon crisis as it developed in many parts of the world.

It is not an exaggeration to say that the controversy leading up to the United Nations Conference on Racism in Geneva (Durban II), held 20–24 April 2009, was partly triggered by the cartoon controversy. A preliminary meeting in Geneva in the United Nations Human Rights Council adopted a resolution in which defamation of religion is strongly condemned (23 voted in favour, 11 against, while 13 abstained). Pakistan introduced the resolution text on behalf of the Organization of the Islamic Conference (54 states).[31]

News articles on this resolution, for example in the *Montreal Gazette* were sometimes illustrated by the usual photos of bearded protesting men (in Pakistan).

As mentioned, the text was modified, although several nations did not take part in the deliberations and others sent low-level delegates.[32]

The results included passages on modern slavery, on the Holocaust being remembered, on the rights of minorities, including the Romany, not to be discriminated against, and much more.

30 See: http://www.un.org/durbanreview2009/.

31 See: http://www.montrealgazette.com/news/body+adopts+resolution+religious+defamation/1431382/story.html.

32 Two important exceptions were the Iranian President Mahmoud Ahmadinejad and the Norwegian Minister of Foreign Affairs, Jonas Gahr Støre. The latter, contrary to several delegates, did not leave the audience as Ahmadinejad delivered his address, but spoke against his views. For a summary of the results from the conference, see http://www.rfi.fr/actuen/articles/112/article_3531.asp. Accessed on 17 August 2009.

Conclusion: An Eye-opener?

The transnational interpretative problems concerning various national or in the case of the European Union, regional, laws were demonstrated on two levels. Exemplified by Shirin M. Mazari, one may suggest that the dormant character of (the remaining) European blasphemy laws was not recognized in parts of the 'non-West' and thus it was easy to label European practices as inconsistent. Secondly, the articles in some European constitutions or punitive laws could at the peak of the controversy in 2006 be interpreted in somewhat different ways, as liberal or absolute, as an opening for sanctions against media expression or simply as legal remnants from a time when religion was a more dominant feature in the everyday lives of Europeans.

Lawsuits against cartoonists had limited support in Europe and no success in court. As mentioned, in Denmark a lawsuit was rejected and in France, where the satire newspaper *Charlie Hebdo* was taken to court, the editors were acquitted.

Furthermore, we observe that in the press coverage, simplifications travel both ways, and that Orientalist and Occidentalist representations *and* self-representations were distinct (and at times rather exclusionist) during the caricature controversy.

During the cartoon crisis, the twelve images transgressed many geographical and cultural borders. But often it was just the ideas of the images that travelled, as many of the people protesting or raising their indignation most likely had never seen the cartoons. What travelled frequently were photographic images of angry and aggressive Muslims protesting them. One particular image, reprinted in the Pakistani press, was of a small but aggressive demonstration in London, where several of the slogans may be characterized as hate speech. Some politicians advocated for police action against the demonstrators, as they labelled some of the posters as incitement to murder and hate speech,[33] and two people, believed to be the organizers, were brought to court for not notifying the police ahead of the demonstration.

In hindsight the whole 'cartoon affair' may be seen as an eye-opener, not only when it comes to variations in religious-leaning practices of law but also when it comes to the variety of interpretations of what free expression entails and what benefits may be reaped from a liberal and open practice of this right. Whether a stronger mutual understanding emerged between some of the communities scattered across the world is another question whose answer is far beyond this chapter.

Further media studies of these issues might concentrate more on the way in which the media in Muslim countries interpret the often parallel judicial practices (secular-leaning versus *Shari'a*-leaning) when it comes to free expression. Furthermore it is worth looking at the way in which overarching laws referring to Islam may restrain alternative liberal interpretations of articles on freedom of expression.

33 See http://news.bbc.co.uk/2/hi/uk_news/4979298.stm and http://en.wikipedia.org/wiki/Islamist_demonstration_outside_Danish_Embassy_in_London_in_2006#The_protest.

References

Ali, T. 2002. *The Clash of Fundamentalisms: Crusades, Jihads and Modernity*. London: Verso.

Benson, R. and Neveu, E. 2005. *Bourdieu and the Journalistic Field*. Cambridge: Polity Press.

Boer, L. 2004. Struggling with –isms: Occidentalism, liberalism, Eurocentrism, Islamism. *Third World Quarterly*, 25, 8:1541–1548.

Buruma, I. and Margalit, A. 2004. *Occidentalism. The West in the Eyes of Its Enemies*. New York: Penguin Press.

Carrier, J.G. (ed.) 1995. *Occidentalism. Images of the West*. Oxford: Clarendon Press.

Chen, Xiaomei 1995. *Occidentalism. A Theory of Counter-Discours in Post-Mao China*. New York: Oxford University Press.

Dayan, D. 2010. 'Beyond media events. Disenchantment, derailment, disruption'. In Couldry, N. *et al.* (eds) *Media Events in a Global Age*. London: Routledge.

Dayan, D. and Katz, E. 1994. *Media Events. The Live Broadcasting of History*. first published 1992. Cambridge, Mass: Harvard University Press.

Eide, E. 2006. The Empire and the Egyptians. *Nordicom Review* 2/2006: 153–169.

—— 2007. Pakistan: Critique, anger and understanding, in *Transnational Media Events. The Mohammed Cartoons and an Imagined Clash of Civilization*, edited by E. Eide, R. Kunelius and A. Phillips. Göteborg: Nordicom, 131–145.

—— 2008. The loop of labelling. Orientalism, Occidentalism and the cartoon crisis, in *Transnational Media Events. The Mohammed Cartoons and an Imagined Clash of Civilization*, edited by E. Eide, R. Kunelius and A. Phillips. Göteborg: Nordicom, 151–173.

—— 2009. Global divides and transnational media literacy, in *Nordicom Review, Media and Global Divides Volume 30, Jubilee Issue June 2009*, edited by U. Carlsson. Gothenburg: Nordicom, 151–163.

Eide, E., Kunelius, R. and Phillips, A. (eds) 2008. *Transnational Media Events. The Mohammed Cartoons and an Imagined Clash of Civilization*. Göteborg: Nordicom.

Fairclough, N. 1995. *Media Discourse*. London: Arnold.

—— 2003. *Analysing Discourse. Textual Analysis for Social Research*. London: Routledge.

Gewertz, D. and Errington, F. 1991. We think, therefore they are? On Occidentalizing the world. *Anthropological Quarterly* 64, 2:80–91.

Hall, S. 1992. The West and the rest: Discourse and power, in *Formations of Modernity*, edited by S. Hall and B. Gieben. Cambridge: Polity Press.

Huntington, S.P. 1993. The clash of civilizations?. *Foreign Affairs* 72, 3:22–50.

—— 1996. *The Clash of Civilizations and the Remaking of the World Order*. London: Touchstone Books.

—— 2006. *Civilisationernes sammenstød* (The clash of civilizations). København: People's Press.

Kunelius, R., Eide, E., Hahn, O. and Schroder, R. (eds) 2007. *Reading the Mohammed Cartoons Controversy, Working Papers in International Journalism.* Dortmund: Projekt Verlag.

Lewis, B. 1990. The roots of the Muslim rage. *Atlantic Monthly*. September issue.

Mazari, S.M. 2006. Exposing freedom myths legally. The News (Pakistan) 8 February.

Moniguet, C. 2006. *Caricatures of Mohammad: The History and Consequences of a Global Manipulation.* Brussels: European Strategic Intelligence and Security Centre.

Phillips, A. 2007. The UK: A very British response, in *Reading the Mohammed Cartoons Controversy, Working Papers in International Journalism*, edited by R. Kunelius, E. Eide, O. Hahn and R. Schroder. Dortmund: Projekt Verlag, 65–79.

Ramonet, I. 1999. *La Tyrannie de la Communication*. Paris: Galilée.

Said, E.W. 1981. *Covering Islam*. London: Routledge and Kegan Paul.

—— 1994. *Culture and Imperialism*. first published 1993. London: Vintage.

—— 1995. *Orientalism*. first published 1978. London: Penguin.

—— 2001. The clash of ignorance. *The Nation* (22 October), 3. Available at: http://www.thenation.com/doc/20011022/said.

—— 2003. The clash of definitions, in *The New Crusades. Constructing the Muslim Enemy*, edited by E. Qureshi and M.A. Sells. New York: Columbia University Press, 68–88.

Saleh, I. 2007. Coverage of professional disparities and religious disruptions, in *Reading the Mohammed Cartoons Controversy, Working Papers in International Journalism*, edited by R. Kunelius, E. Eide, O. Hahn and R. Schroder. Dortmund: Projekt Verlag, 119–131.

Sardar, Z. 2004. Why do they hate us? *New Statesman* (4 October).

Tate, S. 2005. Whose Occident? Methodological parochialism in research on the West. *Scottish Geographic Journal* 121:4.

Zhengrong, Hu and Zheng Liang 2007. China: A controlled practice, in *Reading the Mohammed Cartoons Controversy, Working Papers in International Journalism*, edited by R. Kunelius, E. Eide, O. Hahn and R. Schroder. Dortmund: Projekt Verlag, 169–177.

Chapter 13

The Globalization of the Insult: Freedom of Expression meets Cosmopolitan Thinking

Thomas Hylland Eriksen[1]

> All are equal and all are different.
>
> Ulrich Beck, Cosmopolitan Vision

It is difficult to argue against the view that human rights, as defined in the Universal Declaration of Human Rights of 1948, currently rule the waves in the discourses on transnational justice and global values. No other common denominators appear as likely candidates for a globally shared set of moral coordinates. Anyone with an ambition to be taken seriously in the transnational discourses over democracy, religion or for that matter the future of humanity, needs to pay their dues to the Universal Declaration. This is particularly true as regards political rights and not least those referring to individuals and their right to express personal views and to make their own life decisions. Any suggestion to the effect that the freedom of expression should perhaps be limited somewhat in order to accommodate the views and sensibilities of people who do not share the worldview of liberal individualists, is severely and often aggressively criticized in the public spheres of most parts of the world and certainly in the North Atlantic region. After the collapse of Marxism, competition is thin on the ground in the international discourse, notwithstanding the persistence of deeply held religious worldviews which may contradict and are on occasion seen by their adherents to trump individual human rights.

The gospel of human rights represents a set of common denominators but it lacks a social theory. Human beings may (in theory) be equipped with certain inalienable rights but rights are not sufficient to fill a life with meaningful substance. The thinness of rights appears as a skeletal scaffolding compared with the thickness of lived experience. Very often, there is no conflict; although even a full knowledge of the norms that regulate people's behaviour does not enable us to predict how they will act (because agency is informed by much more than norms), that does not mean that actual behaviour is necessarily in conflict with the norms. Besides, human rights must always be contextualized, understood and interpreted against the backdrop of local circumstances. It is nevertheless an indisputable fact that events in the world of lived experience may under certain

1 The author would like to thank the editors for thoughtful and very useful comments on the first version of this chapter.

conditions be seen to violate human rights; that is, conflicts between local custom and Universalist rights may arise. Examples of such contradictions are numerous, from the traditions of indigenous peoples to practices followed by literal-minded adherents of religions in complex societies.

The tension in social theory between liberal and communitarian positions sometimes simply reflects differences in emphasis – culture is somewhat more important than rights or vice versa – but it may also be a result of deeper differences between social ontologies. Briefly, liberals hold that individuals create societies, while communitarians argue that on the contrary, individuals *are created by* societies. As many years of philosophical and political debate have shown, this distinction is not trifling. If the communitarians are right, the thickness of lived culture is a necessary prerequisite for personhood and is therefore logically and ontologically prior to rights thinking (which is itself a product of a cultural world); if the liberals are right, then the respect for the integrity of the individual should serve as a bulwark against transgressions committed in the name of culture (or religion) and individual rights should overrule cultural peculiarities.

Unreformed communitarians are hard to come by in contemporary mainstream intellectual life but certain communitarian interpretations of human rights remain academically respectable and influential (for example, Kymlicka 2007). While it has become unfashionable to defend cultural relativism as an ethical stance, opinion remains divided as to the legitimacy of group rights and, more generally, the relationship between group and individual in the contemporary world. However, since the very existence of groups (as corporate subjects and not mere statistical categories) cannot be taken for granted, the individual tends to be foregrounded in law and normative theory. Public debates and controversies may concern intellectual property rights (Kasten 2004), cultural and linguistic rights, as well as multicultural dilemmas ranging from language policies in schools to the tension between individualist agency and arranged marriages among non-European immigrants in North Atlantic societies (Baumann 1999), but there is also a fraught relationship between customary practices and formal legal systems based on individual rights thinking in many third world countries (see Hellum *et al.* 2007 for cases).

In the following, I shall relate the human rights discourse to a recently revived social philosophy with a respectable lineage but which is sometimes at odds with human rights thinking which foregrounds the individual at the expense of collective representations and cultural values, namely the tradition of cosmopolitanism. The term 'cosmopolitanism', deriving from the Greek *cosmos* and *polis* (the world and the city), can be understood in a variety of ways and is often glossed as 'world citizenship', that is a condition where one regards the entire world as one's home. This notion can be traced back to ancient Athens; a classic statement on cosmopolitanism, quoted by Tzvetan Todorov (1982:250), derives from the medieval Franciscan monk Hugo of St Victor, who wrote: 'The man who holds his country sweet is only a raw beginning; the man for whom each country is as his own is already strong; but only the man for whom the whole world is a foreign country, is perfect'. Todorov adds that he borrowed the quotation from Edward Said, a Christian Palestinian living in the United States of America, who in turn had found it in the work of Erich Auerbach, a German exiled to Turkey. Todorov is himself, naturally, a Bulgarian exile writing in French from Paris.

Cosmopolitanism need not, however, entail universal familiarity nor universal foreignness. One may perfectly well adhere to a localized and emotionally deeply held cultural identity and simultaneously support and embody cosmopolitan values. It is a common misunderstanding that a cosmopolitan view somehow precludes cultural identity; quite the contrary, it implies the recognition of the existence of distinct cultural worlds. According to the cosmopolitan view, people are in various respects different; they hold different values, believe in different gods (or none) and adhere to different sets of norms. In spite of these differences, however, they can communicate with each other. Yet, the fact that we can understand each other across cultural differences does not hold out a promise of ultimate consensus: although we understand each other, we may remain different. This is the point made by Claudio Magris (1989) in his rich and appropriately meandering essay on the cultural history of the Danube. He points out that a fascist is not someone who has intimate friends, who loves his *Heimat*, the local folk music, the country's nineteenth-century romantic poets, and so on, but someone who is incapable of seeing others, who love *their* home village, folk music and so on, as equals.

The cosmopolitan position, thus, is far from incompatible with cultural rootedness and commitment to tradition but entails recognition of the equality of discrete life-worlds. Moreover, it is relevant to the present discussion that cosmopolitanism acknowledges the importance of cultural identity for normative orientations, in other words that human rights are in themselves insufficient to account for norms and values at an operational level. Human rights provide a framework but custom and local traditions supply the substance. On occasion, the latter may conflict with the former. There is thus a possible tension here, reminiscent of the liberalism–cosmopolitanism debate, which is arguably being deepened and bridged simultaneously on a planet whose inhabitants increasingly find themselves divided by a shared destiny.

It should be emphasized here that I deal with the human rights discourse and the cosmopolitan worldview in this context as ideal types. Several bids to bridge the gap between recognition of difference and the universalism of rights thinking exist, not least in legal anthropology but for the sake of the argument, they are not discussed here.

Implications of Globalization

It is an empirical fact that human rights, notwithstanding their origins in Enlightenment thought, have been and continue to be globally disseminated as an ideal. Yet, it is also a fact that many of the organizations and individuals who demand equal rights worldwide do not do so as universal, context-free human beings but as a special kind of human being, as indigenous peoples, as Muslims, as women, and so on. In other words, rights thinking is supplemented by contextual factors; the question is how to negotiate this relationship.

Globalization is pervasive and has, among other things, economic, political and cultural dimensions, fuelled to no small degree by communication technology. Recent and current changes in the social and cultural dynamics of the world sometimes appear to call for an entirely new conceptual apparatus, and the sociologist John Urry (2000), for one, suggests replacing the term 'society' with 'mobility', as the latter term, in his view, is a better starting-point for conceptualizing and modelling social processes in the contemporary world. Change is fast and creates frictions owing to increased and accelerated contact where there was formerly none. In 2007, few had heard about Facebook. In 2010, Facebook and/or LinkedIn membership is considered *de rigueur* among the networking classes, although it has partly been superseded by Twitter. The verb 'to google' would have been meaningless a decade ago and is now common and generally understood in the same classes. Some important dimensions of the contemporary world, highlighting the speed and compass of changes, were mentioned almost in passing by Manuel Castells already in 1998, in a footnote towards the end of the final volume of his trilogy, *The Information Society*:

> Why is this a new world? … Chips and computers are new; ubiquitous, mobile telecommunications are new, genetic engineering is new; electronically integrated, global financial markets working in real time are new; an inter-linked capitalist economy embracing the whole planet, and not only some of its segments, is new; a majority of the urban labor force in knowledge and information processing in advanced economies is new; a majority of urban population in the planet is new; the demise of the Soviet Empire, the fading away of communism, and the end of the Cold War are new; the rise of the Asian Pacific as an equal partner in the global economy is new; the widespread challenge to patriarchalism is new; the universal consciousness on ecological preservation is new; and the emergence of a network society, based on a space of flows, and on timeless time, is historically new (Castells 1998:336).

A few years later, he could have added the advent of deterritorialized warfare and political battles involving the question of humanly induced climate change to the list. He might also have spoken of post-Fordist flexible accumulation (Harvey 1989) and mass migration (Castles and Davidson 2003). Be this as it may, Castells adds, at the end of his lengthy footnote, that it does not really matter whether all this is new or not; his point is that this is our world and therefore we should study it. (I disagree. It does matter what is new and what isn't, if we are going to make sense of the contemporary world, not least since different parts of culture change at different speeds.)

In contemporary transnational communication, there are in principle no longer any delays. It is instantaneous. The implications for rights discourses and issues concerning cosmopolitan values and practices are dramatic, and to this we now move through a few examples indicating a new world order of communication and rights discourse.

The Globalization of the Insult

In 2003, a middle-aged Afghan man named Shah Mohammad Rais arrived in Oslo amidst massive media coverage. Already prior to leaving the airport, he told the journalists present that a book, originally published in Norway in 2002 but shortly afterwards translated into many languages, had led to a flood of rumours in his hometown of Kabul, and had created a dangerous situation for him and his family. The book had brought shame to his family, he explained, and since it, according to him, exposed intimate and private details about his family's domestic life, he ran the risk of being victim to violent acts of revenge at home. For one thing, he claimed, he feared that someone might set fire to his bookshop.

One of the faces of globalization which is becoming more and more common, is the globalization of insults, frequently corroborated by clashes between different sets of cultural values, in this case the confrontation between Scandinavian feminism and the male honour code characteristic of Afghan society. Rais had felt dishonoured and betrayed by the journalist Åsne Seierstad when she described his and his family's private life in considerable detail in her book, *The Bookseller of Kabul* (orig. *Bokhandleren i Kabul*, Seierstad 2002), sprinkling her journalism with fictionalized passages about the inner life of her hosts. Possibly, she had not expected the family, whose hospitality she had depended on for months while doing research for the book, to learn what she had written about them. Perhaps she had not expected the book to be translated into English; in fact, Rais was initially informed about the book by another Norwegian journalist, who showed him a rough English translation of some chapters before the translation was out. But even if the book had only been published in Norwegian, the Afghan diaspora community in Norway would in all likelihood have communicated with acquaintances in Kabul about its contents.

The supposition that the book might not become known to people in remote, war-torn Afghanistan is not very surprising. After all, Europeans have always written what they felt like about people in remote places, with Europeans and not the remote peoples as their intended readership, without having to fear sanctions. For centuries, the natives had no way of speaking back. In the current era of global modernity, by contrast, 'former tribals' use classic anthropological texts to 'learn about their own culture' and as documentation to combat Western stereotypes about them, and draw on transnational rights discourses in order to strengthen their case. In this particular case, the positive freedom ('freedom to') of expression is confronted with the negative freedom ('freedom from') of protection from defamation.

The controversy around Colin Turnbull's, *The Mountain People* (Turnbull 1972) exemplifies the turning point or the transition from a colonial to a post-colonial field of discourse. In this grim but deeply moving book, written in a popular style by an anthropologist, Turnbull describes a society on the verge of total breakdown. Owing largely to drought and their enforced displacement following the Uganda government's decision to make a national park, the Ik (or Teuso), as the group were called, found themselves in an extremely precarious situation and, as a result, Turnbull suggests their social and cultural institutions were collapsing. Tradition, norms and religion were dissipating, kinship organization ceased to function and the situation, as depicted in his book, was reminiscent of a Hobbesian state of nature.

The book received a great deal of attention, not least outside anthropology, and Peter Brook adapted it for the stage in 1975. However, the German linguist Bernd Heine, who worked among the Ik in 1983, reported findings which were seriously at odds with Turnbull's, to the extent that he was 'at times … under the impression that I was dealing with an entirely different people' (Heine 1985). More to the point, Heine elaborates on the Ik's reactions to Turnbull's publications:

> After they had been informed by the Roman Catholic mission, Kaabong, of the content of Turnbull's publications, they were shocked about the way their name had been 'spoilt' in them, and they were reluctant to provide any more information to white researchers. At a meeting I had with the elders of Kamion, Moruatap, Lomoli'j and Nawa'dou [Ik villages] on 27 February 1983, I was asked whether it was not possible to take legal action against Turnbull. Should he ever dare to come back to Ik country they would force him 'to eat his own feces' (Heine 1985:3).

The Ik lacked the necessary resources to initiate a court case against the anthropologist but their reaction was an early, significant response to the monopoly of representation against which very many intellectuals and not a few non-European peoples have since reacted, arguing in effect for a redistribution of the means of communication. Alex de Waal (1993) has suggested that the Ik would have had a fairly strong legal case against Turnbull and would probably have been able to stop sales of the book through a court injunction.

The world has shrunk considerably since the controversy between Turnbull and the Ik, which never reached the stage of the direct confrontation, but was mediated through intermediate persons, media and the passage of several years. An academic debate about the merits and shortcomings of *The Mountain People* viewed as a work of anthropology (which Turnbull in fact came close to denying that it was) had no importance for the Ik.

The arrival of bookseller Rais in Norway indicated that a new era had begun. Like *The Mountain People*, *The Bookseller of Kabul* was a popular book written in a journalistic style, and although the author had no academic credentials (unlike Turnbull), she used participant-observation method to collect information. Critics have pointed out that the fictionalization of the informants, through introspective methods and speculative conjunctures, weakens its authenticity but many thousands of readers worldwide would appear to disagree. Rais's main objection to the book is that it is defamatory of his family and he has also accused Seierstad of abusing his hospitality, given that he had expected a very different portrayal of himself and his family. In spite of difficulties in obtaining a visa, Rais visited Norway again in 2006 and by 2009 he and his family are still pressing for a legal case against Seierstad.

In principle, anything being written in a particular place now has the entire world as a potential readership and is being read differently by different groups of readers who are positioned in various ways to the text. When the author Jostein Gaarder (of *Sophie's World* fame) in 2006 published a highly critical opinion article in a Norwegian newspaper, about Israel, he had not expected it to be translated and publicized worldwide. This, in effect, was what happened in the space of a few weeks and Gaarder was flabbergasted by the accusations of anti-semitism, especially from Germany and Israel, which doubtless somewhat tarnished his reputation.

As information flows ever more freely and faster between countries and regions, the Iks of the near future will not even require a plane ticket to make their indignation known. The Lord's Resistance Army in Northern Uganda, active slightly to the west of the Ik homelands, follow the Premier League on satellite television and many support Arsenal since this London club has a cannon in its logo. On the instantaneously interconnected planet on which we now live, twelve cartoons published in a Danish newspaper may result in global outrage and lead to anything from sharp editorials to violent street demonstrations, from Indonesia to Morocco. Domestic discourses about the cartoon affair of 2006 display great variations both between and within countries – Muslim and non-Muslim – and the affair nicely summarizes the argument about human rights, globalization and cosmopolitanism which I began to sketch above. To this controversy we therefore turn. (C.f., Eide's chapter in this book, also Eide *et al.* 2008).

Some Bare (and not so Bare) Facts

In the summer of 2005, Flemming Rose, the cultural editor of Denmark's largest subscription newspaper, *Jyllands-Posten* (described by Christopher Hitchens as a newspaper 'nobody had heard of'), discovered that the Danish author Kåre Bluitgen had written a children's book about the life of Muhammad but was unable to find an artist willing to illustrate it. The Danish public sphere had been shaken by the murder of the Dutch filmmaker Theo van Gogh in Amsterdam a year earlier and the ban on depicting Muhammad in Sunni Islam was well known. The book was, incidentally, published in 2006, beautifully illustrated by an anonymous artist (Bluitgen 2006).

Rose decided to invite the leading newspaper cartoonists of the country to make cartoons depicting the Prophet, in order to demonstrate that the freedom of expression was a non-negotiable and absolute human right in liberal Denmark or in his own words, to 'find out how far the self-imposed censorship had gone'. Twelve of the forty gave a positive response and the resulting cartoons were published in the weekend edition of *Jyllands-Posten* on 30 September 2005.

The cartoons could be said to range from the harmless to the potentially deeply insulting (although the general ban on depicting the Prophet in Sunni Islam must be kept in mind, meaning that any drawing of Muhammad might in principle be seen as offensive). One of the cartoonists used the competition as a pretext for criticizing *Jyllands-Posten*'s antagonistic approach to religious pluralism in Denmark. His drawing depicts a dark-haired schoolboy called Mohammad (from 7a, Valby School) and the text on the blackboard reads (in Persian, with Arabic script): 'The journalists at *Jyllands-Posten* are a bunch of reactionary agitators'. Several of the others must be judged harmless. One comments on the chasm between Islam and terrorism by depicting a bedraggled group of suicide bombers arriving at Heaven's Gate, only to be met by an apologetic Prophet who says: 'Sorry boys, we've run out of virgins'. Another anticipates the reactions to the cartoons: some angry, armed men appear, ready to go out and kill, when the Prophet, holding up a sheet of paper, raises his hand and says, 'Easy friends, when all is said and done, it's just a rough sketch made by an infidel from southern Jutland'.

A few of the cartoons appear to be less benign. The most infamous one is the drawing of Muhammad wearing a bomb in the shape of a turban on his head. Yet the message is not necessarily that Muhammad was a terrorist but could also be that the religion he founded is about to become the victim of terrorists who give it a bad reputation (the person about to blow up, after all, is Muhammad himself). Yet the only obviously insulting of the twelve cartoons, in my interpretation, is the one depicting Muhammad with a lifted dagger, his eyes concealed, apparently with the missing piece of fabric from the burka worn by the women standing behind him. This is an unambiguously negative comment on gender relations and the concept of *jihad* in Islam.

There was no immediate outrage following the publication of the cartoons. Only when journalists from other newspapers began to ask conservative *imams* in the main Danish cities about their views, some of the latter said that the cartoons insulted all Muslims of the world. A demonstration was organized in October in Copenhagen, led by the now deceased Danish *imam,* Ahmed Abu Laban. The demonstration was not, incidentally, all about the cartoons but was directed against the perceived growing Islamophobia in Danish society.

With other Muslim leaders from Denmark, Abu Laban afterwards travelled to several Muslim countries, asking for support in protesting to the Danish state. Hearing about this, the Danish populist leader, Pia Kjærsgaard, who's Danish People's Party supported the right-of-centre coalition government, claimed that these Muslims were traitors.

The most tangible result of the trip to the Muslim countries was a letter of protest sent by eleven Muslim governments to the Danish Prime Minister, Anders Fogh Rasmussen, asking him to meet with their ambassadors to explain the situation. Rasmussen declined, simply stating that it was not the government's business to interfere with the press. In this, Rasmussen clearly placed the decontextualized liberal freedom of expression above the cosmopolitan principle of the need for recognition and dialogue across cultural boundaries.

In December 2005, the Organization of the Islamic Conference and the Arab League called for a general boycott against Denmark. Unverified rumours began to circulate in the Arabic-speaking world, about Bluitgen's book being a 'government-commissioned new Koran'. Some of the cartoonists received threats.

In January 2006, a relatively unknown Norwegian publication republished the cartoons. This magazine has a modest circulation and is published by conservative Christians and it was a publication few had heard about, even in Norway, before it reprinted the Danish cartoons.

As a result of this, however, Norway was increasingly perceived as being complicit with Denmark in the conspiracy against Islam. In fact, the general secretary of the Norwegian Press Association received death threats because he was wrongly identified as the man who had defamed the Prophet Mohammed (all he had done was to ascertain the newspaper's right to publish the cartoons). By February, protests in many countries had turned violent. Embassies were burnt down in Damascus and Beirut; Libya closed its embassy in Copenhagen, armed men stormed the European Union offices in the Gaza strip and there were angry demonstrations in many countries with substantial Muslim populations. During the riots in early February, people were killed in Gaza, in Libya, in Pakistan and elsewhere (but, ironically, not in Europe) – only in Nigeria, 38 people were reported killed during anti-cartoon riots.

At the same time, the cartoons were reprinted as an act of solidarity in several other countries; *Die Zeit*, *The Times of India*, *France-Soir*, *La Stampa*, *El Periodico* and *El Mundo*, to mention a few; even the BBC showed the cartoons on television.

Also at the same time, however, Danish and Norwegian authorities were feeling increasingly uneasy. The Norwegian Foreign Minister, Jonas Gahr Støre, made a public apology to Muslims on a trip to Palestine in January, stating that the freedom of expression was a strongly held value in Norwegian society but that this did not mean that one was justified in insulting others. In this, he tried to strike a balance between the freedom of expression (human rights) and the need for respect and recognition (cosmopolitanism). As things got out of hand, even *Jyllands-Posten* apologized 'for having offended many Muslims', the Danish Prime Minister mumbled his apologies as he realized that Muslim countries were boycotting Lego, Bang and Olufsen and Danish butter; and the conservative Protestant who edited *Magazinet* had a reconciliation meeting with leaders of the Norwegian Islamic Council. By this time, however, the affair had gained momentum, and the rioters in the Muslim countries did not closely follow developments in Northern Europe. Most of them had probably not even seen the cartoons.

The public debates, the demonstrations, the accusations, the riots and anger flared up suddenly, and vanished in the same way. By early March, the cartoon controversy appeared to have died down and, in spite of temporary effects such as the cancellation of a Danish state visit to India because the Indian government felt Mr Rasmussen had 'become too controversial' in April, there were no indications that Denmark's international reputation had suffered.

Some Context

Before I begin the analysis, some additional contextual information may be helpful. First of all, it should be noted that an Egyptian newspaper actually reprinted the cartoons as early as October 2005. Nobody in the Arab world demanded a boycott of Egyptian goods for that reason. A Jordanian weekly, *Al-Shihan*, published three of them in February 2006, along with the rhetorical question: What harms Islam the most, these drawings or images of violent Muslim hostage-takers in Iraq? (The editor was dismissed, the newspaper removed from the kiosks.) It may also be of some interest that *Jyllands-Posten* was offered some satirical depictions of Jesus Christ in 2003, made by the Danish artist Christoffer Zieler. The Sunday editor wrote, in his reply to Zieler: 'As a matter of fact, I do not think that the readers of *Jyllands-Posten* will enjoy these cartoons. Actually, I think they will lead to an outrage. Therefore, I will not publish them' (Larsen and Seidenfaden 2006:264). One may moreover suspect that a few Danes, in spite of their suddenly vehement support of the freedom of expression, would have been annoyed if a Muslim cartoonist had made a few such caricatures and had them published in a leading newspaper – even if there is no ban on depicting Jesus in Christianity.

It should also be kept in mind that the actual number of demonstrators was modest: 300 in Pakistan, 400 in Indonesia, 200 in Tripoli and even fewer in Damascus. In other words, a very limited number of people – some radical *imams* and their followers in Denmark, a few hundred youths in Muslim countries, a couple of editors who disliked Islam – proved themselves capable of setting political and civil society agendas in many parts of the world for several weeks, and doubtless contributed to the growing polarization between Muslims and others in several countries.

A factor which most of the non-Scandinavian commentators failed to take into account is the heightened tension between Denmark's Muslims and mainstream Danish society following the change in government in 2001, when a conservative government supported by the right-wing Danish People's Party took the reins. Denmark is in this respect not just another West European country; it has in recent years introduced legislation on minority issues seen by many as draconian, affecting both new immigration and forms of integration into Danish society for immigrants. The reactions to the cartoons among many Danish Muslims, led by

Abu Laban, must in this way be seen as a pretext for addressing other problems they experience in Danish society. In a detailed study of the controversy, Larsen and Seidenfaden (2006) argue that the sharp turn to the right in Danish politics, where the conservative government depends on support from the right-wing populist *Dansk Folkeparti* (The Danish People's Party), explains much of the dynamics of the affair: Danish Muslims felt disenfranchised and leading Danish media had for years taken a hard line on political Islam and in general focused intensively on problems with Muslims in Danish society.

As a result of the polarization resulting from the cartoon affair, Islamophobic Danes and militant Islamists were given ample media space, at the expense of almost everybody else. Abu Laban himself said to a German journalist in February: 'I have to thank the government for its stubbornness'. His formerly marginal congregation grew rapidly in 2006. Neither Islamists nor the Danish People's Party and its sympathizers see it as being in their interest to depict Danish Muslims as ordinary Danes. In the interview with *Die Zeit,* quoted from above, Abu Laban says that a Muslim:

> ... could never be a normal citizen of a Western state. He makes a 'security contract' with the secular state, but as a true believer he can never accept secularism – the separation of religion and state. He must always remain loyal to the highest religious law, the *Shari'a*. 'We Muslims must use freedom of speech,' says the *imam*, 'to the extent that it serves the goals of Islam' (Lau 2006).

However, Abu Laban is also quoted as having said, in the same period, 'I condemn every violent act against the Danish military or others' (Larsen and Seidenfaden 2006:142).

Der Spiegel's Henryk M. Broder, thinking along similar lines as Lau, states that 'Unfortunately, the paper [*Jyllands-Posten*] apologized for the Muhammad-critical cartoons and democratic values lost out to totalitarian ideology' (*Spiegel*, 1 February 2006). This is a view which in no uncertain terms places the freedom of expression above the principles of respect and recognition.

Cosmopolitan and Human Rights Positions

More complex positions are nevertheless widespread and several of them are relevant for a discussion about cosmopolitanism. We may provisionally divide the positions on the affair in two, the confrontational and the conciliatory, which overlap partly with the duality between human rights principles and cosmopolitan thinking. As shown already, the caricatures were not published merely as a matter of principle: *Jyllands-Posten* had refused to print caricatures of Jesus, and they were within their rights to do so, since the freedom of expression does not oblige one to print anything. The editor of the Norwegian *Magazinet* was, until the cartoon controversy, a staunch supporter of a law against blasphemy in Norway but he subsequently changed his view on this issue. On the other side, Muslims who reacted with violence against the caricatures were clearly not interested in promoting either cosmopolitan values or the freedom of expression.

There can be several reasons for rejecting the middle ground, just as there can be different middle grounds. If we concentrate on Danish (and, to a lesser extent, Norwegian) society, leaving the problems of the Arab and Muslim worlds aside for now (see Eide *et al.* 2008), it may be said a priori that those who defended the view that the controversy proves the existence of an insurmountable gulf between 'us' and 'them', demonstrated limited faith in the possibility of a society based simultaneously on shared values and different values; in other words, they rejected a cosmopolitan ideal of dialogue and mutual understanding which does not mechanically lead to agreement and similarity.

A few examples of this kind of attitude follow as illustrations.

- In late January, the Norwegian Progress Party (a large populist party) demanded that the government cease to have contact with the Norwegian Islamic council, since the latter was opposed to printing the cartoons.
- On 2 February, Mullah Krekar, a controversial Kurdish religious leader who has lived in Norway for extended periods, said to a newspaper that the publication of the cartoons was tantamount to 'a declaration of war against Islam'.
- The well-known social scientist Johan Galtung said a day later, to another newspaper, that one must expect terrorist attacks in Norway and Denmark now. He saw the publication of the cartoons as an insensitive use of the freedom of expression and compared it to publishing a cartoon which depicts sex between the Virgin Mary and the Holy Ghost. (And yet it must be pointed out that such cartoons doubtless exist.)
- The Danish government's refusal to meet ambassadors from Muslim countries could equally be seen as an indication of an attitude precluding the possibility of mutual understanding. (On the other hand, the Danish government at one point requested Arab governments to apologize for the burning of the Danish flag.)

These views seem to deny the possibility of a middle ground. Alternative views are even more diverse.

On 10 February, a Norwegian non-governmental organization devoted to problems of ethnic discrimination, *Antirasistisk senter*, organized a demonstration in favour of freedom of expression, against violence and for respect. Their position, which did not attract much attention from the media, was complex in that it argued that a condition for practising freedom of expression in a culturally diverse society would be mutual respect. Now of course it is impossible to legislate for or against respect, which may imply that cosmopolitan ideals cannot be embedded in the law, only as informal norms.

The famous Muslim academic, Tariq Ramadan, writing in the *International Herald Tribune*, elaborates on a similar position:

> What we need now on both sides is an understanding that this is not a legal issue or an issue of rights. Free speech is a right in Europe and legally protected. No one should contest this. At the same time, there should be an understanding that the complexion of European society has changed with immigrants from diverse cultures. Because of that, there should be sensitivity to Muslims and others living in Europe (Tariq Ramadan, *International Herald Tribune*, 5 February 2006).

Note his use of the term *sensitivity*. Compare this with the critic, Christopher Hitchens, writing on the website Slate (www.slate.com). He first reminds the readers that Arab newspapers routinely print anti-Jewish cartoons and adds, in the climactic part of the brief article: 'I am not asking for the right to slaughter a pig in a synagogue or mosque or to relieve myself on a "holy" book. But I will not be told I can't eat pork, and I will not respect those who burn books on a regular basis'.

This is another complex position. Hitchens concedes that synagogues and mosques may be a special kind of building for certain people but that he is not required to respect them any more than faithful believers can be expected to respect him. This position, veering towards mutual indifference, is compatible with cosmopolitanism given certain conditions, to which I shall return.

Most of the lengthier opinion articles that were published in the Danish and Norwegian press about the controversy may be classified as 'conciliatory' or 'complex' in their attitude. Although there was disagreement over the good sense in publishing the cartoons, few believed that it should have been illegal. There was also disagreement over the use of boycott as a way of expressing disgust; but boycott has been used by liberals and socialists in the North Atlantic part of the world in the recent past as well, most famously in the international campaign against apartheid and even today, there are people who will not buy Israeli goods. This kind of disagreement is compatible with cosmopolitanism.

A Muslim writing in a Norwegian newspaper pointed out that there exists a set of ethical guidelines for the Norwegian press, known as the 'Be cautious poster' (*Vær varsom-plakaten*), where (in § 4.3) it says that one shall show respect for people's personal peculiarities, private life, race, nationality and religion. Within (Sunni) Islam, the writer adds, it is an absolute and incontestable sin to depict Mohammed. A possible response to this view is that it may be a sin to you, but to me 'it ain't'.

The Danish liberal Member of Parliament, Naser Khader, who describes himself as an 'ultra-light Muslim', called for the establishment of a network of 'cultural Muslims' and pragmatic Muslims who saw their religion as just one of their several identities. In an interview, Khader said, 'The Mohammed cartoon dispute also has a positive side. Now we know where the radicals stand. It's up to us moderates to develop an alternative. What is at stake is no less than the soul of Islam'. In fact, a trilingual (Arabic, Danish and English) website was set up by 'moderate Danish Muslims' under the heading 'It's enough now!'(*Nu er det nok!*), with a mission statement saying that 'everything can now be discussed and criticized', adding that the Muhammad cartoons were a provocation but that one cannot prohibit such statements in a liberal society.

Substantial segments of the Danish and Norwegian populations (just how substantial one cannot know) believe that it was 'unwise' to publish the Muhammad cartoons, while others think that it is exactly for this kind of purpose that freedom of the press exists. As I shall argue, the latter position (sometimes called 'freedom of expression fundamentalism') is incompatible with cosmopolitanism.

Interestingly, some prominent North American reactions have been more in line with Egyptian columnists than with Danish members of the government. Bill Clinton was quoted as having commented: 'None of us are totally free of stereotypes about people of different races, different ethnic groups, and different religions. ... There was this appalling example in Northern Europe, in Denmark, ... these totally outrageous cartoons against Islam'. He may not have seen the cartoons (perhaps one or two could reasonably be described as 'outrageous'), but that is not the point.

Notwithstanding the predominance of nuanced and complex positions on both sides – for example, the Lebanese Prime Minister, Fouad Saniora, said, in a comment on the destruction of the Danish consulate in Beirut, that 'this is absolutely not the way we express our opinions' – the debate took place chiefly on the terms of the antagonists. The controversy might easily be invoked by enemies of cosmopolitanism as evidence that societies can only be cohesive if they are based on sameness.

The rapid escalation of the conflict from December to the beginning of February looks like a classic instance of Batesonian schismogenesis (Bateson 1972), a model explaining the emergence of 'evil spirals' or 'vicious circles'. On one side, the extremists argued: 'See, we told you, the West is against Islam'. On the other side, the other kind of extremist said, 'See, Muslims can't be integrated into Europe and they are destroying our values by not accepting what we stand for'. From this starting point, the conflict began to escalate.

Bateson applied the concept of schismogenesis to as diverse phenomena as alcoholism, gang violence and arms races. Convinced that the cause of some of the most widespread forms of schismogenesis was an error in the dominant Western mode of thought – the error of individualism – Bateson wrote that if, for example, boasting is an element in the relationship between group A and group B, then:

> ... it is likely, if boasting is a response to boasting, that each group will drive the other to an exaggerated emphasis on this pattern, a process which – if it is not checked – only can lead to more and more extreme rivalry and, in the final instance, to enmity and breakdown in the entire system (Bateson 1972:68).

Another example could be a marital conflict. He accuses her of spending too much time outside of the home, so that he rarely gets freshly-ironed shirts and dinner at a set time. She accuses him of trying to control her and of denying her self-realization and an independent career. Unless a third instance, such as a conflict broker, the children's points of view, a new argument or an original perspective, is drawn in, the relationship may well deteriorate right up to the point of divorce.

The limitations of classic system theory are evident here. There was no shortage of 'rational' third instances or alternative framings of the situation in the cartoon affair. Quite the opposite: no chauvinistic or antagonistic statement was made in the European public spheres without immediate counterstatements adding nuance, correcting mistakes and making appeals to dialogue, respect and tolerance. What must be understood, before considering the possibilities of cosmopolitanism, is why certain views and statements become more powerful than others. Batesonian or other system theory cannot answer this question. As I have argued earlier in a book about the enemy image of Islam (Eriksen 2001), in order to understand the disappointment and occasional rage encountered in Muslim societies, it is necessary to look not at the relations of production but at the relations of communication. Humiliation, a result of disrespect, is a key term here. It is a common view among Muslims that they are not taken seriously, not listened to, not treated as equals. That is certainly a widespread perception in contemporary Denmark. Asymmetrical relations of communication result in one party feeling that it is not being heard. Thus Danes may say to the Muslims that you can say whatever you like about our gods and we say whatever we like about yours, and we then have equality. Quite apart from the fact that Danes are generally secular and Muslims are generally religious, and that there is a religious ban on depicting the Prophet in Sunni Islam.

Many Muslims see this as a bogus equality since the power of definition is unequally distributed and also because their religion contains notions of sacredness which are more fundamental than liberal rights. This inequality partly accounts for the violence in some reactions and the calls for moderation in the use of the freedom of expression among others. An image that comes to mind is that reported in the press in 2005, about a demonstration in Afghanistan following a rumour that American marines in Guantánamo had urinated on the Holy Qur'an. The report led to a public enquiry and the soldier who had done the urinating admitted it but explained that he had really just urinated on a prisoner, and that a few drops accidentally fell on the Qur'an. This is the kind of world inhabited subjectively by many politically-conscious Muslims.

Historically, caricatures have usually been 'a weapon of the weak' used to humiliate and shame powerful groups but it can also be a weapon of the strong, as in the case of anti-Semite caricatures in Germany before and during the Second World War. In this context, given the geopolitical situation and the situation of Muslims in Western Europe (and, perhaps in particular, in Denmark), there can be no doubt how the cartoons were perceived there.

Concerning the controversy around *The Bookseller of Kabul*, different normative positions are also conceivable. Leaving the question of personal defamation and the possible infliction of danger to Mr Rais and his family aside, one may ask what kinds of depictions of 'other peoples' are feasible. Written in an orientalist mode, the book has a Western intended readership. This is, legally speaking, unproblematic. On the other hand, it may well be asked, and this question is a constitutive one in post-colonial studies, whether such a literary mode is productive of conviviality in a shrunken world. When this question is raised, moving beyond a rights discourse (and beyond the orbit of law), the issues pertain to cosmopolitan norms, which are bound to be informal, lest liberal political rights are jeopardized. Cultural recognition can to some extent be sanctioned by law but this is not the case regarding the respect of others. In this realm, it is difficult to see the possibility of moving beyond appeals to reasonableness, which may or may not be taken into consideration.

Limits of Legislation

Global uniformity at the level of values is not realistic, notwithstanding the almost unanimous support of the Universal Declaration of Human Rights. Given that a newspaper feature in an obscure North European country could lead to riots and violence as far afield as Nigeria and Afghanistan, it is clear that disagreements over values – verbal as well as non-verbal – are irreducibly transnational. If fundamental disagreement is deemed dangerous, then it might seem that the only solution is global ethics based on a set of common denominators ensuring that nobody is ever offended. This would, incidentally, be the ultimate result of the position Hitchens attacks, where respect and consideration lead to massive self-censorship and where the tolerant are instructed to respect the intolerant. In such a world, where offensive messages are globalized as easily as e-mails, many essential debates would become private and might even go underground, for fear of offending the sensibilities of others. It would be reminiscent, on a huge scale, of the dinner party organized by Mr Fielding in E.M. Forster's *A Passage to India*, where our good Englishman worries about the menu – the guests have different religions and subscribe to various food taboos. In the end, the public sphere would be left empty under such a regime. Another option would consist in exploring the possibilities of living with difference, that is to say the project of cosmopolitanism as it has been formulated in Europe since Montaigne but especially since Kant.

Let us suppose that secularized Danes were to take the religiosity of Muslims seriously and treat it with respect, much as they treat their old parents with respect. In that case, they would easily know how to maneuvre in order not to offend them. Not even trying to maneuvre indicates a strong inclination not to live in the same society, even if one lives next door to each other.

The kind of cosmopolitan attitude leading to restraint can be compared to the underlying reasoning behind the ban on smoking in public, which has in recent years been implemented in many parts of the world. Supposing that I smoke and you do not, and we are in a room together, I might just tell you that if I smoke and you don't, we both enjoy our liberal freedom. This is the problem of the cartoon controversy and the simplistic liberal responses to offended reactions among some Muslims. Muhammad cartoons to them are like tobacco smoke to an asthmatic.

Cosmopolitanism presupposes the acknowledgment of living in the same society, which confers not only rights but also responsibilities. When Salman Rushdie's Indian publishers were offered *The Satanic Verses*, they were uncertain as to what to do, given the already controversial reputation of the book, so they asked Khushwant Singh for advice. Singh is an unrepentant liberal in Indian public life, having written a great number of satirical and sometimes serious books, articles and columns all over the country since just after the Second World War. He hates sectarianism and enjoys his whisky in a very public way. Surprisingly perhaps, Khushwant Singh recommended that Rushdie's book should not be published. His reasoning was that the few members of the Indian cultural elite who would really enjoy it could get it from England anyway and if it were to be published in India, the result was likely to be riots and unnecessary deaths (Waldrop 1999). And so the book was not published in India and this may be seen as a clear victory for a cosmopolitan attitude that transcends mere liberalism and acknowledges that difference necessitates respect.

Conclusion

In a review of Kwame Anthony Appiah's *Cosmopolitanism* (Appiah 2006) John Gray states: 'As a position in ethical theory, cosmopolitanism is distinct from relativism and universalism. It affirms the possibility of mutual understanding between adherents to different moralities but without holding out the promise of any ultimate consensus' (Gray 2006).

In other words, fervent missionary activity is not, according to this view, compatible with cosmopolitanism, nor is an ethical position which assumes that there is but one good life. The question asked by liberals may be why they should tolerate intolerance; the answer is that they are not asked to do so. They are only asked to coexist with and collaborate with people of different persuasions when the need arises. Most conflicts involving immigrants in European cities are of a practical nature: Why do the parents of immigrant children, active in sports, so rarely take part in the community work – organizing raffles and fleamarkets, selling hot dogs on match days and so on – which are essential to raise money for the children? Why do immigrant parents let their children play noisily outside late in the evening? Why do native Europeans never invite their immigrant neighbours for a cup of tea? It is this kind of everyday problem that creates coldness and distance between natives and newcomers – I have yet to hear of a single conflict between ethnic Scandinavians and immigrants that directly involved differences in religious beliefs. The main flaw in many accounts of cosmopolitanism consists in their reliance on dialogue, verbal exchange, mutual cognitive understanding, and so on. In my own immediate neighbourhood, we don't really care which political party the neighbour votes for and we don't know if they have any religious beliefs or if they love European classical music as much as we do, nor do we care, as long as they take their turn shovelling snow in our common courtyard in the winter months. Cosmopolitanism may degenerate into missionary liberalism but it may also degenerate into indifference. As long as there are practical tasks at hand, which need to be handled collectively, this is not a danger. If anything, it is the lack of such tasks that prevent cosmopolitanism in North Atlantic societies, not the lack of things to disagree or agree about in the media. Principled liberal individualists like Hitchens can perfectly well live in a cosmopolitan society without caring about other people's beliefs and religious practices but only in so far as he engages in common activities with them. 'Rational discourse', which both Hitchens and Ramadan believe in, cannot be an ultimate solution. There is nothing like getting your hands dirty together. It could be said that violence begins where language ends but it may just as well be said that violence begins where interaction ends. As the examples of the cartoon affair and the bookseller book have shown, it is difficult to legislate in favour of cosmopolitan views and practices without limiting civil rights beyond what is considered acceptable in liberal societies. So the most effective method for promoting cosmopolitanism uses – perhaps paradoxically – the same practices that also lead to frictions, namely increased contact, dialogue and interaction, but based on the principles of recognition rather than suspicion.

References

Appiah, K.A. 2006. *Cosmopolitanism: Ethics in a World of Strangers*. New York: Norton.

Bateson, G. 1972. *Steps to an Ecology of Mind*. New York: Ballantine.

Baumann, G. 1999. *The Multicultural Riddle: Rethinking National, Ethnic and Religious Identities*. London: Routledge.

Beck, U. 2006. *The Cosmopolitan Vision*. Cambridge: Polity.

Bluitgen, K. 2006. *Koranen og profeten Muhammeds liv* (The Koran and the Life of the Prophet Muhammad). Copenhagen: Høst and Søn.

Castells, M. 1998. *End of Millennium*. Vol 3 in The Information Age. Oxford: Blackwell.

Castles, S. and Davidson, A. 2000. *Citizenship and Migration: Globalization and the Politics of Belonging*. London: Palgrave Macmillan.

Dworkin, R. 2006. The right to ridicule. *New York Review of Books*, 23 March.

Eide, E., Kunelius, R. and Phillips, A. (eds) 2008. *Transnational Media Events. The Mohammed Cartoons and an Imagined Clash of Civilization*. Göteborg: Nordicom.

Eriksen, T.H. 2001. *Bak fiendebildet: Politisk islam og verden etter 11. september* (Behind the enemy image: Political Islam and the world after 9/11). Oslo: Cappelen.

Gray, J. 2006. Easier said than done. *The Nation*, 30 January.

Harvey, D. 1989. *The Condition of Postmodernity*. Oxford: Blackwell.

Heine, B. 1985. 'The Mountain People': Some notes on the Ik of North-Eastern Uganda. *Africa* 5(1): 3–16.

Hellum, A., Stewart, J., Ali, S.S. and Tsanga, A. (eds) 2007. *Human Rights, Plural Legalities and Gendered Realities*. Harare: Weaver.

Hitchens, C. 2006. The case for mocking religion. *Slate*. 4 February. Available at: www.slate.com.

Kasten, E. (ed.) 2004. *Properties of Culture – Culture as Property*. Berlin: Dietrich Reimer Verlag.

Kymlicka, W. 2007. *Multicultural Odysseys: Navigating the New International Politics of Diversity*. Oxford: Oxford University Press.

Larsen, R.E. and Seidenfaden, T. 2006. *Karikaturkrisen: En undersøgelse af baggrund og ansvar* (The Cartoon Crisis: An Investigation of Background and Responsibility). Copenhagen: Gyldendal.

Lau, J. 2006. Allah und der Humor. *Die Zeit*, 1 February.

Magris, C. 1989. *Danube*. New York: Farrar, Strauss, Giroux.

Ramadan, T. 2006. Free speech and civic responsability. *International Herald Tribune*, 5 February.

Seierstad, Å. 2002. *Bokhandleren i Kabul*. Oslo: Cappelen.

Todorov, T. 1982. *La Conquête de l'Amerique: La Question de l'Autre*. Paris: Seuil.

Turnbull, C. 1972. *The Mountain People*. London: Cape.

Urry, J. 2000. *Sociology Beyond Societies: Mobilities for the Twenty-First Century*. London: Routledge.

de Waal, A. 1993. In the disaster zone. *Times Literary Supplement*, 16 July.

Waldrop, A. 1999. Gud, og jeg vet ikke hva. Samtale med Khushwant Singh. ('God, and I don't know what. A conversation with Khushwant Singh') *Samtiden* No 5/6:112–122.

Index

www.ingramcontent.com/pod-product-compliance
Ingram Content Group UK Ltd.
Pitfield, Milton Keynes, MK11 3LW, UK
UKHW022009180926
475701UK00003B/279

* 9 7 8 1 1 3 8 2 6 1 0 6 8 *